FUNDAMENTALS OF DATABASE MANAGEMENT SYSTEMS

FUNDAMENTALS OF DATABASE MANAGEMENT SYSTEMS

Mark L. Gillenson

Fogelman College of Business and Economics
University of Memphis

WILEY

John Wiley & Sons, Inc.

CREDITS

ACQUISITIONS EDITOR: Beth Golub
MARKETING MANAGER: Gitti Lindner
PRODUCTION EDITOR: Sujin Hong
DESIGNER: Dawn L. Stanley
ILLUSTRATION EDITOR: Ana Melhorn
MANAGING EDITOR: Kevin Dodds
PRODUCTION MANAGEMENT SERVICES: Leyh Publishing LLC
COVER IMAGE: Photo by Glenn D. Chambers. © Ducks Unlimited, Inc.
Image reproduced with permission

This book was set in 10/12 Times New Roman by Leyh Publishing LLC, and printed and bound by Donnelley/Willard. The cover was printed by Phoenix Color Corp.

This book is printed on acid free paper. ∞

ISBN 0-471-26297-8 (US)
ISBN 0-471-65925-8 (WIE)

Printed in the United States of America

10 9 8 7 6 5 4 3 2 1

To my loves
Leslie, Rochelle, and Caroline

CONTENTS

PREFACE

PURPOSE OF THIS BOOK

A course in database management has become well established as a required course in both undergraduate and graduate management information systems degree programs. This is as it should be considering the central position that the database field holds in the information systems environment. Indeed, a solid understanding of the fundamentals of database is crucial for success in the information systems field. An IS professional should be able to talk to the users in a business setting, ask the right questions about the nature of their entities, their attributes, and the relationships among them, and quickly react to their existing data and database designs as being properly structured or not. An IS professional should be able to design new databases with the confidence that they will serve their owners and users well. An IS professional should be able to guide a company in the best use of the various database-related technologies.

Over the years, at the same time that database management has increased in importance, it has also increased tremendously in breadth. In addition to such fundamental topics as data modeling, relational database concepts, logical and physical database design, and SQL, a basic set of database topics today includes object-oriented database, data administration, data security, distributed database, data warehousing, and Web database, among others. The dilemma faced by database instructors and by database books is to cover as much of this material as is reasonably possible so that students will come away with a solid background in the fundamentals without being overwhelmed by the tremendous breadth and depth of the field. Being exposed to too much material in too short a time period at the expense of developing a sound foundation is of no value to anyone. I believe that a one-semester course in database management should provide a firm grounding in the fundamentals of database and provide a solid survey of the major database subfields, while deliberately not being encyclopedic in its coverage.

KEY FEATURES OF THIS BOOK

With the above realities and goals in mind, this book has several key features:

- It is designed to be a carefully and clearly written, friendly, narrative introduction to the subject of database management that can reasonably be completed in a one-semester course.

- It provides a clear understanding of the fundamentals of database while at the same time providing a broad survey of all the major topics of the field. It is an applied book of important basic concepts and practical material that can be used immediately in business.
- It makes heavy use of examples. There are four major examples that are used throughout the text where appropriate, plus two minicases included among the chapter exercises at the end of every chapter. Having multiple examples solidifies the material and helps students to see the point despite the peculiarities of a particular example.
- It starts with the basics of data and file structures and then builds up in a progressive, step-by-step way through the distinguishing characteristics of database.
- It includes a story and accompanying photograph of a real company's real use of database management at the beginning of every chapter. This is both for motivational purposes and to give the book a more practical, real-world feel.
- It has a chapter on SQL that concentrates on the data retrieval aspect and applies to essentially every relational database product on the market.

ORGANIZATION OF THIS BOOK

The book effectively divides into two halves. After the introduction in Chapter 1, Chapters 2 and 3 lay the foundation with file structures and data modeling. Chapter 4 describes the fundamental concepts of database and contrasts them with ordinary files. Importantly, this is done separately from and prior to the discussion of relational database. Chapters 5 and 6 explain the major concepts of relational database. In turn, this is done separately from and prior to the discussion of logical database design in Chapter 7 and physical database design (yes, a whole chapter on this subject) in Chapter 8. Chapter 9 is the chapter on SQL which, for a book of this size, also serves as the chapter on data retrieval. General database concepts, relational database concepts, and relational database design are handled independently to bring the students along gradually and deliberately with the goal of a solid understanding at the end. Note that Chapter 9 on SQL can be covered either where it is, after the chapters on logical and physical database design, or before those two chapters, without any disruption in the content. I know that some instructors will prefer it one way and some the other and that's fine. The book will work either way.

Then, in the second half of the book, each chapter describes one or more of the major database subfields. These latter chapters are generally independent and, for the most part, can be approached in any order. They include Chapter 10 on object-oriented database; Chapter 11 on data administration, database administration, and data dictionaries; Chapter 12 on security, backup and recovery, and concurrency; Chapter 13 on client/server database and distributed database; Chapter 14 on the data warehouse; and Chapter 15 on database and the Internet.

SUPPLEMENTS

Web site www.wiley.com/college/gillenson

The Web site includes several resources designed to aid the learning process:

- PowerPoint slides for each chapter that instructors can use as is or tailor as they wish and that students can use both to take notes on in the classroom and to help with their studying at home.
- Quizzes for each chapter that students can take on their own to test their knowledge.
- For instructors: The Instructor's Manual, written by the author. For each chapter it includes a guide to presenting the chapter, discussion stimulation points, and answers to every question, exercise, and minicase at the end of each chapter.
- For instructors: The Test Bank, written by the author. Questions are organized by chapter and are designed to test the level of understanding of the chapter's concepts, as well as such basic knowledge as the definitions of key terms presented in the chapter.

ACKNOWLEDGMENTS

I would like to thank the reviewers of the manuscript for their time, efforts, and insightful comments:

Thomas Sandman, California State University–Sacramento
Ashraf Shirani, San Jose State University
Shamsul Chowdhury, Roosevelt University
Peter Weiss, George Washington University
Reza Barkhi, Virginia Tech
Anita Whitehill, Foothill College
Amita Goyal Chin, Virginia Commonwealth University
Mary Ann Robbert, Bentley College
Vincent Yen, Wright State University
Constance Knapp, Pace University
Zachary Wong, Sonoma State University
Nancy Davidson, Auburn University at Montgomery
James Burkman, Texas Tech University
Subhasish Dasgupta, George Washington University
Suhong Li, Bryant College

In addition, I would like to acknowledge and thank several people who read and provided helpful comments on specific chapters and portions of the manuscript: Mark Cooper of FedEx Corp., Satish Puranam of the University of Memphis, Trent Sanders, now of Bowling Green State University, and David Tegarden of Virginia Tech.

I would also like to thank the people and companies who agreed to participate in the corporate and government database management vignettes that appear at the beginning of each chapter and, in some cases, later in the chapters. I strongly believe that business students should not have to study subjects like database management in a vacuum. Rather, they should be regularly reminded of the ways in which real companies put these concepts and techniques to use. Whether the products involved are power tools, auto parts, toys, or books, it is important to always remember that database management supports these businesses in which billions of dollars are at stake every year. Thus, the people and companies who participated in these vignettes have significantly added to the educational experience that the students using this book will have.

Finally, I would like to thank the crew at John Wiley & Sons for their professionalism and continuous support: Beth Lang Golub, my most expert editor and friend and her excellent staff; Marc Periou, my local Wiley sales representative who provided encouragement and helpful advice; and Sujin Hong, who oversaw the production of this book. A special thank you goes to Image Archive Manager Ken Liao who provided extraordinary support regarding the photography in the book's corporate vignettes.

Mark L. Gillenson
Memphis, TN
November 2003

ABOUT THE AUTHOR

Dr. Mark L. Gillenson has been practicing, researching, teaching, writing, and, most importantly, thinking, about data and database management for over twenty-five years, split between working for the IBM Corporation and being a professor in the academic world. While working for IBM, he designed databases for IBM's corporate headquarters, consulted on database issues for some of IBM's largest customers, taught database management at the prestigious IBM Systems Research Institute in New York, and conducted database seminars throughout the United States and on four continents. In one such seminar, he taught introduction to database to an IBM development group that went on to develop one of IBM's first relational database management system products, SQL/DS.

Dr. Gillenson conducted some of the earliest studies on data and database administration and has written extensively about the subject as well as about database design. He is an associate editor of the *Journal of Database Management,* with which he has been associated since its inception. This is his third book on database management, all published by John Wiley & Sons, Inc. He has also written *Strategic Planing, Systems Analysis, and Database Design* (1984) with Robert Goldberg and *Database Step-by-Step* (1985, 1990).

Dr. Gillenson is currently a professor of MIS in the Fogelman College of Business and Economics of The University of Memphis. His degrees are from Rensselaer Polytechnic Institute and The Ohio State University.

Oh, and speaking of interesting kinds of data, as a graduate student Dr. Gillenson invented the world's first computerized facial compositor and codeveloped an early computer graphics system that, among other things, was used to produce some of the special effects in the first *Star Wars* movie.

CHAPTER 1

DATA: THE NEW CORPORATE RESOURCE

CHAPTER OBJECTIVES

After learning the material in this chapter, you will be able to:

✔ Explain why humankind's interest in data goes back to ancient times.
✔ Describe how data needs have historically driven many information technology developments.
✔ Describe the evolution of data storage media during the last century.
✔ Relate the idea of data as a corporate resource that can be used to gain a competitive advantage to the development of the database management systems environment.

Photo courtesy of The Home Depot

THE HOME DEPOT

Founded in 1978, The Home Depot is the world's largest home improvement retailer. Headquartered in Atlanta, Georgia, the company currently operates over 1,484 stores in the United States, Canada, Mexico, and Puerto Rico. Each store's inventory ranges from 40,000–50,000 different kinds of building, home improvement, and

1

lawn and garden products. The company sells to both do-it-yourselfers and construction professionals.

The Home Depot uses a multi-level relational database to keep track of its store inventory. Known as the "Store Inventory Management System," the application was developed starting in 1994 as a replacement for an older store inventory system. This system is based on Informix databases running on a Hewlett-Packard/Unix platform in the stores. Near real-time inventory updates are sent from each store to a DB2 database running on an IBM 390 system at the company's Atlanta corporate headquarters.

This classic inventory application features automated product ordering at each store and then tracks the receiving of the goods on the loading dock. It also manages transfers of goods between stores, price changes, shelf label creation, reporting, and returns to vendors. The "cash registers" are point-of-sale terminals that scan the product bar codes during customer checkout and automatically update the on-hand inventory quantities of the goods for sale in the stores. An interesting feature is mobile computers that are rolled around the store on carts to check inventory and account for "shrinkage" due to stolen, misplaced, and miscounted merchandise.

The database at corporate headquarters accumulates eighteen months of sales (point-of-sale) history. This data is used by many departments, including merchandising, finance, store operations, and loss prevention. Home Depot also centralizes its customer and order databases. This information is used by call centers that need to see customer information from an enterprise view. Home Depot is currently building an Enterprise Data Warehouse, which will enable business analysts and executives to have ready access to key business indicators.

Printed by permission of The Home Depot.

What a fascinating world we live in today! Technological advances are all around us in virtually every aspect of our daily lives. From cellular telephones to satellite television to advanced aircraft to modern medicine to computers—especially computers—high tech is with us wherever we look. Businesses of every description and size rely on computers and the information systems they support to a degree that would have been unimaginable just a few short years ago. Businesses routinely use automated manufacturing and inventory control techniques, automated financial transaction procedures, and high-tech marketing tools. As consumers, we take it for granted that by simply calling our banks, insurance companies, and department stores we can instantly get up-to-the-minute information on our accounts. And everyone, businesses and consumers alike, have come to rely on the Internet for instant worldwide communications. Beneath the surface, the foundation for all of this activity is data: the stored facts that we need to manage all of our human endeavors.

This book is about **data.** It's about how to think about data in a highly organized and deliberate way. It's about how to store data efficiently and about how to retrieve it effectively. It's about ways of managing data so that the exact data that we need will be there when we need it. It's about the concept of assembling data into a highly organized collection called a **database** and about the sophisticated software known as a **database management system** that controls the database and oversees the **database environment.** It's about the various approaches that people have taken to database management and about the roles that people have assumed in the database environment. The Home Depot's Store Inventory Management System is a perfect example of how a modern company can use a database management system to collect, organize, and use data to great advantage. We will see many more such real-world examples of data usage throughout this book.

Computers came into existence because we needed help in processing and using the massive amounts of data that we have been accumulating. Is the converse true? Could data exist without computers? The answer to this question is a resounding "yes." In fact, data has existed for thousands of years in some very interesting, if by today's standards crude, forms. Furthermore, some very key points in the history of the development of computing devices were driven not by an inspiration about computing for computing's sake, but by a real need to efficiently handle a pesky data management problem. Let's begin by tracing some of these historical milestones in the evolution of data and data management.

THE HISTORY OF DATA

The Origins of Data

People have been interested in data for at least the past 12,000 years. Although today we often associate the concept of data with the computer, historically, there have been many more primitive methods of data storage and handling.

In ancient times in the Middle East, shepherds kept track of their flocks with pebbles (Figure 1.1). As each sheep left its pen to graze, the shepherd placed one pebble in a small sack. When all of the sheep had left, the shepherd had a record of how many sheep were out grazing. When the sheep returned, the shepherd discarded one pebble for each animal, and if there were more pebbles than sheep, he knew that some of his sheep still hadn't returned or were missing. This was, indeed, a primitive but legitimate example of data storage and retrieval. It is important to realize that the count of the number of sheep going out and coming back in was all that the shepherd cared about in his "business environment" and that his primitive data storage and retrieval system satisfied his needs.

➤ **Figure 1.1**
Shepherd using pebbles to keep track of sheep

Excavations in the Zagros region of Iran, dated to 8500 B.C., have unearthed clay **tokens** or "counters" that we think were used for record keeping in primitive forms of accounting. Such tokens have been found in sites from present-day Turkey to Pakistan and as far afield as the present-day Khartoum in Sudan, dating to as long ago as 7000 B.C. By 3000 B.C., at the present-day city of Susa in Iran, the use of such tokens had reached a greater level of sophistication. Tokens, with special markings on them (Figure 1.2) were sealed in hollow clay vessels that accompanied commercial goods in transit. These primitive bills of lading certified the contents of the shipments. The tokens represented the quantity of goods being shipped and, obviously, no one could tamper with them without breaking open the clay vessel. Inscriptions on the outside of the vessels and the seals of the parties involved provided a further record. The external inscriptions included words or concepts such as "deposited," "transferred," and "removed."

At about the same time that the Susa culture existed, people in the city-state of Uruk in Sumeria kept records in clay texts. With pictographs, numerals, and ideographs, they described land sales and business transactions involving bread, beer, sheep, cattle, and clothing. Other Neolithic means of record keeping included storing tallies as cuts and notches in wooden sticks and as knots in rope. The former continued in use in England as late as the medieval period, South American Indians used the latter.

Data Through the Ages

As with Susa and Uruk, much of the very early interest in data can be traced to the rise of cities. Simple subsistence hunting, gathering, and, later, farming had only limited use for the concept of data. But when people live in cities they tend to specialize in the goods and services they produce. They become dependent on each other, **bartering** and using money to trade these goods and services for mutual

➤ **Figure 1.2**
Ancient clay tokens used to record goods in transit

survival. This trade encouraged **record keeping**—the recording of data-to keep track of how much a person has produced and what it can be bartered or sold for.

As time went on, more and different kinds of data and records were kept. These included calendars, census data, surveys, land ownership records, marriage records, records of church contributions, and family trees (Figure 1.3). Increasingly sophisticated merchants had to keep track of inventories, shipments, and wage payments in addition to production data. In addition, as farming went beyond the subsistence level and progressed to the feudal manor stage, there was a need to keep data on the amount of produce to consume, to barter with, and to keep as seed for the following year.

The Crusades took place from the late eleventh to the late thirteenth centuries. One side effect of the Crusades was a broader view of the world from the perspective of the Europeans, with an accompanying increase in interest in trade. A common method of trade in that era was the establishment of temporary partnerships among merchants, ships captains, and owners to facilitate commercial voyages. That increased level of commercial sophistication brought with it another round of increasingly complex record keeping: specifically, **double-entry bookkeeping.**

Double-entry bookkeeping originated in the trading centers of fourteenth-century Italy. The earliest known example is from a merchant in Genoa and dates to the year 1340. Its use spread gradually, but it was not until 1494, in Venice (about twenty-five years after the first movable type printing press in Venice came into use), that a Franciscan monk named Luca Pacioli published his *Summa de Arithmetica, Geometrica, Proportioni et Proportionalita.* That work had an important effect in spreading the use of double-entry bookkeeping. Of course, as a separate issue, the increasing use of paper and the printing press furthered the advance of record keeping as well.

As the dominance of the Italian merchants declined, other countries became more active in trade and thus with data and record keeping. Furthermore, as the use of temporary trading partnerships declined, and more stable long-term mercantile organizations were established, other types of data became necessary. For example, annual as opposed to venture-by-venture statements of profit and loss were needed.

➤ **Figure 1.3**
New types of data with the advance of civilization

In 1673 the Code of Commerce in France required that every businessman draw up a **balance sheet** every two years. Thus the data had to be periodically accumulated for reporting purposes.

Early Data Problems Spawn Calculating Devices

It was also in the seventeenth century that people began to take an interest in devices that could "automatically" *process their data,* if only in a rudimentary way. Blaise Pascal produced one of the earliest and best known such devices in France in the 1640s, reputedly to help his father keep track of the data associated with his job as a tax collector (Figure 1.4). It was a small box that contained interlocking gears and was capable of doing addition and subtraction. This was the forerunner of today's mechanical automobile odometers.

In 1805 Joseph Marie Jacquard of France invented a device that automatically reproduced patterns during the textile weaving process. The heart of the device was a series of cards with holes punched in them; the holes allowed strands of material to be interwoven in a sequence that produced the desired pattern (Figure 1.5). Although Jacquard's loom wasn't a **calculating device** as such, his method of storing fabric patterns, a form of graphic data, as holes in **punched cards** was a very clever means of **data storage,** which would have great importance for computing devices to follow. Charles Babbage, a nineteenth-century English mathematician and inventor picked up Jacquard's concept of storing data in punched cards. Beginning in 1833, Babbage began to think about an invention that he called the Analytical Engine. He never completed it (the state of the art of machinery was not developed enough), but included in its design were many

➤ **Figure 1.4**
Blaise Pascal and his adding machine

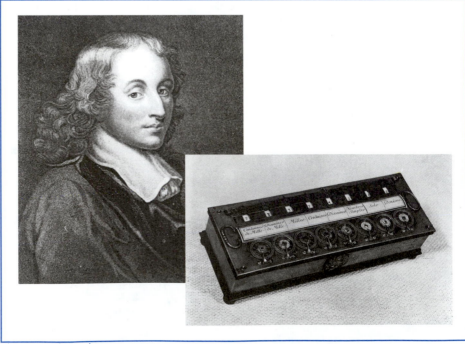

Photo courtesy of IBM Archives

➤ **Figure 1.5**

The Jacquard loom recorded patterns in punched-cards

Photo courtesy of IBM Archives

of the principles of modern computers. The Analytical Engine was to consist of a "store" for holding data items and a "mill" for operating upon them. Babbage was very impressed by Jacquard's work with punched cards. In fact, the Analytical Engine was to be able to store calculation instructions in punched cards. These would be fed into the machine together with punched cards containing data, operate on that data, and produce the desired result.

Swamped with Data

In the late 1800s, an enormous (for that time) data storage and retrieval problem and greatly improved machining technology ushered in the era of modern **information processing.** The 1880 U.S. **Census** took about seven years to compile by hand. With a rapidly expanding population fueled by massive immigration, it was estimated that if the same manual techniques were used, the compilation of the 1890 Census would not be completed until after the 1900 Census data had begun to be collected. The solution to processing the census data was provided by a government engineer named Herman Hollerith. Basing his work on Jacquard's punched card concept, he arranged to have the census data stored in punched cards. He built devices to punch the holes into cards and devices to sort the cards (Figure 1.6). Wire brushes touching the cards completed circuits when they came across the holes and advanced counters. The equipment came to be classified as **electro-mechanical**—electro because it was powered by electricity and mechanical because the electricity powered mechanical counters that tabulated the data. By using Hollerith's equipment, the total population count of the 1890 Census was completed one month after all of the data was in. The complete set of tabulations, including data on questions that had never before even been practical to ask, took two years. In 1896 Hollerith formed the Tabulating Machine Company to produce and commercially market his devices. That company, combined with several others, eventually formed what is today the International Business Machines Corporation (IBM).

Toward the turn of the century, the immigrants kept coming and the U.S. population kept expanding. The census bureau, while using Hollerith's equipment, continued experimenting on its own to produce even more advanced data tabulating machinery. One of its engineers, James Powers, developed devices to automatically feed cards into the equipment and to automatically print results. In 1911 he established the Powers Tabulating Machine Company, which eventually formed the

➤ **Figure 1.6**
Herman Hollerith and his
tabulator/sorter, circa 1890

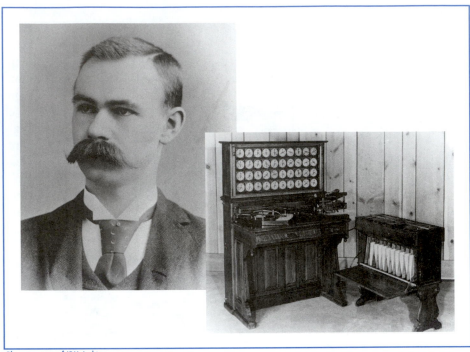

Photo courtesy of IBM Archives

basis for the UNIVAC division of the Sperry Corporation, which eventually became the Unisys Corporation.

From the days of Hollerith and Powers through the 1940s, commercial data processing was performed on a variety of electromechanical punched card based devices, including calculators, punches, sorters, collators, and printers. The data was stored in punched cards, while the processing instructions were implemented as collections of wires plugged into specially designed boards, which in turn were inserted into slots in the electromechanical devices. Electromechanical equipment overlapped with **electronic computers,** which were introduced commercially in the mid-1950s.

The introduction of electronic computers in the mid-1950s coincided with a tremendous boom in economic development, which raised the level of data storage and retrieval requirements another notch. This post–World War II era was a time of rapid commercial growth in the United States and of rebuilding in Europe and the Far East. From this point onward, the furious pace of new data storage and retrieval requirements as more and more commercial functions and procedures were automated and as technological advances were made in computing devices has been one big blur. From this point onward, it would be virtually impossible to tie advances in computing devices to specific, landmark data storage and retrieval needs.

Modern Data Storage Media

Paralleling the growth of equipment to process data was the development of new media on which to store the data. The earliest form of modern data storage was

punched paper tape, which was introduced in the 1870s and 1880s in conjunction with early teletype equipment. Of course, we've already seen that Hollerith in the 1890s and Powers in the early 1900s used punched cards as a storage medium. Indeed, punched cards were the only data storage medium used in the increasingly sophisticated electromechanical accounting machines of the 1920s, 1930s, and 1940s. They were still used extensively in the early computers of the 1950s and 1960s and could even be found well into the 1970s, in smaller information systems installations, though to a progressively reduced degree.

The middle to late 1930s saw the beginning of the era of erasable magnetic storage media, with Bell Laboratories experimenting with magnetic tape for sound storage. By the late 1940s, early work was done on the use of magnetic tape for recording data. By 1950, several companies, including RCA and Raytheon, were developing the **magnetic tape** concept for commercial use. Both UNIVAC and Raytheon offered commercially available magnetic tape units in 1952, followed by IBM in 1953 (Figure 1.7). During the mid-1950s and into the mid-1960s, magnetic tape gradually became the dominant data storage medium in computers. Magnetic tape technology has been continually improved since then and is still in limited use today, particularly for archived data.

The original concept that eventually grew into the **magnetic disk** actually began to be developed at MIT in the late 1930s and early 1940s. By the early 1950s, several companies, including UNIVAC, IBM, and Control Data, had developed prototypes of **magnetic drums,** which were the forerunners of magnetic disk technology. In 1953 IBM began work on its 305 RAMAC (Random Access Memory Accounting Machine) fixed disk storage device. By 1954 there was a multi-platter version, which became commercially available in 1956 (Figure 1.8).

During the mid-1960s, a massive conversion from tape to magnetic disk as the preeminent data storage medium began to take place; disk storage is still the data storage medium of choice today. After the early fixed disks, the disk storage environment became geared toward the removable disk pack philosophy, with a dozen or more packs being juggled on and off a single drive as a common ratio. But with the increasingly tighter environmental controls that fixed disks permitted, more data per square inch (or square centimeter) could be stored on fixed disk devices. Today, the **disk drives** on mainframes and servers, as well as the fixed disks or "hard drives" of PCs, are all nonremovable, sealed units. But, of course, the removable disk concept has stayed with us in the

> **Figure 1.7**
> Early magnetic tape drive, circa 1953

Photo courtesy of IBM Archives

➤ **Figure 1.8**
IBM RAMAC disk storage device, circa 1956

Photo courtesy of IBM Archives

form of PC diskettes and the Iomega Corporation's Zip Disks. These have been joined by the laser-based, optical technology **compact disk** (CD), which was introduced as a data storage medium in 1985. Originally, data could only be recorded on them at the factory, and once created, they were nonerasable. Now, data can be recorded on them, erased, and rerecorded in a standard PC.

DATA IN TODAY'S INFORMATION SYSTEMS ENVIRONMENT

Using Data for Competitive Advantage

Today's computers are technological marvels. Their speed, compactness, ease of use, price as related to capability, and, yes, their data storage capacities, are truly amazing. And yet, our fundamental interest in computers is no different from the interest the ancient Middle Eastern shepherds had in their pebbles and sacks: they are the vehicles we need to store and utilize the data that is important to us in our environment.

Indeed, data has become indispensable to every kind of modern business and government organization. Data, the applications that process the data, and the computers on which the applications run are fundamental to every aspect of every kind of endeavor. When speaking of **corporate resources,** people used to list such items as capital, plant and equipment, inventory, personnel, and patents. Today, any such list of corporate resources must include the corporation's data. It has even been suggested that data is the most important corporate resource because it describes all of the others.

Data can give a company a crucial **competitive advantage.** We routinely speak of data and the information derived from it as competitive weapons in hotly contested industries. For example, FedEx had a significant competitive advantage when it first provided access to its package tracking data on its Web site. Then, once one company in an industry develops a new application that takes advantage of its data, the other companies in the industry are forced to match it to remain competitive. This cycle continually moves the use of data to ever higher levels, making it an even more important corporate resource than it was before. Examples of this abound. Banks provide their customers with online access to their accounts. Package shipping companies provide up-to-the-minute information on the whereabouts of a package. Retailers send manufacturers product sales data that the manufacturers use to adjust inventories and production cycles. Manufacturers automatically send their parts suppliers inventory data and expect the suppliers to use the data to keep a steady stream of parts flowing.

Problems in Storing and Accessing Data

But being able to store and to provide efficient access to a company's data while also maintaining its accuracy so that it can be used to competitive advantage is anything but simple. Several factors make it a major challenge. First and foremost, the volume or amount of data that companies have is massive and growing all the time. Wal-Mart estimates that its data warehouse (a type of database we will explore later) alone contains 70 terabytes (trillions of characters) of data and is constantly growing larger. The number of people who want access to the data is also growing. At one time, only a select group of a company's own employees were concerned with retrieving its data, but this has changed. Now, not only do vastly larger numbers of companies' employees demand access to the companies' data but so also do the companies' customers and trading partners. All major banks today provide their depositors with Internet access to their accounts. Increasingly, tightly linked "supply chains" are requiring that companies provide other companies, such as their suppliers and customers, with access to their data.

The combination of huge volumes of data and large numbers of people demanding access to it has created a major performance challenge. How do you sift through so much data for so many people and provide them with the data they want in an acceptably small amount of time? How much patience would you have with an insurance company that kept you on the phone for five or ten minutes while it retrieved claim data about which you had a question? The tremendous advances in computer hardware, including data storage hardware have helped; indeed, it would have been impossible to reach the stage that we have attained in information systems without them. But as the hardware continues to improve, the volume of data and the number of people who want access to it are also increasing, making for a continuing struggle to provide them with acceptable response times.

Other factors that enter into data storage and retrieval include data security, data privacy, and backup and recovery. Data security involves a company protecting its data from theft, malicious destruction, deliberate attempts at making phony changes to the data (e.g., someone trying to increase his own bank account balance), and even accidental damage by the company's own employees. Data privacy implies ensuring that even employees who normally have access to the company's data (much less outsiders) are given access only to the specific data that they need in their work. Put another way, sensitive data such as employee salary data and personal customer data should only be accessible by employees whose job functions require it. Backup and recovery means the ability to reconstruct data if it is lost or corrupted, say in a hardware failure. The extreme case of backup and recovery is known as disaster recovery when an information system is destroyed by fire, a hurricane, or other calamity.

Then, there is a whole other dimension involving maintaining the accuracy of a company's data. Historically, and in many cases even today, the same data is stored several, sometimes many, times within a company's information system. Why does this happen? For several reasons. Many companies are simply not organized to share data among multiple applications. Every time a new application is written, new data files are created to store its data. As recently as the early 1990s, I spoke to a database administration manager (more will be said on this type of position later) in the securities industry who told me that one of the reasons he was hired was to reduce duplicate data which appeared in as many as sixty to seventy files! Furthermore, depending on how database files are designed, data can even be duplicated within a single file. We will explore this issue much more in this book, but for now, suffice it to say that duplicate data, either in multiple files or in a single file, can cause major data accuracy problems.

Data as a Corporate Resource

Every corporate resource has to be carefully managed in order for a company to keep track of it, protect it, and distribute it to those people and purposes in the company that need it. Furthermore, public companies have a responsibility to their shareholders to competently manage the company's assets. Can you imagine a company's money just sort of out there somewhere without being carefully managed? The chief financial officer with a staff of accountants and financial professionals is responsible for the money, with outside accounting firms providing independent audits of it. Typically, vice presidents of personnel and their staffs are responsible for the administrative functions that are necessary to manage employee affairs; production managers at various levels are responsible for parts inventories; and so on. Data is no exception.

But data may just be the most difficult corporate resource to manage. In data, we have a resource of tremendous volume, billions, trillions, and more individual pieces of data, each piece of which is different from the next. And it has the characteristic that much of it is in a state of change at any one time. It's not as if we're talking about managing a company's employees. Even the largest companies have only a few hundred thousand of them, and they don't change all that frequently. Or the money that a company has: sure, there is a lot of it, but it's all the same in the sense that a dollar that goes to payroll is the same kind of dollar that goes to paying a supplier for raw materials.

As far back as the early to mid-1960s, barely ten years after the introduction of commercially viable electronic computers, some forward-looking companies began to realize that storing each application's data separately, in simple files, was becoming problematic and was not going to work in the long run, for precisely the reasons that we've talked about: the increasing volume of data (even way back then), the increasing demand for data access, the need for data security, privacy, backup and recovery, and the desire to share data and cut down on data redundancy. Several things were becoming clear. The task was going to require a new kind of software to help manage the data and progressively faster hardware to keep up with the increasing volume of data and data access demands. In terms of personnel, data management specialists would have to be developed, educated, and given the responsibility for managing the data as a corporate resource.

Out of this need was born a new kind of software, the database management system (DBMS), and a new category of personnel, with titles like database administrator and data management specialist. And, yes, hardware has progressively gotten faster and cheaper for the degree of performance that it provides. The integration of these advances adds up to much more than the simple sum of their parts. They add up to the database environment.

The Database Environment

Back in the early 1960s, the emphasis in what was then called data processing was on programming. Data was not much more than a necessary afterthought in the application development process and in the running of the data processing installation. There was a good reason for this. By today's standards, the rudimentary computers of the time had very small main memories and very simplistic operating systems. Even relatively basic application programs had to be shoehorned into main memory using low-level programming techniques and a lot of cleverness. But then, as we progressed further into the 1960s and beyond, two events occurred simultaneously that caused this picture to change forever. One was that main memories progressively became larger and cheaper and operating systems became much more powerful. Second, computers progressively became faster and cheaper on a price/performance basis. All of these changes had the effect of permitting the use of higher level programming languages that were easier for a larger number of personnel to use, allowing at least some of the emphasis to shift elsewhere. Well, nature hates a vacuum, and at the same time that all of this was happening, companies began to see the value of thinking of data as a corporate resource and using it as a competitive weapon.

The result was the development of database management systems (DBMS) software and the creation of the "database environment." Supported by ever improved hardware and specialized database personnel, the database environment is designed to largely correct all the problems of the nondatabase environment. It encourages data sharing and the control of data redundancy, with important improvements in data accuracy. It permits the storage of vast volumes of data with acceptable access and response times for database queries. And it provides the tools to control data security, data privacy, and backup and recovery.

This book is a straightforward introduction to the fundamentals of database in the current information systems environment. It is designed to teach you the important concepts of the database approach and to teach you specific skills, such as how to design relational databases, how to improve database performance, and how to retrieve data from relational databases using the Structured Query Language (SQL). In addition, as you proceed through the book, you will explore such topics as entity-relationship diagrams, object-oriented databases, database administration, distributed databases, data warehousing, Internet database issues, and others.

We will start with the basics and take a step-by-step approach to exploring all of the various components of the database environment. Each chapter progressively adds more to an understanding of both the technical and managerial aspects of the field. Database is a very powerful concept. Overall it provides ingenious solutions to a set of very difficult problems. As a result, it tends to be a multifaceted and complex subject, which can appear difficult when one attempts to swallow it in one gulp. But database is approachable and understandable if we proceed carefully, cautiously, and progressively step by step. It is an understanding that no one involved in information systems can afford to be without.

KEY TERMS

Balance sheet
Bartering
Calculating devices
Census
Compact disk
Competitive advantage
Corporate resource
Data
Data storage

Database
Database environment
Database management system
Disk drive
Double-entry bookkeeping
Electromechanical equipment
Electronic computer
Information processing
Magnetic disk

Magnetic drum
Magnetic tape
Punched cards
Punched paper tape
Record keeping
Tally
Token

QUESTIONS

1. What did the Middle Eastern shepherds' pebbles and sacks, Pascal's calculating device, and Hollerith's punched card devices all have in common?

2. What did the growth of cities have to do with the need for data?

3. What did the growth of trade have to do with the need for data?

4. What did Jacquard's textile weaving device have to do with the development of data?

5. Choose what you believe to be the:

   a. One most important
   b. Two most important
   c. Three most important landmark events in the history of data. Defend your choices.

6. Do you think that computing devices would have been developed even if specific data needs had not come along? Why or why not?

7. What did the need for data among ancient Middle Eastern shepherds have in common with the need for data among modern corporations?

8. List several problems in storing and accessing data in today's large corporations. Which do you think is the most important? Why?

9. How important of an issue do you think data accuracy is? Explain.

10. How important of a corporate resource is data compared to other corporate resources? Explain.

11. What factors led to the development of database management systems?

EXERCISES

1. Draw a timeline showing the landmark events in the history of data from ancient times to the present day. Do not include the development of computing devices in this timeline.

2. Draw a timeline for the last four hundred years, comparing landmark events in the history of data to landmark events in the development of computing devices.

3. Draw a timeline for the last two hundred years comparing the development of computing devices to the development of data storage media.

4. Invent a fictitious company in *one* of the following industries and list several ways in which the company can use data to gain a competitive advantage.

   a. Banking
   b. Insurance
   c. Manufacturing
   d. Airline

5. Invent a fictitious company in *one* of the following industries and describe the relationship between data as a corporate resource and the company's other corporate resources.

   a. Banking
   b. Insurance
   c. Manufacturing
   d. Airline

MINICASES

1. Throughout the world, vacation cruises on increasingly larger ships have been steadily growing in popularity. People like the all-inclusive price for food, room, and entertainment, the variety of shipboard activities, and the ability to unpack just once and still visit several different places on their vacation. The first of the two minicases that will be used throughout this book is the story of Happy Cruise Lines. Happy Cruise Lines has several ships and operates (begins its cruises) from a number of ports. It has a variety of vacation cruise itineraries, each involving several ports-of-call. The company wants to keep track of both its past and future cruises and of the passengers who sailed on past cruises and are booked on future cruises. Actually, you can think of a cruise line as simply a somewhat specialized case of any passenger transportation company, including airlines, trains, and buses. Beyond that, a cruise line is, after all, a business, and like any other business of any kind it must be concerned about its finances, employees, equipment, and so forth.

   a. Using this introductory description of (and hints about) Happy Cruise Lines, make a list of the things in Happy Cruise Lines' business environment about which you think the company would want to maintain data. Do some or all of these qualify as corporate resources? Explain.

   b. We've just begun to talk about data, but even at this early stage develop some ideas of how the data that you identified in part (a) can be used by Happy Cruise Lines to gain a competitive advantage over other cruise lines.

2. Sports are universally enjoyed activities around the globe. Whether the sport is a team or an individual sport, whether a person is a participant or a spectator, and whether the sport is played at the amateur or professional level, people of all ages and interests can enjoy this kind of activity in one way or another. Furthermore, professional sports today is a big business involving very large sums of money. And so, the second of the two minicases that will be used throughout this book is the story of the professional Super Baseball League. Like any sports league, the Super Baseball League wants to maintain information about its teams, coaches, players, and equipment, among other things. If you are not particularly familiar with baseball or simply prefer another sport, most of the issues that will come up in this minicase easily translate to any team sport at the amateur, college, or professional level. After all, all team sports have teams, coaches, players, fans, equipment, and so forth. When specialized equipment or other baseball-specific items come up, we will explain them.

   a. Using this introductory description of (and hints about) the Super Baseball League, make a list of the things in the Super Baseball League's business environment about which you think the league would want to maintain data. Do some or all of these qualify as corporate resources, where the term is broadened to include the resources of a sports league? Explain.

   b. We've just begun to talk about data, but even at this early stage develop some ideas of how the data that you identified in part (a) can be used by the Super Baseball League to gain a competitive advantage over other sports leagues for the fans' interest and entertainment dollars (or Euros, pesos, yen, etc.).

CHAPTER 2

SIMPLE FILE STORAGE AND RETRIEVAL

CHAPTER OBJECTIVES

After learning the material in this chapter, you will be able to:

- ✔ Discuss the nature of data.
- ✔ Define data-related terms such as entity and attribute and storage-related terms such as field, record, and file.
- ✔ Identify the four basic operations performed on stored data.
- ✔ Compare sequential access of data with direct access of data.
- ✔ Describe how a disk device works.
- ✔ Describe the principles of file organizations and access methods.
- ✔ Describe how simple linear indexes and B+-tree indexes work.
- ✔ Describe how hashed files work.

Photo Courtesy of Landau Uniforms

LANDAU UNIFORMS

Landau Uniforms is a premier supplier of professional apparel to the healthcare community, offering a comprehensive line of healthcare uniforms and related apparel. Headquartered in Olive Branch, Mississippi, the company, which dates back to 1938, has continuously expanded its operations both domestically and internationally and today includes corporate apparel among its products. Landau sells its apparel though authorized dealers throughout the U.S. and abroad.

Controlling Landau's product flow in its warehouse is a sophisticated information system that is anchored in database management. Their order filling system, which was implemented in 2001, is called the Garment Sortation System. It begins with taking orders which are then queued in preparation for "waves" of as many as eighty orders to be filled simultaneously. Each order is assigned a bin at the end of a highly automated conveyor line. The garments for the orders are picked from the shelves and placed onto the beginning of the conveyor line. Scanning devices then automatically direct the bar-coded garments into the correct bin. When an order is completed, it is boxed and sealed. The box then goes on another conveyor where it is automatically weighed, a shipping label is printed and attached to it, and it is routed to one of several shipping docks, depending on which shipper is being used. In addition, a bill is automatically generated and sent to the customer. In fact, for its more sophisticated customers, Landau bills them electronically using an electronic data interchange (EDI) system.

There are two underlying relational databases. The initial order processing is handled using a DB2 database running on an IBM "i" series computer. The orders are passed on to the Garment Sortation System's Oracle database running on PCs. The shipping is once again under the control of the DB2/"i" series system. The relational tables include an order table, a customer table, a style master table, and, of course, a garment table with 2.4 million records.

Printed by permission of Landau Uniforms

Every major technological advance in every field has been preceded by a series of steppingstones, and database is no exception. The historical progression outlined in Chapter 1 stressed the increasing importance of data in the development of civilization. It also described early and continuing efforts to develop devices for storing data. Does that mean we're ready to talk about database? Not quite. There are some fundamental ideas and definitions relating to data that apply whether or not the data is stored in a modern database. It is extremely important to gain a solid grasp of these concepts about what data is, and how to store and retrieve it, before we go on to deal with the subject of database.

WHAT IS DATA?

Important Objects and Facts

What is data? To start, what is a single piece of data? A single piece of data is a single fact about something that interests us. Think about the world around you, about your environment. In any environment there are things that are important to you, and there are facts about those things that are worth remembering. A "thing" can be an obvious object like an automobile or a piece of furniture. But the concept of an object is broad enough to include a person, an organization like a company, or an event that took place like a particular meeting. A fact can be any characteristic of an object. In a university environment it may be the fact that student Gloria Thomas has completed ninety-six credits; or it may be the fact that Professor Howard Gold graduated from Ohio State University; or it may be the fact that English 349 is being held in Room 830 of Alumni Hall. In a commercial environment, it may be the fact that employee John Baker's employee number is 137; or it may be the fact that one of a company's suppliers, the Superior Products Company, is located in Chicago; or it may be the fact that the refrigerator with serial number 958304 was manufactured on November 5, 2004.

Usually, we have many facts to describe something of interest to us in our environment. For example, let's consider the facts that might interest us about that employee of ours, John Baker. Our company is a sales-oriented company and John Baker is one of our salespersons. As mentioned above, we want to remember that his employee number (which we will now call his salesperson number) is 137. We are also interested in the facts that his commission percentage on the sales he makes is 10 percent, his home city is Detroit, his home state is Michigan, his office number is 1284, and he was hired in 1995. There are, of course, reasons that we need to keep track of these facts about John Baker, such as generating his paycheck every week. It certainly seems reasonable to collect all of the facts about Baker that we need and to hold all of them together. Figure 2.1 shows all of these facts about John Baker presented in an organized way.

RECORDS AND FILES

Since we have to generate a paycheck each week for every employee in our company, not just for Baker, we are obviously going to need a collection of facts such as those in Figure 2.1 for every one of our employees. Figure 2.2 shows a portion of that collection.

Let's start introducing some terminology along with some additional concepts. What we have been loosely referring to as a "thing" or "object" in our environment that we want to keep track of is called an **entity.** Remember that this is the real physical object or event, not the facts about it. John Baker, the real, living, breathing person whom you can go over to and touch, is an entity. A collection of entities of the same type (e.g., all of the company's employees) is called an **entity set.** An **attribute** is a property of, a characteristic of, or a fact that we know about an entity. Each characteristic or property of John Baker, including his salesperson number 137, his name, city of Detroit, state of Michigan, office number 1284, commission percentage 10, and year of hire 1995, are all attributes of John Baker. Some attributes have unique values within an entity set. For example, the salesperson numbers are unique within the salesperson entity set, meaning each salesperson has a different salesperson number. We can use the fact that salesperson numbers are unique to distinguish between the different salespersons.

Using the structure in Figure 2.2, we can define some standard file structure terms and relate them to the terms *entity, entity set,* and *attribute.* Each row in Figure 2.2 describes a single entity. Specifically, each row contains all of the facts

➤ **Figure 2.1**
Facts about salesperson Baker

Salesperson Number	Salesperson Name	City	State	Office Number	Commission Percentage	Year of Hire
137	Baker	Detroit	MI	1284	10	1995

➤ **Figure 2.2**
Salesperson file

Salesperson Number	Salesperson Name	City	State	Office Number	Commission Percentage	Year of Hire
119	Taylor	New York	NY	1211	15	2003
137	Baker	Detroit	MI	1284	10	1995
186	Adams	Dallas	TX	1253	15	2001
204	Dickens	Dallas	TX	1209	10	1998
255	Lincoln	Atlanta	GA	1268	20	2003
361	Carlyle	Detroit	MI	1227	20	2001
420	Green	Tucson	AZ	1263	10	1993

that we know about a particular entity. The first row contains all of the facts about salesperson 119, the second row contains all of the facts about salesperson 137, and so on. Each row of a structure like this is called a **record.** The columns, representing the facts, are called **fields.** The entire structure is called a **file.** The file in Figure 2.2, which is about the most basic kind of file imaginable, is often called a simple file or a **simple linear file** (linear because it is a collection of records listed one after the other in a long line). Since the salesperson attribute is unique, the salesperson field values can be used to distinguish the individual records of the file. Loosely speaking, at this point, the salesperson number field can be referred to as the **key field** or **key** of the file.

Tying together the two kinds of terminology that we have developed, we see that a record of a file describes an entity, a whole file contains the descriptions of an entire entity set, and a field of a record contains an attribute of the entity described by that record. In Figure 2.2, each row is a record that describes an entity, specifically a single salesperson. The whole file, row-by-row or record-by-record, describes each salesperson in the collection of salespersons. Each column of the file represents a different attribute of salespersons. At the row or entity level, the salesperson name field for the third row of the file indicates that the third salesperson, salesperson 186 has Adams as his salesperson name attribute, that is, he is named Adams.

One last terminology issue is the difference between the terms *type* and *occurrence.* Let's talk about it in the context of a record. If you look at a file, like that of Figure 2.2, there are two ways to describe "a record." One, which is referred to as the *record type,* is a structural description of each and every record in the file. Thus we would describe the salesperson record type as a record consisting of a salesperson number field, a salesperson name field, a city field, and so forth. This is a general description of what any of the salesperson records looks like. The other way of describing a record is referred to as a *record occurrence* or a *record instance.* A specific record of the salesperson file is a record occurrence or instance. Thus, we would say that, for example, the set of values {186, Adams, Dallas, TX, 1253, 15, 2001} is an occurrence of the salesperson record type.

BASIC CONCEPTS IN STORING AND RETRIEVING DATA

Having established the idea of a file and its records, we can now, in simple terms at this point, envision a company's data as a large collection of files. The next step is to discuss how we might want to access data from these files and otherwise manipulate the data in them.

Retrieving and Manipulating Data

Four fundamental operations can be performed on stored data, whether it is stored in the form of a simple linear file, such as that of Figure 2.2, or in any other form. The four are:

- **Retrieve or Read**
- **Insert**
- **Delete**
- **Update**

It is convenient to think of each of these operations as basically involving one record at a time, although in practice they can involve several records at one time, as we will see later in the book. Retrieving or reading a record means looking at a record's contents without changing it. For example, using the Salesperson file of Figure 2.2, we might read the record for salesperson 204 because we want to find out what year she was hired. Insertion means adding a new record to the file, as when a new salesperson is hired. Deletion means deleting a record from the file, as when a salesperson leaves the company. Updating means changing one or more of a record's field values, for example, if we want to increase salesperson 420's commission percentage from 10 to 15. There is clearly a distinction between retrieving or reading data and the other three operations. Retrieving data allows a user to refer to the data for some business purpose *without changing it.* All of the other three operations involve changing the data. Different topics in this book will focus on one or another of these operations simply because a particular one of the four operations may be more important to a particular topic than the others.

One particularly important concept concerning data retrieval is that while information systems applications come in a countless number of variations, there are fundamentally only two kinds of access to stored data that any of them require. These two ways of retrieving data are known as **sequential access** and **direct access.**

Sequential Access   The term *sequential access* means the retrieval of all or a portion of the records of a file one after another, in some sequence, starting from the beginning, until all of the required records have been retrieved. This could mean all of the records of the file, if that is the goal, or all of the records up to some point, such as up to the point that a record being searched for is found. The records will be retrieved in some order, and there are two possibilities for this retrieval. In **physical sequential access,** the records are retrieved, one after the other, just as they are stored on the disk device. (More will be said about these devices shortly.) In **logical sequential access,** the records are retrieved in an order based on the values of one or a combination of the fields.

Assuming the records of the Salesperson file of Figure 2.2 are stored on the disk in the order shown in the figure, if they are retrieved in physical sequence they will be retrieved in the order shown in the figure. However, if, for example, they were to be retrieved in logical sequence based on the Salesperson Name field, then the record for Adams would be retrieved first, followed by the record for Baker, followed by the record for Carlyle, and so on in alphabetic order. An example of an application that would require the physical sequential retrieval of the records of this file would be payroll processing every week. If the company wants to generate a payroll check for each salesperson in the order of their salesperson numbers, it can very simply retrieve the records physically in sequential order, since that's the order in which they were stored on the disk. If the company wants to produce the checks in the order of the salespersons' names, it will have to perform a logical sequential retrieval based on the Salesperson Name field. It can do so either by sorting the records on the Salesperson Name field or by using an index (see below) that is built on this field.

We said that sequential access could involve retrieving a portion of the records of a file. This sense of sequential retrieval usually means starting from the beginning of the file and searching every record, in sequence, until finding a particular record that is being sought. Obviously, this could take a long time for even a moderately large file and so is not a particularly desirable kind of operation, which leads to the concept of direct access.

Direct Access   The other mode of access is *direct access*—the retrieval of a single record of a file or a subset of the records of a file based on one or more values of a field or a combination of fields in the file. For example, in the Salesperson file of Figure 2.2, if we need to retrieve the record for salesperson 204 to find out her year of hire, we will perform a direct access operation on the file specifying that we want the record with a value of 204 in the Salesperson Number field. How do we know that we would retrieve only one record? Because the Salesperson Number field is the unique, key field of the file, there can only be one record (or none) with any one particular value. Another possibility is that we want to retrieve the records for all of the salespersons with a commission percentage of 10. The subset of the records retrieved would consist of the records for salespersons 137, 204, and 420.

Direct access is a crucial concept in information systems today. If you telephone a bank with a question about your account, you will not be happy having to wait on the phone while the bank's information system performs a sequential access of its customer file until it finds your record. Clearly, this example calls for direct access. The vast majority of information systems operations that all companies perform today require direct access. Two elements are needed to be able to accomplish direct access: a hardware storage device that will accommodate it and software that will take advantage of the hardware's capabilities and store and retrieve the data in such a way that it accomplishes direct access. Direct access is such a critically important concept to the field of database that the rest of this chapter will be devoted to these two elements.

DISK STORAGE

The Need for Disk Storage

Computers execute programs and process data in their main or **primary memory.** Primary memory is very fast and certainly does permit direct access, but it has several drawbacks:

- It is relatively expensive.
- It is not transportable (that is, you can't remove it from the computer and carry it away with you, as you can a diskette).
- It is volatile. When you turn the computer off, you lose whatever data is stored in it.

Because of these shortcomings, the vast volume of data and the programs that process them are held on secondary memory devices. Data is loaded from secondary memory into primary memory when required for processing (as are programs when they are to be executed). A loose analogy can be drawn between primary and secondary memory in a computer system and a person's brain and a library (Figure 2.3). The brain cannot possibly hold all of the information that a person might need,

➤ **Figure 2.3**
Primary and secondary
memory are like a brain
and a library

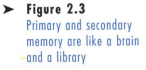

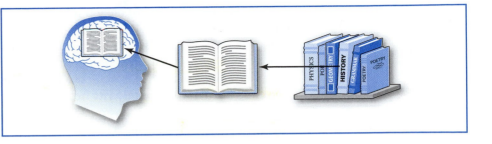

➤ **Figure 2.3**
Primary and secondary memory are like a brain and a library

but let's say a large library can. So when a person needs some particular information that's not in her brain at the moment, she finds a book in the library that has the information and, by reading it, transfers the information from the book into her brain. Secondary memory devices in use today include compact disks and magnetic tape, but by far the predominant secondary memory technology in use today is magnetic disk or simply disk.

How Disk Storage Works

The Structure of Disk Devices   Disks come in a variety of types and capacities, ranging from 3.5 inch **diskettes** that hold 1.44 million bytes of data on a single, plastic disk or **platter,** to large, multi-platter, aluminum or ceramic disk units that hold many billions of bytes of data. Some disks, like the PC diskettes, are designed to be removable; others, such as the **fixed** or **hard disk drives** in PCs and the disks associated with larger computers are designed to be nonremovable. The platters have a metallic coating that can be magnetized, and this is how the data is stored, bit-by-bit. Disks are very fast in terms of storage and retrieval times (although not nearly as fast as primary memory), provide a direct access capability to the data, are less expensive than primary memory units on a byte-by-byte basis, and are nonvolatile (when you turn off the computer or remove the diskette, you don't lose the data on the disk).

It is important to see how data is arranged on disks to understand how they provide a direct access capability. It is also important because making certain decisions as to how to arrange file or database storage on a disk can seriously affect the performance of the applications using the data, an issue that we will address later in the book under the heading of "physical database design."

In the large disk devices used with mainframe computers and midsized servers (as well as the hard drives or fixed disks in PCs), several disk platters are stacked together, and mounted on a central spindle, with some space in between them (Figure 2.4). In common usage, even a multiplatter arrangement like this is simply referred to as "the disk." Each of the two surfaces of a platter is a recording surface on which data can be stored. (*Note:* In some of these

➤ **Figure 2.4**
The platters of a disk are mounted on a central spindle

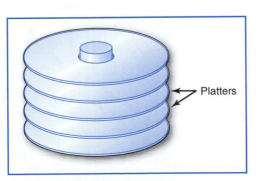

Platters

devices, the upper surface of the top-most platter and the lower surface of the bottom-most platter are not used for storing data. We will make this assumption in the following text and figures.) This arrangement of platters spins at high speed in the disk drive. The basic disk drive (there are more complex variations) has one **access arm mechanism** with arms that can reach in between the disks (Figure 2.5). At the end of each arm are two **read/write heads,** one for storing and retrieving data from the recording surface above the arm and the other for the surface below the arm, as shown in the figure. It is important to know and understand that the entire access arm mechanism always moves as a unit in and out among the disk platters, so that the read/write heads are always lined up exactly one above the other in a straight line. The platters spin, all together as a single unit, on the central spindle, at a high velocity. The spinning of the platters and the ability of the access arm mechanism to move in and out allow the read/write heads to be located over any piece of data on the entire unit, many times each second, and this is what mechanically provides the direct access capability.

Tracks On a recording surface, data is stored, serially by bit, in concentric circles known as **tracks** (Figure 2.6). There may be fewer than one hundred or several hundred tracks on each recording surface, depending on the particular device. In some devices each track holds the same amount of data while in others, the longer outer tracks hold more data than the shorter inner tracks. The tracks on a recording surface are numbered track 0, track 1, track 2, and so on. How would you store the Salesperson file of Figure 2.2 on a disk (and let's assume there are many more records in the file than are shown in Figure 2.2)? You might assume

➤ **Figure 2.5**
A disk drive with its access arm mechanism and read/write heads

➤ **Figure 2.6**
Tracks on a recording surface

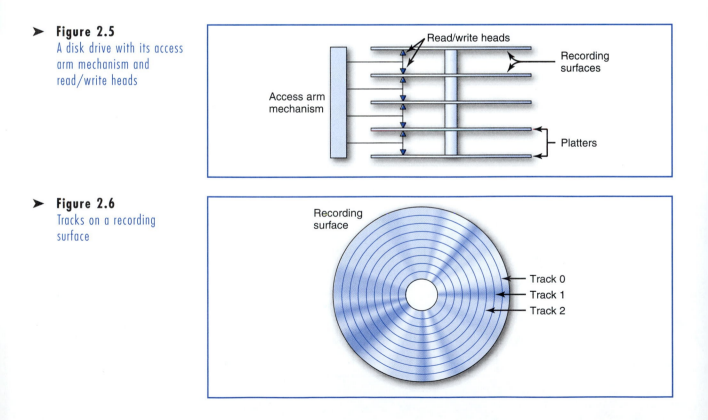

that you would fill up the first track on a particular surface, then fill up the next track on the surface, then the next, and so on until you had filled an entire surface. Then you would move on to the next surface. At first, this sounds reasonable and perhaps even obvious. But it turns out to be problematic. Every time you move from one track to the next on a surface, the device's access arm mechanism has to move. That's the only way that the read/write head, which can only read or write one track at a time, can get from one track to another on a given recording surface. But the access arm mechanism's movement is a slow, mechanical motion compared to the electronic processing speeds in the computer's central processing unit (CPU) and main memory. There is a better way to store the file!

Cylinders   Figure 2.7 shows the disk's access arm mechanism positioned so that the read/write head for recording surface 0 is positioned at that surface's track 76. Since the entire access arm mechanism moves as a unit and the read/write heads are always one over the other in a line, the read/write head for recording surface 1 is positioned at that surface's track 76, too. In fact, each surface's read/write head is positioned over its track 76. If you could picture the collection of each surface's track 76, one above the other, they would seem to take the shape of a cylinder (Figure 2.8). Indeed, each collection of tracks, one from each recording surface, one directly above the other, is known as a **cylinder.** Notice that the number of cylinders in a disk is equal to the number of tracks on any one of its recording surfaces.

If we want to number the cylinders in a disk, which seems like a reasonable thing to do, it is certainly convenient to give a cylinder the number corresponding to the track numbers that make it up. Thus the cylinder in Figure 2.8, which is made up of track 76 from each recording surface, will be numbered and called cylinder 76. There is one more point to make. So far, the numbering that we have looked at

➤ **Figure 2.7**
Each read/write head positioned over track 76 of its recording surface

➤ **Figure 2.8**
The collection of each recording surface's track 76 looks like a cylinder. This collection of tracks is called cylinder 76

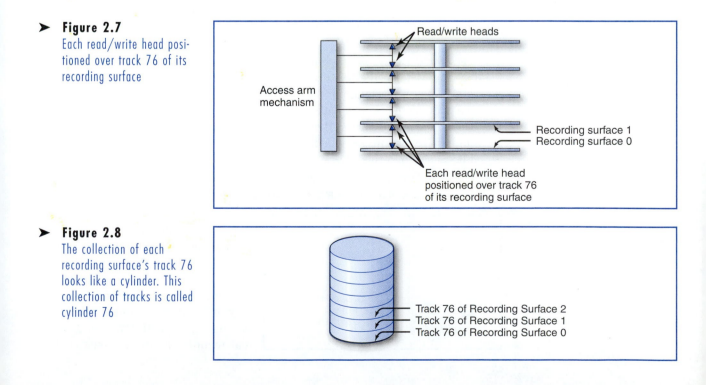

has been the numbering of the tracks on the recording surfaces which has also led to the numbering of the cylinders. But once we have established a cylinder, it is also necessary to number the tracks within the cylinder (Figure 2.9). Typically, these are numbered 0, 1, ..., n, which corresponds to the numbers of the recording surfaces. What will "n" be? That's the same question as how many tracks are there in a cylinder, but we've already answered that question. Since each recording surface "contributes" one track to each cylinder, the number of tracks in a cylinder is the same as the number of recording surfaces in a disk. The bottom line is that you have to remember that we are going to number the tracks across a recording surface and then, *perpendicular to that,* we are also going to number the tracks in a cylinder.

Why is the concept of the cylinder important? Because in storing or retrieving data on a disk, you can move from one track of a cylinder to another *without having to move the access arm mechanism.* The operation of turning off one read/write head and turning on another is an electrical switch that takes almost no time compared to the time it takes to move the access arm mechanism. Thus the ideal way to store data on a disk is to fill up one cylinder and then move on to the next cylinder, and so on. This speeds up the applications that use the data considerably. Incidentally, this may seem important only when reading files sequentially, as opposed to when performing the more important direct access operations. But we will see later in the book that in many database situations closely related pieces of data will have to be accessed together, and so storing them in such a way that they can be retrieved quickly can be a big advantage.

Steps in Finding and Transferring Data   To further clarify and summarize the way these disk devices work, there are four major steps or timing considerations in the transfer of data from a disk to primary memory:

1. **Seek Time:** The time it takes to move the access arm mechanism to the correct cylinder from whatever cylinder it's currently positioned at.
2. **Head Switching:** Selecting the read/write head to access the required track of the cylinder.
3. **Rotational Delay:** Waiting for the desired data on the track to arrive under the read/write head as the disk is spinning. On the average, this takes half the time of one full rotation of the disk. That's because, as the disk is spinning, at one extreme the needed data might have just arrived under the read/write head at the instant the head was turned on while at the other extreme you might have just missed it and have to wait for a full rotation. On the average, it takes half of a rotation.
4. **Transfer Time:** The time to actually move the data from the disk to primary memory once steps 1–3 have been completed.

➤ **Figure 2.9**
Cylinder 76's tracks

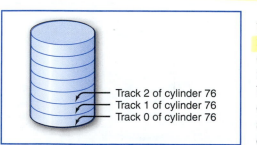

Track 2 of cylinder 76
Track 1 of cylinder 76
Track 0 of cylinder 76

One last point. Each record in the file in Figure 2.2 is called a **logical record.** Since the rate of processing data in the CPU is much faster than the rate at which data can be brought in from secondary memory, it is often advisable to transfer several, consecutively stored, logical records at a time. Once such a

physical record or **block** of several logical records has been brought into primary memory from the disk, each logical record can be examined and processed as necessary by the executing program.

FILE ORGANIZATIONS AND ACCESS METHODS

The Goal: Locating a Record

At this point we have established that we might want to retrieve the records of a file on either a sequential or a direct access basis. We have also established that disk devices are capable of storing records in some logical sequence, if we wish, and are capable of accessing records in the middle of a file. But that's still not enough to accomplish direct access.

Say that a file consists of many thousands or even a few million records. Further, say that there is a single record that you want to retrieve and you know the value of its unique identifier, its key. The question is, how do you know where it is on the disk? The disk device may be capable of going directly into the middle of a file to pull out a record, but how does it know where that particular record is? Remember, what we're trying to avoid is having it read through the file in sequence until finding the record being sought. It's not magic (nothing in a computer ever is), and it is important to have a basic understanding of each of the steps in working with simple files, including this step, before we talk about database. This brings us to the subject known as file organization and access methods, which refers to the way that we store the records of a file on the disk and the way that we retrieve them. We refer to the way that we store the data for subsequent retrieval as the **file organization.** The way that we retrieve the data, based on it being stored in a particular file organization, is called the **access method.** (Note in passing that the terms file organization and access method are often used synonymously, but this is technically incorrect.)

What we are primarily concerned with is how to achieve direct access of the records of a file, since this is the predominant mode of file operation today. In terms of file organizations and access methods, we can achieve direct access in two ways. One involves the use of a tool known as an **index.** The other is based on a way of storing and retrieving records known as a **hashing method.** The idea is that if we know the value of a field of a record that we want to retrieve, the index or hashing method will pinpoint its location in the file and instruct the hardware mechanisms of the disk device where to find it.

The Index

The interesting thing about the concept of an index is that while we are interested in it as a tool to provide direct access to the records in files, the principle involved is exactly the same as that governing the index in the back of a book. After all, a book is a storage medium for information about some subject. And in both books and files, we want to be able to find some portion of the contents "directly" without having to scan sequentially from the beginning of the book or file until we find it. With a book, we really have three choices for finding a particular portion of the contents. One is a sequential scan of every page starting from the beginning of the book until the desired content is found. The second is using the table of contents. The table of contents in the front of the book merely summarizes what is in the book by major topics and is written in the same order as the material in the book. To use the table of contents, you have to scan through it from the beginning and because the items included in it are summarized and written at a pretty high level, there is a good chance that you won't find what you're looking for. Even if you do, you will typically be directed to a page in the vicinity of the topic you're looking for, not to the exact page. The third choice is to use the index in the back of the book. The index is arranged alphabetically by item. As humans, we have the ability to efficiently do a quick search through the index, using the fact that the items in it are in alphabetic order, to quickly home in on the topic of interest. Then what? Next to the located item in the index appears a page number. Think of the page number as the address of the item you're looking for. In fact, it is a "direct pointer" to the page in the book where the material appears. You proceed directly to that page and find the material there (Figure 2.10).

The index in the back of a book has three key elements that are also characteristic of information systems indexes:

- The items of interest are copied over into the index, but the original text is not disturbed in any way.
- The items copied over into the index are sorted; they are alphabetized in the case of the index in the back of a book.
- Each item in the index is associated with a "pointer"; in the case of a book's index, this is a page number pointing to the place in the text where the item can be found.

Simple Linear Index The indexes used in information systems come in a variety of types and styles. We will start with what is called a **simple linear index** because it is relatively easy to understand and is very close in structure to the index in the back of a book. On the right-hand side of Figure 2.11 is the Salesperson file. As before, it is in order by the unique Salesperson Number field. It is reasonable

> **Figure 2.10**
> The index in a book

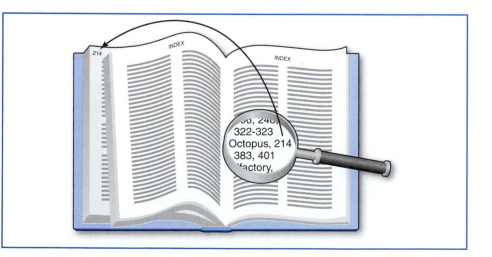

> **Figure 2.11**
Salesperson file on the right with index built over the Salesperson Name field, on the left

Index			Salesperson File			
Salesperson Name	Record Address		Record Number	Salesperson Number	Salesperson Name	City
Adams	3		1	119	Taylor	New York
Baker	2		2	137	Baker	Detroit
Carlyle	6		3	186	Adams	Dallas
Dickens	4		4	204	Dickens	Dallas
Green	7		5	255	Lincoln	Atlanta
Lincoln	5		6	361	Carlyle	Detroit
Taylor	1		7	420	Green	Tucson

to assume that the records of this file are stored on the disk in the sequence shown in Figure 2.11. (We note in passing that retrieving the records in physical sequence, as they are stored on the disk, would also have the effect of retrieving them in logical sequence by salesperson number, since they were in order by salesperson number when they were stored.) Figure 2.11 also shows that we have numbered the records of the file with a Record Number or a Relative Record Number ("relative" because the record number is relative to the beginning of the file). These record numbers are a handy way of referring to the records of the file, and the use of such record numbers is considered another way of "physically" locating a record in a file, just as a cylinder and track address is a physical address.

On the left hand-side of Figure 2.11 is an index built over the Salesperson Name field of the Salesperson file. Notice that the three rules for building an index in a book were observed here, too. The indexed items were copied over from the file to the index and the file was not disturbed in any way. The items in the index were sorted. Finally, each indexed item was associated with a physical address, in this case the relative record number (the equivalent of a page number in a book) of the record of the Salesperson file from which it came. The first index record shows Adams 3 because the record of the Salesperson file with salesperson name Adams is at relative record location 3 in the Salesperson file. Notice the similarity between this index and the index in the back of a book. Just as you would quickly find an item that you are looking for in a book's index because the items are in alphabetic order, a programmed procedure could quickly find one of the salespersons' names in the index because they are in sorted order. Then, just as the item that you found in the book's index would have a page number next to it telling you where to look for the detailed information you seek, the index record in the index of Figure 2.11 has the relative record number of the record of the Salesperson file that has the information, that is, the record, that you are looking for.

Figure 2.12, with an index built over the City field, demonstrates another point about indexes. An index can be built over a field with nonunique values.

Figure 2.13 shows the Salesperson file with an index built over the Salesperson Number field. This is an important concept known as an "indexed-sequential file." In an indexed-sequential file, the file is stored on the disk in order based on a set of field values (in this case the salesperson numbers), and an index is built *over that same field*. This allows both sequential and direct access by the

➤ **Figure 2.12**
Salesperson file on the right with index built over the City field, on the left

Index			Salesperson File			
City	Record Address		Record Number	Salesperson Number	Salesperson Name	City
Atlanta	5		1	119	Taylor	New York
Dallas	3		2	137	Baker	Detroit
Dallas	4		3	186	Adams	Dallas
Detroit	2		4	204	Dickens	Dallas
Detroit	6		5	255	Lincoln	Atlanta
New York	1		6	361	Carlyle	Detroit
Tucson	7		7	420	Green	Tucson

➤ **Figure 2.13**
Salesperson file on the right with index built over the Salesperson Number field, on the left

Index			Salesperson File			
Salesperson Number	Record Address		Record Number	Salesperson Number	Salesperson Name	City
119	1		1	119	Taylor	New York
137	2		2	137	Baker	Detroit
186	3		3	186	Adams	Dallas
204	4		4	204	Dickens	Dallas
255	5		5	255	Lincoln	Atlanta
361	6		6	361	Carlyle	Detroit
420	7		7	420	Green	Tucson

key field, which can be an advantage when applications with different retrieval requirements share the file. The odd thing about this index is that since the Salesperson file was already in sequence by the Salesperson Number field, when the salesperson numbers were copied over into the index they were already in sorted order! Further, for the same reason, the record addresses are also in order. In fact, in Figure 2.13, the Salesperson Number field in the Salesperson file, with the list of relative record numbers next to it, appears to be identical to the index. Then, why bother having an index built over the Salesperson Number field at all? In principle, the reason is that when the search algorithm processes the salesperson numbers, they have to be in primary memory. Again, in principle, it would be much more efficient to bring the smaller index into primary memory for this purpose than to bring the entire Salesperson file in, just to process the Salesperson Number field.

Why, in the last couple of sentences, did we keep using the phrase "in principle"? The answer to this question is closely tied to the question of whether simple linear indexes are practical for use in even moderately sized information systems applications. And the answer is that they are not. One reason (and here is where the "in principle" from the last paragraph comes in) is that even if the simple linear index is made up of just two columns, it would still be clumsy to try to move all of it or even parts of it into primary memory to use it in a search. At best, it would require many read operations to the disk on which the index is located. The second reason has to do with inserting new disk records. Once again, look at the Salesperson file and the index of Figure 2.11. Say that a new salesperson named French is hired and is assigned salesperson number 452. Her record can be inserted at the end of the Salesperson file where it would become record number 8. But the index would have to be updated, too. An index record, French 8, would have to be inserted between the index records for Dickens and Green to maintain the crucial alphabetic or sorted sequence of the index (Figure 2.14). The problem is that there is no obvious way to accomplish that insertion unless we move all of the index records from Green to Taylor down one record position. In even a moderate-sized file, that would clearly be impractical!

Indeed, the simple linear index is not a good solution for indexing the records of a file. This leads us to another kind of index that *is suitable* for indexing even very large files, the B+-tree index.

B+-Tree Index   The **B+-tree index,** in its many variations (and there are many, including one called the B*-tree), is far and away the most common data indexing system in use today. Assume that the Salesperson file now includes records for several hundred salespersons. Figure 2.15 is a variation of how the B+-tree index works. The figure shows the salesperson records arranged, in sequence, by the Salesperson Number field on ten cylinders, numbered 1–10, of a disk. Above the ten cylinders is an arrangement of special index records in what is known as a "tree." There is a single index record, known as the "root," at the top, with "branches" leading down from it to other "nodes." Sometimes the lowestlevel nodes are called "leaves." In terms of the terminology, think of it as a real tree turned upside-down with the roots clumped into a single point at the top (Figure 2.16). Alternately, you can think of it as a family tree, which normally has this kind of top-to-bottom orientation.

Notice the following about the index records in the tree:

- The index records contain salesperson number key values *copied from* certain of the salesperson records.
- Each key value in the tree is associated with a pointer that is the address of either a lower level index record or a cylinder containing the salesperson records.

➤ **Figure 2.14**
Salesperson file with the insertion of a record for #452 French. But how can you squeeze the index record into the proper sequence?

Index			Salesperson File			
Salesperson Name	Record Address		Record Number	Salesperson Number	Salesperson Name	City
Adams	3		1	119	Taylor	New York
Baker	2		2	137	Baker	Detroit
Carlyle	6		3	186	Adams	Dallas
Dickens	4		4	204	Dickens	Dallas
Green	7		5	255	Lincoln	Atlanta
Lincoln	5		6	361	Carlyle	Detroit
Taylor	1		7	420	Green	Tucson
			8	452	French	New York
French 8		?				

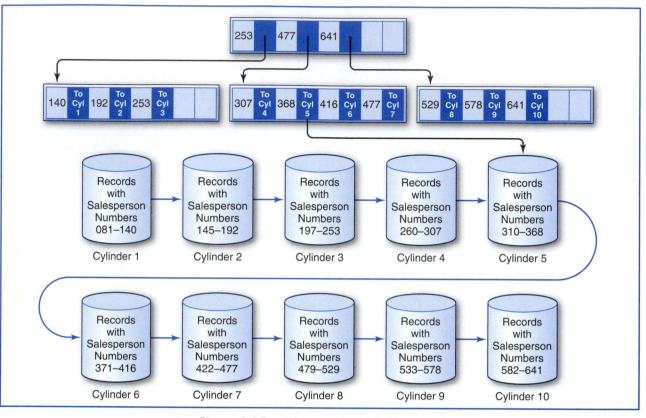

➤ **Figure 2.15** Salesperson file with a B+-tree index

- Each index record, at every level of the tree, contains space for the same number of key value/pointer pairs (four in this example). This index record capacity is arbitrary, but once it is set, it must be the same for every index record at every level of the index.

- Each index record is at least half full (i.e., in this example each actually contains at least two key value/pointer pairs).

How are the key values in the index tree constructed, and how are the pointers arranged? The lowest level of the tree contains the highest key value of the salesperson records on each of the ten data cylinders. That's why there are ten key values in the lowest level of the index tree. Each of those ten key values has a pointer to the data cylinder from which it was copied. For example, the leftmost index record on the lowest level of the tree contains key values 140, 192, and 253, which are the highest key values on cylinders 1, 2, and 3, respectively. The root index record contains the highest key value of each of the index records at the next (which happens to be the last in this case) level down. Looking down from the root index record, notice that 253 is the highest key value of the first index record at the next level down and so on for key values 477 and 641 in the root.

Let's say that you wanted to perform a direct access for the record for salesperson 361. A stored search routine would start at the root and scan its key values from

➤ **Figure 2.16**
A real tree, upside down, with the roots clumped together into a single point

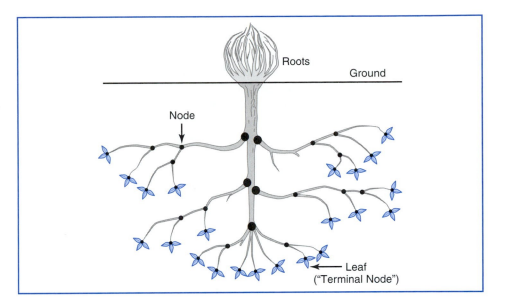

left to right, looking for the first key value higher than or equal to 361, the key value for which you are searching. Starting from the left, we see that the first key value in the root higher than or equal to 361 is 477. The routine would then follow the pointer associated with key value 477 to the second of the three index records at the next level. The search would be repeated in that index record, following the same rules. This time, key value 368 is the first one from the left, higher than or equal to 361. The routine would then follow the pointer associated with key value 368 to cylinder 5. Additional search cues within the cylinder could then point to the track and possibly even the position on the track at which the record for salesperson 361 would be found.

Several additional points can be noted about this B+-tree arrangement:

- The tree index is small and can be kept in main memory indefinitely for a frequently accessed file.
- The file and index of Figure 2.15 fit the definition of an indexed-sequential file, because the file is stored in sequence by the salesperson numbers and the index is built over the Salesperson Number field.
- The file can be retrieved in sequence by salesperson number by pointing from the end of one cylinder to the beginning of the next, which is typically done without even using the tree index.
- B+-tree indexes can be and are routinely used to index nonkey, nonunique fields, although the tree can be deeper and/or the structures at the end of the tree can be more complicated.
- In general, the storage unit for groups of records can be (as in the above example) but does not have to be the cylinder or any other physical device subunit.

The final point to make about B+-tree indexes is that, unlike simple linear indexes, they are designed to comfortably handle the insertion of new records into the file and to handle record deletion. The principle for this is based on the idea of unit splits and contractions, both at the record storage and index tree level. For example, say that a new record with salesperson number 365 must be inserted. Starting from the root and following the same procedure for a record search, the computer determines that this record should be located on cylinder 5 in order to maintain the sequence of the records based on the salesperson number key. If there is room on the track on that cylinder that it should go into to maintain the sequence, the other records can be shifted over and there is no problem. If the track it should go into is full but another track on the cylinder has been left empty as a reserve, then the set of records on the full track plus the one for 365 can be "split," with half of them staying on the original track and the other half moving to the reserve track. There would also have to be a mechanism to maintain the proper sequence of the tracks within the cylinder as the split may have thrown it off.

But suppose that cylinder 5 is completely full. Then the collection of records on the entire cylinder has to be split between cylinder 5 and an empty reserve cylinder, say cylinder 11 (Figure 2.17). That's fine, except that the key value of 368 in the tree index's lowest level still points to cylinder 5, while the record with key value 368 is now on cylinder 11. Furthermore, there is no key value/pointer pair representing cylinder 11 in the tree index, at all! If the lowest level index record containing key value 368 had room in it, a pointer to the new cylinder could be added and the keys in the key value/pointer pairs adjusted. But, as can be seen in Figure 2.15, there is no room in that index record.

Figure 2.18 shows how this situation is handled. The index record, into which the key for the new cylinder should go (the middle of the three index records at the lower level), which happens to be full, is split into two index records. The now five instead of four key values and their associated pointers are divided, as equally as possible, between them. But in Figure 2.15, there were three key values in the record at the next level up (which happens to be the root), and now there are four index records instead of the previous three at the lower

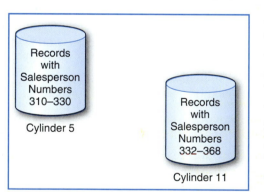

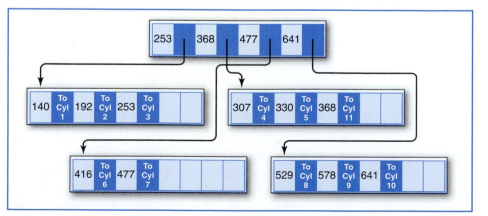

level. As shown in Figure 2.18, the empty space in the root index record is used to accommodate the new, fourth index record at the lower level. What would have happened if the root index record had already been full? It would have split in half, and a new root at the next level up would have been created, expanding the index tree from two levels of index records to three levels.

Remember the following about indexes in general:

- An index can be built over any field of a file, whether or not the file is in physical sequence based on that or any other field. The field does not have to have unique values.
- An index can be built on a single field, but it can also be built on a combination of fields. For example, an index could be built on the combination of City and State in the Salesperson file of Figure 2.2.
- In addition to its direct access capability, an index can be used to retrieve the records of a file in logical sequence based on the indexed field. For example, the index in Figure 2.11 could be used to retrieve the records of the Salesperson file in sequence by salesperson name. Since the index is in sequence by salesperson name, a simple scan of the index from beginning to end lists the relative record numbers of the salesperson records in order by salesperson name.
- Many separate indexes into a file can exist simultaneously, each based on a different field or combination of fields of the file. The indexes are quite independent of each other.
- When a new record is inserted into a file, an existing record is deleted, or an indexed field is updated, all of the affected indexes must be updated.

Hashed Files

There are many applications in which all file accesses must be done on a direct basis; speed is of the essence, and there is no particular need for the file to be organized in sequence by the values of any of its fields. An approach to file organization and access that fits this bill is the **hashed file.** The basic ideas include the following:

- The number of records in a file is estimated, and enough space is reserved on a disk to hold them.
- Additional space is reserved for additional **overflow records.**
- To determine where to insert a particular record of the file, the record's key value is converted by a **hashing routine** into one of the reserved record locations on the disk.
- To subsequently find and retrieve the record, the same hashing routine is applied to the key value during the search.

Say, for example, that our company has 50 salespersons and that we have reserved enough space on the disk for their 50 records. There are many hashing routines, but the most common is known as the **division-remainder method.** In this method, we divide the key value of the record that we want to insert or retrieve by the number of record locations that we have reserved. Remember long division with its quotient and remainder? We perform the division, discard the quotient, and use the remainder to tell us where to locate the record. Why the remainder?

Because the remainder is tailor-made to point to one of the storage locations. If, as in this example, we have 50 storage locations and divide a key value by that number, 50, we will get a remainder that is a whole number between 0 and 49. The value of the quotient doesn't matter. If we number the 50 storage locations 0–49 and store a record at the location dictated by its "hashed" key value, we have clearly developed a way to store and then locate the records, and a very fast way, at that! There's only one problem. More than one key value can hash to the same location. When this happens, we say that a *collision* has occurred and the two key values involved are known as "synonyms."

Figure 2.19 shows a storage area that can hold 50 salesperson records plus space for overflow records. (We will not go into how to map this space onto the cylinders and tracks of a disk, but it can easily be done.) The main record storage locations are numbered 0–49; the overflow locations begin at position 50. An additional field for a **synonym pointer** has been added to every record location. Let's start by storing the record for salesperson 186. Dividing 186 by the number of record locations, 50, yields a quotient of 3 (which we don't care about) and a remainder of 36. So, as shown in the figure, we store the record for salesperson 186 at record location 36. Next, we want to store the record for salesperson 361. This time the hashing routine gives a remainder of 11, and, as shown in the figure, that's where the record goes. The next record to be stored is the record for salesperson 436. The hashing routine produces a remainder of 36. The procedure tries to store the record at location 36 but finds another record is already stored there.

To solve this problem, the procedure stores the new record at one of the overflow record locations, say number 50. It then indicates this by storing that location number in the synonym pointer field of record 36. When another collision occurs

➤ **Figure 2.19**
The Salesperson file stored as a hashed file

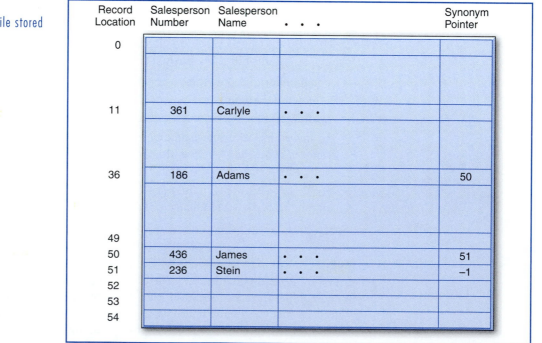

Record Location	Salesperson Number	Salesperson Name	. . .	Synonym Pointer
0				
11	361	Carlyle	. . .	
36	186	Adams	. . .	50
49				
50	436	James	. . .	51
51	236	Stein	. . .	−1
52				
53				
54				

with the insertion of salesperson 236, this record is stored at the next overflow location and its location is stored at location 50, the location of the last record that "hashed" to 36.

Subsequently, if an attempt is made to retrieve the record for salesperson 186, the key value hashes to 36, and, indeed, the record for salesperson 186 is found at location 36. If an attempt is made to retrieve the record for salesperson 436, the key hashes to 36, but another record (the one for salesperson 186) is found at location 36. The procedure then follows the synonym pointer at the end of location 36 to location 50, where it finds the record for salesperson 436. A search for salesperson 236's record would follow the same procedure. Key value 236 would hash to location 36, but another record would be found there. The synonym pointer in the record at location 36 points to location 50, but another record, 436, is found there, too. The synonym pointer in the record at location 50 points to location 51, where the desired record is found.

There are a few other points to make about hashed files:

- The way that the hashing algorithm scatters records within the storage space disallows any sequential storage based on a set of field values.
- A file can only be hashed once, based on the values of a single field or a single combination of fields. This is because the essence of the hashing concept includes the physical placement of the records based on the result of the hashing routine. A record can't be located in one place based on the hash of one field and then at the same time be placed somewhere else based on the hash of another field. It can't be in two places at once!
- If a file is hashed on one field, direct access based on another field can be achieved by building an index on the other field.
- Many hashing routines have been developed. The goal is to minimize the number of collisions and synonyms which can obviously slow down retrieval performance. In practice, several hashing routines are tested on a file to determine the best "fit." Even a relatively simple procedure like the division-remainder method can be fine-tuned. In this method, experience has shown that once the number of storage locations has been determined, it would be better to choose a slightly higher number, specifically the next higher prime number or number not evenly divisible by any number less than 20.
- A hashed file must occasionally be **reorganized** after so many collisions have occurred that performance is degraded to an unacceptable level. A new storage area with a new number of storage locations is chosen, and the process starts all over again.
- Figure 2.19 shows a value of -1 in the synonym pointer field of the record for salesperson 236 at storage location 51. This is an end-of-chain marker. It is certainly possible that a search could be conducted for a record, say with key value 386, that does not exist in the file. Key value 386 would hash to 36 and the chain would be followed to location 50 and then to location 51. Some signal must then be set up at the end of the chain to indicate that there are no more records stored in the file that hash to 36, so that the search can be declared over and a "not found" condition indicated. (A negative number is a viable signal because there can't be a negative record location!)

KEY TERMS

Access arm mechanism
Access method
Attribute
Block
B+-tree index
Collision
Cylinder
Delete
Direct access
Diskette
Division-remainder method
Entity
Entity set
Fact
Field
File
File organization

Fixed disk drive
Hard disk drive
Hashed file
Hashing method
Hashing routine
Head switching
Index
Insert
Key
Key field
Logical record
Logical sequential access
Overflow records
Physical record
Physical sequential access
Platter
Primary memory

Read
Read/write head
Record
Reorganization
Retrieve
Rotational delay
Seek time
Sequential access
Simple linear file
Simple linear index
Synonym
Synonym pointer
Track
Transfer time
Update

QUESTIONS

1. What is data? Do you think the word "data" should be treated as a singular or plural word? Why?

2. Name some entities and their attributes in a university environment.

3. Name some entities and attributes in an insurance company environment.

4. Name some entities and attributes in a furniture store environment.

5. What is the relationship between:
   a. An entity and a record?
   b. An attribute and a field?
   c. An entity set and a file?

6. What is the difference between a record type and an occurrence of that record? Give some examples.

7. Name the four basic operations on stored data. In what important way is one, in particular, different from the other three?

8. What is sequential access? What is direct access? Which of the two is more important in today's business environment? Why?

9. Give an example of and describe an application that would require sequential access in:
   a. The university environment.
   b. The insurance company environment.
   c. The furniture store environment.

10. Give an example of and describe an application that would require direct access in:

a. The university environment
b. The insurance company environment
c. The furniture store environment

11. Discuss the reasons for having both primary and secondary memories in a computer system.

12. Describe the following disk concepts or components.
   a. Platter and recording surface
   b. Track
   c. Cylinder
   d. Read/write head
   e. Access arm mechanism

13. Why is it important to store files on a cylinder-by-cylinder basis?

14. Describe the four steps in the transfer of data from disk to primary memory.

15. What is a file organization? What is an access method? What do they accomplish?

16. What is an index? Compare the concept of the index in a book to an index in an information system.

17. Describe the idea of the simple linear index. What are its shortcomings?

18. What is an indexed-sequential file?

19. Describe the idea of the B+-tree index. What are its advantages in comparison to the simple linear index?

20. Describe how a direct search works using a B+-tree index.

21. Describe what happens to the index tree when you insert new records into a file with a B+-tree index.

22. Answer the following general questions about indexes:

a. Can an index be built over a nonunique field?

b. Can an index be built over a field by which the file is not stored in sequence?

c. Can an index be built over a combination of fields as well as over a single field?

d. Is there a limit to the number of indexes that can be built for a file?

e. How is an index affected when a change is made to a file? Does every change to a file affect every one of its indexes?

f. Can an index be used to achieve sequential access? Explain.

23. Describe the idea of the hashed file. What are its advantages and disadvantages in comparison to indexes?

24. Describe how a direct search works in a hashed file using the division-remainder method of hashing.

25. What is a collision in a hashed file? Why do collisions occur? Why is a collision of concern in the application environment?

EXERCISES

1. A fixed disk consists of six platters. The upper surface of the top-most platter and the lower surface of the bottom-most platter are not used for recording data. There are 120 tracks on each recording surface. How many of each of the following are there in the disk:

a. Recording surfaces?

b. Cylinders?

c. Tracks per cylinder?

2. A fixed disk has 80 cylinders. The tracks in each cylinder are numbered 0-11. The upper surface of the top-most platter and the lower surface of the bottom-most platter are not used for recording data. How many of each of the following are there in the disk:

a. Recording surfaces?

b. Platters?

c. Tracks per recording surface?

3. Consider the B+-tree index below:

a. A record has just been added to cylinder 6, causing a cylinder split. The highest key value on cylinder 6 is now 2156; the highest key value on cylinder 20, the empty reserve cylinder that received half of

cylinder 6's records, is now 2348. Update the tree index accordingly.

b. A record has just been added to cylinder 10, causing a cylinder split. The highest key value on cylinder 10 is now 3780; the highest key value on cylinder 25, the empty reserve cylinder that received half of cylinder 10's records, is now 3900. Update the tree index accordingly. [*Note:* This question is intended to be independent of the question in part (a). Start each of parts (a) and (b) from the figure shown.]

4. A hashed file has space for 70 records. Relative record numbers of 0–69 label each of the 70 record positions. In addition, there is space for several overflow (synonym) records. Draw a picture of the file, and using the division-remainder method, store records with each of the following four digit keys, accounting for collisions as necessary:

a. 4000

b. 5207

c. 0360

d. 1410

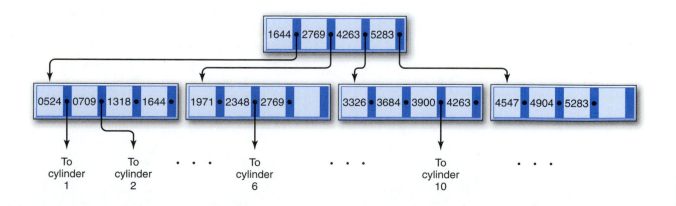

MINICASES

1. Happy Cruise Lines.

   a. Consider the Happy Cruise Lines Sailor file shown below. It lists all of the sailors on the company's cruise ships by their unique sailor identification number, their name, the unique identification number of the ship they currently work on, their home country, and their job title.

Sailor File				
Sailor Number	Sailor Name	Ship Number	Home Country	Job Title
00536	John Smith	009	USA	Purser
00732	Ling Chang	012	China	Engineer
06988	Maria Gonzalez	020	Mexico	Purser
16490	Prashant Kumar	005	India	Navigator
18535	Alan Jones	009	UK	Cruise Director
20254	Jane Adams	012	USA	Captain
23981	Rene Lopez	020	Philippines	Captain
27467	Fred Jones	020	UK	Waiter
27941	Alain DuMont	009	France	Captain
28184	Susan Moore	009	Canada	Wine Steward
31775	James Collins	012	USA	Waiter
32856	Sarah McLachlan	012	Ireland	Cabin Steward

   i. Describe the file's record type.
   ii. Show a record occurrence.
   iii. Describe the set or range of values that the Ship Number field can take.
   iv. Describe the set or range of values that the Home Country field can take.

   b. Assume that the records of the Sailor file are physically stored in the order shown.
   i. Retrieve all of the records of the file physically sequentially.
   ii. Retrieve all of the records of the file logically sequentially based on the Sailor Name field.
   iii. Retrieve all of the records of the file logically sequentially based on the Sailor Number field.
   iv. Retrieve all of the records of the file logically sequentially based on the Ship Number field.
   v. Perform a direct retrieval of the records with a Sailor Number field value of 27467.
   vi. Perform a direct retrieval of the records with a

   Ship Number field value of 020.
   vii. Perform a direct retrieval of the records with a Job Title field value of Captain.

   c. Create a simple linear index for the Sailor file based on:
   i. The Sailor Name field
   ii. The Sailor Number field
   iii. The Ship Number field
   iv. The combination of the Ship Number and the Job Title fields

   d. Construct a B+-tree index of the type shown in this chapter for the Sailor file, *assuming that now there are many more records than are shown above.* The file and the index have the following characteristics:

   - The file is stored on nine cylinders of the disk. The highest key values on the nine cylinders, in order, are:
     Cylinder 1: 02653
     Cylinder 2: 07784
     Cylinder 3: 13957
     Cylinder 4: 18002
     Cylinder 5: 22529
     Cylinder 6: 27486
     Cylinder 7: 35800
     Cylinder 8: 41633
     Cylinder 9: 48374
   - Each index record can hold four key value/pointer pairs.
   - There are three index records at the lowest level of the tree index.

   e. The same as part (d) above, but now there are four index records at the lowest level of the tree index.

   f. The same as part (d) above, but each index record can hold two key value/pointer pairs and there are five index records at the lowest level of the tree index.

2. The Super Baseball League.

   a. Consider the Super Baseball League Player file shown below. It lists all of the players in the league by their unique player identification number, their name, age, the year they joined the league, and the team on which they are currently playing.

Player File				
Player Number	Player Name	Age	First Year	Team Number
1538	Fred Williams	23	2003	12
1882	Tom Parker	29	2000	35
2071	Juan Gomez	33	1990	12
2364	Steve Smith	24	2002	20
2757	Tim Jones	37	1988	18
3186	Dave Lester	29	1998	18
3200	Rod Smith	25	2002	20
3834	Chico Lopez	24	2003	12
4950	Chris Vernon	26	2003	15
5296	Barry Morton	30	1995	35

  i. Describe the file's record type.
  ii. Show a record occurrence.
  iii. Describe the set or range of values that the Player Number field can take.
  iv. Describe the set or range of values that the First Year field can take.

b. Assume that the records of the Player file are physically stored in the order shown.

  i. Retrieve all of the records of the file physically sequentially.
  ii. Retrieve all of the records of the file logically sequentially based on the Player Name field.
  iii. Retrieve all of the records of the file logically sequentially based on the Player Number field.
  iv. Retrieve all of the records of the file logically sequentially based on the Team Number field.
  v. Perform a direct retrieval of the records with a Player Number field value of 3834.
  vi. Perform a direct retrieval of the records with a Team Number field value of 20.

  vii. Perform a direct retrieval of the records with an Age field value of 24.

c. Create a simple linear index for the Player file based on:

  i. The Team Number field.
  ii. The Player Name field.
  iii. The Player Number field.
  iv. The combination of the Team Number and the Player Number fields.

d. Construct a B+-tree index of the type shown in this chapter for the Player file, *assuming that now there are many more records than are shown above*. The file and the index have the following characteristics:

  • The file is stored on eight cylinders of the disk. The highest key values on the eight cylinders, in order, are:

  Cylinder 1: 1427
  Cylinder 2: 1965
  Cylinder 3: 2848
  Cylinder 4: 3721
  Cylinder 5: 4508
  Cylinder 6: 5396
  Cylinder 7: 6530
  Cylinder 8: 7442

  • Each index record can hold four key value/pointer pairs.
  • There are three index records at the lowest level of the tree index.

e. The same as part (d) above, but now there are four index records at the lowest level of the tree index.

f. The same as part (d) above, but each index record can hold two key value/pointer pairs and there are four index records at the lowest level of the tree index.

CHAPTER 3

DATA MODELING

CHAPTER OBJECTIVES

After learning the material in this chapter, you will be able to:

✔ Explain the concept and practical use of data modeling.
✔ Recognize which relationships in the business environment are unary, binary, and ternary relationships.
✔ Describe one-to-one, one-to-many, and many-to-many unary, binary, and ternary relationships.
✔ Recognize and describe intersection data.
✔ Model data in business environments by drawing entity-relationship diagrams that involve unary, binary, and ternary relationships.

Photo Courtesy of The Walt Disney Company

THE WALT DISNEY COMPANY

The Walt Disney Company is world-famous for its many entertainment ventures but it is especially identified with its theme parks. First there was Disneyland in Los Angeles, then the mammoth Walt Disney World in Orlando. These were followed by parks in Paris and Tokyo, and one now under development in Hong Kong. The Disney theme parks are so well-run that they create a wonderful feeling of natural harmony with everyone and everything being in the right place at the right time. When you're there, it's too much fun to stop to think about how all of this is organized and carried off with such precision. But is it any wonder to learn that database plays a major part?

One of the Disney theme parks' interesting database applications keeps track of all of the costumes worn by the workers or "cast members" in the parks. The system is called the Garment Utilization System or GUS (which was also the name of one of the mice that helped Cinderella sew her dress!). Managing these costumes is no small task. Virtually all of the cast members, from the actors and dancers to the ride operators, wear some kind of costume. Disneyland in Los Angeles has 684,000 costume parts (each costume is typically made up of several garments) each of which is uniquely bar-coded, for its 46,000 cast members. The numbers in Orlando are three million garments and 90,000 cast members. Using bar-code scanning, GUS tracks the life cycle of every garment. This includes the points in time when a garment is in the storage facility, is checked-out to a cast member, is in the laundry, or is out for repair (in house or at a vendor). In addition to managing the day-to-day movements of the costumes, the system also provides a rich data analysis capability. The industrial engineers in Disney's business planning group use the accumulated data to decide how many garments to keep in stock and how many people to have staffing the garment check-out windows based on the expected wait times. They also use the data to determine whether certain fabrics or the garments made by specific manufacturers are not holding up well through a reasonable number of uses or of launderings.

GUS, which was inaugurated at Disneyland in Los Angeles in 1998 and then again at Walt Disney World in Orlando in 2002, replaced a manual system in which the costume data was written on index cards. It is implemented in Microsoft's SQL Server DBMS and runs on a Compaq server. It is also linked to an SAP personnel database to help maintain the status of the cast members. If GUS is ever down, the process shifts to a Palm Pilot-based backup system, which can later update the database. For purposes of keeping track of the costume parts and cast members, not surprisingly, there is a relational table for costume parts with one record for each garment and there is a table for cast members with one record for each cast member. The costume parts records include the type of garment, its size, color, and even such details as whether its use is restricted to a particular cast member and whether it requires a special laundry detergent. Correspondingly, the cast member records include the person's clothing sizes and other specific garment requirements.

Ultimately, GUS' database precision serves several purposes in addition to its fundamental managerial value. The Walt Disney Company feels that consistency in how its visitors or "guests" look at a given ride gives them an important comfort level. Clearly, GUS provides that consistency in the costuming aspect. In addition, GUS takes the worry out of an important part of each cast member's workday. One of Disney's creeds is that the company strives to take good care of its cast members so that they will take good care of Disney's guests. Database management is a crucial tool in making this work so well.

Printed by permission of The Walt Disney Company

There are several preliminary steps that we have to take before discussing database management. In the last chapter, we established the concept of the entity and the idea of storing data about entities in simple linear files. Then we distinguished sequential access from direct access. From there we developed a foundation for accomplishing direct access of data from simple linear files both from the hardware side with disk technology and from the software side with index and hashing-based file organizations and access methods.

Before beginning our discussion of database management, however, there is yet one more preliminary to cover, one more direction from which to approach the subject. If Chapter 2 approached the subject from the technology side, this chapter, on data modeling, will approach it from the business side. Before considering database management, we have to explore the different ways that entities can relate to each other as they always do in the real world. Furthermore, we have to devise a way of recording, of diagramming, the entities and the ways in which they interrelate in the business environment. This is the essence of **data modeling.**

INTRODUCTION

The diagramming technique that we will use is called the **entity-relationship** or **E-R model.** It is well named, for it diagrams entities (together with their attributes) and the relationships between them. Actually, there are many variations of **E-R diagrams,** and drawing them is as much an art as a science. We will take the best ideas from several of these variations, add a few of our own, and come up with an E-R diagramming technique that does the job and is reasonably easy to work with.

In Chapter 2, we defined an entity as an object or event in our environment that we want to keep track of and we defined an attribute as a property or characteristic of an entity. Figure 3.1, with its rectangular shape, represents a type of entity. The name of the entity type (SALESPERSON) is set in caps above the separator line. The entity type's attributes are shown below the separator line. An asterisk denotes the one or more attributes that constitute the entity type's **unique identifier** (*).

In the real world, entities never really stand alone; they are typically associated with each other. Parents are associated with their children, automobile parts are associated with the finished automobile in which they are installed, firefighters are associated with the fire engines to which they are assigned, and so forth. Recognizing and recording the associations among entities provide a far richer description of an environment than recording the entities alone. In order to intelligently and usefully deal with the associations or **relationships** between entities, we have to recognize that there are several different kinds of relationships and several different aspects of describing them. The most basic way of categorizing a relationship is by the number of entity types involved.

BINARY RELATIONSHIPS

What Is a Binary Relationship?

The simplest kind of relationship is known as the **binary relationship**—a relationship between two entity types. Figure 3.2 shows a small E-R diagram with a binary relationship between two entity types, salespersons and products. The diamond-shaped box represents the relationship. The E-R diagram in Figure 3.2 tells us that a salesperson "sells" products. Conversely, products are sold by salespersons. That's good information, but we can do better than that with a very small increase in effort. Just knowing that a salesperson sells products leaves open several obvious and important questions. Is a particular salesperson allowed to sell only one kind of product, or two, or three, or all of the available products? Can a particular product be sold by only a single salesperson or by all of the salespersons? Might we want to keep track of a new salesperson who has just joined the company but has not been assigned to sell any products yet (assuming that there is indeed a restriction on which salespersons can sell which products)?

➤ **Figure 3.1**
An E-R model entity and its attributes

SALESPERSON

*Salesperson Number
Salesperson Name
Commission Percentage
Year of Hire

One Salesperson

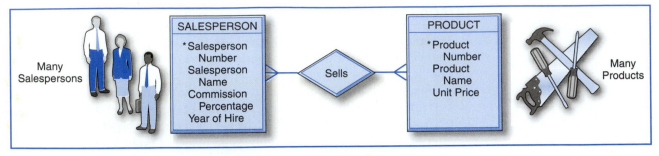

➤ **Figure 3.2** A binary relationship

Cardinality

One-to-One Binary Relationship Figure 3.3 shows three binary relationships of different **cardinalities,** representing the *maximum* number of entities that can be involved in a particular relationship. Figure 3.3a shows a **one-to-one (1-1) binary relationship,** which means that a single occurrence of one entity type can be associated with a single occurrence of the other entity type and vice versa. A

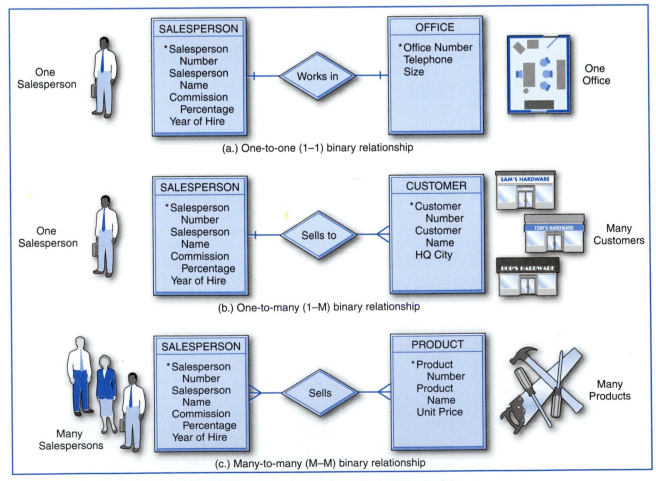

(a.) One-to-one (1–1) binary relationship

(b.) One-to-many (1–M) binary relationship

(c.) Many-to-many (M–M) binary relationship

➤ **Figure 3.3** Binary relationships with cardinalities

particular salesperson is assigned to one office. Conversely, a particular office (they are all private offices) has just one salesperson assigned to it. Note the "bar" or "one" symbol on either end of the relationship in the diagram indicating the maximum one cardinality. The way to read these diagrams is to start at one entity, read the relationship in the diamond, pick up the cardinality *on the other side of the diamond near the second entity,* and then finally reach the other entity. Thus, Figure 3.3a, reading from left to right, says, "A salesperson works in one (really at most one, since it is a maximum) office." The bar or one symbol involved in this statement is the one just to the left of the office entity box. Conversely, reading from right to left, "An office is worked in by (is assigned to) one salesperson."

One-to-Many Binary Relationship   Associations can also be multiple in nature. Figure 3.3b shows a **one-to-many (1–M) binary relationship** between salespersons and customers. The "crow's foot" device attached to the customer entity box represents the multiple association. Reading from left to right, the diagram indicates that a salesperson sells to many customers. (Note that "many," as the maximum number of occurrences that can be involved, means a number that can be 1, 2, 3, ... n. It also means that the number is not restricted to being *exactly* one, which would require the "one" or "bar" symbol instead of the crow's foot.) Reading from right to left, it says that a customer is sold to by only one salesperson. This is reasonable, indicating that in this company each salesperson has an exclusive territory and thus each customer can only be sold to by one salesperson from the company.

Many-to-Many Binary Relationship   Figure 3.3c shows a **many-to-many (M–M) binary relationship** between salespersons and products. A salesperson is authorized to sell many products; a product can be sold by many salespersons. By the way, sometimes "many" can be either an exact number or have a known maximum, in either the 1–M or M–M case. For example, a company rule may set a limit of a maximum of ten customers in a sales territory. Then the "many" in the 1–M relationship of Figure 3.3b can never be more than ten (a salesperson can have many customers but not more than ten). Sometimes people will include this exact number or maximum next to or even instead of the crow's foot on the E-R diagram.

Modality

Figure 3.4 shows the addition of the **modality**—the *minimum* number of entity occurrences that can be involved in a relationship. In our particular salesperson environment, every salesperson must be assigned to an office. On the other hand, a given office might be empty or it might be in use by exactly one salesperson. This situation is recorded in Figure 3.4a, where the "inner" symbol, which can be a zero or a one, represents the modality—the minimum—and the "outer" symbol, which can be a one or a crow's foot, represents the cardinality—the maximum. Reading Figure 3.4a from left to right tells us that a salesperson works in a minimum of one and a maximum of one office, which is another way of saying *exactly one* office. Reading from right to left, an office may be worked in or assigned to a minimum of no salespersons (i.e., the office is empty) or a maximum of one salesperson.

Similarly, Figure 3.4b indicates that a salesperson may have no customers or many customers. How could a salesperson have no customers? What are we pay-

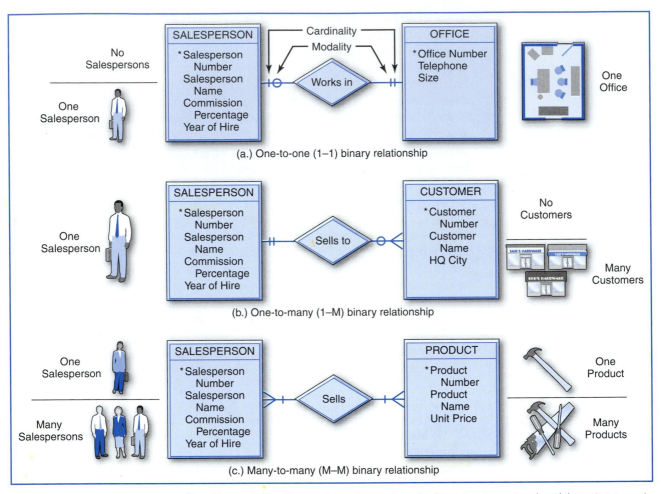

(a.) One-to-one (1–1) binary relationship

(b.) One-to-many (1–M) binary relationship

(c.) Many-to-many (M–M) binary relationship

➤ **Figure 3.4** Binary relationships with cardinalities (maximums) and modalities (minimums)

ing her for? Actually, this allows for the case in which we have just hired a new salesperson and have not as yet assigned her a territory or any customers. On the other hand, a customer is always assigned to exactly one salesperson. We never want a customer to be without a salesperson—how would they buy anything from us when they need to? We never want to be in a position of losing sales! If a salesperson leaves the company, the company's procedures require that another salesperson or, temporarily, a sales manager be immediately assigned the departing salesperson's customers. Figure 3.4c says that each salesperson is authorized to sell at least one or many of our products and each product can be sold by at least one or many of our salespersons. This includes the extreme, but not surprising, case in which each salesperson is authorized to sell all of the products and each product can be sold by all of the salespersons.

More About Many-to-Many Relationships

Intersection Data Generally, we think of attributes as facts about entities. Each salesperson has a salesperson number, a name, a commission percentage, and a year of hire. At the entity occurrence level, for example, one of the salespersons has salesperson number 528, the name Jane Adams, a commission percentage of 15 percent, and the year of hire of 2003. In an E-R diagram, these attributes are written or drawn together with the entity, as in Figure 3.1 and the succeeding figures. This certainly appears to be very natural and obvious. Are there ever any circumstances in which an attribute can describe something other than an entity?

Consider the many-to-many relationship between salespersons and products in Figure 3.4c. As usual, salespersons are described by their salesperson number, name, commission percentage, and year of hire. Products are described by their product number, name, and unit price. But what if there is a requirement to keep track of the number of units, call it "quantity," *of a particular product that a particular salesperson has sold?* Can we add the quantity attribute to the product entity box? No, because while a particular product has a single product number, product name, and unit price, there will be lots of quantities, one for each salesperson selling the product. Can we add the quantity attribute to the salesperson entity box? No, because while a particular salesperson has a single salesperson number, salesperson name, commission percentage, and year of hire, there will be lots of quantities, one for each product that the salesperson sells. It makes no sense to try to put the quantity attribute in either the salesperson entity box or the product entity box. While each salesperson has a single salesperson number, name, and so forth, each salesperson has many quantities, one for each product he sells. Similarly, while each product has a single product number, product name, and so forth, each product has many quantities, one for each salesperson who sells that product. But an entity box in an E-R diagram is designed to list the attributes that simply and directly describe the entity, with no complications involving other entities. Putting quantity in either the salesperson or the product entity box just will not work.

The quantity attribute doesn't describe either the salesperson alone or the product alone. It describes the combination of a particular occurrence of one entity type and a particular occurrence of the other entity type. The quantity 170 doesn't make sense as a description or characteristic of salesperson number 137 alone. She sold many different kinds of products. To which one does the quantity 170 refer? Similarly, the quantity 170 doesn't make sense as a description or characteristic of product number 24013 alone. It was sold by many different salespersons.

In fact, the quantity 170 falls at the *intersection* of salesperson number 170 and product number 24013. It describes the combination of or the association between that particular salesperson and that particular product, and it is known as **intersection data.** Figure 3.5 shows the many-to-many relationship between salespersons and products with the intersection data, quantity, represented in a special five-sided intersection data box. Notice that the intersection data box is attached to the relationship diamond between the two entity boxes. That is the natural place for it to be drawn. Pictorially, it looks like it is at the intersection between the two entities, but there is more to it than that. The intersection data *describes the relationship between the two entities.* We know that an occurrence of the Sells relationship specifies that salesperson 137 has sold some of product 24013. The quantity 170 is an attribute of that relationship occurrence further describing the relationship. We know not only that salesperson 137 sold some of product 24013 but also *how many units* of that product that salesperson sold.

➤ **Figure 3.5**

Many-to-many binary
relationship with
intersection data

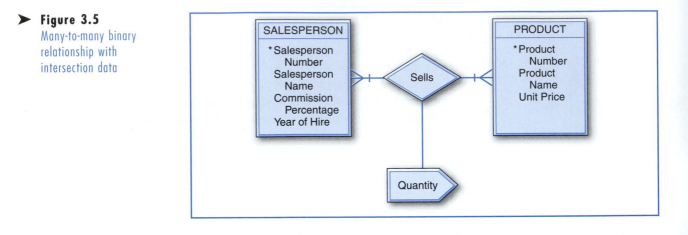

Associative Entity   Since we know that entities can have attributes and now we
see that many-to-many relationships can have attributes, does that mean that entities
and many-to-many relationships can in some sense be treated in the same way within
E-R diagrams? Indeed they can, although it is a matter of choice and not a requirement! Figure 3.6 shows the many-to-many relationship Sells converted into the **associative entity** Sale. An occurrence of the Sale associative entity does exactly what the
many-to-many relationship did: it indicates a relationship between a salesperson and
a product, specifically sales, and includes any intersection data that describes that relationship. Note very, very carefully the reversal of the cardinalities and modalities when
the many-to-many relationship is converted to an associative entity. Sale is now a kind
of entity in its own right, and you must think of the new relationships as follows. A
salesperson can be involved in many sales (where in this case "sale" means that a
salesperson has been involved in selling a type of product over some period of time),
but a particular "sale" can only involve one salesperson! Similarly, a product can be
involved in many sales, but a particular sale can involve only one product.

If the many-to-many relationship E-R diagram style of Figure 3.5 is equivalent
to the associative entity style of Figure 3.6, which one should you use? This is one
of those instances in which this type of diagramming is an art with a lot of leeway
for personal taste. The fact is that you can use either one, but you may find yourself working for a company that has set standards for these diagrams and expects
you to use the one that has been chosen for its standards.

The Unique Identifier in Many-to-Many Relationships   Since, as we
have just seen, a many-to-many relationship can appear to be a kind of an

➤ **Figure 3.6**

Associative entity with
intersection data

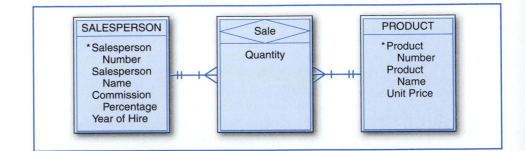

entity, complete with attributes, it also follows that it should have a unique identifier, like other entities. (If this seems a little strange or even unnecessary here, it will become essential later in the book when we actually design databases based on these E-R diagrams.) In its most basic form, the unique identifier of the many-to-many relationship or the associative entity is the combination of the unique identifiers of the two entities in the many-to-many relationship. So, the unique identifier of the many-to-many relationship of Figure 3.5 or the associative entity of Figure 3.6 is the combination of the Salesperson Number and Product Number attributes.

Sometimes, an additional attribute or attributes must be added to this combination to produce uniqueness. This often involves a time element. For example, if we wanted to keep track of the sales on a weekly basis, we would have to have a date attribute or a week number attribute as intersection data and the unique identifier would be Salesperson Number, Product Number, and Date. If we want to know how many units of each product were sold by each salesperson each week, the combination of Salesperson Number and Product Number would not be unique because for a particular salesperson and a particular product, the combination of those two values would be the same each week! Date must be added to produce uniqueness, not to mention to make it clear which week a particular value of the Quantity attribute applies to a particular salesperson product combination.

The third and last possibility occurs when the nature of the associative entity is such that it has its own unique identifier. For example, a company might specify a unique serial number for each sales record, in which case the combination of Salesperson Number, Product Number, and Date isn't needed. Another example would be the many-to-many relationship between motorists and police officers who give traffic tickets for moving violations. (Hopefully it's not *too* many for each motorist!) The unique identifier could be the combination of police officer number and motorist driver's license number plus perhaps date and time. But, typically, each traffic ticket has a unique serial number, and this would serve as the unique identifier.

UNARY RELATIONSHIPS

Unary relationships associate occurrences of an entity type with other occurrences of the *same* entity type. Take the entity person, for example. One person may be married to another person and vice versa. One person may be the parent of other people; conversely, a person may have another person as one of his parents.

One-to-One Unary Relationship

Figure 3.7a shows the one-to-one unary relationship called Backup involving the salesperson entity. The salespersons are organized in pairs as backup to each other when one is away from work. Following one of the links, say the one that extends from the right side of the salesperson entity box, we can say that salesperson number 137 backs up salesperson number 186. Then, going in the other direction, salesperson number 186 backs up salesperson 137. Notice that in each direction the modality of one rather than zero forbids the situation of a salesperson not having a backup.

One-to-Many Unary Relationship

Some of the salespersons are also sales managers, managing other salespersons. A sales manager can manage several other salespersons. Further, there can be several levels of sales managers, that is, several low-level sales managers can be managed by a higher-level sales manager. Each salesperson (or sales manager) is managed by exactly one sales manager. This situation describes a one-to-many unary relationship. Consider Figure 3.7b and follow the downward branch out of

➤ **Figure 3.7**
Unary relationships

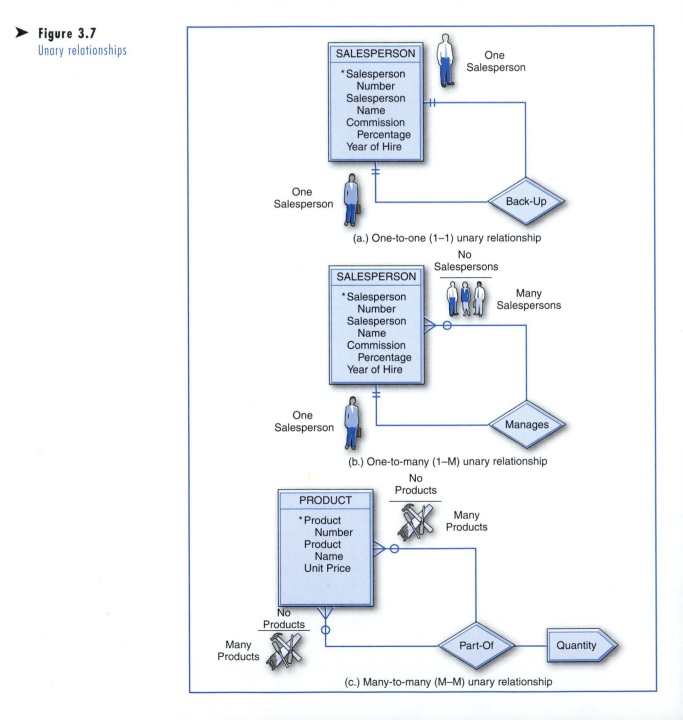

(a.) One-to-one (1–1) unary relationship

(b.) One-to-many (1–M) unary relationship

(c.) Many-to-many (M–M) unary relationship

its salesperson entity box. It says that a salesperson manages zero to many other salespersons, meaning that a salesperson may not be a sales manager (the zero modality case) or may be a sales manager with several subordinate salespersons (the many cardinality case). Following the branch that extends from the right side of the salesperson entity box, the diagram says that a salesperson is managed by exactly one other salesperson (who, of course, must be a sales manager).

Many-to-Many Unary Relationship

Unary relationships also come in the many-to-many variety. One classic example of a many-to-many unary relationship is known as the bill of materials problem. Consider a complex mechanical object like an automobile, an airplane, or a large factory machine tool. Any such object is made of basic parts like nuts and bolts that are used to make other components or subassemblies of the object. Small subassemblies and basic parts go together to make bigger subassemblies, and so on until ultimately they form the entire object. Each basic part and each sub-assembly can be thought of as a "part" of the object. Then, the parts are in a many-to-many unary relationship to each other. Any one particular part can be made up of several other parts, while at the same time itself being a component of several other parts.

In Figure 3.7c, think of the products sold in hardware and home improvement stores. Basic items like hammers and wrenches can be combined and sold as sets. Larger tool sets can be composed of smaller sets plus additional single tools. All of these single tools and sets of all sizes can be classified as products. Thus, as shown in Figure 3.7c, a product can be part of no other products or part of several other products. Going in the reverse direction, a product can be composed of no other products or can be composed of several other products.

TERNARY RELATIONSHIPS

A **ternary relationship** involves three different entity types. Assume for the moment that any salesperson can sell to any customer. Then, Figure 3.8 shows the most general, many-to-many-to-many ternary relationship between salespersons, customers, and products. It means that we know which salesperson sold which product to which customer. Each sale has intersection data consisting of the date of the sale and the number of units of the product sold.

EXAMPLES

The General Hardware Company

Figure 3.9 is the E-R diagram for the General Hardware Company, parts of which we have been using throughout this chapter. General Hardware is a wholesaler and distributor of various manufacturers' tools and other hardware products. Its customers are hardware and home improvement stores, which in turn sell the products at retail to individual consumers. Again, as a middleman it buys its goods from the manufacturers and then sells them to the retail stores. How exactly does General Hardware operate? Now that we know something about E-R diagrams, let's see if we can figure it out from Figure 3.9!

Begin with the SALESPERSON entity box in the middle on the left. SALES-PERSON has four attributes, with one of them, Salesperson Number, serving as the

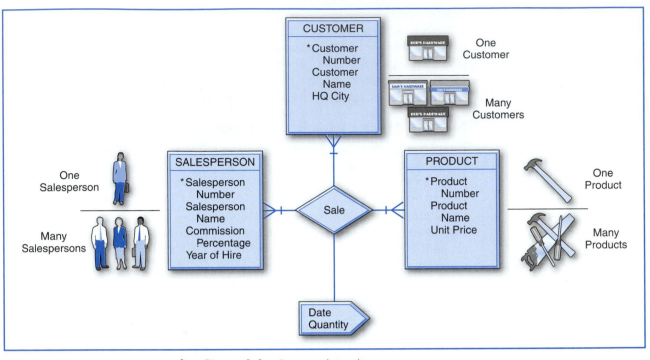

➤ **Figure 3.8**   Ternary relationship

unique identifier of the salespersons. Looking upwards from SALESPERSON, a salesperson works in exactly one office (indicated by the double ones or bars encountered on the way to the OFFICE entity). OFFICE has three attributes; Office Number is the unique identifier. Looking back downwards from the OFFICE entity box, an office has either no salespersons working in it (the zero modality symbol) or one salesperson (the one or bar cardinality symbol). Starting again at the SALESPERSON entity box and moving to the right, a salesperson has no customers or many customers. (Remember that the customers are hardware or home improvement stores.) The CUSTOMER entity has three attributes; Customer Number is the unique identifier. In the reverse direction, a customer must have exactly one salesperson.

From the CUSTOMER entity downward is the CUSTOMER EMPLOYEE entity. According to the figure, a customer must have at least one but can have many employees. An employee works for exactly one customer. This is actually a special situation. General Hardware has an interest only in maintaining data about the people who are its customers' employees as long as their employer remains a customer of General Hardware. If a particular hardware store or home improvement chain stops buying goods from General Hardware, then General Hardware no longer cares about that store's or chain's employees. Furthermore, while General Hardware assumes that each of its customers assigns their employees unique employee numbers, those numbers *can only be assumed to be unique within that customer store or chain*. Thus the unique identifier for a customer employee must be the combination of the Customer Number and the Employee Number attributes. In this situation, CUSTOMER EMPLOYEE is called a *dependent entity*. As shown in the CUSTOMER EMPLOYEE entity box in

➤ **Figure 3.9**
The General Hardware
Company E-R diagram

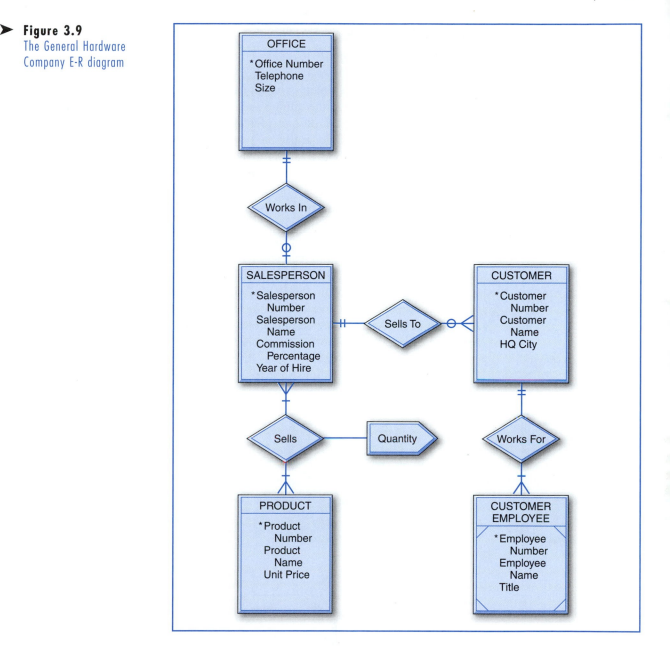

Figure 3.9, a dependent entity is distinguished by a diagonal hash mark in each corner of its attribute area.

Returning to the SALESPERSON entity box and looking downward, there is a many-to-many relationship between salespersons and products. A salesperson is authorized to sell at least one and possibly (probably, in this case) many products. A product is sold by at least one and possibly many salespersons. The PRODUCT entity has three attributes, with Product Number being the unique identifier. The attribute Quantity is intersection data in the many-to-many relationship, meaning that the company is interested in keeping track of how many units of each product each salesperson has sold.

Good Reading Bookstores

Figure 3.10 shows the E-R diagram for Good Reading Bookstores, a chain of bookstores that wants to keep track of the books it sells, their publishers, their authors, and the customers who buy them. The BOOK entity has four attributes; Book Number is the unique identifier. A book has exactly one publisher. Publisher Name is the unique identifier of the PUBLISHER entity. A publisher may have (and generally has) published many books that Good Reading carries; however, Good Reading also wants to be able to keep track of some publishers that currently have no books in Good Reading's inventory. (Note the zero modality symbol from PUBLISHER towards BOOK.) A book must have at least one author but can have many (where in this case "many" means a few, generally two or three, at most). For a person to be of interest to Good Reading as an author, she must have written at least one and possibly many books that Good Reading carries. Note that there is a many-to-many relationship between the BOOK and AUTHOR entities but no intersection data. Looking downward from the BOOK entity box, a book that Good Reading carries may not as yet have been bought by any of its customers (maybe it just came out) or may have been bought by many of its customers. For a customer to be of interest to Good Reading, he must have bought at least one book and possibly (hopefully!) many. Date, Price, and Quantity are intersection data in the many-to-many relationship between the BOOK and CUSTOMER entities.

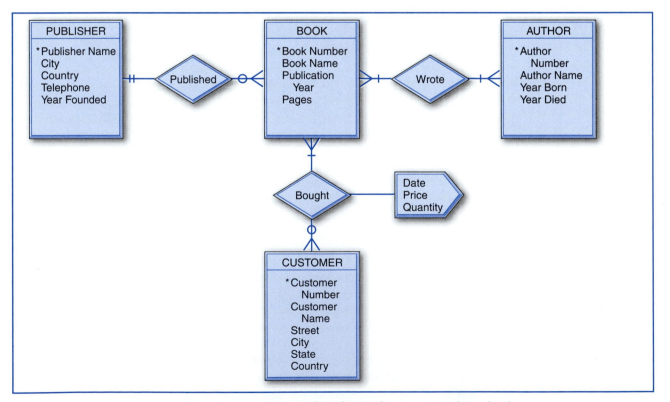

➤ **Figure 3.10** Good Reading Bookstores entity-relationship diagram

Does this make sense? Might a customer have bought several copies of the same book on the same date? After all, that's what the presence of the Quantity attribute implies. Might she have then bought more copies of the same book on a later date? Yes to both questions! A grandmother bought a copy of a book for each of three of her grandchildren one day, and they liked it so much that she returned and bought five more copies of the same book for her other five grandchildren several days later.

World Music Association

The World Music Association (WMA) is an organization that maintains information about its member orchestras and the recordings they have made. The WMA E-R diagram of Figure 3.11 shows the information about the orchestras and their musicians across the top and the information about the recordings in the rest of the diagram. Each orchestra has at least one and possibly many musicians. (In this case, the modality expressing "at least one" is a technicality. Certainly, an orchestra must have many musicians.) A musician may not work for any orchestra (perhaps he is currently unemployed, but WMA wants to keep track of him, anyway) or works for just one orchestra. A musician may not be a college graduate or may have several college degrees. A degree belongs to just one musician. (For the moment we will ignore the possibility that more than one musician earned the same degree from the same university in the same year.) Since the DEGREE entity is dependent on the MUSICIAN entity, the unique identifier for DEGREE is the combination of the Musician Number and Degree (e.g., B.A.) attributes.

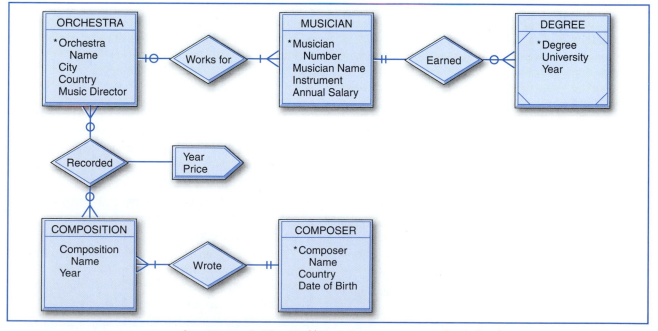

➤ **Figure 3.11** World Music Association entity-relationship diagram

Looking downward from the ORCHESTRA entity box, an orchestra may have made no recordings of a particular composition or may have made many. In the reverse direction, a composition may not have been recorded by any orchestra (but we still want to maintain data about it) or may have been recorded by many orchestras. For a particular recording, we note the year of the recording and the retail price, as intersection data of the many-to-many relationship. A composer may have several compositions to his credit but must have at least one to be of interest to WMA. A composition is associated with exactly one composer.

Lucky Rent-A-Car

Lucky Rent-A-Car's business environment is, obviously, centered around its cars. This is literally true in its E-R diagram, shown in Figure 3.12. A car was manufactured by exactly one manufacturer. A manufacturer manufactured at least one and generally many of Lucky's cars. A car has had many maintenance events (but a brand new car may not have had any yet). A car may not have been rented to any customers (again, the case of a brand new car) or to many customers. A customer may have rented many cars from Lucky and to be in Lucky's business environment must have rented at least one. Rental Date, Return Date, and Total Cost are intersection data to the many-to-many relationship between CAR and CUSTOMER.

KEY TERMS

Associative entity	Entity-relationship (E-R) model	One-to-one relationship
Binary relationship	Intersection data	Relationship
Cardinality	Many-to-many relationship	Ternary relationship
Data modeling	Modality	Unary relationship
Entity-relationship (E-R) diagram	One-to-many relationship	Unique identifier

QUESTIONS

1. What is data modeling? Why is it important?

2. What is the entity-relationship model?

3. What is a relationship?

4. What is the difference between a unary relationship, a binary relationship, and a ternary relationship?

5. Explain and compare the cardinality of a relationship and the modality of a relationship.

6. Explain the difference between a one-to-one, a one-to-many, and a many-to-many binary relationship.

7. What is intersection data in a many-to-many binary relationship? What does the intersection data describe?

8. Can a many-to-many binary relationship have no intersection data? Explain.

9. Can intersection data be placed in the entity box of one of the two entities in the many-to-many relationship? Explain.

10. What is an associative entity? How does intersection data relate to an associative entity?

11. Describe the three cases of unique identifiers for associative entities.

12. Describe the concept of the unary relationship.

13. Explain how a unary relationship can be described as one-to-one, one-to-many, and many-to-many if there is only one entity type involved in the relationship.

14. Describe the ternary relationship concept.

15. Can a ternary relationship have intersection data? Explain.

16. What is a dependent entity? (See the description in the General Hardware example.)

➤ **Figure 3.12**
Lucky Rent-A-Car entity-
relationship diagram

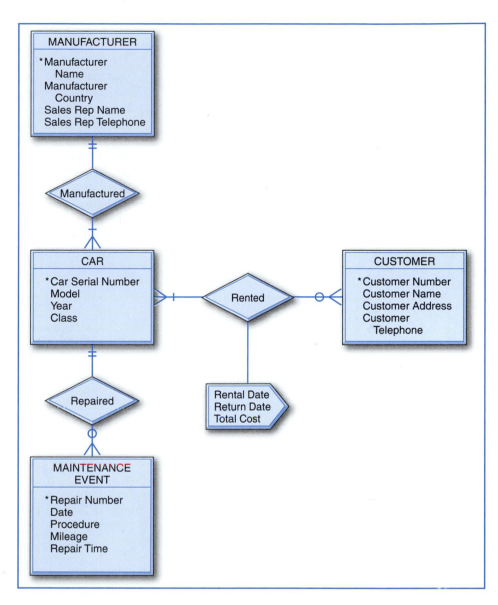

EXERCISES

1. Draw an entity-relationship diagram that describes the following business environment.

   The city of Chicago, Illinois, wants to maintain information about its extensive system of high schools, including its teachers and their university degrees, its students, administrators, and the subjects that it teaches.

   Each school has a unique name, plus an address, telephone number, year built, and size in square feet. Students have a student number, name, home address, home telephone number, current grade, and age. With regard to a student's school assignment, the school system is only interested in keeping track of which school a student *currently* attends. Each school has several administrators, such as the principal and assistant principals. Administrators are identified by an employee number and also have a name, telephone number, and office number.

   Teachers are also identified by an employee number, and each has a name, age, subject specialty such as English (assume only one per teacher), and the year that they entered the school system. Teachers tend to periodically move from school to school, and the school system wants to keep track of the *history* of which schools the teacher has taught in, including the current school. Included will be the year in which the teacher entered the school and the highest pay rate that the teacher attained at the school. The school system wants to keep track of the universities that each teacher attended, including the degrees earned and the years in which they were earned. The school system wants to record each university's name, address, year founded, and Internet URL (address). Some teachers, as department heads, supervise other teachers. The school system wants to keep track of these supervisory relationships but only for teachers' *current* supervisors.

The school system also wants to keep track of the subjects that it offers (e.g., French I, Algebra III, etc.). Each subject has a unique subject number, a subject name, the grade level in which it is normally taught, and the year in which it was introduced in the school system. The school system wants to keep track of which teacher taught which student which subject, including the year this happened and the grade received.

2. The following entity-relationship diagram describes the business environment of Video Centers of Europe, Ltd. (VCE), which is a chain of videotape and DVD rental stores. Write a verbal description of how VCE conducts its business, based on this E-R diagram:

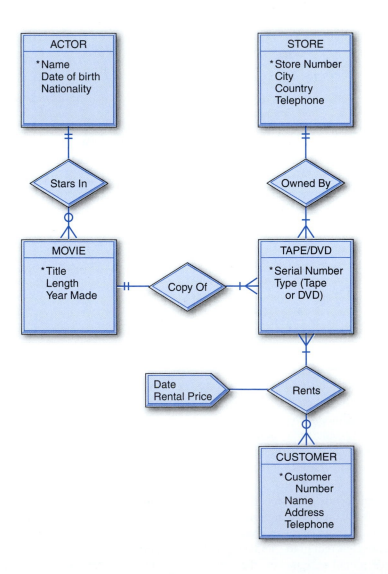

MINICASES

1. Draw an entity-relationship diagram that describes the following business environment.

   Happy Cruise Lines has several ships and a variety of cruise itineraries, each involving several ports-of-call. The company wants to maintain information on the sailors who *currently* work on each of its ships. It also wants to keep track of both its past and future cruises and of the passengers who sailed on the earlier cruises and are booked on the future cruises.

   Each ship has at least one and, of course, normally many sailors on it. The unique identifier of each ship is its ship number. Other ship attributes include ship name, weight, year built, and passenger capacity. Each sailor has a unique sailor identification number, as well as a name, date of birth, and nationality. Some of the sailors are in supervisory positions, supervising several other sailors. Each sailor reports to just one supervisor. A cruise is identified by a unique cruise serial number. Other cruise descriptors include a sailing date, a return date, and a departure port (which is also the cruise's ending point). Clearly, a cruise involves exactly one ship; over time a ship sails on many cruises, but there is a requirement to be able to list a new ship that has not as yet sailed on any cruises at all. Each cruise stops at at least one and usually several ports-of-call, each of which is normally host to many cruises over time. In addition, the company wants to maintain information about ports that it has not as yet used in its cruises but may use in the future. A port is identified by its name and the country that it is in. Other information about a port includes its population, whether a passport is required for the passengers to disembark there, and its current docking fee, which is assumed to be the same for all ships. Passenger information includes a unique passenger number, name, home address, nationality, and date of birth. A cruise typically has many passengers on it (certainly at least one). Hoping for return business, the company assumes that each passenger may have sailed on several of its cruises (and/or may be booked for a future cruise). For a person to be of interest to the company, he or she must have sailed on or be booked on at least one of the company's cruises. The company wants to keep track of how much money each passenger paid for (or will pay for) each of their cruises, as well as their satisfaction rating of the cruise, if it has been completed.

2. Draw an entity-relationship diagram that describes the following business environment.

   The Super Baseball League wants to maintain information about its teams, their coaches, players, and bats. The information about players is historic. For each team, the league wants to keep track of all of the players who have ever played on the team, including the current players. For each player, it wants to know about every team the player ever played for. On the other hand, coach affiliation and bat information is current only.

   The league wants to keep track of each team's team number, which is unique, its name, the city in which it is based, and the name of its manager. Coaches have a name (which is only assumed to be unique within its team) and a telephone number. Coaches have units of work experience, which are described by the type of experience and the number of years of that type of experience. Bats are described by their serial numbers (which are only unique within a team) and their manufacturer's name. Players have a player number that is unique across the league, a name, and an age.

   A team has at least one and usually several coaches. A coach works for only one team. Each coach has several units of work experience or may have none. Each unit of work experience is associated with the coach to whom it belongs. Each team owns at least one and generally many bats. Currently and historically, each team has and has had many players. To be of interest to the league, a player must have played on at least one and possibly many teams during his career. Further, the league wants to keep track of the number of years that a player has played on a team and the batting average that he compiled on that team.

CHAPTER 4

THE DATABASE MANAGEMENT SYSTEM CONCEPT

CHAPTER OBJECTIVES

After learning the material in this chapter, you will be able to:

✔ Discuss the problems encountered in a nondatabase information systems environment.
✔ List the five basic principles of the database concept.
✔ Describe how data can be considered to be a manageable resource.
✔ List the three problems created by data redundancy.
✔ Describe the nature of data redundancy among many files.
✔ Explain the relationship between data integration and data redundancy in one file.
✔ State the primary defining feature of a database management system.
✔ Explain why the ability to store multiple relationships is an important feature of the database approach.
✔ Explain why providing support for such control issues as data security, backup and recovery, and concurrency is an important feature of the database approach.
✔ Explain why providing support for data independence is an important feature of the database approach.

Photo Courtesy of Memphis Light, Gas, and Water Division

MEMPHIS LIGHT, GAS, AND WATER

Memphis Light, Gas, and Water (MLGW) is the largest "three-service" (electricity, natural gas, and water) municipal utility system in the United States. It serves over 400,000 customers in Memphis and Shelby County, Tennessee, and has 2,600 employees. MLGW is the largest of the 159 distributors of the federal Tennessee Valley Authority's electricity output. It brings in natural gas via commercial pipelines, and it supplies water from a natural aquifer beneath the city of Memphis.

Like any supplier of electricity, MLGW is particularly sensitive to electrical outages. It has developed a two-stage application system to determine the causes of outages and to dispatch crews to fix them. The first stage is the Computer-Aided Restoration of Electric Service (CARES) system, which was introduced in 1996. Beginning with call-in patterns as customers report outages, CARES uses automated data from MLGW's electric grid, wiring patterns to substations, and other information, to function as an expert system to determine the location and nature of the problem. It then feeds its conclusion to the second-stage Mobile Dispatching System (MDS), which was introduced in 1999. MDS sends a repair person to an individual customer's location if that is all that has been affected or sends a crew to a malfunctioning or damaged piece of equipment in the grid that is affecting an entire neighborhood. There is a feedback loop in which the repair person or crew reports back to indicate whether the problem has been fixed or a higher-level crew is required to fix it.

The CARES and MDS systems are supported by an Oracle database running on Hewlett-Packard and Compaq Alpha UNIX platforms. The database includes a wide range of tables: a Customer Call table has one record per customer reporting call; an Outage table has one record per outage; a Transformer table that has one record for each transformer in the grid; a Device table for other devices in the grid. These can also interface to the Customer Information System which has a Customer table with one record for each of the over 400,000 customers. In addition to its operational value, CARES and other systems feed a System Reliability Monitoring database which generates reports on outages and can be queried to gain further knowledge of outage patterns for improving the grid.

Printed by permission of Memphis Light, Gas, and Water

Before the database concept was developed, all data in information systems (then generally referred to as data processing systems) was stored in simple linear files. Some applications and their programs required data from only one file. Other applications required data from several files. Some of the more complex applications used data extracted from one file as the search argument (the item to be found) for extracting data from another file. Generally, files were created for a single application and were used only for that application. There was no sharing of files or of data among applications, and, as a result, the same data often appeared redundantly in multiple files. In addition to this situation of data redundancy among multiple files, a lack of sophistication in the design of individual files often led to data redundancy within those individual files.

As information systems continued to grow in importance, a number of the ground rules began to change. Hardware became cheaper—much cheaper relative to the computing power that it provided. Software development took on a more standardized, "structured" form. Large backlogs of new applications to be implemented built up, making the huge amount of time spent on maintaining existing programs more and more unacceptable. It became increasingly clear that the lack of a focus on data was one of the major factors in the program maintenance dilemma that developed. Furthermore, the redundant data across multiple files and even within individual files was causing data accuracy nightmares (which will be explained further in this chapter) just as companies were relying more and more on their information systems to substantially manage their businesses. As we will begin to see in this chapter, the technology that came to the rescue was the database management system.

Summarizing, the problems included:

- Data was stored in different formats in different files.
- Data was often not shared among different programs that needed it, necessitating the duplication of data in redundant files.
- Little was understood about file design, resulting in redundant data within individual files.
- Files often could not be rebuilt after being damaged by a software error or a hardware failure.
- Data was not secure and was vulnerable to theft or malicious mischief by people inside or outside of the company.
- Programs were usually written in such a manner that if the way that the data was stored changed, the program had to be modified to continue working.
- Changes in everything from access methods to tax tables required programming changes.

This chapter will describe these problems in detail and show how the database concept overcame them and set the stage for a vastly improved information systems environment.

THE DATABASE CONCEPT

The database concept is one of the most powerful, enduring technologies of the information systems environment. It encompasses a variety of technical and managerial issues and features that are at the heart of today's information systems scene. In order to get started and begin to develop the deep understanding of database that we seek, we will focus on five issues that establish a set of basic principles of the database concept:

1. The creation of a **data-centric environment** in which a company's data can truly be thought of as a significant corporate resource. A key feature of this environment is the ability to share data among those inside and outside of the company who require access to it.
2. The ability to achieve **data integration** while at the same time storing data in a nonredundant fashion. This, alone, is the central, defining feature of the database approach.
3. The ability to store data representing entities involved in multiple relationships without introducing **data redundancy** or other structural problems.
4. The establishment of an environment that manages certain data control issues, such as data security, backup and recovery, and concurrency control.
5. The establishment of an environment that permits a high degree of data independence.

Data as a Manageable Resource

Broadly speaking, the information systems environment consists of several components, including hardware, networks, applications software, systems software, people, and data. The relative degree of focus placed on each of these components has varied over time. In particular, the amount of attention paid to data has undergone a radical transformation. In the earlier days of "data processing," most of the time and emphasis in application development was spent on the programs, rather than on the data and data structures. Hardware was expensive, and the size of main memory was extremely limited by today's standards. Programming was a new discipline, and there was much to be learned about it in order to achieve the goal of efficient processing. Standards for effective programming were unknown. In this environment, the treatment of the data was hardly the highest priority concern.

At the same time, as more and more corporate functions at the operational, tactical, and strategic levels became dependent on information systems, data increasingly became recognized as an important corporate resource. Furthermore, the corporate community became increasingly convinced that a firm's data about its products, manufacturing processes, customers, suppliers, employees, and competitors could, with proper storage and use, provide a significant competitive advantage to the firm.

Money, plant and equipment, inventories, and people are all important enterprise resources, and, indeed, a great deal of effort has always been expended to manage them. As corporations began to realize that data is also an important enterprise resource, it became increasingly clear that data would have to be managed in an organized way, too (Figure 4.1). What was needed was a **software utility** that could manage and protect data while providing controlled, shared access to it so that it could fulfill its destiny as a critical **corporate resource.** Out of this need was born the database management system.

As we look to the future and look back at the developments of the last few years, we see several phenomena that emphasize the importance of data and demand that it be carefully managed as a corporate resource. These include reengineering, electronic commerce, and **enterprise resource planning (ERP) systems** that have placed an even greater emphasis on data. In reengineering, data and information systems are aggressively used to redesign business processes for

➤ **Figure 4.1**
Corporate resources

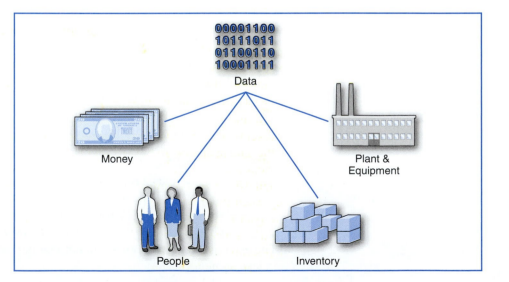

maximum efficiency. At the heart of every electronic commerce Web site is a database through which companies and their customers transact business. Another very important development was that of ERP systems, which are collections of application programs built around a central shared database. ERP systems very much embody the principles of shared data and of data as a corporate resource.

Data Integration and Data Redundancy

Data integration and data redundancy, each in its own right, are critical issues in the field of database management.

- Data integration refers to the ability to tie together pieces of related data within an information system. If a record in one file contains customer name, address, and telephone data and a record in another file contains sales data about an item that the customer has purchased, there may come a time when we want to contact the customer about the purchased item.

- Data redundancy refers to the same fact about the business environment being stored more than once within an information system. While data integration is clearly a positive feature of a database management system, data redundancy is a negative feature (except for performance reasons under certain circumstances that will be discussed later in this book).

In terms of the data structures used in database management systems, data integration and data redundancy are tied together and will be discussed together in this section of the book.

Data stored in an information system describes the real-world business environment. Put another way, the data is a reflection of the environment. Over the years that information systems have become increasingly sophisticated, they and the data that they contain have revolutionized the ways that we conduct virtually all aspects of business. But as valuable as the data is, if the data is duplicated and stored multiple times within a company's information systems facilities, it can result in a nightmare of poor performance, lack of trust in the data's accuracy, and a reduced level of competitiveness in the marketplace. Data redundancy and the problems it causes can occur within a single file or across multiple files.

The problems caused by data redundancy are threefold.

- First, the redundant data takes up a great deal of extra disk space. This alone can be quite significant.

- Second, if the redundant data has to be updated, it takes additional time to do so since, if done correctly, every copy of the redundant data must be updated. This can be a major performance issue.

- Third and potentially the most significant is the potential for data integrity problems. The term data integrity refers to the accuracy of the data. Obviously, if the data in an information system is inaccurate, it and the whole information system are of limited value. The problem with redundant data, whether in a single file or across multiple files, occurs when it has to be updated (or possibly when it is first stored). If data is held redundantly and all of the copies of the data record being updated are not correctly updated to the new values, clearly a data integrity problem exists. There is an old saying that has some applicability here, "The person with one watch always knows what time it is. The person with several watches is never quite sure" (Figure 4.2).

➤ **Figure 4.2**
With several watches
the correct time might
not be clear

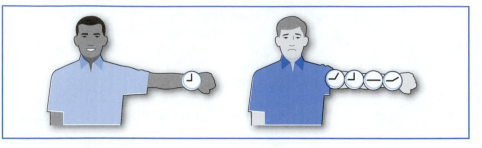

➤ **Figure 4.3**
Three files with
redundant data

Sales file		
Customer Number	Customer Name	Customer Address
2746795	John Jones	123 Elm Street

Accounts Receivable file		
Customer Number	Customer Name	Customer Address
2746795	John Jones	123 Elm Street

Credit file		
Customer Number	Customer Name	Customer Address
2746795	John Jones	123 Elm Street

➤ **Figure 4.4**
Three files with a data
integrity problem

Sales file		
Customer Number	Customer Name	Customer Address
2746795	John Jones	456 Oak Street

Accounts Receivable file		
Customer Number	Customer Name	Customer Address
2746795	John Jones	456 Oak Street

Credit file		
Customer Number	Customer Name	Customer Address
2746795	John Jones	123 Elm Street

Data Redundancy Among Many Files Beginning with data redundancy across multiple files, consider the following situation involving customer names and addresses. Frequently, different departments in an enterprise in the course of their normal everyday work need the same data. For example, the sales department, the accounts receivable department, and the credit department may need customer name and address data. Often, the solution to this multiple need is redundant data. The sales department has its own stored file that, among other things, contains the customer name and address; the same is true of the accounts receivable and credit departments (Figure 4.3).

One day, customer John Jones, who currently lives at 123 Elm Street, moves to 456 Oak Street. If his address is updated in two of the files but not the third, then the company's data is inconsistent (Figure 4.4). Two of the files indicate that John Jones lives at 456 Oak Street, but one file still shows him living at 123 Elm Street. The company can no longer trust its information system. How could this happen? It could have been a software or a hardware error. But more likely it was because whoever received the new information and was responsible for updating one or two of the files simply did not know the third one existed. As mentioned earlier, at various times in information systems history, it has not been unusual in large companies for the same data to be held redundantly in sixty or seventy files! Thus the possibility of data integrity problems is great.

Multiple file redundancy initially poses more of a managerial issue than single file redundancy but also has technical implications. The issue is managerial to the extent that a company's management does not encourage data sharing among departments and their applications. But the issue is technical when it comes to the reality of whether the company's software systems are capable of providing shared access to the data without compromising performance and data security.

Data Integration and Data Redundancy Within One File   Data redundancy in a single file results in exactly the same three problems that resulted from data redundancy in multiple files: wasted storage space, extra time on data update, and the potential for data integrity problems. To begin developing this scenario, consider Figure 4.5, which shows two files from the General Hardware Company information system. General Hardware is a wholesaler of hardware, tools, and related items. Its customers are hardware stores, home improvement stores, and department stores, or chains of such stores. Figure 4.5a shows the Salesperson file, which has one record for each of General Hardware's salespersons. Salesperson Number is the unique identifying "key" field and as such is underlined in the figure. Clearly, there is no data redundancy in this file. There is one record for each salesperson, and each individual fact about a salesperson is listed once in the salesperson's record.

Figure 4.5b shows General Hardware's Customer file. Customer Number is the unique key field. Again, there is no data redundancy, but two questions have to be answered regarding the Salesperson Number field appearing in this file. First, why

➤ **Figure 4.5**
General Hardware
Company files

(a) Salesperson file

Salesperson Number	Salesperson Name	Commission Percentage	Year of Hire
137	Baker	10	1995
186	Adams	15	2001
204	Dickens	10	1998
361	Carlyle	20	2001

(b) Customer file

Customer Number	Customer Name	Salesperson Number	HQ City
0121	Main St. Hardware	137	New York
0839	Jane's Stores	186	Chicago
0933	ABC Home Stores	137	Los Angeles
1047	Acme Hardware Store	137	Los Angeles
1525	Fred's Tool Stores	361	Atlanta
1700	XYZ Stores	361	Washington
1826	City Hardware	137	New York
2198	Western Hardware	204	New York
2267	Central Stores	186	New York

is it there? After all, it seems that it already had a good home as the unique, iden-tifying field of the Salesperson file. The Salesperson Number field appears in the Customer file to record which salesperson is responsible for a given customer account. In fact, there is a one-to-many relationship between salespersons and cus-tomers. A salesperson can and generally does have several customer accounts, while each customer is serviced by only one General Hardware salesperson. The second question involves the data in the Salesperson Number field in the Customer file. For example, salesperson number 137 appears in four of the records (plus once in the first record of the Salesperson file). Does this constitute data redundancy? The answer is no. For data to be redundant (and there will be examples of data redundancy coming up shortly), the same fact about the business environment must be recorded more than once. The appearance of salesperson number 137 in the first record of the Salesperson file establishes 137 as the identifier of one of the sales-persons. The appearance of salesperson number 137 in the first record of the Customer file indicates that salesperson number 137 is responsible for customer number 0121. This is a different fact about the business environment. The appear-ance of salesperson number 137 in the third record of the Customer file indicates that salesperson number 137 is responsible for customer number 0933. This is yet another distinct fact about the business environment. And so on through the other appearances of salesperson number 137 in the Customer file.

Retrieving data from each of the files of Figure 4.5 individually is straightfor-ward and can be done on a direct basis if the files are indexed or hashed. Thus, if there is a requirement to find the name or commission percentage or year of hire of salesperson number 204, it can be satisfied by retrieving the record for sales-person number 204 in the Salesperson file. Similarly, if there is a requirement to find the name or responsible salesperson (by salesperson number!) or headquarters city of customer number 1525, we simply retrieve the record for customer number 1525 in the Customer file.

But what if there is a requirement to find the *name* of the salesperson respon-sible for a particular customer account, say for customer number 1525? Can this requirement be satisfied by retrieving data from only one of the two files of Figure 4.5? No, it cannot! The information regarding which salesperson is responsible for which customers is recorded only in the Customer file, and the salesperson names are recorded only in the Salesperson file. Thus, finding the salesperson name will be an exercise in data integration. In order to find the name of the salesperson responsible for a particular customer, first the record for the customer in the Customer file will have to be retrieved. Then, using the sales-person number found in that record, the correct salesperson record can be retrieved from the Salesperson file to find the salesperson name. For example, if there is a need to find the *name* of the salesperson responsible for customer num-ber 1525, the first operation will be to retrieve the record for customer number 1525 in the Customer file. As shown in Figure 4.5b, this would yield salesperson number 361 as the number of the responsible salesperson. Then, accessing the record for salesperson 361 in the Salesperson file of Figure 4.5a determines that the name of the salesperson responsible for customer 1525 is Carlyle. In so doing, the data in the record in the Salesperson file and the data in the record in the Customer file have been integrated, but the data integration process has been awfully laborious.

This kind of custom made, multi-command, multi-file access (which, by the way, could easily require more than two files, depending on the query and the files involved) is clumsy, potentially error prone, and expensive in terms of performance. Although the two files have the benefit of holding data nonredundantly, a good level of data integration is lacking. That is, it is overly difficult to find and retrieve pieces of data in the two files that are related to each other. For example, customer number 1525 and salesperson name Carlyle in the two files in Figure 4.5 are related to each other by virtue of the fact that the two records they are in both include a reference to salesperson number 361. Yet, as shown above, ultimately finding the salesperson name Carlyle by starting with the customer number 1525 is an unacceptably laborious process.

A fair question to ask is, if we knew that data integration was important in this application environment and if we knew that there would be a frequent requirement to find the name of the salesperson responsible for a particular customer, why were the files structured as they were in Figure 4.5 in the first place? An alternative arrangement is shown in Figure 4.6. The single file of Figure 4.6 combines the data in the two files of Figure 4.5.

The file in Figure 4.6 was created by merging the salesperson data from Figure 4.5a into the records of Figure 4.5b, based on corresponding salesperson numbers. As a result, notice that the number of records in the file in Figure 4.6 is identical to the number of records in the Customer file of Figure 4.5b. This is actually a result of the "direction" of the one-to-many relationship in which each salesperson can be associated with several customers. The data was "integrated" in this merge operation. Notice, for example, that in Figure 4.5b, the record for customer number 1525 is associated with salesperson number 361. In turn, in Figure 4.5a, the record for salesperson number 361 is shown to have the name Carlyle. Those two records were merged, based on the common salesperson number, into the record for customer number 1525 in Figure 4.6. (Notice, by the way, that the Salesperson Number field appears twice in Figure 4.6 because it appeared in each of the files of Figure 4.5. The field values in each of those two fields are identical in each record in the file in Figure 4.6, which must be the case since the record merge that created the file in Figure 4.6 was based on those identical values. That being the case, one of the two Salesperson

Figure 4.6
General Hardware Company combined file

Customer Number	Customer Name	Salesperson Number	HQ City	Salesperson Number	Salesperson Name	Commission Percentage	Year of Hire
0121	Main St. Hardware	137	New York	137	Baker	10	1995
0839	Jane's Stores	186	Chicago	186	Adams	15	2001
0933	ABC Home Stores	137	Los Angeles	137	Baker	10	1995
1047	Acme Hardware Store	137	Los Angeles	137	Baker	10	1995
1525	Fred's Tool Stores	361	Atlanta	361	Carlyle	20	2001
1700	XYZ Stores	361	Washington	361	Carlyle	20	2001
1826	City Hardware	137	New York	137	Baker	10	1995
2198	Western Hardware	204	New York	204	Dickens	10	1998
2267	Central Stores	186	New York	186	Adams	15	2001

Number fields in the file in Figure 4.6 could well be deleted without causing any loss of information.)

The file in Figure 4.6 is certainly **well integrated.** Finding the name of the salesperson who is responsible for customer number 1525 now requires a single record access of the record for customer number 1525. The salesperson name, Carlyle, is right there in that record. This appears to be the solution to the earlier multi-file access problem. Unfortunately, integrating the two files caused another problem: data redundancy. Notice in Figure 4.6 that, for example, the fact that salesperson number 137 is named Baker is repeated four times, as are his commission percentage and year of hire. This is indeed data redundancy, for it repeats the same facts about the business environment multiple times within the one file. If a given salesperson is responsible for several customer accounts, then the data about the salesperson *must* appear in several records in the merged or integrated file. It would make no sense from a logical or a retrieval standpoint to specify, for example, the salesperson name, commission percentage, and year of hire for one customer that the salesperson services and not for another. This would imply a nonexistent special relationship between the salesperson and that one customer and would remove the linkage between the salesperson and his other customers. To be complete, the salesperson data must be repeated for every one of his customers.

The combined file in Figure 4.6 also illustrates what have come to be referred to as *anomalies* in poorly structured files. The problems arise when two *different kinds of data,* like salesperson and customer data in this example, are merged into one file. Look at the record in Figure 4.6 for customer number 2198, Western Hardware. The salesperson for this customer is Dickens, salesperson number 204. Look over the table and note that Western Hardware happens to be the only customer that Dickens currently has. If Western Hardware goes out of business or General Hardware stops selling to them and they decide to delete the record for Western Hardware from the file, they will also lose everything they know about Dickens: his commission percentage, his year of hire, even his name associated with his salesperson number, 204. This situation, which is called the **deletion anomaly,** occurs because the salesperson data doesn't have its own file, as in Figure 4.5a. The only place in the combined file of Figure 4.6 that you can store salesperson data is in the records with the customers. If you delete a customer and that record was the only one for that salesperson, the salesperson's data is gone.

Conversely, in the **insertion anomaly,** General Hardware can't record data in the combined file of Figure 4.6 about a new salesperson the company just hired until she is assigned at least one customer. After all, the identifying field of the records of the combined file is Customer Number! Finally, the **update anomaly** notes that the redundant data of the combined file, such as Baker's commission percentage of 10 being repeated four times, must be updated each place it exists when it changes (for example, if Baker is rewarded with an increase to a commission percentage of 15).

There appears to be a very significant tradeoff in the data structures between data integration and data redundancy. The two files of Figure 4.5 are nonredundant but have poor data integration. Finding the name of the salesperson responsible for a particular customer account requires a multi-command, multi-file access that can be slow and error-prone. The merged file of Figure 4.6, in which the data is very well integrated, eliminates the need for a multi-command, multi-file access for this query but is highly data redundant. Neither of these situations is acceptable. A poor level of data integration slows down the company's information systems and perhaps its business as well. Redundant data can cause data accuracy and other problems. Yet the properties of data integration and nonredundant data are both highly desirable. And, while the above example appears to show that the two are hopelessly incompatible, over the years a few—very few—ways have been developed to achieve both goals in a single data management system. This concept is so important that it is the primary defining feature of database management systems:

> A database management system is a software utility for storing and retrieving data that gives the end-user the impression that the data is well integrated even though the data can be stored with no redundancy at all.

Any data storage and retrieval system that does not have this property should not be called a database management system. Notice a couple of fine points in this definition. It says, "data *can* be stored with no redundancy," indicating that nonredundant storage is feasible but not required. In certain situations, particularly those involving performance issues, the database designer may choose to compromise on the issue of data redundancy. The definition also says, "that gives the end-user the *impression* that the data is well integrated." Depending on the approach to database management taken by the particular database management system, data can be physically integrated and stored that way on the disk, or it can be integrated at the time that a data retrieval query is executed. In either case, the data will "give the end-user the impression that the data is well integrated." Both of these fine points will be explored further later in this book.

Multiple Relationships

Chapter 3 demonstrated how entities can relate to each other in unary, binary, and ternary one-to-one, one-to-many, and many-to-many relationships. A database management system must be able to store data about the entities in a way that reflects and preserves these relationships. Furthermore, this must be accomplished in such a way that it does not compromise the fundamental properties of data integration and nonredundant data storage described above. Consider the following problems with attempting to handle **multiple relationships** in simple linear files, using the binary one-to-many relationship between General Hardware Company's salespersons and customers as an example.

First, the Customer file of Figure 4.5 does the job with its Salesperson Number field. The fact that, for example, salesperson number 137 is associated with four of the customers (it appears in four of the records), while, for example, customer number 1826 has only one salesperson associated with it, demonstrates that the one-to-many relationship has been achieved. However, as has already been shown, the two files of this figure lack an efficient data integration mechanism; that is, trying to link detailed salesperson data with associated customer data is laborious. (Actually, as will be seen later in this book, the structures of Figure 4.5 are quite viable for the relational DBMS environment. In that case, the relational DBMS software will handle the data integration requirement. But without that relational DBMS software, these structures are deficient regarding data integration.) Also, the combined file of Figure 4.6 supports the one-to-many relationship but, of course, introduces data redundancy.

Figure 4.7 shows a "horizontal" solution to the problem. The Salesperson Number field has been removed from the Customer file. Instead, each record in the Salesperson file lists all of the customers, by customer number, that the particular salesperson is responsible for. This could conceivably be implemented as one variable-length field of some sort containing all of the associated customer numbers for each salesperson, or it could be implemented as a series of Customer Number fields. Although this arrangement does represent the one-to-many relationship, it is unacceptable for two reasons. One is that the record length could be highly variable depending on how many customers a particular salesperson is responsible for. This can be tricky from a space management point of view. If a new customer is added to a salesperson's record, the new larger size of the record may preclude its being stored in the same place on the disk that it came from. Placing it somewhere else can cause performance problems in future retrievals. The second reason is that once a given salesperson record is retrieved, the person or program that retrieved it would have a relatively difficult time going through all of the associated customer numbers looking for the one desired. Dealing with simple files like these, the normal expectation is that there will be one value of each field type in each record (e.g., one salesperson number, one salesperson name, and so on). In the arrangement in Figure 4.7, the end-user or supporting software would have to deal with a list of values, that is, of customer numbers, upon retrieving a salesperson record. This would be an unacceptably complex process.

➤ **Figure 4.7**
General Hardware Company combined files: One-to-many relationship horizontal variation

(a) Salesperson file				
Salesperson Number	Salesperson Name	Commission Percentage	Year of Hire	Customer Numbers
137	Baker	10	1995	0121, 0933, 1047, 1826
186	Adams	15	2001	0839, 2267
204	Dickens	10	1998	2198
361	Carlyle	20	2001	1525, 1700

(b) Customer file		
Customer Number	Customer Name	HQ City
0121	Main St. Hardware	New York
0839	Jane's Stores	Chicago
0933	ABC Home Stores	Los Angeles
1047	Acme Hardware Store	Los Angeles
1525	Fred's Tool Stores	Atlanta
1700	XYZ Stores	Washington
1826	City Hardware	New York
2198	Western Hardware	New York
2267	Central Stores	New York

Figure 4.8 shows a "vertical" solution to the problem. In a single file, each salesperson record is immediately followed by the records for all of the customers for which the salesperson is responsible. Although this does preserve the one-to-many relationship, the complexities involved in a system that has to manage multiple record types in a single file make this solution unacceptable, too.

A database management system must be able to handle all of the various unary, binary, and ternary relationships in a logical and efficient way that does not introduce data redundancy or interfere with data integration. The database management system approaches that have been developed and are in use today all satisfy this requirement. In particular, the way that the relational approach to database management handles it will be explained in detail.

Data Control Issues

The people responsible for managing the data in an information systems environment must be concerned with several **data control issues,** regardless of which database management system approach is in use. It is even true if no database management system is in use, that is, if the data is merely stored in simple files. Most prominent among these data control issues are data security, backup and recovery, and concurrency control (Figure 4.9). These issues are introduced here and will be covered in more depth later in this book. These data control issues are considered in this discussion of the essence of the database management system concept because such systems should be expected to handle these issues on a common basis for all of the data stored in the system's databases.

Computer security has become a very broad topic with many facets and concerns, including protecting the physical hardware environment, defending against hacker attacks, encrypting data transmitted over networks, educating employees on the importance of protecting the company's data, and many more. All computer security

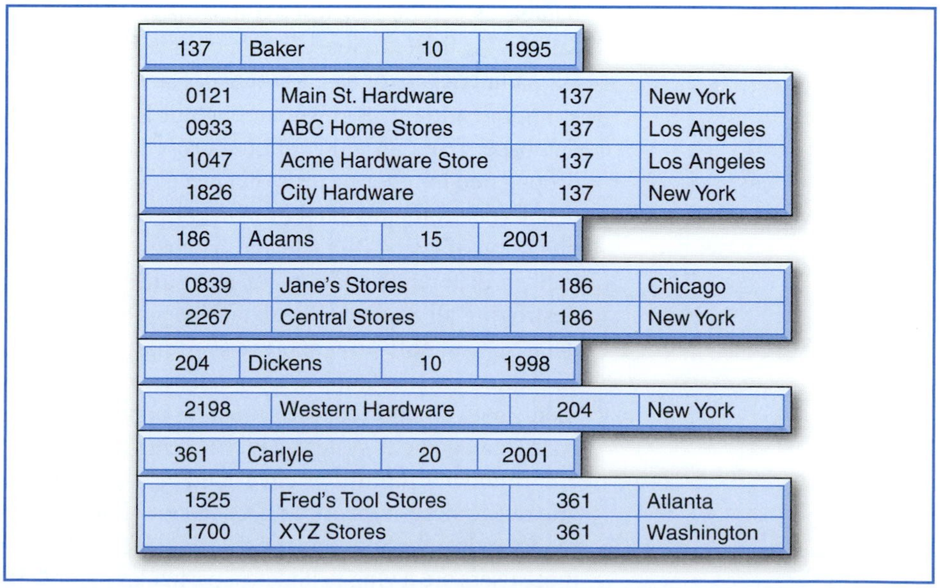

> **Figure 4.8**
> General Hardware Company combined files: One-to-many relationship vertical variation

➤ **Figure 4.9**
Three data control issues

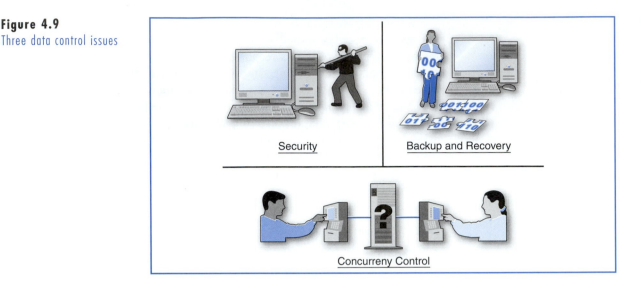

Security

Backup and Recovery

Concurreny Control

exposures potentially affect a company's data. Some exposures represent direct threats to data while others are more indirect. For example, the theft of transmitted data is a direct threat to data, while a computer virus, depending on its nature, may corrupt programs and systems in such a way that the data is affected on an incidental or delayed basis. The types of direct threats to data include outright theft of the data, unauthorized exposure of the data, malicious corruption of the data, unauthorized updates of the data, and loss of the data. Protecting a company's data assets has become a responsibility that is shared by its operating systems, by special security utility software, and by its database management systems. All database management systems incorporate features that are designed to help protect the data in their databases.

Data can be lost or corrupted in any of a variety of ways and not just from the data security exposures just mentioned. Entire files, portions of databases, or entire databases can be lost when a disk drive suffers a massive accidental or deliberate failure. At the extreme, all of a company's data can be lost to a disaster such as a fire, a hurricane, or an earthquake. Hackers, computer viruses, or even poorly written application programs can corrupt from a few to all of the records of a file or database. Even an unintentional error in entering data into a single record can be propagated to other records that use its values as input into the creation of their values. Every company (and even every personal computer user) must have more than one copy of every data file and database. Furthermore, some of the copies must be kept in different buildings, or even different cities, to prevent a catastrophe from destroying all copies of the data. The process of using this duplicate data, plus other data, special software, and even specially designed disk devices to recover lost or corrupted data, is known as backup and recovery. As a key issue in data management, backup and recovery must be considered and incorporated within the database management system environment.

In today's multi-user environment, it is quite common for two or more users to attempt to access the same data record simultaneously. If they are merely trying to read the data without updating it, this does not cause a problem. However, if two or more users are trying to update a particular record simultaneously, say a bank account balance or the number of available seats on an airline flight, they run the risk of generating what is known as a **concurrency problem.** In this situation, the updates can interfere with each other in such a way that the resulting data values will be incorrect. This intolerable possibility must be guarded against and, once again, the database management system must be designed to protect its databases from such an eventuality.

A fundamental premise of the database concept is that these three data control issues—data security, backup and recovery, and concurrency—must be managed by or coordinated with the database management system. This means that when a new application program is written for the database environment, the programmers can concentrate on the details of the application and not have to worry about writing code to manage these data control issues. It also means that there is a good comfort level that the potential problems caused by these issues are under control since they are being managed by long-tested components of the DBMS. Finally, it means that the functions are standard for all of the data in the environment, which leads to easier management and economies of scale in assigning and training personnel to be responsible for the data. This kind of commonality of control is a hallmark of the database approach.

Data Independence

In the earlier days of "data processing," many decisions involving the way that application programs were written were made in concert with the specific file designs and the choice of file organization and access method used. The program logic itself was dependent upon the way in which the data was stored. The **data dependence** was often so strong that if for any reason the storage characteristics of the data had to be changed, the program itself had to be modified, often extensively. That characteristic of the data storage and programming environments was very undesirable because of the time and expense involved in such efforts. In practice, storage structures sometimes have to change to reflect improved storage techniques, application changes, attempts at sharing data, and performance tuning, to name a few reasons. Thus it would be highly desirable to have a data storage and programming environment in which as many types of changes in the data structure as possible would not require changes in the application programs that use them. This goal of data independence is an objective of today's database management systems.

DBMS APPROACHES

We have established a set of principles for the database concept and have stated that a database management system is a software utility that embodies those concepts. The next question concerns the nature of a DBMS in terms of how it organizes data and how it permits its retrieval. Considering that the database concept is such a crucial component of the information systems environment and that a huge profit motive must be tied up with it, you might think that many people have worked on the problem over the years and come up with many different approaches to designing DBMSs. It's true that many very bright people have worked on this problem for a long time, but, interestingly, you can count the number of different viable approaches that have emerged on the fingers of one hand. In particular, the central issue of providing a nonredundant data environment that also looks as though it is integrated is a very hard nut to crack. Let's just say that we're fortunate that even a small number of practical ways to solve this problem have been discovered.

Basically, there are four major DBMS approaches. They are:

- Hierarchical
- Network
- Relational
- Object-oriented

The hierarchical and network approaches to database are both called navigational approaches because of the way that programs have to "navigate" through hierarchies and networks of data to find the data they need. Both of these technologies were developed in the 1960s and, relative to the other approaches, are somewhat similar in structure. IBM's Information Management System (IMS), a DBMS based on the hierarchical approach, was released in 1969. It was followed in the early 1970s by several network-based DBMSs developed by such computer manufacturers of the time as UNIVAC, Honeywell, Burroughs, and Control Data. There was also a network-based DBMS called Integrated Data Management Store (IDMS) produced by an independent software vendor originally called Cullinane Systems, which was eventually absorbed into Computer Associates. These navigational DBMSs, which were suitable only for mainframe computers, were an elegant solution to the redundancy/integration problem at the time that they were developed. But they were complex, difficult to work with in many respects, and, as we have said, required a mainframe computer. Now often called legacy systems, interestingly some of them have survived to this very day for certain applications that require a lot of data and fast data response times.

The relational database approach became commercially viable in about 1980. After several years of user experimentation, it became the preferred DBMS approach and it has remained so ever since. Chapters 5–9 of this book, as well as portions of later chapters, are devoted to the relational approach. The object-oriented approach has proven useful for a variety of niche applications and will be discussed in Chapter 10 of this book. It is interesting to note that some of the key object-oriented database concepts have found their way into some of the mainstream relational DBMSs and some are described as taking a hybrid object/relational approach to database.

KEY TERMS

Backup and recovery	Data integrity problem	Manageable resource
Computer security	Data redundancy	Multiple relationships
Concurrency control	Data retrieval	Software utility
Concurrency problem	Data security	Update anomaly
Corporate resource	Data-centric environment	Well integrated
Data control issues	Deletion anomaly	
Data dependence	Enterprise resource planning (ERP)	
Data independence	system	
Data integration	Insertion anomaly	

QUESTIONS

1. Should data be considered a true corporate resource? Why or why not? Compare and contrast data to other corporate resources (capital, plant and equipment, personnel, etc.) in terms of importance, intrinsic value, and modes of use.

2. Defend or refute the following statement: "Data is the most important corporate resource because it describes all of the others."

3. What are the two kinds of data redundancy, and what are the three types of problems that they cause in the information systems environment?

4. What factors might lead to redundant data across multiple files? Is the problem managerial or technical in nature?

5. Describe the apparent tradeoff between data redundancy and data integration in simple linear files.

6. In your own words, describe the key quality of a DBMS that sets it apart from other data handling systems.

7. Do you think that the single file redundancy problem is more serious, less serious, or about the same as the multi-file redundancy problem? Why?

8. What are the two defining goals of a database management system?

9. What expectation should there be for a database management system with regards to handling multiple relationships? Why?

10. What problems are associated with "horizontal" and "vertical" solutions to the handling of multiple relationships that were described in the chapter?

11. What expectation should there be for a database management system with regard to handling data control issues such as data security, backup and recovery, and concurrency control? Why?

12. What would the alternative be if database management systems were not designed to handle data control issues such as data security, backup and recovery, and concurrency control?

13. What is data independence? Why is it desirable?

14. What expectation should there be for a database management system with regard to data independence? Why?

15. What are the four major DBMS approaches? Which approaches are used the most and least today?

EXERCISES

1. Consider a hospital in which each doctor is responsible for many patients while each patient is cared for by just one doctor. Each doctor has a unique employee number, a name, telephone number, and office number. Each patient has a unique patient number, a name, home address, and home telephone number.

   a. What kind of relationship is there between doctors and patients?

   b. Develop sample doctor and patient data and construct two relational tables in the style of Figure 4.5 in which to store your sample data.

   c. Do any fields have to be added to one or the other of the two tables to record the relationship between doctors and patients? Explain.

   d. Merge these two tables into one, as in the style of Figure 4.6. Does this create any problems with the data? Explain.

2. The Dynamic Chemicals Corporation keeps track of its customers and its orders. Customers typically have several outstanding orders, while each order was generated by a single customer. Each customer has a unique customer number, a customer name, address, and telephone number. An order has a unique order number, a date, and a total cost.

   a. What kind of relationship is there between customers and orders?

   b. Develop sample customer and order data and construct two relational tables in the style of Figure 4.5 in which to store your sample data.

   c. Do any fields have to be added to one or the other of the two tables to record the relationship between customers and orders? Explain.

   d. Merge these two tables into one, as in the style of Figure 4.6. Does this create any problems with the data? Explain.

MINICASES

1. Answer the following questions based on the following two tables from Happy Cruise Lines' relational database.

(a) Ship table			
Ship Number	Ship Name	Year Built	Weight (Tons)
005	Sea Joy	1999	80,000
009	Ocean IV	2003	75,000
012	Prince Al	2004	90,000
020	Queen Shirley	1999	80,000

(b) Crew Member table				
Sailor Number	Sailor Name	Ship Number	Home Country	Job Title
00536	John Smith	009	USA	Purser
00732	Ling Chang	012	China	Engineer
06988	Maria Gonzalez	020	Mexico	Purser
16490	Prashant Kumar	005	India	Navigator
18535	Alan Jones	009	UK	Cruise Director
20254	Jane Adams	012	USA	Captain
23981	Rene Lopez	020	Philippines	Captain
27467	Fred Jones	020	UK	Waiter
27941	Alain DuMont	009	France	Captain
28184	Susan Moore	009	Canada	Wine Steward
31775	James Collins	012	USA	Waiter
32856	Sarah McLachlan	012	Ireland	Cabin Steward

a. The value 009 appears as a ship number once in the SHIP table and four times in the CREW MEMBER table. Does this constitute data redundancy? Explain.

b. Merge the SHIP and CREW MEMBER tables based on the common ship number field (in a manner similar to Figure 4.6 for the General Hardware database). Is the merged table an improvement over the two separate tables in terms of:
   i. Data redundancy? Explain.
   ii. Data integration? Explain.

c. Explain why the Ship Number field is in the CREW MEMBER table.

d. Explain why ship number 012 appears three times in the CREW MEMBER table.

e. How many tables must be accessed to find:

i. The year that ship number 012 was built?
ii. The home country of sailor number 27941?
iii. The name of the ship on which sailor number 18535 is employed?

f. Describe the procedure for finding the weight of the ship on which sailor number 00536 is employed.

g. What is the mechanism for recording the one-to-many relationship between crew members and ships in the Happy Cruise Lines database, above?

2. Answer the following questions based on the following two tables from the Super Baseball League's relational database.

(a) Team table			
Team Number	Team Name	City	Manager
137	Eagles	Orlando	Smith
275	Cowboys	San Jose	Jones
294	Statesmen	Springfield	Edwards
368	Pandas	El Paso	Adams
422	Sharks	Jackson	Vega

(b) Player table				
Player Number	Player Name	Age	Position	Team Number
1209	Steve Marks	24	Catcher	294
1254	Roscoe Gomez	19	Pitcher	422
1536	Mark Norton	32	First Baseman	368
1953	Alan Randall	24	Pitcher	137
2753	John Harbor	22	Shortstop	294
2843	John Yancy	27	Center Fielder	137
3002	Stuart Clark	20	Catcher	422
3274	Lefty Smith	31	Third Baseman	137
3388	Kevin Taylor	25	Shortstop	294
3740	Juan Vidora	25	Catcher	368

a. The value 294 appears as a team number once in the TEAM table and three times in the PLAYER table. Does this constitute data redundancy? Explain.

b. Merge the TEAM and PLAYER tables based on the common Team Number field (in a manner similar to Figure 4.6 for the General Hardware database). Is the merged table an improvement over the two separate tables in terms of:

i. Data redundancy? Explain.

ii. Data integration? Explain.

c. Explain why the Team Number field is in the PLAYER table.

d. Explain why team number 422 appears twice in the PLAYER table.

e. How many tables must be accessed to find:

i. The age of player number 1953?

ii. The name of the team on which player number 3388 plays?

iii. The number of the team on which player number 3388 plays?

f. Describe the procedure for finding the name of the city in which player number 3002 is based.

g. What is the mechanism for recording the one-to-many relationship between players and teams in the Super Baseball League database above?

CHAPTER 5

THE RELATIONAL DATABASE MODEL: INTRODUCTION

CHAPTER OBJECTIVES

After learning the material in this chapter, you will be able to:

✔ Explain why the relational database model became practical in about 1980.
✔ Define such basic relational database terms as relation and tuple.
✔ Describe the major types of keys including primary, candidate, and foreign.
✔ Describe how one-to-one, one-to-many, and many-to-many binary relationships are implemented in a relational database.
✔ Describe how relational data retrieval is accomplished in concept with the select, project, and join operators.
✔ Understand how the join operator facilitates data integration in relational database.

A Black & Decker power saw

BLACK & DECKER

Black & Decker is one of the world's largest producers of electric power tools and power tool accessories, is among the largest-selling residential lock manufacturers in the United States, and is a major manufacturer of faucets sold in the United States. It is also the world's largest producer of certain types of technology-based industrial fastening systems. The company's brand names include Black & Decker and DeWalt power tools,

Emhart Teknologies, Kwikset locks and other home security products, and Price Pfister plumbing fixtures. Based in Towson, Maryland, Black & Decker has manufacturing plants in ten countries and markets its products in over 100 countries around the globe.

One of the major factors in Black & Decker's Power Tools Division's leadership position is its highly advanced, database-focused information system that assures a steady and accurate supply of raw materials to the manufacturing floor. Using Manugistics' Demand and Supply Planning software, the system forecasts demand for Black & Decker's power tools and then generates a raw material supply plan based on the forecast and on the company's manufacturing capacity. These results are fed into SAP's Plant Planning System that takes into account suppliers' capabilities and lead-time constraints to set up orders for the raw materials.

Both the Manugistics and SAP software use Oracle databases to keep track of all of the data involved in these processes. Black & Decker runs the system, which became fully integrated in 1998, on clustered Compaq Alphas. The databases are also shared by the company's purchasing, receiving, finance, and accounting departments, assuring very high degrees of accuracy and speed throughout the company's operations and procedures. Included among the major database tables that support this information system are a material master table, a vendor master table, a bill-of-materials table (that indicates which parts go into making which other parts), a routing table (that indicates the work stations that the part will move through during manufacturing), planning, purchase order, customer, and other tables.

Printed by permission of Black & Decker

In 1970, Dr. Edgar F. (Ted) Codd of IBM published a paper entitled "A Relational Model of Data for Large Shared Data Banks" in *Communications of the ACM*. This paper marked the beginning of the field of relational database. During the 1970s, the relational approach to database progressed from being a technical curiosity to a subject of serious interest in the information systems community. But it was not until the early 1980s that commercially viable relational database management systems became available. There were two basic reasons for this lag. One was that while relational database was very tempting in concept, it was not easily applicable in a real-world environment for reasons related to performance, which we will discuss later in Chapter 8. The second reason was that at exactly the time that Codd's paper was published, the earlier hierarchical and network database management systems were just coming onto the commercial scene and were the focus of intense marketing efforts by the software and hardware vendors of the day.

Several factors converged in the early 1980s to begin turning the tide toward relational database. One was that the performance issues that held back its adoption in the 1970s began to be resolved. Another was that after a decade of use of hierarchical and network database management systems, information systems professionals were interested in finding an alternative that would help simplify the database design process and produce database structures that were easier to use and understand at all levels. At this time, too, there was increasing interest in having a DBMS environment that would allow easier, more intuitive access to the data by an increasingly broad range of personnel. Finally, the early 1980s saw the advent of the **personal computer (PC).** As software developers began trying to create all manner of applications and supporting software utilities for the PC, it quickly became clear that the existing hierarchical and network database approaches would not work in the PC environment, for two reasons. One was that these DBMSs were simply too large to store and use on the early PCs. The other was that they were too complex to be used by the very broad array of noninformation systems professionals to whom the PCs were targeted.

Today, the relational approach to database management is by far the primary database management approach used in all levels of information systems and for most application purposes from accounting to banking to manufacturing to sales on the World Wide Web. Relational database management is represented today by such products as Microsoft Access and SQL Server, Oracle, Sybase, and IBM's DB2 and Informix. While these and other relational database systems have different features and implementations, they all share a common data structure philosophy and a common data access tool: Structured Query Language (SQL) (often pronounced "sequel"). This chapter will focus on the basic concepts of how data is stored and retrieved in a relational database by a relational DBMS. The following chapter, Chapter 6, will discuss some additional relational database concepts; Chapter 7 will describe logical database design; Chapter 8 will go into physical database design; and Chapter 9 will be devoted to SQL, primarily to its use in retrieving data from a relational database. *As explained in the Preface, it is important to note that Chapter 9 on SQL can be read and studied before the two design chapters, Chapters 7 and 8, without any loss of content or continuity.*

THE RELATIONAL DATABASE CONCEPT

Relational Terminology

In spite of the apparent conflict between non-redundant, linear file data storage and data integration demonstrated in the previous chapter, the concept of having the relative simplicity of simple, linear files or structures that resemble them in a true database environment is very desirable. After all, the linear file arrangement is the most basic and commonly used data structure available. This is precisely one of the advantages of relational database.

To begin with, consider the data structure used in relational databases. In a relational database, the data *appears* to be stored in what we have been referring to as simple, linear files. Following the conventions of the area of mathematics on which relational database is based, we will begin calling those simple linear files **relations,** although in common practice they are also referred to as tables. In the terminology of files, each **row** is called a record, while in a relation, each row is called a **tuple.** In files, each **column** is called a field, while in a relation each column is called an **attribute.** In practice, in speaking about relational database, it is common for people to use relation, table, and file synonymously. Similarly, tuple, row, and record are often used synonymously, as are attribute, column, and field, (Figure 5.1). We will use an appropriate term in each particular situation during our discussion. In particular, we will use the term relation in this chapter and the next, in which we are talking about relational database concepts. Following common usage, we will generally use the term table in the more applied parts of the book, such as in the corporate database stories in each chapter and in the discussion of SQL in Chapter 9.

➤ **Figure 5.1**
Relational database
terminology

Attribute (or Column or Field)		Relation (or Table or File)	
Student Number	Student Name	Class	Major
03657	Robert Shaw	Senior	Biology
05114	Gloria Stuart	Freshman	English
05950	Fred Simpson	Junior	Mathematics
12746	W. Shin	Junior	English
15887	Pedro Marcos	Senior	History
19462	H. Yamato	Sophomore	French
21682	Mary Jones	Freshman	Chemistry
24276	Steven Baker	Sophomore	History

Tuple (or Row or Record)

Technical differences exist between the concept of a file and the concept of a relation (which is why we say that in a relational database the data only *appears* to be stored in structures that look like files). The differences include:

- The columns of a relation can be arranged in any order without affecting the meaning of the data. This is not true of a file.
- Similarly, the rows of a relation can be arranged in any order, which is not true of a file.
- Every row/column position, sometimes referred to as a cell, can have only a single value, which is not necessarily true in a file.
- No two rows of a relation are identical, which is not necessarily true in a file.

A relational database is simply a collection of relations that, as a group, contain the data that describes a particular business environment.

Primary and Candidate Keys

Primary Keys   Figure 5.2 contains two relations, the SALESPERSON relation and the CUSTOMER relation, from General Hardware Company's relational database. The SALESPERSON relation has four rows, each representing one salesperson. Also, the SALESPERSON relation has four columns, each representing a characteristic of salespersons. Similarly, the CUSTOMER relation has nine rows, each representing a customer, and four columns.

A relation always has a unique **primary key.** A primary key (sometimes shortened in practice to just "the key") is an attribute or a group of attributes whose values are unique throughout all of the rows of the relation. The primary key represents the characteristic of a collection of entities that uniquely identifies each one. For example, in the situation described by the relations of Figure 5.2, each salesperson has been assigned a unique salesperson number and each customer has been assigned a unique customer number. Therefore the Salesperson Number attribute is the primary key of the SALESPERSON relation, and the Customer Number attribute is the primary key of the CUSTOMER relation. As shown in Figure 5.2, we will start marking the primary key attribute(s) with a single, solid underline.

➤ **Figure 5.2**
General Hardware Company
relational database

(a) SALESPERSON relation

Salesperson Number	Salesperson Name	Commission Percentage	Year of Hire
137	Baker	10	1995
186	Adams	15	2001
204	Dickens	10	1998
361	Carlyle	20	2001

(b) CUSTOMER relation

Customer Number	Customer Name	Salesperson Number	HQ City
0121	Main St. Hardware	137	New York
0839	Jane's Stores	186	Chicago
0933	ABC Home Stores	137	Los Angeles
1047	Acme Hardware Store	137	Los Angeles
1525	Fred's Tool Stores	361	Atlanta
1700	XYZ Stores	361	Washington
1826	City Hardware	137	New York
2198	Western Hardware	204	New York
2267	Central Stores	186	New York

The number of attributes involved in the primary key is always the minimum number of attributes that provide the uniqueness quality. For example, in the SALESPERSON relation, it would make no sense to have the combination of Salesperson Number and Salesperson Name as the primary key because Salesperson Number is unique by itself. However, consider the situation of a SALESPERSON relation that does not include a Salesperson Number attribute, but instead has a First Name attribute, a Middle Name attribute, and a Last Name attribute. The primary key might then be the combination of the First, Middle, and Last Name attributes. (Assuming this would always produce a unique combination of values. If it did not, then a fourth attribute could be added to the relation and to the primary key as a sequence field to produce, for example, John Alan Smith #1, John Alan Smith #2, and so forth.) Some attribute or combination of attributes of a relation has to be unique and can serve as the unique primary key, since, by definition, no two rows can be identical. In the worst case, all of the relation's attributes combined could serve as the primary key if necessary (but this situation is uncommon in practice).

Candidate Keys   If a relation has more than one attribute or minimum group of attributes that represents a way of uniquely identifying the entities, then they are each called a *candidate key*. (Actually, if there is only one unique attribute or minimum group of attributes, it can also be called a candidate key.) For example, in a personnel relation, an Employee Number attribute and a Social Security number attribute (each of which is obviously unique) would each be a candidate key of that relation. When there is more than one candidate key, one of them must be chosen to be the primary key of the relation. That is where the term candidate key comes from since each one is a candidate for selection as the primary key. The decision of which candidate key to pick to be the primary key is typically based on which one will be the best for the purposes of the applications that will use the relation and the database. Sometimes the term **alternate key** is used to describe a candidate key that was not chosen to be the primary key of the relation (Figure 5.3).

Foreign Keys and Binary Relationships

Foreign Keys   If in a collection of relations that make up a relational database, an attribute or group of attributes serves as the primary key of one relation and also appears in another relation, then it is called a *foreign key* in that other relation. Thus Salesperson Number, which is the primary key of the SALESPERSON relation, is considered a foreign key in the CUSTOMER relation (Figure 5.4). As shown in Figure 5.4, we will start marking the Foreign Key attribute(s) with a dashed underline. The concept of the foreign key is crucial in relational database, because the foreign key is the mechanism that ties relations together to represent unary, binary, and ternary relationships. We begin the discussion by considering how binary relationships are stored in relational databases. These are both the most common and the easiest to deal with. The unary and ternary relationships will come later. Recall from the discussion of the entity-relationship model that the three kinds of binary relationships among the entities in the business environment are the one-to-one, one-to-many, and many-to-many relationships. The first case is the one-to-many relationship, which is typically the most common of the three.

➤ **Figure 5.3**
Candidate keys become either primary or alternate keys

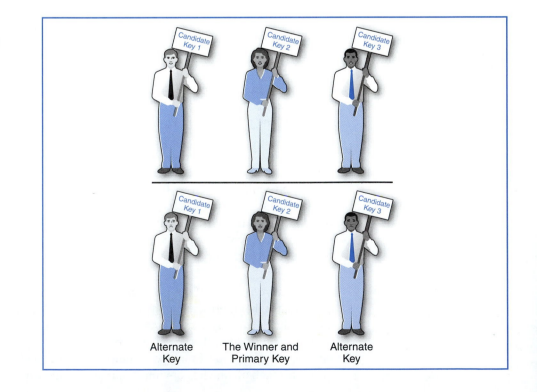

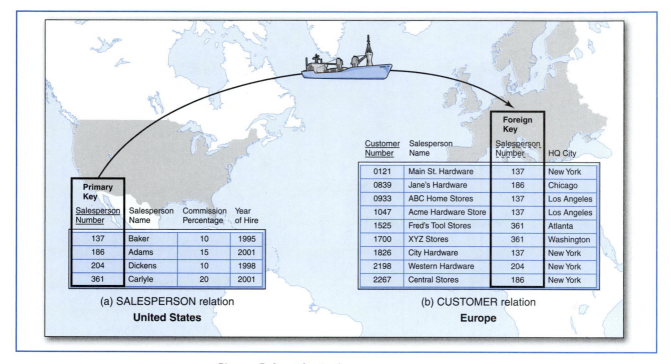

(a) SALESPERSON relation
United States

(b) CUSTOMER relation
Europe

Figure 5.4 A foreign key

One-to-Many Binary Relationship Consider the SALESPERSON and CUS-TOMER relations of Figure 5.2, repeated in Figure 5.4. As one would expect in most sales-oriented companies, notice that each salesperson is responsible for several customers, while each customer has a single salesperson as their point of contact with General Hardware. This one-to-many binary relationship can be represented as:

Salesperson ◄───►► Customer

For example, the Salesperson Number attribute of the CUSTOMER relation shows that salesperson 137 is responsible for customers 0121, 0933, 1047, and 1826. Looking at it from the point of view of the customer, the same relation shows that the only salesperson associated with customer 0121 is salesperson 137 (Figure 5.5). This last point has to be true. After all, there is only one record for each customer in the CUSTOMER relation (the Customer Number attribute is unique since it is the relation's primary key), and there is only one place to put a salesperson number in it. The bottom line is that the Salesperson Number foreign key in the CUSTOMER relation effectively establishes the one-to-many relationship between salespersons and customers.

Notice that, in this case, the primary key of the SALESPERSON relation and the corresponding foreign key in the CUSTOMER relation both have the same **attribute name,** Salesperson Number. This will often be the case, but it does not have to be. What is necessary is that both attributes have the same **domain of values;** that is they must both have values of the same type, such as, in this case, three-digit whole numbers that are the identifiers for salespersons.

➤ **Figure 5.5**

A salesperson and his
four customers

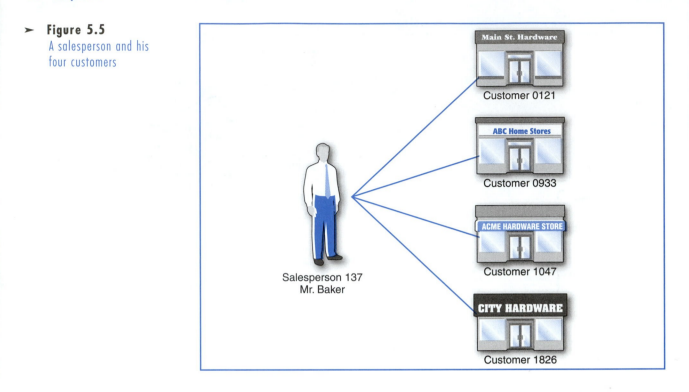

It is the presence of a salesperson number in a customer record that indicates which salesperson the customer is associated with. Fundamentally, that is why the Salesperson Number attribute is in the CUSTOMER relation, and that is the essence of its being a foreign key in that relation. Later in the book, we will discuss database design issues in detail. But for now, note that when building a one-to-many relationship into a relational database, it will always be the case that the unique identifier of the entity on the "one side" of the relationship (Salesperson Number, in this example) will be placed as a foreign key in the relation representing the entity on the "many side" of the relationship (the CUSTOMER relation, in this example).

Here's something else about foreign keys. In some situations a relation doesn't have a single, unique attribute to serve as its primary key. Then, it requires a combination of two or more attributes to reach uniqueness and serve as its primary key. Sometimes one or more of the attributes in that combination can be a foreign key! Yes, when this happens, a foreign key is actually part of the relation's primary key! This was not the case in the CUSTOMER relation of Figure 5.2b. In this relation, the primary key only consists of one attribute, Customer Number, which is unique all by itself. The foreign key, Salesperson Number, is clearly not a part of the primary key.

Here is an example of a situation in which a foreign key is part of a relation's primary key. Figure 5.6 adds the CUSTOMER EMPLOYEE relation (Figure 5.6c), to the General Hardware database. Remember that General Hardware's customers are the hardware stores, home improvement stores, or chains of such stores that it supplies. Figure 5.6c, the CUSTOMER EMPLOYEE relation, lists the employees of each of General Hardware's customers. In fact, there is a one-to-many relationship between customers and customer employees. A customer (like a hardware store) has many employees, but an employee, a person, works in only one store:

Customer ⟷➤➤ Customer Employee

> **Figure 5.6**
> General Hardware Company relational database including the CUSTOMER EMPLOYEE relation

(a) SALESPERSON relation

Salesperson Number	Salesperson Name	Commission Percentage	Year of Hire
137	Baker	10	1995
186	Adams	15	2001
204	Dickens	10	1998
361	Carlyle	20	2001

(b) CUSTOMER relation

Customer Number	Customer Name	Salesperson Number	HQ City
0121	Main St. Hardware	137	New York
0839	Jane's Stores	186	Chicago
0933	ABC Home Stores	137	Los Angeles
1047	Acme Hardware Store	137	Los Angeles
1525	Fred's Tool Stores	361	Atlanta
1700	XYZ Stores	361	Washington
1826	City Hardware	137	New York
2198	Western Hardware	204	New York
2267	Central Stores	186	New York

(c) CUSTOMER EMPLOYEE relation

Customer Number	Employee Number	Employee Name	Title
0121	27498	Smith	Co-Owner
0121	30441	Garcia	Co-Owner
0933	25270	Chen	VP Sales
0933	30441	Levy	Sales Manager
0933	48285	Morton	President
1525	33779	Baker	Sales Manager
2198	27470	Smith	President
2198	30441	Jones	VP Sales
2198	33779	Garcia	VP Personnel
2198	35268	Kaplan	Senior Accountant

For example, Figure 5.6c shows that customer 2198 has four employees—Smith, Jones, Garcia, and Kaplan. Each of those people is assumed to work for only one customer company, customer 2198. Following the rule we developed for setting up a one-to-many relationship with a foreign key, the Customer attribute must appear in the CUSTOMER EMPLOYEE relation as a foreign key, and indeed it does.

Now, what about finding a legitimate primary key for the CUSTOMER EMPLOYEE relation? The assumption here is that employee numbers *are only unique within a company*; they are not unique across all of the customer companies.

Thus, as shown in the CUSTOMER EMPLOYEE relation of Figure 5.6c, there can be an employee of customer number 0121 who is employee number 30441 in that company's employee numbering system, an employee of customer number 0933 who is employee number 30441 in that company's system, and also an employee of customer number 2198 who is also employee number 30441. That being the case, the Employee Number is not a **unique attribute** in this relation. Neither it nor any other single attribute of the CUSTOMER EMPLOYEE relation is unique and can serve, alone, as the relation's primary key. But the combination of Customer Number and Employee Number is unique. After all, we know that customer numbers are unique and that within each customer company, employee numbers are unique. That means that, as shown in Figure 5.6c, the combination of Customer Number and Employee Number can be and is the relation's primary key. That also means that Customer Number is both a foreign key in the CUSTOMER EMPLOYEE relation *and* a part of its primary key. As shown in Figure 5.6c, we will start marking attributes that are both a foreign key and a part of the primary key with an underline consisting of a dashed line over a solid line.

Many-to-Many Binary Relationship

Storing the Many-to-Many Binary Relationship Figure 5.7 expands the General Hardware database by adding two more relations: the PRODUCT relation (Figure 5.7d), and the SALES relation (Figure 5.7e). The PRODUCT relation simply lists the products that General Hardware sells, one row per product, with Product Number as the unique identifier and thus the primary key of the relation. Each of General Hardware's salespersons can sell any or all of the company's products, and each product can be sold by any or all of its salespersons. Therefore the relationship between salespersons and products is a many-to-many relationship.

Salesperson ◄◄——————►► Product

So, the database will somehow have to keep track of this many-to-many relationship between salespersons and products. The way that a many-to-many relationship is represented in a relational database is by the creation of an additional relation, in this example, the SALES relation in Figure 5.7e. The SALES relation of Figure 5.7e is intended to record the *lifetime* sales of a particular product by a particular salesperson. Thus there will be a single row in the relation for each applicable combination of salesperson and product (i.e., when a particular salesperson *has actually sold* some of the particular product). For example, the first row of the SALES relation indicates that salesperson 137 has sold product 19440. Since it is sufficient to record that fact once, the combination of the Salesperson Number and Product Number attributes always produces unique values. So, in this case, the new relation created to record the many-to-many relationship will have as its primary key the combined, unique identifiers of the two entities in the many-to-many relationship. That's why, in this example, the Salesperson Number and Product Number attributes both appear in the SALES relation. Each of the two is a foreign key in the SALES relation since each is the primary key of another relation in the database. The combination of these two attributes is unique and, combined, they comprise the primary key of the newly created SALES relation.

> **Figure 5.7**
> General Hardware Company relational database including the PRODUCT and SALES relation

(a) SALESPERSON relation

Salesperson Number	Salesperson Name	Commission Percentage	Year of Hire
137	Baker	10	1995
186	Adams	15	2001
204	Dickens	10	1998
361	Carlyle	20	2001

(b) CUSTOMER relation

Customer Number	Customer Name	Salesperson Number	HQ City
0121	Main St. Hardware	137	New York
0839	Jane's Stores	186	Chicago
0933	ABC Home Stores	137	Los Angeles
1047	Acme Hardware Store	137	Los Angeles
1525	Fred's Tool Stores	361	Atlanta
1700	XYZ Stores	361	Washington
1826	City Hardware	137	New York
2198	Western Hardware	204	New York
2267	Central Stores	186	New York

(c) CUSTOMER EMPLOYEE relation

Customer Number	Employee Number	Employee Name	Title
0121	27498	Smith	Co-Owner
0121	30441	Garcia	Co-Owner
0933	25270	Chen	VP Sales
0933	30441	Levy	Sales Manager
0933	48285	Morton	President
1525	33779	Baker	Sales Manager
2198	27470	Smith	President
2198	30441	Jones	VP Sales
2198	33779	Garcia	VP Personnel
2198	35268	Kaplan	Senior Accountant

(Continues)

The new SALES relation of Figure 5.7e effectively records the many-to-many relationship between salespersons and products. This is illustrated from the "salesperson side" of the many-to-many relationship by looking at the first three rows of the SALES relation and seeing that salesperson 137 sells products 19440, 24013, and 26722. It is illustrated from the "product side" of the many-to-many relationship by scanning down the Product Number column of the SALES relation, looking for the value 19440, and seeing that product 19440 is sold by salespersons 137 and 186 (Figure 5.8).

➤ **Figure 5.7 (Continued)**
General Hardware Company relational database including the PRODUCT and SALES relation

(d) PRODUCT relation		
Product Number	Product Name	Unit Price
16386	Wrench	12.95
19440	Hammer	17.50
21765	Drill	32.99
24013	Saw	26.25
26722	Pliers	11.50

(e) SALES relation		
Salesperson Number	Product Number	Quantity
137	19440	473
137	24013	170
137	26722	688
186	16386	1,745
186	19440	2,529
186	21765	1,962
186	24013	3,071
204	21765	809
204	26722	734
361	16386	3,729
361	21765	3,110
361	26722	2,738

Intersection Data What about the Quantity attribute in the SALES relation? In addition to keeping track of which salespersons have sold which products, General Hardware wants to record *how many* of each particular product each salesperson has sold since the product was introduced or since the salesperson joined the company. So, it sounds like there has to be a Quantity attribute. And, an attribute describes an entity, right? Then, which entity does the Quantity attribute describe? Does it describe salespersons the way the Year of Hire does in the SALESPERSON relation? Does it describe products the way Unit Price does in the PRODUCT relation? Each salesperson has exactly one date of hire, and each product has exactly one unit price. But a salesperson doesn't have just one quantity associated with her because she sells many products, and similarly, a product doesn't have just one quantity associated with it because it is sold by many salespersons.

➤ **Figure 5.8**
Many-to-many relationship between salespersons and products as shown in the SALES relation

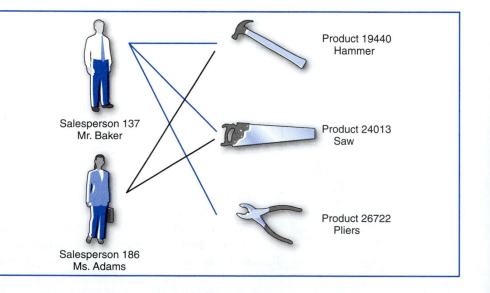

While year of hire is clearly a characteristic of salespersons and unit price is clearly a characteristic of products, quantity is a characteristic of *the relationship between salesperson and product*. For example, the fact that salesperson 137 appears in the first row of the SALES relation of Figure 5.7e along with product 19440 indicates that he has a history of selling this product. But do we know more about his history of selling it? Yes! That first row of Figure 5.7e indicates that salesperson 137 has sold 473 units of product 19440. Quantity *describes the many-to-many relationship* between salespersons and products. In a sense, it falls at the intersection between the two entities and is called intersection data (Figure 5.9).

Since the many-to-many relationship has its own relation in the database and since it can have attributes, does that mean that we should think of it as a kind of entity? Yes! Many people do just that and refer to it as an associative entity, a concept that we first described when discussing data modeling in Chapter 3.

Additional Many-to-Many Concepts Before leaving the subject of many-to-many relationships, there are a few more important points to make. First, will the combination of the two primary keys representing the two entities in the many-to-many relationship always serve as a unique identifier or primary key in the additional relation representing the many-to-many relationship? That depends on the precise nature of the many-to-many relationship. For example, in the situation of the SALES relation in Figure 5.7e, the combination of the two entity identifier attributes works perfectly as the primary key, as described above. But what if General Hardware decides that it wants to keep track of each salesperson's *annual* sales of each product instead of their *lifetime* sales? Fairly obviously, a new attribute, Year, would have to

➤ **Figure 5.9**
Intersection data that indicates that salesperson 137 has sold 473 units of product 19440

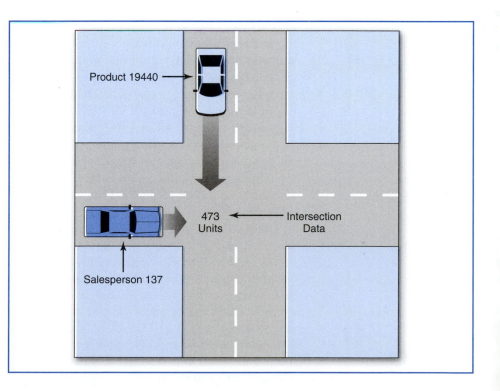

➤ **Figure 5.10**
Modified SALES relation
of the General Hardware
Company relational data-
base, including a Year
attribute

SALES relation (modified)			
Salesperson Number	Product Number	Year	Quantity
137	19440	1999	132
137	19440	2000	168
137	19440	2001	173
137	24013	2000	52
137	24013	2001	118
137	26722	1999	140
137	26722	2000	203
137	26722	2001	345
186	16386	1998	250
186	16386	1999	245
186	16386	2000	581
186	16386	2001	669

be added to the SALES relation, as shown in Figure 5.10. Moreover, as demonstrated by a few sample rows of that relation, the combination of Salesperson Number and Product Number is no longer unique. For example, salesperson 137 sold many units of product 19440 in each of 1999, 2000, and 2001. The first three records of the relation all have the salesperson number, product number combination of 137, 19440. The way to solve the problem in this instance is to add the Year attribute to the Salesperson Number and Product Number attributes to form a three-attribute, unique, primary key. It is quite common in practice to have to add such a "timestamp" to a relation storing a many-to-many relationship in order to attain uniqueness and have a legitimate primary key. Sometimes, as in the example in Figure 5.10, this is accomplished with a Year attribute. A Date attribute is required if the data may be stored two or more times in a year. A Time attribute is required if the data may be stored more than once in a day.

Next is the question of why an additional relation is necessary to represent a many-to-many relationship. For example, could the many-to-many relationship between salespersons and products be represented in either the SALESPERSON or PRODUCT relation? The answer is no! If, for instance, you tried to represent the many-to-many relationship in the SALESPERSON relation, you would have to list all of the products (by Product Number) that a particular salesperson has sold in that salesperson's record. Furthermore, in some way you would have to carry the Quantity intersection data along with it. For example, in the SALESPERSON relation, the row for salesperson 137 would have to be extended to include products 19440, 24013, and 26722, plus the associated intersection data (Figure 5.11a). Alternately, one could envision a single additional attribute in the SALESPERSON relation into which all of the related product number and intersection data for each salesperson would somehow be stuffed (Figure 5.11b), although, aside from other problems, this would violate the rule about every cell in a relation having only a single value. In either case, it would be unworkable. Because, in general, each salesperson has been involved in selling different numbers of product types, each record of the SALESPERSON relation would be a different length. Furthermore, additions, deletions, and updates of product/quantity pairs would be a nightmare. Also, trying to access the related data from the "product side," for example, looking for all of the salespersons who have sold a particular product, would be very difficult. And, incidentally, trying to make this work by putting the salesperson data into the PRODUCT relation, instead of putting the product data into the SALESPERSON relation as in Figure 5.11, would generate an identical set of problems. No, the only way that's workable is to

(a) Additional Product and Quantity columns

Salesperson Number	Salesperson Name	Commission Percentage	Year of Hire	Product	Qty	Product	Qty	Product	Qty	Product	Qty
137	Baker	10	1995	19440	473	24013	170	26722	688		
186	Adams	15	2001	16386	1745	19440	2529	21765	1962	24013	3071
204	Dickens	10	1998	21765	809	26722	734				
361	Carlyle	20	2001	16386	3729	21765	3110	26722	2738		

(b) One additional column for Product and Quantity Pairs

Salesperson Number	Salesperson Name	Commission Percentage	Year of Hire	Product and Quantity Pairs
137	Baker	10	1995	(19440, 473) (24013, 170) (26722, 688)
186	Adams	15	2001	(16386, 1745) (19440, 2529) (21765, 1962) (24013, 3071)
204	Dickens	10	1998	(21765, 809) (26722, 734)
361	Carlyle	20	2001	(16386, 3729) (21765, 3110) (26722, 2738)

➤ **Figure 5.11**   *Unacceptable ways of storing a binary many-to-many relationship*

create an additional relation to represent the many-to-many relationship. Each combination of a related salesperson and product has its own record, making the insertion, deletion, and update of related items feasible, providing a clear location for intersection data, and avoiding the issue of variable-length records.

Finally, there is the question of whether an additional relation is required to represent a many-to-many relationship in the case where there is no intersection data. For example, suppose that General Hardware wants to track which salespersons have sold which products but has no interest in how many units of each product they have sold. The SALES relation of Figure 5.7e would then have only the Salesperson Number and Product Number attributes (Figure 5.12). Could this information be stored in some way other than with the additional SALES relation? The answer is that the additional relation is still required. Note that in the preceding explanation, of why an additional relation is necessary in general to represent a many-to-many relationship, the intersection data played only a small role. The issues would still be there, even without intersection data.

One-to-One Binary Relationship   After considering one-to-many and many-to-many binary relationships in relational databases, the remaining binary relationship is the one-to-one relationship. Each of General Hardware's salespersons has exactly one office, and each office is occupied by exactly one salesperson (Figure 5.13).

Salesperson ⟵⟶ Office

Figure 5.14 shows the addition of the OFFICE relation (Figure 5.14f) to the General Hardware relational database. The SALESPERSON relation has the Office Number attribute as a foreign key so that the company can look up the record for a salesperson and see to which office she is assigned. Because this is a one-to-one relationship and each salesperson has only one office, the company can also scan down

➤ **Figure 5.12**
The many-to-many
SALES relation without
intersection data

SALES relation (without intersection data)	
Salesperson Number	Product Number
137	19440
137	24013
137	26722
186	16386
186	19440
186	21765
186	24013
204	21765
204	26722
361	16386
361	21765
361	26722

the Office Number column of the SALESPERSON relation, find a particular office number (which can only appear once, since it's a one-to-one relationship), and see which salesperson is assigned to that office. In general, this is the way that one-to-one binary relationships are built into relational databases. The unique identifier, the primary key, of one of the two entities in the one-to-one relationship is inserted into the other entity's relation as a foreign key. The question of which of the two entities is chosen as the "donor" of its primary key and which is chosen as the "recipient" will be discussed further when we talk about logical design in Chapter 7.

But there is another interesting question about this arrangement. Could the SALESPERSON and OFFICE relations of Figure 5.14 be combined into one relation? After all, a salesperson has only one office and an office has only one salesperson assigned to it. So, if an office and its unique identifier, Office Number, "belongs" to

➤ **Figure 5.13**
A one-to-one binary
relationship

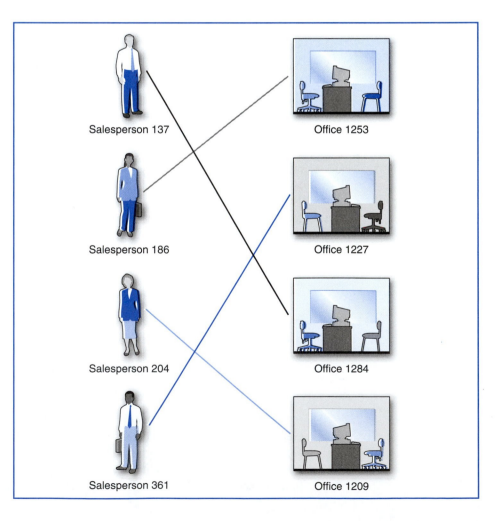

Salesperson 137   Office 1253

Salesperson 186   Office 1227

Salesperson 204   Office 1284

Salesperson 361   Office 1209

> **Figure 5.14**
> General Hardware Company relational database including the OFFICE relation

(a) SALESPERSON relation

Salesperson Number	Salesperson Name	Commission Percentage	Year of Hire	Office Number
137	Baker	10	1995	1284
186	Adams	15	2001	1253
204	Dickens	10	1998	1209
361	Carlyle	20	2001	1227

(b) CUSTOMER relation

Customer Number	Customer Name	Salesperson Number	HQ City
0121	Main St. Hardware	137	New York
0839	Jane's Stores	186	Chicago
0933	ABC Home Stores	137	Los Angeles
1047	Acme Hardware Store	137	Los Angeles
1525	Fred's Tool Stores	361	Atlanta
1700	XYZ Stores	361	Washington
1826	City Hardware	137	New York
2198	Western Hardware	204	New York
2267	Central Stores	186	New York

(c) CUSTOMER EMPLOYEE relation

Customer Number	Employee Number	Employee Name	Title
0121	27498	Smith	Co-Owner
0121	30441	Garcia	Co-Owner
0933	25270	Chen	VP Sales
0933	30441	Levy	Sales Manager
0933	48285	Morton	President
1525	33779	Baker	Sales Manager
2198	27470	Smith	President
2198	30441	Jones	VP Sales
2198	33779	Garcia	VP Personnel
2198	35268	Kaplan	Senior Accountant

(Continues)

one particular salesperson, so does that office's Telephone Number and Size. Indeed, when we want to be able to contact a salesperson, we ask for *her phone number*, not for "her office's phone number!" So, could we combine the SALESPERSON and OFFICE relations of Figure 5.14 into the single relation of Figure 5.15? The answer is, it's possible in some cases, but you have to be very careful about making such a decision. In the General Hardware case, how would you store an *unoccupied* office in the database? The relation of Figure 5.15 only

➤ **Figure 5.14 (Continued)**
General Hardware Company relational database including the OFFICE relation

(d) PRODUCT relation

Product Number	Product Name	Unit Price
16386	Wrench	12.95
19440	Hammer	17.50
21765	Drill	32.99
24013	Saw	26.25
26722	Pliers	11.50

(e) SALES relation

Salesperson Number	Product Number	Quantity
137	19440	473
137	24013	170
137	26722	688
186	16386	1,745
186	19440	2,529
186	21765	1,962
186	24013	3,071
204	21765	809
204	26722	734
361	16386	3,729
361	21765	3,110
361	26722	2,738

(f) OFFICE relation

Office Number	Telephone	Size (sq. ft.)
1253	901-555-4276	120
1227	901-555-0364	100
1284	901-555-7335	120
1209	901-555-3108	95

allows data about an office to be stored if the office is *occupied*. After all, the primary key of Figure 5.15's relation is Salesperson Number! You can't have a record with office data in it and no salesperson data. A case where it might work is a database of U.S. states and their governors. Every state *always* has exactly one governor, and anyone who is a governor *must* be associated with one state. There can't be a state without a governor or a governor without a state.

At any rate, in practice, there are a variety of reasons for keeping the two relations involved in the one-to-one relationship separate. It may be that because each of the two entities involved is considered sufficiently important in its own right, it simply adds clarity to the database. It may be because most users at any one time seek data about only one of the two entities. It may have to do with splitting the data between different geographic sites. It can even be done for system performance purposes in the case where the records would be unacceptably long if the data was all contained in one relation. These issues will be discussed later in this book, but at this point it is important to have at least a basic idea of the intricacies of the one-to-one relationship.

DATA RETRIEVAL FROM A RELATIONAL DATABASE

Extracting Data from a Relation

Thus far, the discussion has concentrated on how a relational database is structured, but building relations and loading them with data is only half of the story. The other half is the effort to retrieve the data in a way that is helpful and beneficial to the business organization that built the database. If the database management system did not provide any particular help with this effort, then the problem would revert to simply writing a program in some programming language to retrieve data from the relations, treating them as if they were simple, linear files. But the crucial point

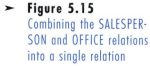

➤ **Figure 5.15**
Combining the SALESPER-
SON and OFFICE relations
into a single relation

Combined SALESPERSON/OFFICE relation						
Salesperson Number	Salesperson Name	Commission Percentage	Year of Hire	Office Number	Telephone	Size (sq. ft.)
137	Baker	10	1995	1284	901-555-7335	120
186	Adams	15	2001	1253	901-555-4276	120
204	Dickens	10	1998	1209	901-555-3108	95
361	Carlyle	20	2001	1227	901-555-0364	100

is that a major, defining feature of a relational DBMS is the ability to accept high-level **data retrieval** commands, process them against the database's relations, and return the desired data. The data retrieval mechanism is a built-in part of the DBMS and does not have to be written from scratch by every program that uses the database. As we shall soon see, this is true even to the extent of matching related records in different relations (integrating data), as in the earlier example of finding the *name* of the salesperson on a particular customer account. We shall address what relational retrieval might look like, first in terms of single relations and then across multiple relations.

Since a relation can be viewed as a tabular or rectangular arrangement of data values, it would seem to make sense to want to approach data retrieval horizontally, vertically, or in a combination of the two. To take a horizontal slice of a relation implies retrieving one or more rows of the relation. In effect, that's an expression for retrieving one or more records or retrieving the data about one or more entities. Taking a vertical slice of a relation means retrieving one or more entire columns of the relation (down through all of its rows). Taken in combination, we can retrieve one or more columns of one or more rows, the minimum of which is a single column of a single row, or a single attribute value of a single record. That's as fine a sense of retrieval, as we would ever want.

Using terminology from a database formalism called **relational algebra,** and an informal, hypothetical command style for now, there are two commands called *Select* and *Project,* which are capable of the kinds of horizontal and vertical manipulations that were just suggested. (*Note:* The use of the word "Select" here is *not* the same as its use in the SQL data retrieval language, which we will discuss later in this book.)

The Relational Select Operator

Consider the database of Figure 5.14 and its SALESPERSON relation (Figure 5.14a). To begin with, suppose that we want to find the row or record for salesperson number 204. In a very straightforward way, the informal command might be:

Select rows from the SALESPERSON relation in which Salesperson Number = 204.

The result would be:

Salesperson Number	Salesperson Name	Commission Percentage	Year of Hire
204	Dickens	10	1998

Notice that the result of the Select operation is itself a relation, in this case consisting of only one row. *The result of a relational operation will always be a relation,* whether it consists of many rows with many columns or one row with one column (i.e., a single attribute value).

In order to retrieve all of the records with a common value in a particular (nonunique) attribute, for example, all of the salespersons with a commission percentage of 10, the command looks the same as when dealing with a unique attribute:

Select rows from the SALESPERSON relation in which Commission Percentage = 10.

But the result of the operation may include several rows:

Salesperson Number	Salesperson Name	Commission Percentage	Year of Hire
137	Baker	10	1995
204	Dickens	10	1998

If the requirement is to retrieve the entire relation, the command would be: Select all rows from the SALESPERSON relation.

The Relational Project Operator

To retrieve what we referred to earlier as a vertical slice of the relation requires the **Project operator.** For example, to retrieve the number and name of each salesperson in the file, the command might look like:

Project the Salesperson Number and Salesperson Name over the SALESPERSON relation.

The result will be a long, narrow relation:

Salesperson Number	Salesperson Name
137	Baker
186	Adams
204	Dickens
361	Carlyle

If we project a nonunique attribute, then a decision must be made as to whether or not we want duplicates in the result (although, since the result is itself a relation, technically there should not be any duplicate rows). For example, whether:

Project the Year of Hire over the SALESPERSON relation.

Produces:

Year of Hire
1995
2001
1998
2001

or (eliminating the duplicates in the identical rows) produces:

Year of Hire

1995

2001

1998

would depend on exactly how this hypothetical, informal command language was implemented.

Combination of the Relational Select and Project Operators

More powerful still is the combination of the Select and Project operators. Suppose we apply them serially, with the relation that results from one operation being used as the input to the next operation. For example, to retrieve the numbers and names of the salespersons working on a 10 percent commission, we would issue:

> Select rows from the SALESPERSON relation in which Commission Percentage = 10.
>
> Project the Salesperson Number and Salesperson Name over that result.

The first command "selects out" the rows for salespersons 137 and 204. Then the second command "projects" the salesperson numbers and names from those two rows, resulting in:

Salesperson Number	Salesperson Name
137	Baker
204	Dickens

The following combination illustrates the ability to retrieve a single attribute value. Suppose that there is a need to find the year of hire of salesperson number 204. Since Salesperson Number is a unique attribute, only one row of the relation can possibly be involved. Since the goal is to find one attribute value in that row, the result must be just that: a single attribute value. The command is:

> Select rows from the SALESPERSON relation in which Salesperson Number = 204.
>
> Project the Year of Hire over that result.

The result is the single value:

Year of Hire

1998

Extracting Data Across Multiple Relations: Data Integration

In Chapter 4, the issue of data integration was broached, and the concept was defined. First, the data in the Salesperson and Customer files of Figure 4.5 was shown to be **nonredundant.** Then it was shown that **integrating data** would require the extraction of data from one file and the use of that extracted data as a search argument to find the sought-after data in the other file. For example, recall that finding the name of the salesperson who was responsible for customer number 1525 required finding the salesperson number in customer 1525's record in the Customer file (i.e., salesperson number 361) and then using that salesperson number as a search argument in the Salesperson file to discover that the sought-after name was Carlyle. The alternative was the combined file of Figure 4.6 that introduced data redundancy.

A fundamental premise of the database approach is that a DBMS must be able to store data nonredundantly while also providing a data integration facility. But it seems that we may have a problem here. Since relations appear to be largely similar in structure to simple, linear files, do the lessons learned from the files of Figure 4.5 and Figure 4.6 lead to the conclusion that it is impossible to simultaneously have nonredundant data storage and data integration with relations in a relational database?

> In fact, one of the elegant features of relational DBMSs is that they automate the cross-relation data extraction process in such a way that it appears that the data in the relations is integrated while also remaining nonredundant.

The data integration takes place at the time that a relational query is processed by the relational DBMS for solution. This is a unique feature of relational database and is substantially different from the functional equivalents in the older navigational database systems and in some of the newer object-oriented database systems. In both the older and newer systems, the data integration is much more tightly built into the data structure itself. In relational algebra terms, the integration function is known as the *Join* command.

Now, focus on the SALESPERSON and CUSTOMER relations of Figure 5.14, which outwardly look just like the Salesperson and Customer files of Figure 4.5. Adding the **Join operator** to our hypothetical, informal command style, consider the following commands designed to find the *name* of the salesperson responsible for customer number 1525. Again, this was the query that seemed to be so problematic in Chapter 4.

> Join the SALESPERSON relation and the CUSTOMER relation, using the Salesperson Number of each as the join fields.
> Select rows from that result in which Customer Number = 1525.
> Project the Salesperson Name over that last result.

Obviously, the first sentence represents the use of the join command. The join operation will take advantage of the common Salesperson Number attribute, which for this purpose is called the *join field,* in both relations. The Salesperson Number attribute is, of course, the primary key of the SALESPERSON relation and is a foreign key in the CUSTOMER relation. Remember that the point of the foreign key is to represent a one-to-many (in this case) relationship between salespersons and customers. Some rows of the SALESPERSON relation *are related* to some rows of the CUSTOMER relation by virtue of their having the same salesperson number. The Salesperson Number attribute serves to identify each salesperson in the SALESPERSON relation, while the Salesperson Number attribute in the CUSTOMER relation indicates which salesperson is responsible for a particular customer. Thus the rows of the two relations that have identical Salesperson Number values are *related*. It is these related rows that the join operation will bring together for the purpose of satisfying the query that was posed.

The join operation tries to find matches between the join field values of the rows in the two relations. For example, it finds a match between the Salesperson Number value of 137 in the first row of the SALESPERSON relation and the Salesperson Number value of 137 in the first, third, fourth, and seventh rows of the CUSTOMER relation. When it finds such a pair of rows, it takes all of the attribute values from both rows and creates a single new row out of them in the resultant relation. In its most basic form, as shown here, the join is truly an exhaustive operation, comparing every row of one relation to every row of the other relation, looking for a match in the join fields. (Comparing every possible combination of two sets, in this case rows from the two relations, is known as the Cartesian product.) So the result of the join command, the first of the three commands in the example command sequence we're executing, is:

Salesperson Number	Salesperson Name	Commission Percentage	Year of Hire	Customer Number	Customer Name	Salesperson Number	HQ City
137	Baker	10	1995	0121	Main St. Hardware	137	New York
137	Baker	10	1995	0933	ABC Home Stores	137	Los Angeles
137	Baker	10	1995	1047	Acme Hardware Store	137	Los Angeles
137	Baker	10	1995	1826	City Hardware	137	New York
186	Adams	15	2001	0839	Jane's Stores	186	Chicago
186	Adams	15	2001	2267	Central Stores	186	New York
204	Dickens	10	1998	2198	Western Hardware	204	New York
361	Carlyle	20	2001	1525	Fred's Tool Stores	361	Atlanta
361	Carlyle	20	2001	1700	XYZ Stores	361	Washington

Notice that the first and seventh columns are identical in all of their values, row by row. They represent the Salesperson Number attributes from the SALESPERSON and CUSTOMER relations, respectively. Remember that two rows from the SALESPERSON and CUSTOMER relations would not be combined together to form a row in the resultant relation unless their two join field values were identical in the first place. This leads to identical values of the two Salesperson Number attributes within each of the rows of the resultant relation. This type of join is called an **equijoin.** If, as seems reasonable, one of the two identical join columns is eliminated in the process, the result is called a **natural join.**

Continuing with the command sequence to eventually find the name of the salesperson responsible for customer number 1525, the next part of the command issued is:

Select rows from that result (the relation that resulted from the join) in which Customer Number = 1525.

This produces:

Salesperson Number	Salesperson Name	Commission Percentage	Year of Hire	Customer Number	Customer Name	Salesperson Number	HQ City
361	Carlyle	20	2001	1525	Fred's Tool Stores	361	Atlanta

Finally, we issue the third command:
Project the Salesperson Name over that last result.

and get:

Carlyle

Notice that the process could have been streamlined considerably if the relational DBMS had more "intelligence" built into it. The query dealt with only a single customer, customer 1525, and there is only one row for each customer in the CUSTOMER relation, since Customer Number is the unique key attribute. Therefore, the query only needed to look at one row in the CUSTOMER relation, the one for customer 1525. Since this row only references one salesperson, salesperson 361, it follows that, in turn, it only needed to look at one row in the SALESPERSON relation, the one for salesperson 1525. This type of performance issue in relational query processing will be covered later in this book in the chapter on physical database design (Chapter 8).

EXAMPLE: GOOD READING BOOKSTORES

Figure 5.16 shows the relational database for the Good Reading Bookstores example that was described earlier in the book. Since publishers are in a one-to-many relationship to books, the primary key of the PUBLISHER relation, Publisher Name, is inserted into the BOOK relation as a foreign key. There are two many-to-many relationships. One, between books and authors, keeps track of which authors wrote which books. Recall that a book can have multiple authors and a particular author may have written or partly written many books. The other many-to-many relationship, between books and customers, records which customers bought which books.

The WRITING relation handles the many-to-many relationship between books and authors. The primary key is the combination of Book Number and Author Number. There is no intersection data! Could there be a reason for having intersection data in this relation? If, for example, this database belonged to a publisher instead of a bookstore chain, an intersection data attribute might be Royalty Percentage; that is, the percentage of the royalties that a particular author is entitled to for a particular book. The SALE relation takes care of the many-to-many relationship between books and customers. Certainly, Book Number and Customer Number are part of the primary key of the SALE relation, but is the combination of the two the entire primary key? The answer is that it depends on whether the assumption is made that a given customer can or cannot buy copies of a given book on different days. If the assumption is that a customer can only buy copies of a particular book on one single day, then the combination of Book Number and Customer Number is fine as the primary key. If the assumption is that a customer may indeed buy copies of a given book on different days, then the Date attribute must be part of the primary key to achieve uniqueness.

EXAMPLE: WORLD MUSIC ASSOCIATION

Figure 5.17 shows the relational database for the World Music Association example that was described earlier in the book. There is a one-to-many relationship from orchestras to musicians and, in turn, a one-to-many relationship from musicians to degrees. Thus the primary key of the ORCHESTRA relation, Orchestra Name, appears in the MUSICIAN relation as a foreign key. In turn, the primary key of the

> **Figure 5.16**
> Good Reading Bookstores
> relational database

```
┌──────────────────────────────────────────────────────────────────┐
│  ┌────────────────────────────────────────────────────────────┐   │
│  │                      PUBLISHER relation                     │   │
│  │  ──────────────────────────────────────────────────────     │   │
│  │  Publisher                                          Year     │   │
│  │  Name        City       Country     Telephone    Founded     │   │
│  └────────────────────────────────────────────────────────────┘   │
│                                                                    │
│  ┌────────────────────────────────────────────────────────────┐   │
│  │                       AUTHOR relation                       │   │
│  │  ──────────────────────────────────────────────────────     │   │
│  │  Author        Author          Year          Year           │   │
│  │  Number        Name            Born          Died           │   │
│  └────────────────────────────────────────────────────────────┘   │
│                                                                    │
│  ┌────────────────────────────────────────────────────────────┐   │
│  │                        BOOK relation                        │   │
│  │  ──────────────────────────────────────────────────────     │   │
│  │  Book        Book        Publication              Publisher  │   │
│  │  Number      Name         Year        Pages       Name       │   │
│  └────────────────────────────────────────────────────────────┘   │
│                                                                    │
│  ┌────────────────────────────────────────────────────────────┐   │
│  │                      CUSTOMER relation                      │   │
│  │  ──────────────────────────────────────────────────────     │   │
│  │  Customer    Customer                                        │   │
│  │  Number      Name       Street    City    State   Country    │   │
│  └────────────────────────────────────────────────────────────┘   │
│                                                                    │
│  ┌──────────────────────────────┐                                 │
│  │       WRITING relation        │                                │
│  │  ──────────────────────────    │                               │
│  │  Book            Author        │                                │
│  │  Number          Number        │                                │
│  └──────────────────────────────┘                                 │
│                                                                    │
│  ┌────────────────────────────────────────────────────────────┐   │
│  │                        SALE relation                        │   │
│  │  ──────────────────────────────────────────────────────     │   │
│  │  Book        Customer                                        │   │
│  │  Number      Number      Date       Price      Quantity      │   │
│  └────────────────────────────────────────────────────────────┘   │
└──────────────────────────────────────────────────────────────────┘
```

MUSICIAN relation, Musician Number, appears in the DEGREE relation as a foreign key. In fact, since the Degree attribute is only unique within a musician, the Musician Number attribute and the Degree attribute together serve as the compound primary key of the DEGREE relation. The one-to-many relationship from composers to compositions requires that the primary key of the COMPOSER relation, Composer Name, appear as a foreign key in the COMPOSITION relation.

The many-to-many relationship between orchestras and compositions indicates which orchestras have recorded which compositions and which compositions have been recorded by which orchestras. As a many-to-many relationship, it requires that an additional relation be created. The primary key of this new, RECORDING relation has three attributes: Orchestra Name, Composition Name, and Year. Orchestra Name is the unique identifier of orchestras. Composition Name is the unique identifier of compositions. Since a particular orchestra could have recorded a particular composition multiple times in different years (although we assume that this is limited to once per year), Year must also be part of the primary key of the RECORDING relation to provide uniqueness. The Price attribute is then intersection data in the RECORDING relation.

➤ **Figure 5.17**
World Music Association
relational database

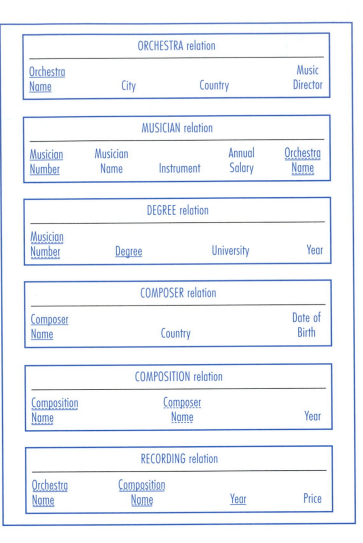

EXAMPLE: LUCKY RENT-A-CAR

Figure 5.18 shows the relational database for the Lucky Rent-A-Car example that was described earlier in the book. There is a one-to-many relationship from manufacturers to cars and another one-to-many relationship from cars to maintenance events. The former requires the manufacturer primary key, Manufacturer Name, to be placed in the CAR relation as a foreign key. The latter requires the car primary key, Car Serial Number, to be placed in the MAINTENANCE relation as a foreign key. The many-to-many relationship between cars and customers requires the creation of a new relation, the RENTAL relation. Each record of the RENTAL relation records the rental of a particular car by a particular customer. Note that the combination of the Car Serial Number and Customer Number attributes is not sufficient as the primary key of the RENTAL relation. A given customer might have rented a given car more than once. Adding Rental Date to the primary key achieves the needed uniqueness.

➤ **Figure 5.18**
Lucky Rent-A-Car relational
database

```
┌─────────────────────────────────────────────────────────────────┐
│   ┌─────────────────────────────────────────────────────────┐     │
│   │               MANUFACTURER relation                      │     │
│   │─────────────────────────────────────────────────────────│     │
│   │  Manufacturer    Manufacturer    Sales Rep    Sales Rep  │     │
│   │  Name            Country         Name         Telephone  │     │
│   └─────────────────────────────────────────────────────────┘     │
│                                                                    │
│     ┌───────────────────────────────────────────────────┐        │
│     │                  CAR Relation                      │        │
│     │───────────────────────────────────────────────────│        │
│     │  Car Serial                              Manufacturer│       │
│     │  Number      Model      Year     Class    Name      │        │
│     └───────────────────────────────────────────────────┘        │
│                                                                    │
│     ┌───────────────────────────────────────────────────┐        │
│     │                MAINTENANCE relation                │        │
│     │───────────────────────────────────────────────────│        │
│     │  Repair    Car Serial                        Repair │        │
│     │  Number    Number    Date   Procedure  Mileage Time │        │
│     └───────────────────────────────────────────────────┘        │
│                                                                    │
│     ┌───────────────────────────────────────────────────┐        │
│     │                 CUSTOMER relation                  │        │
│     │───────────────────────────────────────────────────│        │
│     │  Customer    Customer    Customer     Customer     │        │
│     │  Number      Name        Address      Telephone    │        │
│     └───────────────────────────────────────────────────┘        │
│                                                                    │
│     ┌───────────────────────────────────────────────────┐        │
│     │                  RENTAL relation                   │        │
│     │───────────────────────────────────────────────────│        │
│     │  Car Serial   Customer    Rental    Return   Total │        │
│     │  Number       Number      Date      Date     Cost  │        │
│     └───────────────────────────────────────────────────┘        │
└─────────────────────────────────────────────────────────────────┘
```

KEY TERMS

Alternate key
Attribute
Attribute name
Candidate key
Cell
Column
Data retrieval
Domain of values
Equijoin

Foreign key
Integrating data
Intersection data
Join operator
Natural join
Nonredundant data
Personal computer (PC)
Primary key
Project operator

Relation
Relational algebra
Relational database
Row
Select operator
Tuple
Unique attribute

QUESTIONS

1. Why was the commercial introduction of relational database delayed during the 1970s? What factors encouraged its introduction in the early 1980s?

2. How does a relation differ from an ordinary file?

3. Define the terms tuple and attribute.

4. What is a relational database?

5. What are the characteristics of a candidate key?

6. What is a primary key? What is an alternate key?

7. Define the term foreign key.

8. In your own words, describe how foreign keys are used to setup one-to-many binary relationships in relational databases.

9. Describe why an additional relation is needed to represent a many-to-many relationship in a relational database.

10. Describe what intersection data is, what it describes, and why it does not describe a single entity.

11. What is a one-to-one binary relationship?

12. Describe the purpose and capabilities of:
   a. The relational Select operator.
   b. The relational Project operator.
   c. The relational Join operator.

13. Describe how the join operator works.

EXERCISES

1. The main relation of a motor vehicle registration bureau's relational database includes the following attributes:

Vehicle Identification Number	License Plate Number	Owner Serial Number	Manu-facturer	Model	Year	Color

The Vehicle Identification Number is a unique number assigned to the car when it is manufactured.

The License Plate Number is, in effect, a unique number assigned to the car by the government when it is registered.

The Owner Serial Number is a unique identifier of each owner. Each owner can own more than one vehicle.

The other attributes are not unique.

What is/are the candidate key(s) of this relation? If there is more than one candidate key, choose one as the primary key and indicate which is/are the alternate key(s).

2. A relation consists of attributes A, B, C, D, E, F, G, and H. No single attribute has unique values.

The combination of attributes A and E is unique.

The combination of attributes B and D is unique.

The combination of attributes B and G is unique.

Select a primary key for this relation and indicate any alternate keys.

3. In the General Hardware Company relational database of Figure 5.14:
   a. How many foreign keys are there in each of the six relations?
   b. List the foreign keys in each of the six relations.

4. Identify the relations that support many-to-many relationships, the primary keys of those relations, and any intersection data in the General Hardware Company database.

5. Consider the General Hardware Company relational database. Using the informal relational command language described in this chapter, write commands to:
   a. List the product name and unit price of all of the products.

b. List the employee names and titles of all of the employees of customer 2198.

c. Retrieve the record for office number 1284.

d. Retrieve the records for the customers headquartered in Los Angeles.

e. Find the size of office number 1209.

f. Find the name of the salesperson assigned to office number 1209.

g. List the product name and quantity sold of each product sold by salesperson 361.

6. Consider the General Hardware Company relational database and the data stored in it, as shown in Figure 5.14. Find the answer to each of the following queries that are written in the informal relational command language described in this chapter.
   a. Select rows from the CUSTOMER EMPLOYEE relation in which Customer Number = 2198.
   b. Select rows from the CUSTOMER EMPLOYEE relation in which Customer Number = 2198. Project Employee Number and Employee Name over that result.
   c. Select rows from the PRODUCT relation in which Product Number = 21765.
   d. Select rows from the PRODUCT relation in which Product Number = 21765. Project Unit Price over that result.
   e. Join the SALESPERSON and CUSTOMER relations using the Salesperson Number attribute of each as the join fields. Select rows from that result in which Salesperson Name = Baker. Project Customer Name over that result.
   f. Join the PRODUCT relation and the SALES relation using the Product Number attribute of each as the join fields. Select rows in which Product Name = Pliers. Project Salesperson Number and Quantity over that result.

7. For each part of Exercise 6, describe in words what the query is trying to accomplish.

MINICASES

1. Consider the following relational database for Happy Cruise Lines. It keeps track of ships, cruises, ports, and passengers. A "cruise" is a particular sailing of a ship on a particular date. For example, the seven-day journey of the ship Pride of Tampa, that leaves on June 13, 2003, is a cruise. Note the following facts about this environment.

   - Both ship number and ship name are unique in the SHIP relation.

   - A ship goes on many cruises over time. A cruise is associated with a single ship.

   - A port is identified by the combination of port name and country.

   - As indicated by the VISIT relation, a cruise includes visits to several ports and a port is typically included in several cruises.

   - Both Passenger Number and Social Security Number are unique in the PASSENGER relation. A particular person has a single Passenger Number that is used for all of the cruises that she takes.

   - The VOYAGE relation indicates that a person can take many cruises, and a cruise, of course, has many passengers.

SHIP relation				
Ship Number	Ship Name	Ship Builder	Launch Date	Gross Wight

CRUISE relation				
Cruise Number	Start Date	End Date	Cruise Director	Ship Number

PORT relation			
Port Name	Country	Number of Docks	Port Manager

VISIT relation				
Cruise Number	Port Name	Country	Arrival Date	Departure Date

PASSENGER relation				
Passenger Number	Passenger Name	Social Security Number	Home Address	Telephone Number

VOYAGE relation			
Passenger Number	Cruise Number	Stateroom Number	Fare

   a. Identify the candidate keys of each relation.
   b. Identify the primary key and any alternate keys of each relation.
   c. How many foreign keys does each relation have?
   d. Identify the foreign keys of each relation.
   e. Indicate any instances in which a foreign key serves as part of the primary key of the relation in which it is a foreign key. Why does each of those relations require a multi-attribute primary key?
   f. Identify the relations that support many-to-many relationships, the primary keys of those relations, and any intersection data.
   g. Using the informal relational command language described in this chapter, write commands to:
      i. Retrieve the record for passenger number 473942.
      ii. Retrieve the record for the port of Nassau in the Bahamas.
      iii. List all of the ships built by General Shipbuilding, Inc.
      iv. List the port name and number of docks of every port in Mexico.
      v. List the name and number of every ship.
      vi. Who was the cruise director on cruise number 38232?
      vii. What was the gross weight of the ship used for cruise number 39482?
      viii. List the home address of every passenger on cruise number 17543.

2. Super Baseball League

   Consider the following relational database for the Super Baseball League. It keeps track of teams in the league, coaches and players on the teams, work experience of the coaches, bats belonging to each team, and which players have played on which teams. Note the following facts about this environment:

   - The database keeps track of the history of all the teams that each player has played on and all the players who have played on each team.

   - The database only keeps track of the current team that a coach works for.

   - Team Number, Team Name, and Player Number are each unique attributes across the league.

- Coach Name is only unique within a team (and we assume that a team cannot have two coaches of the same name).
- Serial Number (for bats) is only unique within a team.
- In the AFFILIATION relation, the Years attribute indicates the number of years that a player played on a team; the Batting Average is for the years that a player played on a team.

TEAM relation			
Team Number	Team Name	City	Manager

COACH relation		
Team Number	Coach Name	Coach Telephone

WORK EXPERIENCE relation			
Team Number	Coach Name	Experience Type	Years of Experience

BATS relation		
Team Number	Serial Number	Manufacturer

PLAYER relation		
Player Number	Player Name	Age

AFFILIATION relation			
Player Number	Team Number	Years	Batting Average

a. Identify the candidate keys of each relation.

b. Identify the primary key and any alternate keys of each relation.

c. How many foreign keys does each relation have?

d. Identify the foreign keys of each relation.

e. Indicate any instances in which a foreign key serves as part of the primary key of the relation in which it is a foreign key. Why does each of those relations require a multi-attribute primary key?

f. Identify the relations that support many-to-many relationships, the primary keys of those relations, and any intersection data.

g. Assume that we add the following STADIUM relation to the Super Baseball League relational database. Each team has one home stadium, which is what is represented in this relation. Assume that a stadium can serve as the home stadium for only one team. Stadium Name is unique across the league.

STADIUM relation			
Stadium Name	Year Built	Size	Team Number

What kind of binary relationship exists between the STADIUM relation and the TEAM relation? Could the data from the two relations be combined into one without introducing data redundancy? If so, how?

h. Using the informal relational command language described in this chapter, write commands to:

   i. Retrieve the record for team number 12.

   ii. Retrieve the record for Coach Adams on team number 12.

   iii. List the player number and age of every player.

   iv. List the work experience of every coach.

   v. List the work experience of every coach on team number 25.

   vi. Find the age of player number 42459.

   vii. List the serial numbers and manufacturers of all of the Vultures' (the name of a team) bats.

   viii. Find the number of years of college coaching experience that Coach Taylor of the Vultures has.

CHAPTER 6

THE RELATIONAL DATABASE MODEL: ADDITIONAL CONCEPTS

CHAPTER OBJECTIVES

After learning the material in this chapter, you will be able to:

✔ Describe how unary and ternary relationships are implemented in a relational database.

✔ Explain the concept of referential integrity.

✔ Describe how the referential integrity restrict, cascade, and set-to-null delete rules operate in a relational database.

Photo by Permission of the City of Memphis

CITY OF MEMPHIS, TENNESSEE—VEHICLE SERVICE CENTER

The City of Memphis, Tennessee, is the 18th largest city in the United States in both population (650,000) and land area (280 square miles). Memphis was founded in 1819 by General/President Andrew Jackson and others and was incorporated as a city in 1826. Because of its position in the midst of the country's largest cotton farming region and its location on the Mississippi River, Memphis has traditionally been the center of the U.S. cotton industry. It is still the world's largest spot cotton market and is also the world's largest hardwood market. The concept of the grocery supermarket was invented in Memphis in the early

1900s and the concept of the motel chain was invented in Memphis in the 1950s. Today, because of its central location in the country and because of its position as a major transportation hub, Memphis is known as the "Distribution Center" of the United States.

The Vehicle Service Center of the Memphis city government's General Services Division is responsible for all of the city's municipal vehicles, except for Fire Department vehicles. The approximately 4,000 vehicles include everything from police cruisers and sanitation trucks to street cleaners and even lawn mowing tractors. Since 1991, the city has kept track of all of these vehicles with a database application that manages them through their complete lifecycle. New vehicles are entered into the database when they are purchased and they're assigned to a city department. The application then keeps each vehicle's maintenance history, generates automatic reports on maintenance due dates, tracks mileage and gasoline use, and produces monthly reports for the departments listing all of this activity for each of their vehicles. Finally, the system tracks the reassignment of older vehicles and the auctioning of vehicles being disposed of.

Memphis' vehicle tracking system uses an Oracle database running on Dell servers. For vehicle maintenance, the system's major tables include a Vehicle Downtime Detail table with 1.6 million records, a Work Order Job Notes table with 3.3 million records, and a Parts Journal table with 950,000 records.

Printed by permission of the City of Memphis

Chapter 5 defined the basic terminology of relational database and then demonstrated some fundamental ideas about constructing relations in relational databases and manipulating data in them. The discussion focused on relationships between two different entity types, that is, binary relationships. This chapter will go beyond binary relationships into unary and ternary relationships. It will then address the important issue of referential integrity.

RELATIONAL STRUCTURES FOR UNARY AND TERNARY RELATIONSHIPS

Unary One-to-Many Relationships

Let's continue with the General Hardware Company example of Figure 5.14, repeated here for convenience as Figure 6.1. Suppose that General Hardware's salespersons are organized in such a way that some of the salespersons, *in addition to* having their customer responsibilities, serve as the sales managers of other salespersons (Figure 6.2). A salesperson reports to exactly one sales manager, but each salesperson who does serve as a sales manager typically has several salespersons reporting to him. Thus there is a one-to-many relationship within the set or entity type of salespersons.

Salesperson (who is also a sales manager) ◄——►► Salesperson

This is known as a unary one-to-many relationship. It is unary because there is only one entity type involved. It is one-to-many because among the individual entity occurrences, that is, among the salespersons, a particular salesperson reports to one salesperson who is his sales manager, while a salesperson who is a sales manager may have several salespersons reporting to her. Note that, in general, this arrangement can involve as few as two levels of **entity occurrences** or can involve many levels in a

➤ **Figure 6.1**
General Hardware Company
relational database

(a) SALESPERSON relation

Salesperson Number	Salesperson Name	Commission Percentage	Year of Hire	Office Number
137	Baker	10	1995	1284
186	Adams	15	2001	1253
204	Dickens	10	1998	1209
361	Carlyle	20	2001	1227

(b) CUSTOMER relation

Customer Number	Customer Name	Salesperson Number	HQ City
0121	Main St. Hardware	137	New York
0839	Jane's Stores	186	Chicago
0933	ABC Home Stores	137	Los Angeles
1047	Acme Hardware Store	137	Los Angeles
1525	Fred's Tool Stores	361	Atlanta
1700	XYZ Stores	361	Washington
1826	City Hardware	137	New York
2198	Western Hardware	204	New York
2267	Central Stores	186	New York

(c) CUSTOMER EMPLOYEE relation

Customer Number	Employee Number	Employee Name	Title
0121	27498	Smith	Co-Owner
0121	30441	Garcia	Co-Owner
0933	25270	Chen	VP Sales
0933	30441	Levy	Sales Manager
0933	48285	Morton	President
1525	33779	Baker	Sales Manager
2198	27470	Smith	President
2198	30441	Jones	VP Sales
2198	33779	Garcia	VP Personnel
2198	35268	Kaplan	Senior Accountant

(Continues)

hierarchical arrangement. In general, in a company, an employee can report to a manager who in turn reports to a higher-level manager, and so on up to the CEO.

Assume that the General Hardware Company has two levels of sales managers, resulting in a three-level hierarchy. That is, each salesperson reports to a sales manager (who is himself a salesperson), and each sales manager reports to one of several chief sales managers (who is herself a salesperson). Figure 6.3 shows two levels of sales managers plus the salespersons who report to them. For example, salespersons 142, 323, and

➤ **Figure 6.1 (Continued)**
General Hardware Company
relational database

(d) PRODUCT relation

Product Number	Number Name	Unit Price
16386	Wrench	12.95
19440	Hammer	17.50
21765	Drill	32.99
24013	Saw	26.25
26722	Pliers	11.50

(e) SALES relation

Salesperson Number	Product Number	Quantity
137	19440	473
137	24013	170
137	26722	688
186	16386	1745
186	19440	2529
186	21765	1962
186	24013	3071
204	21765	809
204	26722	734
361	16386	3729
361	21765	3110
361	26722	2738

(f) OFFICE relation

Office Number	Telephone	Size (sq. ft.)
1253	901-555-4276	120
1227	901-555-0364	100
1284	901-555-7335	120
1209	901-555-3108	95

411 all report to salesperson (and sales manager) 137. Salespersons 137 and 439, both of whom are sales managers, report to salesperson 186 who is a chief sales manager. As you go upward in the hierarchy, each salesperson is associated with exactly one other salesperson. As you go downward in the hierarchy from any salesperson/sales manager, each salesperson/sales manager is associated with many salespersons below, except for the bottom-level salespersons who are not sales managers and thus have no one reporting to them.

Figure 6.4, which is an expansion of the General Hardware Company SALESPERSON relation in Figure 6.1a, demonstrates how this type of relationship is achieved in a relational database. A one-to-many unary relationship requires the addition of one column to the relation that represents the single entity involved in the unary relationship. In Figure 6.4, the Sales Manager Number attribute is the new attribute that has been added to the SALESPERSON relation. The domain of values of the new column is the same as the domain of values of the relation's primary key. Thus the values in the new Sales Manager Number column will be three-digit whole numbers representing the unique identifiers for salespersons, just like the values in the Salesperson Number column. The value in the new column for a particular row represents the value of the next entity "upward" in the unary one-to-many hierarchy. For example, in the row for salesperson number 323, the sales manager value is 137 because salesperson 323's sales manager is salesperson/sales manager 137, as shown in Figure 6.3. Similarly, the row for salesperson 137, who happens also to be a sales manager, shows salesperson number 186 in its sales manager number column. Salesperson/sales manager 137 reports to chief sales manager 186, also as shown in Figure 6.3. The sales manager column value for salesperson/chief sales manager 186 is blank because the reporting structure happens to end with each chief sales manager; that is, there is nothing "above" salesperson 186 in Figure 6.3.

➤ **Figure 6.2**
Salespersons 142, 323, and 411 reporting to salesperson 137 who is their sales manager

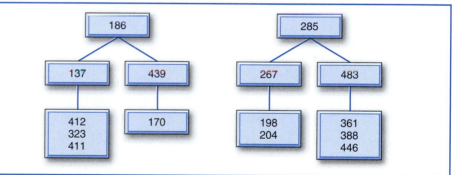

Sales Manager
Salesperson 137

Reports to

Salesperson 142   Salesperson 323   Salesperson 411

➤ **Figure 6.3**
General Hardware Company salesperson reporting hierarchy

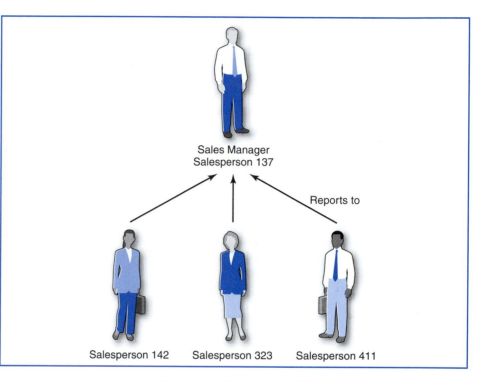

Unary Many-to-Many Relationships

The unary many-to-many relationship is a special case, an example of which has come to be known as the bill of materials problem. Among the entity occurrences of a single entity type, which is what makes this "unary," each particular entity occurrence can be related to many other occurrences, and each of those latter occurrences can, in turn, be related to many other occurrences. Put another way, every entity occurrence can be related to many other occurrences, which, if you think about it, makes this a many-to-many relationship because there is only one entity type involved. (Yes, that sounds a little strange, but keep reading.) The general idea is that in a complex item, say an automobile engine, small parts are assembled together to make a small component or assembly. Then some of those small components or assemblies (and maybe some small parts) are assembled together to make medium-sized components or

➤ **Figure 6.4**
General Hardware Company
SALESPERSON relation
including Sales Manager
Number attribute

SALESPERSON relation				
Salesperson Number	Salesperson Name	Commission Percentage	Year of Hire	Sales Manager Number
137	Baker	10	1995	186
142	Smith	15	2001	137
170	Taylor	18	1992	439
186	Adams	15	2001	
198	Wang	20	1990	267
204	Dickens	10	1998	267
267	Perez	22	2000	285
285	Costello	10	1996	
323	McNamara	15	1995	137
361	Carlyle	20	2001	483
388	Goldberg	20	1997	483
411	Davidson	18	1992	137
439	Warren	10	1996	186
446	Albert	10	2001	483
483	Jones	15	1995	285

assemblies, and so on until the final, top-level "component" is the automobile engine. The key concept here is that an assembly at any level is considered to be both a part made up of smaller units and a unit that can be a component of a larger part. Parts and assemblies at all levels are all considered to be occurrences of the same entity type, and they all have a unique identifier in a single domain of values.

Certainly, this requires an example! Figure 6.5 illustrates this concept using an expansion of General Hardware Company's product set.

Product ◄◄━━━━━━►► Product

The numbers in parentheses in the figure are product numbers. Assume, as is quite reasonable, that General Hardware sells not only individual tools but also sets of tools. Both individual tools and sets of tools are considered to be "products," which also makes sense. As shown in Figure 6.5, General Hardware carries several types (or perhaps sizes) of wrenches, hammers, and drills. Various combinations of wrenches and hammers are sold as wrench and hammer sets. Various combinations of these sets and other tools such as drills are sold as even larger sets. Very importantly, notice the many-to-many nature of this arrangement. For example, the Master Wrench Set (product number 44), looking to its left, *is comprised of* three different wrenches, including Wrench Model A (#11). Conversely, Wrench Model A, looking to its right, *is a component of* two different wrench sets, both the Deluxe Wrench Set (#43) and the Master Wrench Set (#44.) This demonstrates the many-to-many nature of products. Similarly, both the Supreme Tool Set (#53) and the Grand Tool Set (#56) are, obviously, comprised of several smaller sets and tools, while the Deluxe Hammer Set (#48) is a component of both the Supreme Tool Set (#53) and the Grand Tool Set (#56.)

Figure 6.5

General Hardware Company product bill of materials

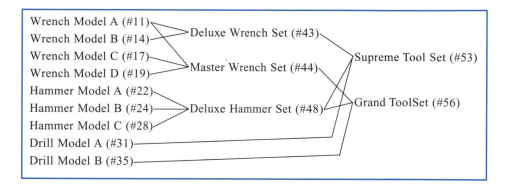

How can this unary many-to-many relationship be represented in a relational database? First of all, note that Figure 6.6 is a modification and expansion of the PRODUCT relation in the General Hardware Company relational database of Figure 6.1d. Notice that the product numbers, matching the product numbers in Figure 6.5, have been reduced to two digits for simplicity in the explanation. Every individual unit item and every set in Figure 6.5 has its own row in the relation in Figure 6.6 because every item and set in Figure 6.5 is a product that General Hardware has for sale.

Now, here is the main point. Just as a binary many-to-many relationship requires the creation of an additional relation in a relational database, so does a unary many-to-many relationship. The new, additional relation is shown in Figure 6.7. It consists of two attributes. The domain of values of *each* column is that of the Product Number column of the PRODUCT relation of Figure 6.6. The relation of Figure 6.7 represents, in a tabular format, the way that the assemblies of Figure 6.5 are constructed. The first two rows of Figure 6.7 literally say that product (assembly) number 43 (the Deluxe Wrench Set) is comprised of products 11 and 14, as indicated in Figure 6.5. Next, product (assembly) 44 is comprised of products 11, 17, and 19. Moving to the last three rows of the relation, product (assembly) 56 is comprised of products 44 and 48, both of which happen to be assemblies, and product 35. Again, notice the many-to-many relationship as it is represented in the relation of Figure 6.7. The first two rows indicate that assembly 43 *is comprised of* two parts. Conversely, the first and third rows indicate that part 11 *is a component of* two different assemblies.

Ternary Relationships

A ternary relationship is a relationship that involves three different entity types. If the entity types are A, B, and C, then we might illustrate this as:

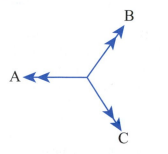

➤ **Figure 6.6**
General Hardware Company
modified PRODUCT relation

PRODUCT relation		
Product Number	Product Name	Unit Price
11	Wrench Model A	12.50
14	Wrench Model B	13.75
17	Wrench Model C	11.62
19	Wrench Model D	15.80
22	Hammer Model A	17.50
24	Hammer Model B	18.00
28	Hammer Model C	19.95
31	Drill Model A	31.25
35	Drill Model B	38.50
43	Deluxe Wrench Set	23.95
44	Master Wrench Set	35.00
48	Deluxe Hammer Set	51.00
53	Supreme Tool Set	100.00
56	Grand Tool Set	109.95

➤ **Figure 6.7**
General Hardware Company
unary many-to-many relation

Assembly	Part
43	11
43	14
44	11
44	17
44	19
48	22
48	24
48	28
53	43
53	48
53	31
56	44
56	48
56	35

In order to demonstrate this concept in the broadest way, using the General Hardware Company database, let's slightly modify part of the General Hardware premise. The assumption has always been that there is a one-to-many relationship between salespersons and customers. A salesperson is responsible for several customers while a customer is in contact with (is sold to by) exactly one of General Hardware's salespersons. For the purposes of describing a general ternary relationship, we are going to temporarily change that premise to a many-to-many relationship between salespersons and customers. That is, we now assume that any salesperson can make a sale to any customer and any customer can buy from any salesperson.

With that change, consider the ternary relationship among salespersons, customers, and products. Such a relationship allows us to keep track of which salesperson sold which product to which customer. This is very significant. In this environment, a salesperson can sell many products and a salesperson can sell to many customers. A product can be sold by many salespersons and can be sold to many customers. A customer can buy many products and can buy from many salespersons. All of this leads to a lot of different possibilities for any given sale. So, it is very important to be able to tie down a particular sale by noting and recording which salesperson sold which product to which customer. For example, we might store the fact that salesperson 137 sold some of product number 24013 to customer 0839 (Figure 6.8).

Relations a, b, and c of Figure 6.9 show the SALESPERSON, CUSTOMER, and PRODUCT relations, respectively, from the General Hardware relational database of Figure 6.1, except for one change. Since there is no longer a one-to-many relationship between salespersons and customers, the Salesperson Number foreign key in the CUSTOMER relation has been removed! The three relations are now all quite independent with no foreign keys in any of them.

Figure 6.9d, the SALES relation, shows how this ternary relationship is represented in a relational database. Much as an additional relation had to be created to accommodate a binary many-to-many relationship, an additional relation has to be created to accommodate a ternary relationship and that relation is Figure 6.9d. Clearly, as in the binary many-to-many case, the primary key of the additional relation will be (at least) the combination of the primary keys of the entities involved

➤ **Figure 6.8**
A ternary relationship

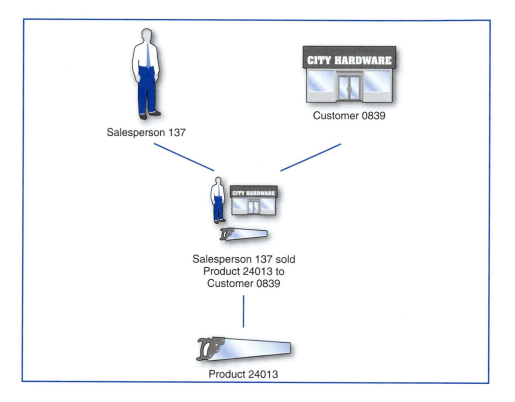

Salesperson 137

Customer 0839

Salesperson 137 sold
Product 24013 to
Customer 0839

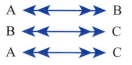

Product 24013

in the relationship. Thus, in Figure 6.9d, the Salesperson Number, Customer Number, and Product Number attributes all appear as foreign keys, and the combination of the three serve as part of the primary key. Why just "part of" the primary key? Because in this example, a particular salesperson may have sold a particular product to a particular customer more than once on different dates. Thus the Date attribute must also be part of the primary key. (We assume that this combination of the three could not have happened more than once on the same date. If it could, then there would also need to be a "time" attribute in the key.) Recall that his situation of needing an additional attribute in the primary key also came up when we discussed binary many-to-many relationships in the last chapter. Finally, the Quantity attribute in Figure 6.9d is intersection data just as it would be in a binary many-to-many relationship. The quantity of the product that the salesperson sold to the customer is clearly an attribute of the ternary relationship, not of any one of the entities.

There is one more important point to make about ternary relationships. In the process of describing the ternary relationship, you may have noticed that, taken two at a time, every pair of the three entities, salespersons, customers, and products, are in a binary many-to-many relationship. In general, this would be shown as:

A ◄◄━━━━━►► B
B ◄◄━━━━━►► C
A ◄◄━━━━━►► C

The question is, are these three many-to-many relationships the equivalent of the ternary relationship? Further, do they provide the same information that the ternary relationship does? The answer to both questions is, no!

➤ **Figure 6.9**
A portion of General Hardware Company relational database modified to demonstrate a ternary relationship

(a) SALESPERSON relation

Salesperson Number	Salesperson Name	Commission Percentage	Year of Hire
137	Baker	10	1995
186	Adams	15	2001
204	Dickens	10	1998
361	Carlyle	20	2001

(b) CUSTOMER relation

Customer Number	Customer Name	HQ City
0121	Main St. Hardware	New York
0839	Jane's Stores	Chicago
0933	ABC Home Stores	Los Angeles
1047	Acme Hardware Store	Los Angeles
1525	Fred's Tool Stores	Atlanta
1700	XYZ Stores	Washington
1826	City Hardware	New York
2198	Western Hardware	New York
2267	Central Stores	New York

(c) PRODUCT relation

Product Number	Product Name	Unit Price
16386	Wrench	12.95
19440	Hammer	17.50
21765	Drill	32.99
24013	Saw	26.25
26722	Pliers	11.50

(d) SALES relation

Salesperson Number	Customer Number	Product Number	Date	Quantity
137	0839	24013	2/21/2002	25
361	1700	16386	2/27/2002	70
137	2267	19440	3/1/2002	40
204	1047	19440	3/1/2002	15
186	0839	26722	3/12/2002	35
137	1700	16386	3/17/2002	65
361	0121	21765	3/21/2002	40
204	2267	19440	4/03/2002	30
204	0839	19440	4/17/2002	20

Again, consider salespersons, customers, and products. You might know that a particular salesperson has made sales to a particular customer. You might also know that a particular salesperson has sold certain products at one time or another. And you might know that a particular customer has bought certain products. But all of that is not the same thing as knowing that a particular salesperson sold a particular product to a particular customer. Still skeptical? Look at Figure 6.10. Parts (a), (b), and (c) of the figure clearly illustrate three many-to-many relationships. They are between (a) salespersons and customers, (b) customers and products, and (c) salespersons and products. Part (a) shows, among other things, that salesperson 137 sold something to customer 0839. Part (b) shows that customer 0839 bought product 19440. Does that mean that we can infer that salesperson 137 sold product 19440 to customer 0839? No! That's a possibility, and, indeed, part c of the figure shows that salesperson 137 did sell product 19440. But part (c) of the figure also shows that salesperson 204 sold product 19440. Is it possible that salesperson 204 sold it to customer 0839? According to part (a), salesperson 204 sold *something* to customer 0839, but it doesn't indicate what. You can go around and around Figure 6.10 and never conclude with certainty that salesperson 137 sold product 19440 to customer 0839. That would require a ternary relationship and a relation like the one in Figure 6.9d. Notice that the last row of Figure 6.9d shows, without a doubt, that it was salesperson 204 who sold product 19440 to customer 0839.

REFERENTIAL INTEGRITY

The Referential Integrity Concept

Thus far in this chapter and the previous one, we have been concerned with how relations are constructed and how data can be retrieved from them. Data retrieval is the operation that clearly provides the ultimate benefit from maintaining a database, but it is not the only operation needed. Certainly, we should expect that, as with any data storage scheme, in addition to retrieving data we must be prepared to perform such data maintenance operations as inserting new records (or rows of a relation), deleting existing records, and updating existing records. All database management systems provide the facilities and commands to accomplish these data maintenance operations. But there are some potential pitfalls regarding these operations that must be dealt with.

The problem is that the logically related (by foreign keys) but physically independent nature of the relations in a relational database exposes the database to the possibility of a particular type of data integrity problem. This problem has come to be known as a **referential integrity** problem because it revolves around the circumstance of trying to *refer* to data in one relation in the database, based on values in another relation.

➤ **Figure 6.10**
Ternary relationship counter-example

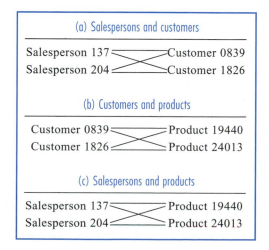

(a) Salespersons and customers

Salesperson 137 ⟋⟍ Customer 0839
Salesperson 204 ⟍⟋ Customer 1826

(b) Customers and products

Customer 0839 ⟋⟍ Product 19440
Customer 1826 ⟍⟋ Product 24013

(c) Salespersons and products

Salesperson 137 ⟋⟍ Product 19440
Salesperson 204 ⟍⟋ Product 24013

(Actually, referential integrity is an issue in all of the DBMS approaches, not just the relational approach. The discussion is placed here because we are focusing on relational database and it is much easier to explain the concept in the context of an example, again the General Hardware database.) Also, while referential integrity problems can surface in any of the three operations that result in changes to the database, insert, delete, and update records, we will mainly use the case of delete to explain the concept while mentioning insert and update where appropriate.

First, consider the situation of **record deletion** in the two relations of Figure 6.11, which is a repeat of Figure 5.2. Suppose that salesperson 361, Carlyle, left the company and that his record was deleted from the SALESPERSON relation. The problem is that there are still two records in the CUSTOMER relation (the records for customers 1525 and 1700) that *refer* to salesperson 361, that is, that have the value 361 in the Salesperson Number foreign key attribute. It is as if Carlyle left the company and his customers have not as yet been reassigned to other salespersons. If a relational join command was issued to join the two relations in order to, for example, find the name of the salesperson responsible for customer 1525, there would be a problem. The relational DBMS would pick up the salesperson number value 361 in the record for customer 1525 in the CUSTOMER relation but would not be able to match 361 to a record in the SALESPERSON relation because there no longer is a record for salesperson 361 in the SALESPERSON relation—it was deleted! Notice that the problem arose because the deleted record, a salesperson record, was on the "one side" of a one-to-many relationship. What about the customer records on the "many side" of the one-to-many relationship? Suppose customer 1047, Acme

► Figure 6.11
General Hardware Company
SALESPERSON and
CUSTOMER relations

(a) SALESPERSON relation

Salesperson Number	Salesperson Name	Commission Percentage	Year of Hire
137	Baker	10	1995
186	Adams	15	2001
204	Dickens	10	1998
361	Carlyle	20	2001

(b) CUSTOMER relation

Customer Number	Customer Name	Salesperson Number	HQ City
0121	Main St. Hardware	137	New York
0839	Jane's Stores	186	Chicago
0933	ABC Home Stores	137	Los Angeles
1047	Acme Hardware Store	137	Los Angeles
1525	Fred's Tool Stores	361	Atlanta
1700	XYZ Stores	361	Washington
1826	City Hardware	137	New York
2198	Western Hardware	204	New York
2267	Central Stores	186	New York

Hardware Store, is no longer one of General Hardware's customers. Deleting the record for customer 1047 in the CUSTOMER relation has no referential integrity exposure. Nothing else in these two relations refers to customer 1047.

Similar referential integrity arguments can be made for the record insertion and update operations, but the issue of whether the exposure is on the "one side" or the "many side" of the one-to-many relationship changes! Again, in the case of deletion, the problem occurred when a record was deleted on the "one side" of the one-to-many relationship. But, for insertion, if a new salesperson record is inserted into the Salesperson relation—that is, a new record is inserted into the "one side" of the one-to-many relationship—there is no problem. All it means is that a new salesperson has joined the company but as yet has no customer responsibility. On the other hand, if a new customer record is inserted into the CUSTOMER relation—that is, a new record is inserted into the "many side" of the one-to-many relationship and it happens to include a salesperson number that does not have a match in the SALESPERSON relation—that would cause the same kind of problem as the deletion example above. Similarly, the update issue would concern updating a foreign key value, that is, a salesperson number in the CUSTOMER relation with a new salesperson number that has no match in the SALESPERSON relation.

The early relational DBMSs did not provide any control mechanisms for referential integrity. The programmers and users were on their own to keep track of it, and this upset many people. This was particularly true because referential integrity issues in the older, hierarchical and network DBMSs were more naturally controlled by the nature of the hierarchical and network data structures on which they were based, at the expense of a degree of flexibility in database design. Modern relational DBMSs provide sophisticated control mechanisms for referential integrity with so-called **delete rules, insert rules,** and **update rules.** These rules are specified between pairs of relations. We will take a look at the three most common delete rules, **restrict, cascade,** and **set-to-null,** to illustrate the problem.

Three Delete Rules

Delete Rule: Restrict   Again, consider the two relations of Figure 6.11. If the delete rule between the two relations is restrict and an attempt is made to delete a record on the "one side" of the one-to-many relationship, the system will forbid the delete to take place if there are any matching foreign key values in the relation on the "many side." For example, if an attempt is made to delete the record for salesperson 361 in the SALESPERSON relation, the system will not permit the deletion to take place because the CUSTOMER relation records for customers 1525 and 1700 include salesperson number 361 as a foreign key value (Figure 6.12). This is as if to say, "You can't delete a salesperson record as long as there are customers for which that salesperson is responsible." This would be a reasonable and necessary course of action in many business situations.

Delete Rule: Cascade   If the delete rule between the two relations is cascade and an attempt is made to delete a record on the "one side" of the relationship, not only will that record be deleted but all of the records on the "many side" of the

➤ **Figure 6.12**
Delete rule: Restrict

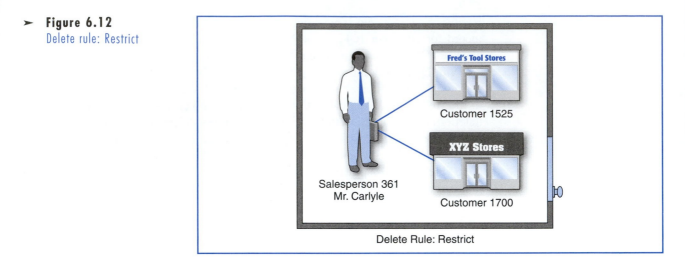

Delete Rule: Restrict

relationship that have a matching foreign key value will also be deleted. That is, the deletion will *cascade* from one relation to the other. For example, if an attempt is made to delete the record for salesperson 361 in the SALESPERSON relation and the delete rule is cascade, that salesperson record will be deleted and so too, automatically, will the records for customers 1525 and 1700 in the CUSTOMER relation because they have 361 as a foreign key value (Figure 6.13). It is as if the assumption is that when a salesperson leaves the company she always takes all of her customers along with her. Although that might be a bit of a stretch in this case, in many other business situations it is not a stretch at all. For example, think about a company that has a main employee relation with name, home address, telephone number, and so on, plus a second relation that lists and describes the several skills of each employee. Certainly, when an employee leaves the company, you would expect to delete both his record in the main employee relation and all of his records in the skills relation.

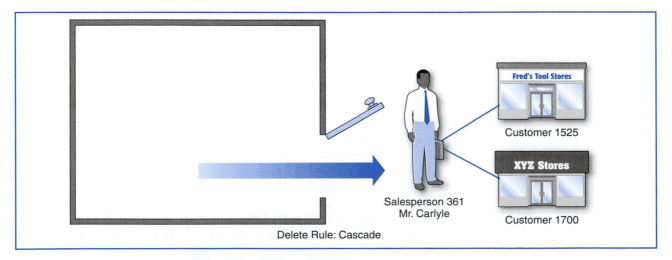

Delete Rule: Cascade

➤ **Figure 6.13** Delete rule: Cascade

Delete Rule: Set-to-Null   If the delete rule between the two relations is set-to-null and an attempt is made to delete a record on the "one side" of the one-to-many relationship, that record will be deleted and the matching foreign key values in the records on the "many side" of the relationship will be changed to null. For example, if an attempt is made to delete the record for salesperson 361 in the SALESPERSON relation, that record will be deleted, and the Salesperson Number attribute values in the records for customers 1525 and 1700 in the CUSTOMER relation will have their Salesperson Number attribute values changed from 361 to null (Figure 6.14). It is as if to say, "You can delete a salesperson record, and we will indicate that, temporarily at least, their former customers are without a salesperson." Obviously, this is the appropriate response in many business situations.

KEY TERMS

Cascade delete rule	Insert rules	Restrict delete rule
Delete rules	Record deletion	Set-to-null delete rule
Entity occurrence	Referential integrity	Update rules

QUESTIONS

1. Describe the concept of the unary one-to-many relationship.

2. How is a unary one-to-many relationship constructed in a relational database?

3. Describe the concept of the unary many-to-many relationship.

4. How is a unary many-to-many relationship constructed in a relational database?

5. Describe the concept of the ternary relationship.

6. How is a ternary relationship constructed in a relational database?

7. Is a ternary relationship the equivalent of the three possible binary relationships among the three entities involved? Explain.

8. Describe the problem of referential integrity.

9. Compare and contrast the three delete rules: restrict, cascade, and set-to-null.

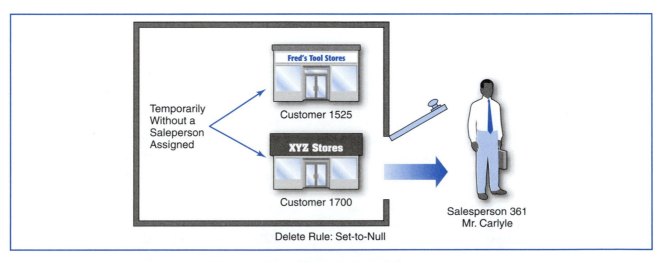

➤ **Figure 6.14**   Delete rule: Set-to-Null

EXERCISES

1. Leslie's Auto Sales has a relational database through which it maintains data on its salespersons, its customers, and the automobiles it sells. Each of these three entity types has a unique attribute identifier. The attributes that it stores are as follows:

   - Salesperson Number (unique), Salesperson Name, Salesperson Telephone, Years with Company.
   - Customer Number (unique), Customer Name, Customer Address, Value of Last Purchase From Us.
   - Vehicle Identification Number (unique), Manufacturer, Model, Year, Sticker Price.

   Leslie's also wants to keep track of which salesperson sold which car to which customer, including the date of the sale and the negotiated price.

   Construct a relational database for Leslie's Auto Sales.

2. The state of New York certifies firefighters throughout the state and must keep track of all of them as well as the state's fire departments. Each fire department has a unique department number, a name, which also identifies its locale (city, county, etc.), the year that it was established, and its main telephone number. Each certified firefighter has a unique firefighter number, a name, year of certification, home telephone number, and a rank (firefighter, fire lieutenant, fire captain, etc.). The state wants to record the fire department for which each firefighter currently works and each firefighter's supervisor. Supervisors are always higher ranking certified firefighters. Construct a relational database for New York's fire departments and firefighters.

3. The ABC Consulting Corporation contracts for projects, which, depending on their size and skill requirements, can be assigned to an individual consultant or to a team of consultants. A consultant or a team can work on several projects simultaneously. Several employees can be organized into a team. Larger teams can consist of a combination of smaller teams, sometimes with additional individual consultants added. This can continue to larger and larger teams. ABC wants to keep track of its consultants, teams, and projects, including which consultant or team is responsible for each project. Each consultant has a unique employee number, plus a name, home address, and telephone number. Each project has a unique project number, plus a name, budgeted cost, and due date. Construct a relational database for

ABC Consulting. *Hint:* You may want to develop an attribute called "responsible party," which can be either a team or an individual consultant. Each project has one responsible party that is responsible for its completion. Or you may want to think of an individual consultant as a potential "team of one" and have the responsibility for each project assigned to a "team," which could then be an individual consultant or a genuine team.

4. Consider the General Hardware Company database of Figure 6.1. Describe the problem of referential integrity in terms of the CUSTOMER and CUSTOMER EMPLOYEE relations if the record for customer 2198 in the CUSTOMER relation is deleted. (Assume that no delete rules exist.)

5. In the General Hardware Company database of Figure 6.1, what would happen if:

   a. The delete rule between the CUSTOMER and CUSTOMER EMPLOYEE relations is restrict and an attempt is made to delete the record for customer 2198 in the CUSTOMER relation?

   b. The delete rule between the CUSTOMER and CUSTOMER EMPLOYEE relations is cascade and an attempt is made to delete the record for customer 2198 in the CUSTOMER relation?

   c. The delete rule between the CUSTOMER and CUSTOMER EMPLOYEE relations is set-to-null and an attempt is made to delete the record for customer 2198 in the CUSTOMER relation?

   d. The delete rule between the CUSTOMER and CUSTOMER EMPLOYEE relations is restrict and an attempt is made to delete the record for employee 33779 of customer 2198 in the CUSTOMER EMPLOYEE relation?

   e. The delete rule between the CUSTOMER and CUSTOMER EMPLOYEE relations is cascade and an attempt is made to delete the record for employee 33779 of customer 2198 in the CUSTOMER EMPLOYEE relation?

   f. The delete rule between the CUSTOMER and CUSTOMER EMPLOYEE relations is set-to-null and an attempt is made to delete the record for employee 33779 of customer 2198 in the CUSTOMER EMPLOYEE relation?

MINICASES

1. Happy Cruise Lines

   a. Look at the Happy Cruise Lines database of Chapter 5, Minicase 1, but, for this question, consider *only* the SHIP, PORT, and PASSENGER relations. The company wants to keep track of which passengers visited which ports on which ships on which dates. Reconstruct these three relations as necessary and/or add additional relation(s) as necessary to store this information.

   b. Consider the following data from the SHIP and CRUISE relations of the Happy Cruise Lines database of Chapter 5, Minicase 1.

SHIP relation				
Ship Number	Ship Name	Ship Builder	Launch Date	Gross Weight
005	Sea Joy	Jones	1999	80,000
009	Ocean IV	Ajax	2003	75,000
012	Prince Al	Ajax	2004	90,000
020	Queen Shirley	Master	1999	80,000

CRUISE relation				
Cruise Number	Start Date	End Date	Cruise Director	Ship Number
21644	7/5/2002	7/12/2002	Smith	009
23007	8/14/2002	8/24/2002	Chen	020
24288	3/28/2003	4/4/2003	Smith	009
26964	7/1/2003	7/11/2003	Gomez	020
27045	7/15/2003	7/22/2003	Adams	012
28532	8/17/2003	8/24/2003	Adams	012
29191	12/20/2003	12/27/2003	Jones	009
29890	1/15/2004	1/22/2004	Levin	020

   What would happen if:

   i. The delete rule between the SHIP and CRUISE relations is restrict and an attempt is made to delete the record for ship number 012 in the SHIP relation?

   ii. The delete rule between the SHIP and CRUISE relations is restrict and an attempt is made to delete the record for ship number 005 in the SHIP relation?

   iii. The delete rule between the SHIP and CRUISE relations is cascade and an attempt is made to delete the record for ship number 012 in the SHIP relation?

   iv. The delete rule between the SHIP and CRUISE relations is cascade and an attempt is made to delete the record for ship number 005 in the SHIP relation?

   v. The delete rule between the SHIP and CRUISE relations is set-to-null and an attempt is made to delete the record for ship number 012 in the SHIP relation?

   vi. The delete rule between the SHIP and CRUISE relations is set-to-null and an attempt is made to delete the record for ship number 005 in the SHIP relation?

   vii. The delete rule between the SHIP and CRUISE relations is restrict and an attempt is made to delete the record for cruise number 26964 in the CRUISE relation?

   viii. The delete rule between the SHIP and CRUISE relations is cascade and an attempt is made to delete the record for cruise number 26964 in the CRUISE relation?

   ix. The delete rule between the SHIP and CRUISE relations is set-to-null and an attempt is made to delete the record for cruise number 26964 in the CRUISE relation?

2. Super Baseball League

   a. In the Super Baseball League database of Chapter 5, Minicase 2, assume that instead of having coaches who are separate from players, now some of the players serve as coaches to other players. A player/coach can have several players whom he coaches. Each player is coached by only one player/coach. Reconstruct the database structure to reflect this change.

   b. In the Super Baseball League database of Chapter 5, Minicase 2, assume that the TEAM relation has a record for team number 17 and that the COACH relation has records for three coaches on that team. What would happen if:

   i. The delete rule between the TEAM and COACH relations is restrict and an attempt is made to delete the record for team 17 in the TEAM relation?

   ii. The delete rule between the TEAM and COACH relations is cascade and an attempt is made to delete the record for team 17 in the TEAM relation?

iii. The delete rule between the TEAM and COACH relations is set-to-null and an attempt is made to delete the record for team 17 in the TEAM relation?

iv. The delete rule between the TEAM and COACH relations is restrict and an attempt is made to delete the record for one of team 17's coaches in the COACH relation?

v. The delete rule between the TEAM and COACH relations is cascade and an attempt is made to delete the record for one of team 17's coaches in the COACH relation?

vi. The delete rule between the TEAM and COACH relations is set-to-null and an attempt is made to delete the record for one of team 17's coaches in the COACH relation?

CHAPTER 7

LOGICAL DATABASE DESIGN

CHAPTER OBJECTIVES

After learning the material in this chapter, you will be able to:
✔ Describe the concept of logical database design.
✔ Design relational databases by converting entity-relationship diagrams into relational tables.
✔ Describe the data normalization process.
✔ Perform the data normalization process.
✔ Test tables for irregularities using the data normalization process.

Photo Courtesy of Ecolab

ECOLAB

Ecolab is a $3 billion-plus developer and marketer of cleaning, sanitizing, pest elimination, and industrial maintenance and repair products and services that was founded in 1923. Its customers include restaurants, hotels, hospitals, food and beverage plants, laundries, schools, and other retail and commercial facilities. Headquartered in St. Paul, Minnesota, Ecolab is truly a global company, operating directly in 70 countries and through distributors, licensees, and export operations in an additional 100 countries. Its domestic and worldwide operations are supported by 20,000 employees and over fifty manufacturing and distribution facilities. A large percentage of the employees are sales and service individuals that work in a mobile, remote environment.

One of Ecolab's applications that has a significant Database component is called "EcoNet." EcoNet enables the large sales and service work force access to information distributed across many databases. EcoNet provides Ecolab's North American sales and service people with a portal into pertinent information needed when interacting with customers for sales and service purposes. EcoNet also enables the standardization of process across the sales and service organizations within the seven various North American business units. This is achieved by having one application get data from different databases.

The system is also used as a sales planning tool. Using EcoNet, a salesperson can access such customer information as past and outstanding invoices, service reports, and order status. The salesperson can also use the system to place new orders. Being Web-based, Econet can be accessed from a home or office PC, from a laptop at the customer location, or even through handheld devices. In addition, customers can view their own data through "My Ecolab.com."

Implemented in 2002, EcoNet uses an interesting mix of databases.

1. The transactional data, including the last six months' orders, is held in a Computer Associates IDMS network-type database. EcoNet accesses this "up-to-the-minute" information using screen scraping technology against the IBM mainframe computer rather than migrating the data "real-time" to a relational DBMS.

2. Completed transaction data is bridged nightly to a data warehouse holding seven years of sales data in IBM DB2 Unix.

3. Summarized Sales tables and Key Performance Indicators are also bridged to Microsoft SQL Server relational databases.

Ecolab is continually looking for additional information to add to the EcoNet application in order to provide their sales and service people with valuable information when interacting with customers.

Logical database design is the process of deciding how to arrange the attributes of the entities in the business environment into database structures, such as the tables of a relational database. The goal of logical database design is to create well-structured tables that properly reflect the company's business environment. The tables will be capable of storing data about the company's entities in a nonredundant manner, and foreign keys will be placed in the tables so that all of the relationships among the entities will be supported. Physical database design, which will be treated in the next chapter, is the process of modifying the logical database design to improve performance.

Historically, a number of techniques have been used for logical database design. In the 1970s, when the hierarchical and network approaches to database management were the only ones available, a technique known as **data normalization** was developed. Although data normalization has some very useful features, it was difficult to apply in that environment. Data normalization can also be used to design relational databases and actually is a better fit for relational databases than it was for the hierarchical and network databases. But as the relational approach to database management and the entity-relationship approach to data modeling both blossomed in the 1980s, a very natural and pleasing approach to logical database design evolved in which rules were developed to convert E-R diagrams into relational tables. Optionally, the result of this process can then be tested with the data normalization technique. Thus this chapter on the logical design of relational databases will proceed in three parts: (1) the conversion of E-R diagrams into relational tables, (2) the data normalization technique, and (3) the use of the data normalization technique to test the tables resulting from the **E-R diagram conversions.**

CONVERTING E-R DIAGRAMS INTO RELATIONAL TABLES

Introduction

The conversion of entity-relationship diagrams to relational tables is surprisingly straightforward, with just a few simple rules to follow. Basically, each entity will convert to a table, plus each many-to-many relationship or associative entity will convert to a table. The only other issue is that during the conversion, certain rules must be followed to ensure that foreign keys appear in their proper places in the tables. We will demonstrate these techniques by methodically converting the E-R diagrams of Chapter 3 into relational tables.

Converting a Simple Entity

Figure 7.1 repeats the simple entity box in Figure 3.1, and Figure 7.2 shows a relational table that is capable of storing the data represented in the entity box. The table simply contains the attributes that were specified in the entity box. Notice that Salesperson Number is underlined to indicate that it is the unique identifier of the entity and the primary key of the table. The more interesting issues and rules come about when, as they almost always are, entities are involved in relationships with other entities.

➤ Figure 7.1
The entity box from Figure 3.1

Converting Entities in Binary Relationships

One-to-One Binary Relationship
Figure 7.3 repeats the one-to-one binary relationship of Figure 3.4a. There are three options for designing tables to represent this data, as shown in Figure 7.4. In Figure 7.4a, the two

➤ Figure 7.2
Conversion of an E-R diagram entity box to a relational table

SALESPERSON			
<u>Salesperson Number</u>	Salesperson Name	Commission Percentage	Year of Hire

➤ **Figure 7.3**
The one-to-one binary
relationship from
Figure 3.4a

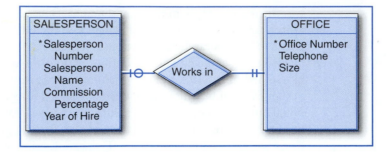

➤ **Figure 7.4**
Conversion of an E-R diagram
with two entities in a one-to-
one binary relationship into
one or two relational tables

SALESPERSON/OFFICE						
Salesperson Number	Salesperson Name	Commission Percentage	Year of Hire	Office Number	Telephone	Size

a. One-to-one binary relationship converted to a single relational table.

SALESPERSON				
Salesperson Number	Salesperson Name	Commission Percentage	Year of Hire	Office Number

OFFICE		
Office Number	Telephone	Size

b. One-to-one binary relationship converted to two relational tables, with the foreign key in the SALESPERSON table.

SALESPERSON			
Salesperson Number	Salesperson Name	Commission Percentage	Year of Hire

OFFICE			
Office Number	Telephone	Salesperson Number	Size

c. One-to-one binary relationship converted to two relational tables, with the foreign key in the OFFICE table.

entities are combined into one relational table. On the one hand, this is possible because the one-to-one relationship means that for one salesperson, there can only be one office associated with him and conversely, for one office there can be only one salesperson. Therefore, a particular salesperson and office combination can fit together in one record, as shown in Figure 7.4a. On the other hand, this design is not a good choice for two reasons. First, the very fact that salesperson and office were drawn in two different entity boxes in the E-R diagram of Figure 7.3 means that they are thought of separately in this business environment and thus should be kept separate in the database. Second is the modality of zero at the salesperson in Figure 7.3. Reading that diagram from right to left, it says that an office might have no one assigned to it. Thus, in the table shown in Figure 7.4a, a few or possibly many record occurrences could have values for the office number, telephone, and size attributes but have the four attributes pertaining to salespersons empty or null! This could result in a lot of wasted storage space, but it is worse than that. If Salesperson Number is declared to be the primary key of the table, this scenario would mean that there would be records with no primary key values, a situation that is clearly not allowed.

Figure 7.4b is a better choice. There are separate tables for the salesperson and office entities. In order to record the relationship (i.e., which salesperson is assigned to which office), the Office Number attribute is placed as a foreign key in the SALESPERSON table. This connects the salespersons with the offices to which they are assigned. Again, look at the modalities in the E-R diagram of Figure 7.3. Reading from left to right, we see that each salesperson is assigned to exactly one office (indicated by the two "ones" adjacent to the office entity). That translates directly into each record in the SALESPERSON table of Figure 7.4b having a value (and a single value at that) for its Office Number foreign key attribute. That's all well and good, but what about the problem of unassigned offices that we mentioned in the last paragraph? In Figure 7.4b, each unassigned office will have a record in the OFFICE table, with Office Number as the primary key, which is fine. Their office numbers will simply not appear as foreign key values in the SALESPERSON table.

Finally, instead of placing Office Number as a foreign key in the SALESPERSON table, could you instead place Salesperson Number as a foreign key in the OFFICE table (Figure 7.4c)? Recall that by reading the E-R diagram of Figure 7.3 from right to left, the modality of zero adjacent to the salesperson entity says that an office might be empty (i.e., it might not be assigned to any salesperson). But as a result some or perhaps many records of the OFFICE table of Figure 7.4c would have no value or a null in their Salesperson Number foreign key attribute positions. Why bother having to deal with this situation when the design in Figure 7.4b avoids it?

Certainly, it follows that if the modalities were reversed, meaning that the zero modality was adjacent to the office entity box and the one modality was adjacent to the salesperson entity box, then the design in Figure 7.4c would be preferable. This would mean that every office must have a salesperson assigned to it, but a salesperson may or may not be assigned to an office. Perhaps lots of the salespersons travel most of the time and don't need offices. By the way, while we're in a "what if" mode, what if the modality was zero *on both sides*? Then we would have to make a judgment call between the designs of Figure 7.4b and Figure 7.4c. If the goal is to minimize the number of null values in the foreign key, then we have to decide whether it is more likely that a salesperson is not assigned to an office (Figure 7.4c is preferable) or that an office is empty (Figure 7.4b is preferable).

One-to-Many Binary Relationship   Figure 7.5 (copied from Figure 3.4b) shows an E-R diagram for a one-to-many binary relationship. Figure 7.6 shows the conversion of this E-R diagram into two relational tables. This is perhaps the simplest case of all. The rule is that the unique identifier of the entity on the "one side" of the one-to-many relationship is placed as a foreign key in the table representing

➤ **Figure 7.5**
The one-to-many binary relationship from Figure 3.4b

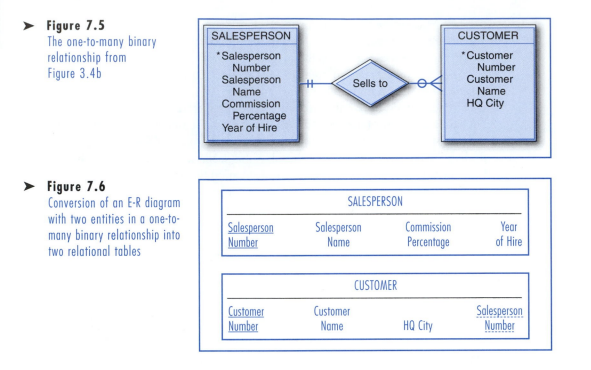

➤ **Figure 7.6**
Conversion of an E-R diagram with two entities in a one-to-many binary relationship into two relational tables

the entity on the "many side." In this case, the Salesperson Number attribute is placed in the CUSTOMER table as a foreign key. Each salesperson has one record in the SALESPERSON table, as does each customer in the CUSTOMER table. The Salesperson Number attribute in the CUSTOMER table links the two, and since the E-R diagram tells us that every customer must have a salesperson, there are no empty attributes in the CUSTOMER table records.

Many-to-Many Binary Relationship Figure 7.7 shows the E-R diagram with the many-to-many binary relationship from Figure 3.5. The equivalent diagram from Chapter 3, using an associative entity, is shown in Figure 7.8. An E-R diagram with two entities in a many-to-many relationship converts to three relational tables, as shown in Figure 7.9. Each of the two entities converts to a table with its own attributes but with no foreign keys (regarding this relationship). The SALESPERSON

➤ **Figure 7.7**
The many-to-many binary relationship from Figure 3.5

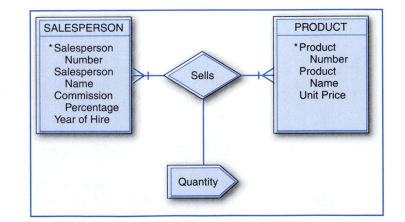

> **Figure 7.8**
> The many-to-many binary relationship with an associative entity from Figure 3.6

> **Figure 7.9**
> Conversion of an E-R diagram in Figure 7.7 (and Figure 7.8) with two entities in a many-to-many binary relationship into three relational tables

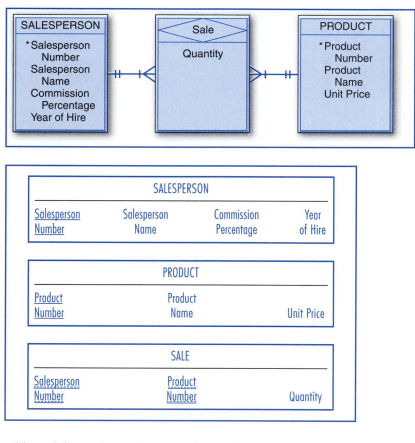

table and the PRODUCT table in Figure 7.9 each contain only the attributes shown in the salesperson and product entity boxes of Figure 7.7 and Figure 7.8.

In addition, there must be a third "many-to-many" table for the many-to-many relationship, the reasons for which were explained in Chapter 5. The primary key of this additional table is the combination of the unique identifiers of the two entities in the many-to-many relationship. Additional attributes consist of the intersection data, Quantity in this example. Also as explained in Chapter 5, in some circumstances additional attributes, such as date and timestamp attributes, must be added to the primary key of the many-to-many table to achieve uniqueness.

Converting Entities in Unary Relationships

One-to-One Unary Relationship Figure 7.10 repeats the E-R diagram with a one-to-one unary relationship from Figure 3.7a. In this case, with only one entity type involved and with a one-to-one relationship, the conversion requires only one table, as shown in Figure 7.11. For a particular salesperson, the Backup Number attribute represents the salesperson number of his backup person—that is, the person who handles his accounts when he is away for any reason.

One-to-Many Unary Relationship The one-to-many unary relationship situation is very similar to the one-to-one unary case. Figure 7.12 repeats the E-R diagram from Figure 3.7b, and Figure 7.13 shows the conversion of this diagram into a relational database. Some employees manage other employees. An employee's manager is recorded in the Manager Number attribute in the table in Figure 7.13. The manager numbers are actually salesperson numbers because, as described earlier in the book, some salespersons are sales managers who manage other salespersons. This arrangement works because each employee has only one manager. For any particular SALESPERSON record, there can only be one value for the Manager Number attribute. However, if you scan down the Manager Number column, a particular value may appear several times because a person can manage several other salespersons.

➤ **Figure 7.10**
The one-to-one unary relationship from Figure 3.7a

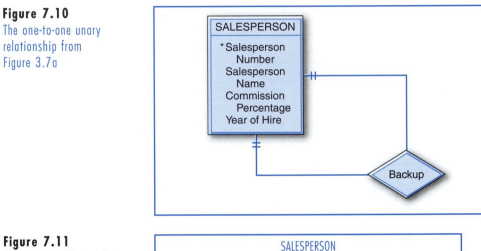

➤ **Figure 7.11**
Conversion of the E-R diagram in Figure 7.10 with a one-to-one unary relationship into a relational table

SALESPERSON				
Salesperson Number	Salesperson Name	Commission Percentage	Year of Hire	Backup Number

➤ **Figure 7.12**
The one-to-many unary relationship from Figure 3.7b

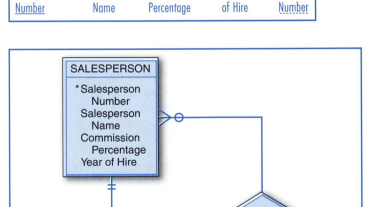

➤ **Figure 7.13**
Conversion of the E-R diagram in Figure 7.12 with a one-to-many unary relationship into a relational table

SALESPERSON				
Salesperson Number	Salesperson Name	Commission Percentage	Year of Hire	Manager

Many-to-Many Unary Relationship Figure 7.14 shows the E-R diagram for the many-to-many unary relationship of Figure 3.7c. As Figure 7.15 indicates, this relationship requires two tables in the conversion. The PRODUCT table has no foreign keys. The COMPONENT table indicates which items go into making up which other items, as was described in the bill-of-materials discussion of Chapter 6. This table also contains any intersection data that might exist in the many-to-many relationship. In this example, the Quantity attribute indicates how many of a particular item go into making up another item.

The fact that we wind up with two tables in this conversion is really not surprising. The general rule is that in the conversion of a many-to-many relationship of *any* degree—unary, binary, or ternary—the number of tables will be equal to the number of entity types (one, two, or three, respectively) plus one more table for the many-to-many relationship. Thus the conversion of the many-to-many unary relationship required two tables, the many-to-many binary relationship three tables, and, as will be shown next, the many-to-many ternary relationship four tables.

Converting Entities in Ternary Relationships

Finally, Figure 7.16 repeats the E-R diagram with the ternary relationship from Figure 3.8. Figure 7.17 shows the four tables necessary for the conversion to relational tables. Notice that the primary key of the SALE table, which is the table added for the many-to-many relationship, is the combination of the unique

➤ **Figure 7.14**
The many-to-many unary relationship from Figure 3.7c

➤ **Figure 7.15**
Conversion of the E-R diagram in Figure 7.14 with a many-to-many unary relationship into two relational tables

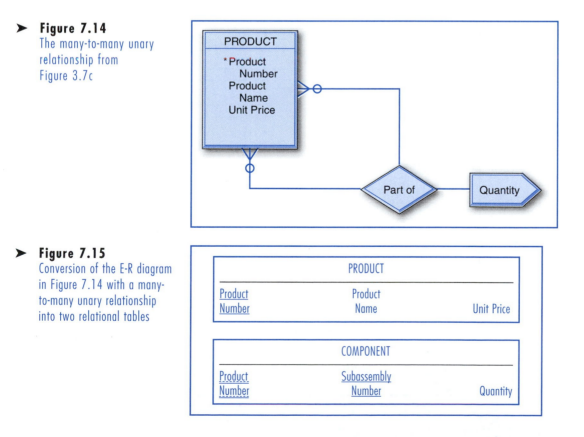

identifiers of the three entities involved, plus the Date attribute. In this case, with the premise being that a particular salesperson can have sold a particular product to a particular customer *on different days*, the Date attribute is needed in the primary key to achieve uniqueness.

➤ **Figure 7.16**
The ternary relationship from Figure 3.8

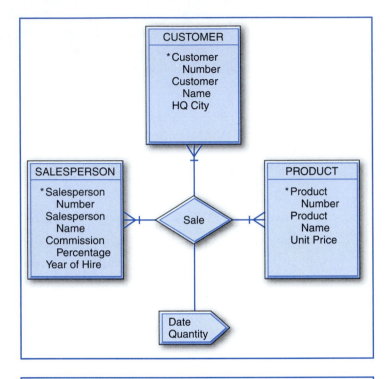

➤ **Figure 7.17**
Conversion of the E-R diagram in Figure 7.16 with three entities in a ternary relationship into four relational tables

SALESPERSON			
Salesperson Number	Salesperson Name	Commission Percentage	Year of Hire

CUSTOMER		
Customer Number	Customer Name	HQ City

PRODUCT		
Product Number	Product Name	Unit Price

SALE				
Salesperson Number	Customer Number	Product Number	Date	Quantity

Designing the General Hardware Company Database

Having explored the specific E-R diagram-to-relational database conversion rules, let's look at a few examples, beginning with the General Hardware Company. Figure 7.18 is the General Hardware E-R diagram. It is convenient to begin the database design process with an important, central E-R diagram entity, such as salesperson, that has relationships with several other entities. Thus the relational database in Figure 7.19 includes a SALESPERSON table with the four salesperson attributes shown in Figure 7.18's salesperson entity box (plus the Office Number attribute, which we will return to shortly). Looking to the right of the salesperson entity box in the E-R diagram, we

➤ **Figure 7.18**
The General Hardware
Company E-R diagram

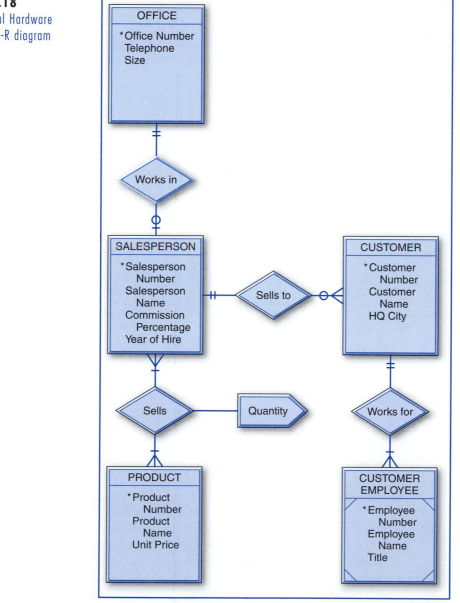

➤ **Figure 7.19**
The General Hardware
Company relational database

SALESPERSON				
Salesperson Number	Salesperson Name	Commission Percentage	Year of Hire	Office Number

CUSTOMER			
Customer Number	Customer Name	Salesperson Number	HQ City

CUSTOMER EMPLOYEE			
Customer Number	Employee Number	Employee Name	Title

PRODUCT		
Product Number	Product Name	Unit Price

SALES		
Salesperson Number	Product Number	Quantity

OFFICE		
Office Number	Telephone	Size

see a one-to-many relationship ("sells to") between salespersons and customers. The database then includes a CUSTOMER table with the Salesperson Number attribute as a foreign key because salesperson is on the "one side" of the one-to-many relationship and customer is on the "many side" of the one-to-many relationship.

Customer employee is a dependent entity of customer, and there is a one-to-many relationship between them. Because of this relationship, the CUSTOMER EMPLOYEE table in the database includes the Customer Number attribute as a foreign key. Furthermore, the Customer Number attribute is part of the primary key of the CUSTOMER EMPLOYEE table because customer employee is a dependent entity and we're told that employee numbers are only unique within a customer.

The PRODUCT table contains the three attributes of the product entity. The many-to-many relationship between the salesperson and product entities is represented by the SALES table in the database. Notice that the combination of the unique identifiers (Salesperson Number and Product Number) of the two entities in the many-to-many relationship is the primary key of the SALES table. Finally, the office entity has its table in the database with its three attributes, which brings us to the presence of the Office Number attribute as a foreign key in the SALESPERSON table. This is needed to maintain the one-to-one binary relationship between salesperson and office. A fair question is, since the relationship is "one" on both sides, why did we decide to put the foreign key in the SALESPERSON table rather than in the OFFICE table? Again, the answer lies in the fact that the modality adjacent to SALESPERSON is zero while the modality adjacent to OFFICE is one. An office may or may not have a salesperson assigned to it, but a salesperson *must* be assigned to an office. The result is that every salesperson must have an associated office number; the Office Number attribute in the SALESPERSON table can't be null. If we reversed it and put the Salesperson Number attribute in the OFFICE table, many of the Salesperson Number attribute values could be null since the zero modality going from office to salesperson tells us that an office can be empty.

One last thought: Why did the PRODUCT table end up without having any foreign keys? Because it is not the "target" (it is not on the "many side") of any one-to-many binary relationship. It is also not involved in a one-to-one binary relationship that would require a foreign key being placed in it. Finally, it is not involved in a unary relationship that would require the primary key to be repeated in the table.

Designing the Good Reading Bookstores Database

The Good Reading Bookstores E-R diagram is repeated in Figure 7.20. Beginning with the central book entity and looking to its left, we see that there is a one-to-many relationship between books and publishers. A publisher publishes many books, but a book is published by just one publisher. The Good Reading Bookstores relational database of Figure 7.21 shows the BOOK and PUBLISHER tables. Publisher Name

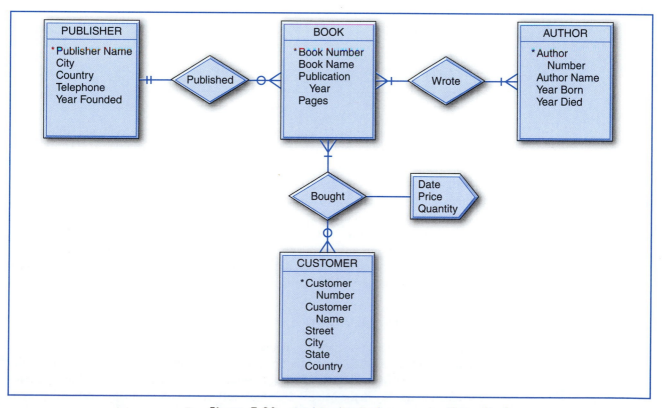

➤ **Figure 7.20** Good Reading Bookstores entity-relationship diagram

➤ **Figure 7.21**
The Good Reading Bookstores
relational database

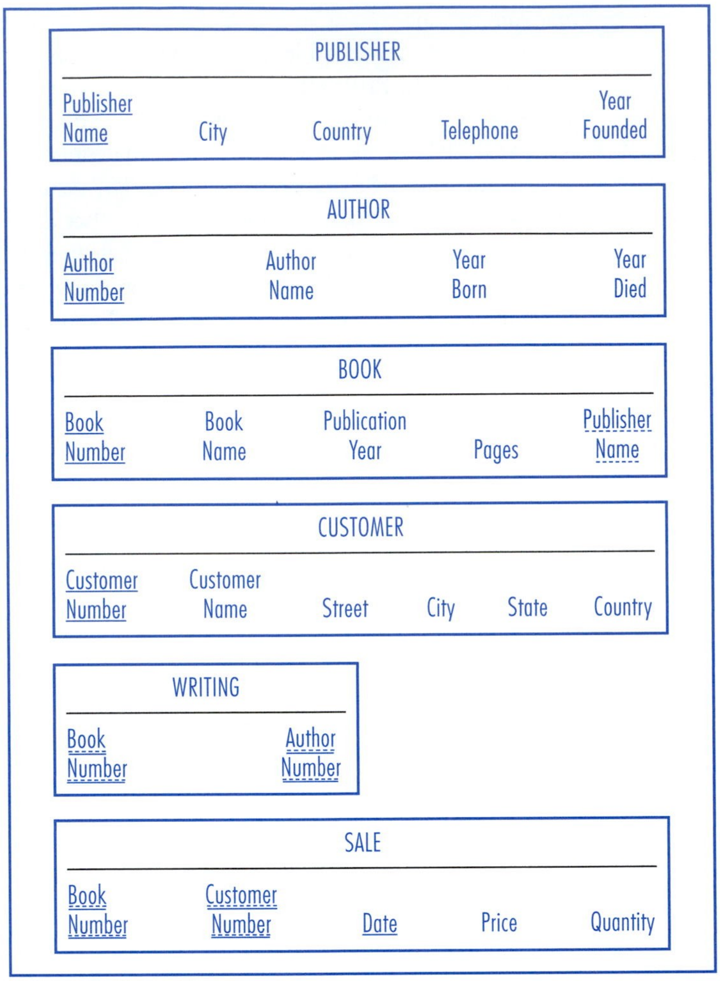

is a foreign key in the BOOK table because publisher is on the "one side" of the one-to-many relationship and book is on the "many side." Next is the AUTHOR table, which is straightforward. The many-to-many binary relationship between books and authors is reflected in the WRITING table, which has no intersection data. Finally, there is the customer entity and the many-to-many relationship between books and customers. Correspondingly, the relational database includes a CUSTOMER table and a SALE table to handle the many-to-many relationship. Notice that the Date, Price, and Quantity attributes appear in the SALE table as intersection data. Also notice that since a customer can buy the same book on more than one day, the Date attribute must be part of the primary key to achieve uniqueness.

Designing the World Music Association Database

The World Music Association E-R diagram in Figure 7.22 shows that the orchestra entity would be a good, central starting point for the database design process. Thus, the relational database in Figure 7.23 begins with the ORCHESTRA table. The Orchestra Name foreign key in the MUSICIAN table reflects the one-to-many relationship from orchestra to musician. Since degree is a dependent entity of musician in a one-to-many

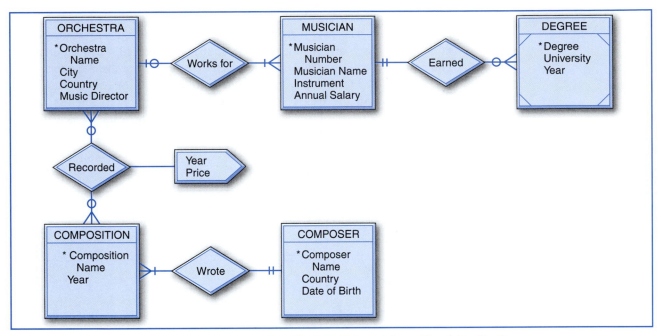

➤ **Figure 7.22** World Music Association entity-relationship diagram

➤ **Figure 7.23**
The World Music Association
relational database

ORCHESTRA			
Orchestra Name	City	Country	Music Director

MUSICIAN				
Musician Number	Musician Name	Instrument	Annual Salary	Orchestra Name

DEGREE			
Musician Number	Degree	University	Year

COMPOSER		
Composer Name	Country	Date of Birth

COMPOSITION		
Composition Name	Composer Name	Year

RECORDING			
Orchestra Name	Composition Name	Year	Price

relationship and degrees (e.g., B.A.) are only unique within a musician, not only does Musician Number appear as a foreign key in the DEGREE table but also it must be part of that table's primary key. Finally, the many-to-many relationship between orchestra and composition is converted into the RECORDING table. Notice that the primary key of the RECORDING table consists of the Orchestra Name, Composition Name, and Year (recorded) attributes. Year (recorded) is included in the primary key because an orchestra may have recorded the same composition in different years. Incidentally, the Year field in the COMPOSITION table is the year the composition was composed.

Designing the Lucky Rent-A-Car Database

Figure 7.24 shows the Lucky Rent-A-Car E-R diagram. The conversion to a relational database structure begins with the car entity and its four attributes, as shown in the

➤ **Figure 7.24**
Lucky Rent-A-Car entity-relationship diagram

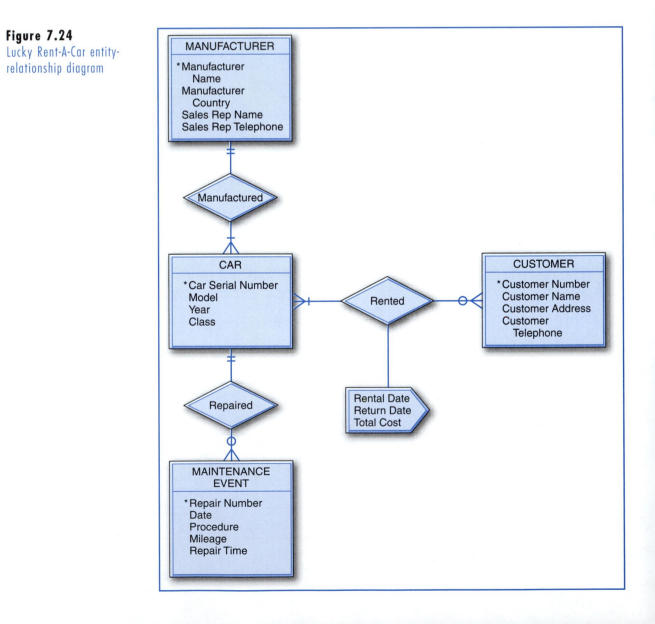

CAR table of the database in Figure 7.25. Because car is on the "many side" of a one-to-many relationship with the manufacturer entity, the CAR table also has the Manufacturer Name attribute as a foreign key. The straightforward one-to-many relationship from car to maintenance event results in a MAINTENANCE EVENT table with Car Serial Number as a foreign key. The customer entity converts to the CUSTOMER table with its four attributes. The many-to-many relationship between car and customer converts to the RENTAL table. Car Serial Number, the unique identifier of the car entity and Customer Number, the unique identifier of the customer entity, plus the Rental Date intersection data attribute form the three-attribute primary key of the RENTAL table, with Return Date and Total Cost as additional intersection data attributes. Rental Date has to be part of the primary key to achieve uniqueness because a particular customer may have rented a particular car on several different dates.

THE DATA NORMALIZATION PROCESS

Data normalization was the earliest formalized database design technique and at one time was the starting point for logical database design. Today, with the popularity of the entity-relationship model and other such diagramming tools, and the ability to convert its diagrams to database structures, data normalization is used more as a check on database structures produced from E-R diagrams than as a full-scale database design technique. That's one of the reasons for learning about data normalization.

➤ **Figure 7.25**
The Lucky Rent-A-Car relational database

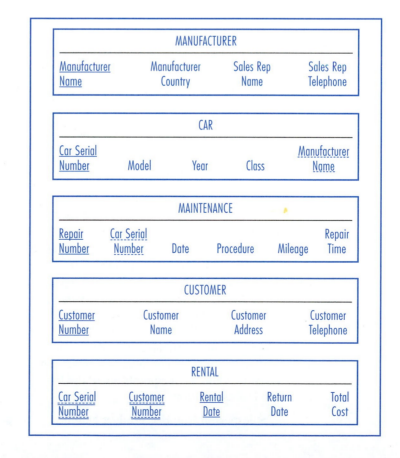

Another reason is that the data normalization process is another way of demonstrating and learning about such important topics as data redundancy, foreign keys, and other ideas that are so central to a solid understanding of database management.

Data normalization is a methodology for organizing attributes into tables so that redundancy among the nonkey attributes is eliminated. Each of the resultant tables deals with a single data focus, which is just another way of saying that each resultant table will describe a single entity type or a single many-to-many relationship. Furthermore, foreign keys will appear exactly where they are needed. In other words, the output of the data normalization process is a properly structured relational database.

Introduction to the Data Normalization Technique

The input required by the data normalization process comes in two parts. One is a list of all the attributes that must be incorporated into the database—that is, all of the attributes in all the entities involved in the business environment under discussion, plus all of the intersection data attributes in all of the many-to-many relationships between these entities. The other input, informally, is a list of all the defining associations between the attributes. Formally, these defining associations are known as *functional dependencies*. And what are defining associations or functional dependencies? They are a means of expressing that the value of one particular attribute is associated with a single, specific value of another attribute. If we know that one of these attributes has a particular value, then the other attribute *must* have some other value. For example, for a particular Salesperson Number, 137, there is exactly one Salesperson Name, Baker, associated with it. Why is this true? In this example, a Salesperson Number uniquely identifies a salesperson and, after all, a person can have only one name! And this is true for every person! Informally, we might say that Salesperson Number *defines* Salesperson Name. If I give you a Salesperson Number, you can give me back the one and only name that goes with it. (It's a little like the concept of independent and dependent variables in mathematics. Take a value of the independent variable, plug it into the formula, and you get back the specific value of the dependent variable associated with that independent variable.) These defining associations are commonly written with a right-pointing arrow like this:

Salesperson Number ⟶ Salesperson Name

In the more formal terms of functional dependencies, Salesperson Number, in general the attribute on the left side is referred to as the *determinant*. Why? Because its value *determines* the value of the attribute on the right side. Conversely, we also say that the attribute on the right is *functionally dependent* on the attribute on the left.

Data normalization is best explained with an example, and this is a good place to start one. In order to demonstrate the main points of the data normalization process, we will modify part of the General Hardware Company business environment and focus on the salesperson and product entities. Let's assume that salespersons are organized into departments and that each department has a manager who is not herself a salesperson. Then the list of attributes that we will consider is shown in Figure 7.26, and the list of defining associations or functional dependencies is shown in Figure 7.27.

Notice a couple of fine points about the list of defining associations in Figure 7.27. The last association:

Salesperson Number, Product Number ⟶ Quantity

➤ **Figure 7.26**
List of attributes for salespersons and products

Salesperson Number
Salesperson Name
Commission
  Percentage
Year of Hire
Department
  Number
Manager Name
Product Number
Product Name
Unit Price
Quantity

shows that the *combination* of two or more attributes may define another attribute. That is, the combination of a particular Salesperson Number and a particular Product Number defines or specifies a particular Quantity. Put another way, in this business context, we know how many units of a particular product a particular salesperson has sold. Another point, which will be important in demonstrating one step of the data normalization process, is that Manager Name is defined, independently, by two different attributes, Salesperson Number and Department Number:

Salesperson Number ———➤ Manager Name
Department Number ———➤ Manager Name

Both of these defining associations are true! If I identify a salesperson by his Salesperson Number, you can tell me who his manager is. Also, if I state a department number, you can tell me who the manager of the department is. How could we wind up with two different ways to define the same attribute? Very easily! It simply means that during the systems analysis process, both of these equally true defining associations were discovered and noted. By the way, the fact that I know the department that a salesperson works in:

Salesperson Number ———➤ Department Number

(and that each of these two attributes independently defines Manager Name) will also be an issue in the data normalization process. More about this later.

Steps in the Data Normalization Process

The data normalization process is known as a decomposition process. Basically, we are going to line up all of the attributes that will be included in the relational database and we are going to start subdividing them into groups that will eventually form the database's tables. Thus we are going to "decompose" the original list of all the attributes into subgroups. To do so, we are going to step through a number

➤ **Figure 7.27**
List of defining associations (functional dependencies) for the attributes of salespersons and products

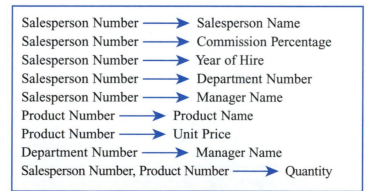

Salesperson Number ———➤ Salesperson Name
Salesperson Number ———➤ Commission Percentage
Salesperson Number ———➤ Year of Hire
Salesperson Number ———➤ Department Number
Salesperson Number ———➤ Manager Name
Product Number ———➤ Product Name
Product Number ———➤ Unit Price
Department Number ———➤ Manager Name
Salesperson Number, Product Number ———➤ Quantity

of **normal forms.** First, we will demonstrate what unnormalized data looks like. After all, if data can exist in several different normal forms, then there should be the possibility of data being in none of the normal forms, too! Then, we will basically work through the three main normal forms in order:

First Normal Form
Second Normal Form
Third Normal Form

There are certain "exception conditions" that have also been described as normal forms. These include Boyce-Codd Normal Form, Fourth Normal Form, and Fifth Normal Form. They are relatively less common in practice and will not be covered here. Here are three additional points to remember:

1. Once the attributes are arranged in third normal form (and if none of the exception conditions is present), the group of tables that they comprise is, in fact, a well-structured relational database with no data redundancy.
2. A group of tables is said to be in a particular normal form if every table in the group is in that normal form.
3. The data normalization process is progressive. If a group of tables is in second normal form, it is also in first normal form. If the tables are in third normal form, they are also in second normal form.

Unnormalized Data Figure 7.28 shows the salesperson and product-related attributes listed in Figure 7.26 arranged in a table with sample data. The salesperson and product data is taken from the General Hardware Company relational database of Figure 5.14, except that Department Number and Manager Name data has

SALESPERSON/PRODUCT table									
Salesperson Number	Product Number	Salesperson Name	Commission Percentage	Year of Hire	Department Number	Manager Name	Product Name	Unit Price	Quantity
137	19440	Baker	10	1995	73	Scott	Hammer	17.50	473
	24013						Saw	26.25	170
	26722						Pliers	11.50	688
186	16386	Adams	15	2001	59	Lopez	Wrench	12.95	1745
	19440						Hammer	17.50	2529
	21765						Drill	32.99	1962
	24013						Saw	26.25	3071
204	21765	Dickens	10	1998	73	Scott	Drill	32.99	809
	26722						Pliers	11.50	734
361	16386	Carlyle	20	2001	73	Scott	Wrench	12.95	3729
	21765						Drill	32.99	3110
	26722						Pliers	11.50	2738

➤ **Figure 7.28** The salesperson and product attributes, unnormalized with sample data

been added. Note that salespersons 137, 204, and 361 are all in department number 73 and that their manager is Scott. Salesperson 186 is in department number 59 and his manager is Lopez.

The table in Figure 7.28 is unnormalized. The table has four records, one for each salesperson. But since each salesperson has sold several products and there is only one record for each salesperson, several attributes of each record must have multiple values. For example, the record for salesperson 137 has three product numbers, 19440, 24013, and 26722, in its Product Number attribute because salesperson 137 has sold all three of those products. Having such multivalued attributes is not permitted in first normal form, and so this table is unnormalized.

First Normal Form   The table in Figure 7.29 is the first normal form representation of the data. The attributes under consideration have been listed in one table, and a primary key has been established. As the sample data of Figure 7.30 shows, the number of records has been increased (compared to the unnormalized representation) so that every attribute of every record has just one value. The multivalued attributes of Figure 7.28 have been eliminated. Indeed, first normal form can be defined as a table in which every attribute value is atomic—that is, no attribute is multivalued.

The combination of the Salesperson Number and Product Number attributes constitutes the primary key of this table. What makes this combination of attributes a legitimate primary key? First, the business context tells us that the combination of the two provides unique identifiers for the records of the table and that there is no single attribute that will do the job. Of course, we have been approaching primary keys in this way all along. Second, in terms of data normalization, according to the list of defining associations or functional dependencies of Figure 7.27, every attribute in the table in either part of the primary key or is defined by one or both attributes of the primary key. Salesperson Name, Commission Percentage, Year of Hire, Department Number, and Manager Name are each defined by Salesperson Number. Product Name and Unit Price are each defined by Product Number. Quantity is defined by the combination of Salesperson Number and Product Number.

Are these two different ways of approaching the primary key selection equivalent? Yes! If the combination of a particular Salesperson Number and a particular Product Number is unique, then it identifies exactly one record of the table. And if it identifies exactly one record of the table, then that record shows the single value of each of the nonkey attributes that is associated with the unique combination of the key attributes. But that is the same thing as saying that each of the nonkey attributes is defined by or is functionally dependent on the primary key! For example, consider the first record of the table in Figure 7.30.

Salesperson Number	Product Number	Salesperson Name	Commission Percentage	Year of Hire	Department Number	Manager Name	Product Name	Unit Price	Quantity
137	19440	Baker	10	1995	73	Scott	Hammer	17.50	473

The combination of Salesperson Number 137 and Product Number 19440 is unique. Only one record in the table can have that combination of Salesperson Number and Product Number values. Therefore, if someone specifies those values,

SALESPERSON/PRODUCT table									
<u>Salesperson</u> <u>Number</u>	<u>Product</u> <u>Number</u>	Salesperson Name	Commission Percentage	Year of Hire	Department Number	Manager Name	Product Name	Unit Price	Quantity

➤ **Figure 7.29** The salesperson and product attributes in first normal form

SALESPERSON/PRODUCT table									
<u>Salesperson</u> <u>Number</u>	<u>Product</u> <u>Number</u>	Salesperson Name	Commission Percentage	Year of Hire	Department Number	Manager Name	Product Name	Unit Price	Quantity
137	19440	Baker	10	1995	73	Scott	Hammer	17.50	473
137	24013	Baker	10	1995	73	Scott	Saw	26.25	170
137	26722	Baker	10	1995	73	Scott	Pliers	11.50	688
186	16386	Adams	15	2001	59	Lopez	Wrench	12.95	1475
186	19440	Adams	15	2001	59	Lopez	Hammer	17.50	2529
186	21765	Adams	15	2001	59	Lopez	Drill	32.99	1962
186	24013	Adams	15	2001	59	Lopez	Saw	26.25	3071
204	21765	Dickens	10	1998	73	Scott	Drill	32.99	809
204	26722	Dickens	10	1998	73	Scott	Pliers	11.50	734
361	16386	Carlyle	20	2001	73	Scott	Wrench	12.95	3729
361	21765	Carlyle	20	2001	73	Scott	Drill	32.99	3110
361	26722	Carlyle	20	2001	73	Scott	Pliers	11.50	2738

➤ **Figure 7.30** The salesperson and product attributes in first normal form with sample data

the only Salesperson Name that can be associated with them is Baker, the only Commission Percentage is 10, and so forth. But that has the same effect as the concept of functional dependency. Since Salesperson Name is functionally dependent on Salesperson Number, given a particular Salesperson Number, say 137, only one Salesperson Name can be associated with it, Baker. Since Commission Percentage is functionally dependent on Salesperson Number, given a particular Salesperson Number, say 137, there can be only one Commission Percentage associated with it, 10. And so forth.

First normal form is merely a starting point in the normalization process. As can immediately be seen from Figure 7.30, first normal form contains a great deal of data redundancy. Three records involve salesperson 137 (the first three records), and so there are three places in which his name is listed as Baker, his commission percentage is listed as 10, and so on. Similarly, two records involve product 19440 (the first and fifth records), and this product's name is listed twice as Hammer and its unit price is listed twice as 17.50. Intuitively, the reason for this is that attributes of two different kinds of entities, salespersons and products, have been mixed together in one table.

Second Normal Form Since data normalization is a decomposition process, the next step will be to decompose the table of Figure 7.29 into smaller tables to eliminate some of its data redundancy. And since we have established that at least some of the redundancy is due to mixing together attributes about salespersons and attributes about products, it seems reasonable to want to separate them out at this stage. Informally, what we are going to do is to look at each of the nonkey attributes of the table in Figure 7.29 and, based on the defining associations of Figure 7.27, decide which attributes of the key are really needed to define it. For example, Salesperson Name really only needs Salesperson Number to define it; it does not need Product Number. Product Name needs only Product Number to define it; it does not need Salesperson Number. Quantity indeed needs both attributes, according to the last defining association of Figure 7.27.

More formally, second normal form, which is what we are heading for, does not allow *partial functional dependencies*. That is, in a table in second normal form, every nonkey attribute must be *fully functionally dependent* on the entire key of that table. In plain language, a nonkey attribute cannot depend on only part of the key, the way that Salesperson Name, Product Name, and most of the other nonkey attributes of Figure 7.29 do.

Figure 7.31 shows the salesperson and product attributes arranged in second normal form. There is a SALESPERSON table in which Salesperson Number is the sole primary key attribute. Every nonkey attribute of the table is fully defined just by Salesperson Number, as can be verified in Figure 7.27. Similarly, the PRODUCT table has Product Number as its sole primary key attribute, and the nonkey attributes of the table are dependent just on it. The QUANTITY table has the combination of Salesperson Number and Product Number as its primary key because its nonkey attribute, Quantity, requires both of them taken together to define it, as indicated in the last defining association of Figure 7.27.

Figure 7.32 shows the sample salesperson and product data arranged in the second normal form structure of Figure 7.31. Indeed, much of the data redundancy visible in Figure 7.30 has been eliminated. Now, only once is salesperson 137's name listed as Baker, his commission percentage listed as 10, and so forth. Only once is product 19440's name listed as Hammer, and its unit price is listed as 17.50.

Second normal form is thus a great improvement over first normal form. But has all of the redundancy been eliminated? In general, that depends on the particular list of attributes and defining associations. It is possible, and in practice it is often the case, that second normal form is completely free of data redundancy. In such a case the second normal form representation is identical to the third normal form representation.

➤ **Figure 7.31**
The salesperson and product attributes in second normal form

SALESPERSON table					
<u>Salesperson Number</u>	Salesperson Name	Commission Percentage	Year of Hire	Department Number	Manager Name

PRODUCT table		
<u>Product Number</u>	Product Name	Unit Price

QUANTITY table		
<u>Salesperson Number</u>	<u>Product Number</u>	Quantity

➤ **Figure 7.32**
The salesperson and product attributes in second normal form with sample data

SALESPERSON table					
Salesperson Number	Salesperson Name	Commission Percentage	Year of Hire	Department Number	Manager Name
137	Baker	10	1995	73	Scott
186	Adams	15	2001	59	Lopez
204	Dickens	10	1998	73	Scott
361	Carlyle	20	2001	73	Scott

PRODUCT table		
Product Number	Product Name	Unit Price
16386	Wrench	12.95
19440	Hammer	17.50
21765	Drill	32.99
24013	Saw	26.25
26722	Pliers	11.50

QUANTITY table		
Salesperson Number	Product Number	Quantity
137	19440	473
137	24013	170
137	26722	688
186	16386	1745
186	19440	2529
186	21765	1962
186	24013	3071
204	21765	809
204	26722	734
361	16386	3729
361	21765	3110
361	26722	2738

A close look at the sample data of Figure 7.32 reveals that the second normal form structure of Figure 7.31 has not eliminated all of the data redundancy. At the right-hand end of the SALESPERSON table, the fact that Scott is the manager of department 73 is repeated three times, and this certainly constitutes redundant data. How could this have happened? Aren't all of the nonkey attributes fully functionally dependent on Salesperson Number? They are, but that is not the nature of the problem. It's true that Salesperson Number defines both Department Number and Manager Name, and that's reasonable. Focusing in on a particular salesperson, I should know what department she is in and what her manager's name is. But, as indicated in the next-to-the-last defining association of Figure 7.27, one of those two attributes defines the other: given a department number, I can tell you who the manager of that department is. In the SALES-PERSON table, one of the nonkey attributes, Department Number, defines another one of the nonkey attributes, Manager Name. This is what is causing the problem.

Third Normal Form   In third normal form, nonkey attributes are not allowed to define other nonkey attributes. Stated more formally, third normal form does not allow *transitive dependencies* in which one nonkey attribute is functionally dependent on another.

Again, there is one example of this in the second normal form representation in Figure 7.31. In the SALESPERSON table, Department Number and Manager Name are both nonkey attributes, and, as shown in the next-to-the-last association in Figure 7.27, Department Number defines Manager Name. Figure 7.33 shows the third normal form representation of the attributes. Note that the SALESPERSON table of Figure 7.31 has been further decomposed into the SALESPERSON and DEPARTMENT tables of Figure 7.33. The Department Number and Department Manager attributes, which were the problem, were split off to form the DEPARTMENT table, but a copy of the Department Number attribute (the primary key attribute of the new DEPARTMENT table) was left behind in the SALESPERSON table. If this had not been done, there no longer would have been a way to indicate which department each salesperson is in.

The sample data for the third normal form structure of Figure 7.33 is shown in Figure 7.34. Now, the fact that Scott is the manager of department 73 is shown only once, in the second record of the DEPARTMENT table. Notice that the Department Number attribute in the SALESPERSON table continues to indicate which department a salesperson is in.

➤ **Figure 7.33**
The salesperson and product attributes in third normal form

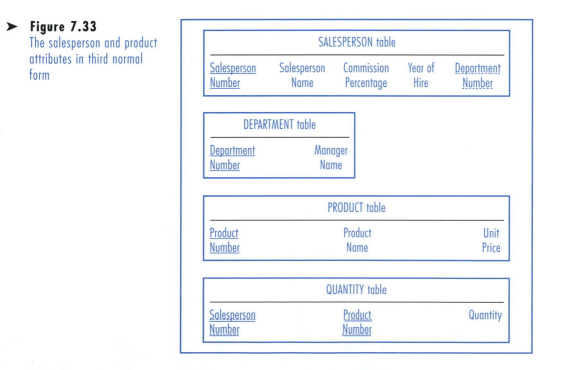

Important points about the third normal form structure of Figure 7.33 are as follows:

1. It is completely free of data redundancy.

2. All foreign keys appear where needed to logically tie together related tables.

➤ **Figure 7.34**
The salesperson and product attributes in third normal form with sample data

SALESPERSON table

Salesperson Number	Salesperson Name	Commission Percentage	Year of Hire	Department Number
137	Baker	10	1995	73
186	Adams	15	2001	59
204	Dickens	10	1998	73
361	Carlyle	20	2001	73

DEPARTMENT table

Department Number	Manager Name
59	Lopez
73	Scott

PRODUCT table

Product Number	Product Name	Unit Price
16386	Wrench	12.95
19440	Hammer	17.50
21765	Drill	32.99
24013	Saw	26.25
26722	Pliers	11.50

QUANTITY Table

Salesperson Number	Product Number	Quantity
137	19440	473
137	24013	170
137	26722	688
186	16386	1745
186	19440	2529
186	21765	1962
186	24013	3071
204	21765	809
204	26722	734
361	16386	3729
361	21765	3110
361	26722	2738

3. It is the same structure that would have been derived from a properly drawn entity-relationship diagram of the same business environment.

Finally, there is one exception to the rule that in third normal form, nonkey attributes are not allowed to define other nonkey attributes. The rule does not hold if the defining nonkey attribute is a candidate key of the table. For the sake of argument here, let's say, that the Salesperson Name attribute is unique. That makes Salesperson Name a candidate key in Figure 7.33's SALESPERSON table. But if Salesperson Name is unique, then it must define Commission Percentage, Year of Hire, and Department Number just as the unique Salesperson Number attribute does. Because it was not chosen to be the primary key of the table, Salesperson Name is technically a nonkey attribute that defines other nonkey attributes. Yet it does not appear from the sample data of Figure 7.34 to be causing any data redundancy problems. Since it was a candidate key, its defining other nonkey attributes is not a problem.

General Hardware Company Example

If the entire General Hardware Company example, including the newly added Department Number and Manager Name attributes, were to be organized for the data normalization process, the list of defining associations or functional dependencies of Figure 7.27 would be expanded to look like Figure 7.35. Several additional interesting functional dependencies in this expanded list are worth pointing out. First, although Salesperson Number is a determinant, defining several other attributes, it is in turn functionally dependent on another attribute, Customer Number:

Customer Number ⟶ Salesperson Number

➤ **Figure 7.35**
List of defining associations (functional dependencies) for the attributes of the General Hardware Company example

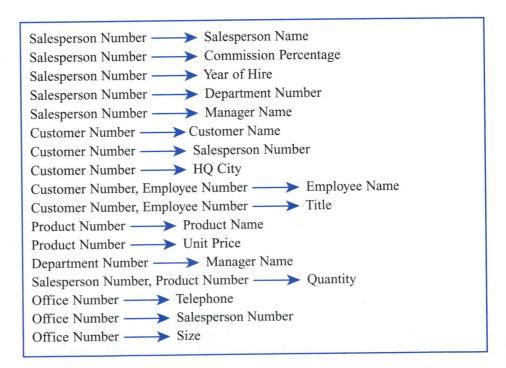

Salesperson Number ⟶ Salesperson Name
Salesperson Number ⟶ Commission Percentage
Salesperson Number ⟶ Year of Hire
Salesperson Number ⟶ Department Number
Salesperson Number ⟶ Manager Name
Customer Number ⟶ Customer Name
Customer Number ⟶ Salesperson Number
Customer Number ⟶ HQ City
Customer Number, Employee Number ⟶ Employee Name
Customer Number, Employee Number ⟶ Title
Product Number ⟶ Product Name
Product Number ⟶ Unit Price
Department Number ⟶ Manager Name
Salesperson Number, Product Number ⟶ Quantity
Office Number ⟶ Telephone
Office Number ⟶ Salesperson Number
Office Number ⟶ Size

As we have already established, this functional dependency makes perfect sense. Given a particular customer, I can tell you which salesperson is responsible for that customer. This is part of the one-to-many relationship between salespersons and customers. The fact that, in the reverse direction, for a particular salesperson there are several customers associated with him makes no difference in this functional dependency analysis. Also, the fact that Salesperson Number is itself a determinant, defining several other attributes, does not matter. Next:

$$\text{Customer Number, Employee Number} \longrightarrow \text{Employee Name}$$
$$\text{Customer Number, Employee Number} \longrightarrow \text{Title}$$

Remember that in the General Hardware business environment, employee numbers are only unique within a customer company. Thus this functional dependency correctly shows that the combination of the Customer Number and Employee Number attributes is required to define the Employee Name and Title attributes.

Figure 7.36 shows the General Hardware Company attributes, including the added Department Number and Manager Name attributes, arranged in first normal form. Moving to second normal form would produce the database structure in Figure 7.19, except that the Department Number and Manager Name attributes would be split out in moving from second to third normal form as has been previously shown.

Good Reading Bookstores Example

In the General Hardware Company example, the table representing the many-to-many relationship between salespersons and products

Salesperson Number	Product Number	Quantity

fell out so easily in the data normalization process because of the presence of the functional dependency needed to define the intersection data attribute, Quantity:

$$\text{Salesperson Number, Product Number} \longrightarrow \text{Quantity}$$

A new twist in the Good Reading Bookstores example is the presence of the many-to-many relationship between the book and author entities with no intersection data. This is shown in the WRITING table of Figure 7.21. The issue is how this can be shown in a functional dependencies list. There are a couple of possibilities. One is to show the two attributes defining "null":

$$\text{Book Number, Author Number} \longrightarrow \text{null}$$

➤ **Figure 7.36**   The General Hardware Company attributes in first normal form

The other is to show paired "multivalued dependencies" in which the attribute on the left determines a *list* of attribute values on the right, instead of the usual single-attribute value on the right. A double-headed arrow is used for this purpose:

Book Number ⟶⟶ Author Number
Author Number ⟶⟶ Book Number

These literally say that given a book number, a list of authors of the book can be produced and that, given an author number, a list of the books that an author has written or co-written can be produced. In either of the two possibilities shown, the null or the paired multivalued dependencies, the notation in the functional dependency list can be used as a signal to split the attributes off into a separate table in moving from first to second normal form.

The other interesting point in the Good Reading Bookstores example involves the many-to-many relationship of the SALE table in Figure 7.21. Recall that Date was an intersection data attribute that, because of the requirements of the company, had to be part of the primary key of the table. This would be handled very simply and naturally with a functional dependency that looks like this:

Book Number, Customer Number, Date ⟶ Quantity

The complete list of functional dependencies is shown in Figure 7.37. First normal form for the Good Reading Bookstores example would consist of the list of its attributes with the following attributes in the primary key:

Publisher Name
Author Number
Book Number
Customer Number
Date

Moving from first to second normal form, including incorporating the rule described above for the many-to-many relationship with no intersection data would directly result in the tables of Figure 7.21. As there are no situations of a nonkey attribute defining another nonkey attribute, this arrangement is already in third normal form.

World Music Association Example

The World Music Association example is straightforward in terms of data normalization. The complete list of functional dependencies is shown in Figure 7.38. Since degree is only unique within a musician, note that two of the functional dependencies are:

Musician Number, Degree ⟶ University
Musician Number, Degree ⟶ Year

The primary key attributes in first normal form are:

Orchestra Name
Musician Number
Degree
Composer Name
Composition Name
Year (recorded)

➤ **Figure 7.37**
List of defining associations (functional dependencies) for the attributes of the Good Reading Bookstores example

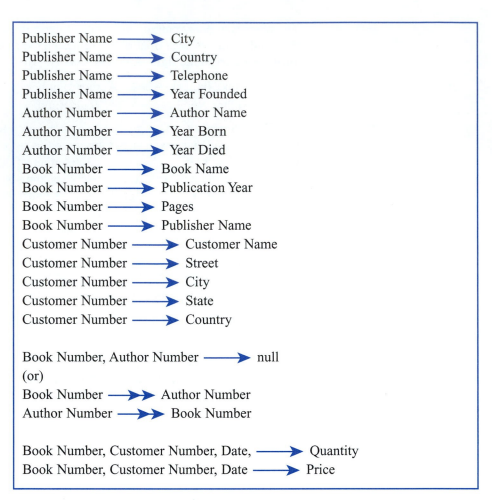

Publisher Name ⟶ City
Publisher Name ⟶ Country
Publisher Name ⟶ Telephone
Publisher Name ⟶ Year Founded
Author Number ⟶ Author Name
Author Number ⟶ Year Born
Author Number ⟶ Year Died
Book Number ⟶ Book Name
Book Number ⟶ Publication Year
Book Number ⟶ Pages
Book Number ⟶ Publisher Name
Customer Number ⟶ Customer Name
Customer Number ⟶ Street
Customer Number ⟶ City
Customer Number ⟶ State
Customer Number ⟶ Country

Book Number, Author Number ⟶ null
(or)
Book Number ⟶⟶ Author Number
Author Number ⟶⟶ Book Number

Book Number, Customer Number, Date, ⟶ Quantity
Book Number, Customer Number, Date ⟶ Price

➤ **Figure 7.38**
List of defining associations (functional dependencies) for the attributes of the World Music Association example

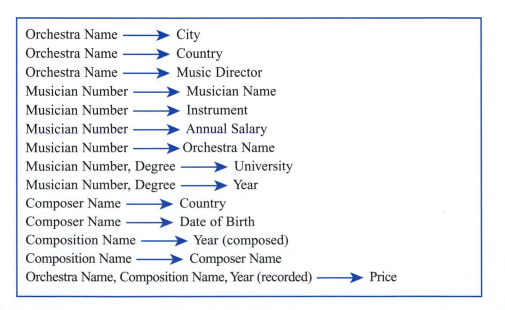

Orchestra Name ⟶ City
Orchestra Name ⟶ Country
Orchestra Name ⟶ Music Director
Musician Number ⟶ Musician Name
Musician Number ⟶ Instrument
Musician Number ⟶ Annual Salary
Musician Number ⟶ Orchestra Name
Musician Number, Degree ⟶ University
Musician Number, Degree ⟶ Year
Composer Name ⟶ Country
Composer Name ⟶ Date of Birth
Composition Name ⟶ Year (composed)
Composition Name ⟶ Composer Name
Orchestra Name, Composition Name, Year (recorded) ⟶ Price

With this in mind, proceeding from first to second normal form will produce the tables in Figure 7.23. These are free of data redundancy and are, indeed, also in third normal form.

Lucky Rent-A-Car Example

Figure 7.39 lists the Lucky Rent-A-Car functional dependencies.

The primary key attributes in first normal form are:

Manufacturer Name

Car Serial Number

Repair Number

Customer Number

Rental Date

Once again, in this case, the conversion from first to second normal form results in a redundancy-free structure (Figure 7.25), which is already in third normal form.

TESTING TABLES CONVERTED FROM E-R DIAGRAMS WITH DATA NORMALIZATION

As we said earlier, logical database design is generally performed today by converting entity-relationship diagrams to relational tables and then checking those tables with the data normalization technique rules. Since we already know that the databases, shown in Figures 7.19, 7.21, 7.23, and 7.25, for the four example business environments we've been working with are in third normal form, there really

➤ **Figure 7.39**
List of defining associations (functional dependencies) for the attributes of the Lucky Rent-A-Car example

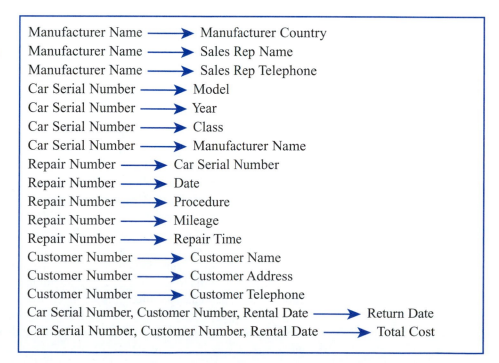

Manufacturer Name ⟶ Manufacturer Country
Manufacturer Name ⟶ Sales Rep Name
Manufacturer Name ⟶ Sales Rep Telephone
Car Serial Number ⟶ Model
Car Serial Number ⟶ Year
Car Serial Number ⟶ Class
Car Serial Number ⟶ Manufacturer Name
Repair Number ⟶ Car Serial Number
Repair Number ⟶ Date
Repair Number ⟶ Procedure
Repair Number ⟶ Mileage
Repair Number ⟶ Repair Time
Customer Number ⟶ Customer Name
Customer Number ⟶ Customer Address
Customer Number ⟶ Customer Telephone
Car Serial Number, Customer Number, Rental Date ⟶ Return Date
Car Serial Number, Customer Number, Rental Date ⟶ Total Cost

isn't much to check. As one example, consider the General Hardware Company database of Figure 7.19.

The basic idea in checking the structural worthiness of relational tables with the data normalization rules is to:

1. Check to see if there are any partial functional dependencies. That is to say, check to see if any nonkey attributes are dependent on or are defined by only part of the table's primary key.
2. Check to see if there are any transitive dependencies. That is to say, check to see if any nonkey attributes are dependent on or are defined by any other nonkey attributes (other than candidate keys).

Both of these can be verified by the business environment's list of defining associations or functional dependencies.

In the SALESPERSON table of Figure 7.19, there is only one attribute, Salesperson Number, in the primary key. Therefore there cannot be any partial functional dependencies. By their very definition, partial functional dependencies require the presence of more than one attribute in the primary key so that a nonkey attribute can be dependent on *only part of the key*! As for transitive dependencies, are any nonkey attributes determined by any other nonkey attributes? No! And even if Salesperson Name is assumed to be a unique attribute and therefore it defines Commission Percentage and Year of Hire, this would be an allowable exception because Salesperson Name, being unique, would be a candidate key. The same analysis can be made for the other General Hardware tables with single-attribute primary keys: the CUSTOMER, PRODUCT, and OFFICE tables of Figure 7.19.

Figure 7.19's CUSTOMER EMPLOYEE table has a two-attribute primary key because Employee Number is only unique within a customer. But then, by the very same logic, the nonkey attributes, Employee Name and Title *must* be dependent on the *entire* key because that is the only way to uniquely identify who we are talking about when we want to know a person's name or title. Analyzing this further, we find that Employee Name cannot be dependent on Employee Number alone because it is not a unique attribute. Functional dependency requires uniqueness from the determining side. And obviously, Employee Name cannot be dependent on Customer Number alone. A customer company has lots of employees, not just one. Therefore Employee Name and Title must be dependent on the entire primary key, and the rule about no partial functional dependencies is satisfied. Since the nonkey attributes, Employee Name and Title, do not define each other, the rule about no transitive dependencies is also satisfied, and thus the table is clearly in third normal form.

In the SALES table of Figure 7.19, there is a two-attribute primary key and only one nonkey attribute. This table exists to represent the many-to-many relationship between salespersons and products. The nonkey attributes, just Quantity in this case, constitute intersection data. *By the definition of intersection data,* these nonkey attributes *must* be dependent on the entire primary key. In any case, there would be a line in the functional dependency list indicating that Quantity is dependent on the combination of the two key attributes. Thus, this table has no partial functional dependencies. Interestingly, since there is only one nonkey attribute, transitive dependencies cannot exist. After all, a table must have at least two nonkey attributes for one nonkey attribute to be dependent on another.

KEY TERMS

Data normalization   First normal form   Second normal form
Entity-relationship diagram conversion   Logical database design   Third normal form

QUESTIONS

1. What is logical database design?
2. What is physical database design and how does it relate to logical database design?
3. In general terms, describe the main logical database design techniques and how they relate to each other.
4. Based on an entity-relationship diagram, how can you determine how many tables there will be in the corresponding relational database?
5. Describe the process for converting entities in each of the following relationships into relational database structures:
   a. One-to-one binary relationship
   b. One-to-many binary relationship
   c. Many-to-many binary relationship
   d. One-to-one unary relationship
   e. Onc-to-many unary rclationship
   f. Many-to-many unary relationship
   g. Ternary relationship
6. Describe the data normalization process, including its specific steps. Why is it referred to as a decomposition process?

7. Explain the following terms:
   a. Functional dependency
   b. Determinant
8. What characterizes unnormalized data? Why is such data problematic?
9. What characterizes tables in first normal form? Why is such data problematic?
10. What is a partial functional dependency? What does the term fully functionally dependent mean?
11. What is the rule for converting tables in first normal form to tables in second normal form?
12. What is the definition of data in second normal form?
13. What is a transitive dependency?
14. What is the rule for converting tables in second normal form to tables in third normal form?
15. What is the definition of data in third normal form?
16. What are the characteristics of data in third normal form?
17. How can data normalization be used to check the results of the E-R diagram-to-relational database conversion process?

EXERCISES

1. Convert the Video Centers of Europe, Ltd., entity-relationship diagram in Exercise 3.2 into a well-structured relational database.
2. Convert the following Central Hospital entity-relationship diagram into a well-structured relational database. (See figure at top of next page.)
3. Video Centers of Europe, Ltd., is a chain of movie DVD rental stores. It must maintain data on the DVDs that it has for rent, the movies that are recorded on the DVDs, its customers, and the actual rentals. Each DVD for rent has a unique serial number. Movie titles and customer numbers are also unique identifiers. Assume that each movie has exactly one "star." Note the difference in the year that the movie was originally filmed as opposed to the date that a DVD—an actual disk—was manufactured.

Some of the attributes and functional dependencies in this environment are as follows:

Attributes

DVD Number
Manufacture Date
Movie Title
Star
Year Filmed
Length [in minutes]
Customer Number
Customer Name
Customer Address
Rental Date
Return Date
Fee Paid

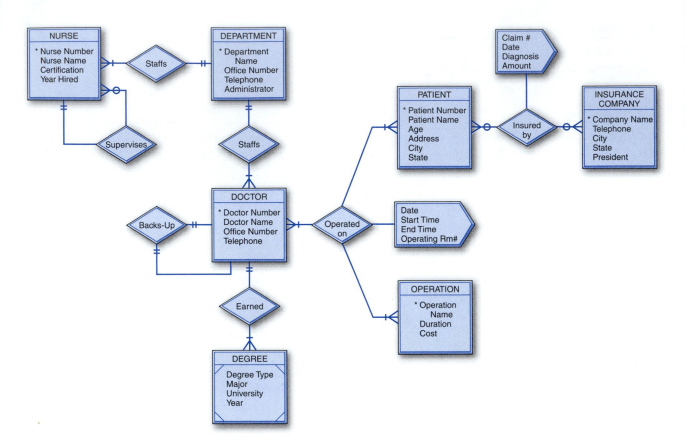

Functional Dependencies

DVD Number ⟶ Movie Title

DVD Number ⟶ Star

DVD Number ⟶ Manufacture Date

Movie Title ⟶ Star

Movie Title ⟶ Length

Movie Title ⟶ Year Filmed

Customer Number ⟶ Customer Name

Customer Number ⟶ Customer Address

DVD Number, Customer Number,
    Rental Date ⟶ Return Date, Fee Paid

For each of the following tables, first write the table's current normal form (as 1NF, 2NF, or 3NF). Then, for those tables that are currently in 1NF or 2NF, reconstruct them as well-structured 3NF tables. Primary key attributes are underlined. Do not assume any functional dependencies other than those shown.

a. <u>Movie Title,</u> Star, Length, Year Filmed.

b. <u>DVD Number, Customer Number, Rental Date,</u> Customer Name, Return Date, Fee Paid.

c. <u>DVD Number,</u> Manufacture Date, Movie Title, Star.

d. <u>Movie Title, Customer Number,</u> Star, Length, Customer Name, Customer Address.

e. <u>DVD Number, Customer Number, Rental Date,</u> Return Date, Fee Paid.

4. The U.S. government wants to keep track of information about states, governors, cities, and mayors. In addition, it wants to maintain data on the various federal agencies and the annual grants that each agency gives to the individual states. Each federal agency is headed by an administrator. Agency names and state names are unique, but city names are only unique within a state. The attributes and functional dependencies in this environment are as follows:

Attributes

State
Governor ID Number
Governor Name
State Flower
City
Mayor ID Number
Mayor Name
City Hall Address
Mayor Telephone
Federal Agency
Administrator
Annual Grant

Functional Dependencies

State  Governor ID Number
State ⟶ Governor Name
State ⟶ State Flower
State, City ⟶ Mayor ID Number
State, City ⟶ Mayor Name
State, City ⟶ City Hall Address

State, City ⟶ Mayor Telephone
Mayor ID Number ⟶ Mayor Name
Mayor ID Number ⟶ Mayor Telephone
Federal Agency ⟶ Administrator
State, City, Federal Agency ⟶ Annual Grant

For each of the following tables, first write the table's current normal form (as 1NF, 2NF, or 3NF). Then, for those tables that are currently in 1NF or 2NF, reconstruct them as well-structured 3NF tables. Primary key attributes are underlined. Do not assume any functional dependencies other than those shown.

a. <u>State, City</u>, Governor Name, Mayor ID Number, Mayor Name, Mayor Telephone.

b. <u>State, City</u>, Mayor Name, Mayor Telephone.

c. <u>State, City, Federal Agency</u>, Governor Name, Administrator, Annual Grant.

d. <u>State, City</u>, Governor Name, State Flower, Mayor Telephone.

e. <u>State, City</u>, City Hall Address, Mayor ID Number, Mayor Name, Mayor Telephone.

MINICASES

1. *Happy Cruise Lines.* Convert the following Happy Cruise Lines entity-relationship diagram into a well-structured relational database. (See figure at top of next page.)

2. *Super Baseball League.* The Super Baseball League wants to keep track of information about its players, its teams, and the minor league teams (which we will call minor league "clubs" to avoid using the word "team" twice). Minor league clubs are not part of the Super Baseball League, but players train in them with the hope of eventually advancing to a team in the Super Baseball League. The intent in this problem is to keep track only of the current team on which a player plays in the Super Baseball League. However, the minor league club data must be historic and include all of the minor league clubs for which a player has played. Team names, minor league club names, manager names, and stadium names are assumed to be unique, as, of course, is player number.

   Design a well-structured relational database for this Super Baseball League environment using the data

normalization technique. Progress from first to second normal form and then from second to third normal form, justifying your design decisions at each step based on the rules of data normalization. The attributes and functional dependencies in this environment are as follows:

Attributes

Player Number
Player Name
Player Age
Team Name
Manager Name
Stadium Name
Minor League Club Name
Minor League Club City
Minor League Club Owner
Minor League Club Year Founded
Start Date
End Date
Batting Average

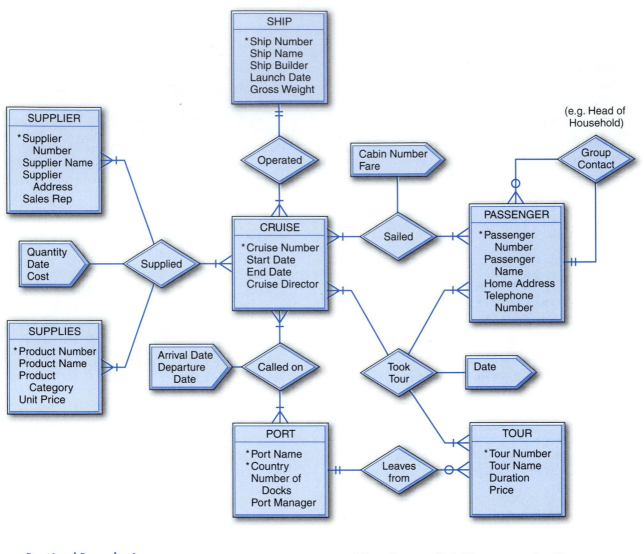

(e.g. Head of Household)

Functional Dependencies

Player Number ——→ Player Name

Player Number ——→ Age

Player Number ——→ Team Name

Player Number ——→ Manager Name

Player Number ——→ Stadium Name

Minor League Club Name ——→ City

Minor League Club Name ——→ Owner

Minor League Club Name ——→ Year Founded

Team Name ——→ Manager Name

Team Name ——→ Stadium Name

Player Number, Minor League Club Name

    ——→ Start Date, End Date, Batting Average

CHAPTER 8

PHYSICAL DATABASE DESIGN

CHAPTER OBJECTIVES

After learning the material in this chapter, you will be able to:
- ✔ Describe the concept of physical database design.
- ✔ List and describe the inputs to the physical database design process.
- ✔ Perform physical database design and improve database performance using a variety of techniques ranging from adding indexes to denormalization.

Photo Courtesy of Ducks Unlimited

DUCKS UNLIMITED

Ducks Unlimited ("DU") is the world's largest wetlands conservation organization. It was founded in 1937 when sportsmen realized that they were seeing fewer ducks on their migratory paths and the cause was found to be the destruction of their wetlands breeding areas. Today, with programs reaching from the arctic tundra of Alaska to the tropical wetlands of Mexico, DU is dedicated, in priority order, to preserving existing wetlands, rebuilding former wetlands, and building new wetlands. DU is a non-profit organization headquartered in Memphis, Tennessee, with regional offices located in the four major North American duck "flyways." DU also works with its affiliated organizations in Canada and Mexico to deliver their mutual conservation mission. DU has 600 employees, over 70,000 volunteers, 756,000 paid members, and over one million total contributors. Currently its annual income exceeds $140 million.

In 1999, Ducks Unlimited introduced a major relational database application that it calls its Conservation System, or "Conserv" for short. Located at its Memphis headquarters, Conserv is a project tracking system that manages both the operational and financial aspects of DU's wetlands conservation projects. In terms of operations, Conserv tracks the phases of each project and the subcontractors performing the work. As for finances, Conserv coordinates the charge-back of subcontractor fees to the "cooperators" (generally federal agencies, landowners, or large contributors) who sponsor the projects.

Conserv is based on the Oracle DBMS and runs on COMPAQ servers. The database has several main tables, including the Project table and the Agreement (with cooperators) table, each of which has several sub-tables. DU employees query the database with Oracle Discoverer to check on how much money has been spent on a project and how much of the expenses have been recovered from the cooperators, as two examples. Each night, Conserv sends data to and receives data from a separate relational database running on an IBM AS/400 system which handles membership data, donor history, and accounting functions such as invoicing and accounts payable. Conserv data can even be sent to a Geographic Information System (GIS) which displays the projects on maps.

Printed by permission of Ducks Unlimited

If computers ran at infinitely fast speeds and data stored on disks could be found and brought into primary memory for processing literally instantly, then logical database design would be the only kind of database design to talk about. Well-structured, redundancy-free third normal form tables are the ideal relational database structures and in a world of infinite speeds would be practical, too. But as fast as computers have become, their speeds are certainly not infinite and the time it takes to find data stored on disks and bring it into primary memory for processing is a crucial issue in whether an application runs as fast as needed. For example, if you telephone your insurance company to ask about a claim that you filed and it takes two minutes for the customer service agent to find the relevant records in the company's information system, you might well become frustrated with the company and question its ability to handle your business competently. Data storage, retrieval, and processing speeds do matter. Regardless of how elegant an application and the database structures it uses are, if the application runs so slowly that it is unacceptable to the business environment, it will be a failure.

Database performance can be adversely affected by a wide variety of factors, as shown in Figure 8.1. Some factors are a result of application requirements, and often the most obvious culprit is the need for joins. Joins are an elegant solution to the need for data integration, but they can be unacceptably slow in many cases. Also, the need to calculate and retrieve the same totals of numeric data over and over again can be a problem in terms of performance. Another factor is the very large data **volume.** Data is the lifeblood of an information system, but when there is a lot of it, care must be taken to store and retrieve it efficiently to maintain acceptable performance. Certain factors involving the structure of the data, such as

➤ **Figure 8.1**

Factors affecting application and database performance

> **Factors Affecting Application and Database Performance**
> - Application Factors
>   - Need for Joins
>   - Need to Calculate Totals
> - Data Factors
>   - Large Data Volumes
> - Database Structure Factors
>   - Lack of Direct Access
>   - Clumsy Primary Keys
> - Data Storage Factors
>   - Related Data Dispersed on Disk
> - Business Environment Factors
>   - Too Many Data Access Operations
>   - Overly Liberal Data Access

the amount of direct access provided and the presence of clumsy, multi-attribute primary keys, can certainly affect performance. If related data in different tables that has to be retrieved together is physically dispersed on the disk, retrieval performance will be slower than if the data is stored physically close together on the disk. Finally, the business environment often presents significant performance challenges. We want data to be shared and to be widely used for the benefit of the business. But a very large number of access operations to the same data can cause a bottleneck that can ruin the performance of an application environment. And giving people access to more data than they need to see can be a security risk.

Physical database design is the process of modifying a database structure to improve the performance of the run-time environment. That is, we are going to modify the third normal form tables produced by the logical database design techniques to make the applications that will use them run faster. A variety of modifications can be made, ranging from simply adding indexes to making major changes to the table structures. Some of the changes, while making some applications run faster, may make other applications that share the data run slower. Some of the changes may even compromise the principle of avoiding data redundancy! We will investigate and explain a number of physical database design techniques in this chapter, pointing out the advantages and disadvantages of each.

INPUTS TO PHYSICAL DATABASE DESIGN

Physical database design starts where logical database design ends. That is, the well-structured relational tables produced by the conversion from entity-relationship diagrams or by the data normalization process form the starting point for physical database design. But these tables are only part of the story. In order to determine how best to modify the tables to improve application performance, a wide range of factors must be considered. The factors will help determine which modification techniques to apply and how to apply them. And, at that, the process is as much art as science. The choices are so numerous and the possible combinations of modifications are so complex that even an experienced designer hopes for a satisfactory but not a perfect solution.

Figure 8.2 lists the inputs to physical database design and thus the factors that are important to it. These inputs naturally fall into several subgroups. First, we will take a look at each of these physical design inputs and factors, one-by-one. Then we will describe a variety of physical database design techniques, explaining how the various inputs and factors influence each technique.

The Tables Produced by the Logical Database Design Process

The tables produced by the logical database design process (which for simplicity we will now refer to as the logical design) form the starting point of the physical database design process. These tables are "pure" in that they reflect all of the data in the business environment, they have no data redundancy, and they have all of the foreign keys in place that are needed to establish all of the relationships in the business environment. Unfortunately, they may present a variety of problems when it comes to performance, as we previously described. Again, for example, without indexes or hashing, there is no support for direct access. Or it is entirely possible that a particular query may require the join of several tables, which may cause an unacceptably slow response from the database. Clearly then, these tables, in their current form, are very likely to be unacceptable from a performance point of view, and that is why we must modify them in physical database design.

➤ **Figure 8.2**
Inputs into the physical database design process

Inputs Into the Physical Database Design Process
- The Tables Produced by the Logical Database Design Process
- Business Environment Requirements
  - Response Time Requirements
  - Throughput Requirements
- Data Characteristics
  - Data Volume Assessment
  - Data Volatility
- Application Characteristics
  - Application Data Requirements
  - Application Priorities
- Operational Requirements
  - Data Security Concerns
  - Backup and Recovery Concerns
- Hardware and Software Characteristics
  - DBMS Characteristics
  - Hardware Characteristics

Business Environment Requirements

Beyond the logical design, the requirements of the business environment lead the list of inputs and factors for the physical database design. These include response time requirements and throughput requirements.

Response Time Requirements **Response time** is the delay from the time that the Enter Key is pressed to execute a query until the result appears on the screen. One of the main factors in deciding how extensively to modify the logical design is establishing what the response time requirements are. Do the major applications that will use the database require two-second response, five-second response, ten-second response, and so on? That is, how much of a delay will a customer telephoning your customer service representatives tolerate when asking a question about her account? How fast a response do the managers in your company expect when looking for information about a customer or the sales results for a particular store or the progress of goods on an assembly line? In addition, different types of applications differ dramatically in response time requirements. Operational environments, including the customer service example, tend to require very fast response. Decision support environments, such as the data warehouse environment that we will discuss later in this book, tend to have relaxed response time requirements.

Throughput Requirements **Throughput** is the measure of how many queries from simultaneous users must be satisfied in a given period of time by the application set and the database that supports it. Clearly, throughput and response time are linked together. The more people who want access to the same data at the same time, the more pressure there is for the system to keep the response time from dropping to an unacceptable level. And the more potential pressure on response time, the more important the physical design task becomes.

Data Characteristics

How much data will be stored in the database and how frequently different parts of it will be updated are important considerations in physical design as well.

Data Volume Assessment How much data will be in the database? Roughly how many records is each table expected to have? Some physical design decisions will hinge on whether a table is expected to have 300 or 30,000 or 3 million records.

Data Volatility **Data volatility** refers to how often stored data is updated. Some data, such as active inventory records that reflect the changes in goods constantly being put into and taken out of inventory, is updated frequently. Some data, such as historic sales records, is never updated (except for data from the latest time period being added to the end of the table). How frequently data is updated, the volatility of the data, is an important factor in making certain physical design decisions.

Application Characteristics

The nature of the applications that will use the data, which applications are the most important to the company, and which data will be accessed by each application form yet another set of inputs and factors in physical design.

Application Data Requirements Exactly which database tables does each application require for its processing? Do the applications require that tables be joined? How many applications and which specific applications will share particular database tables? Are the applications that use a particular table run frequently or infrequently? Questions such as these serve as one indication of how much demand there will be for access to each table and its data. More heavily used tables and tables frequently involved in joins require particular attention in the physical design process.

Application Priorities Typically, tables in a database will be shared by different applications. Sometimes, a modification to a table proposed during physical design that's designed to help the performance of one application hinders the performance of another application. When such a conflict arises, it's important to know which of the two applications is the more critical to the company. Sometimes this can be determined on an increased profit or cost-saving basis. Sometimes it can be based on which application's sponsor has greater political power in the company. But whatever the basis, it is important to note the relative priority of the company's applications for physical design choice considerations.

Operational Requirements: Data Security, Backup and Recovery

Certain physical design decisions can depend on such data management issues as data security and backup and recovery. Data security, which will be discussed later in this book, can include such concerns as protecting data from theft or malicious destruction and making sure that sensitive data is accessible only to those employees of the company who have a "need to know." Backup and recovery, which will also be discussed later, ranges from being able to recover a table or a database that has been corrupted or lost due to hardware or software failure to the recovery of an entire information system after a natural disaster. Sometimes, data security and backup and recovery concerns can affect physical design decisions.

Hardware and Software Characteristics

Finally, the hardware and software environment in which the databases will reside have an important bearing on physical design.

DBMS Characteristics All relational database management systems are similar in that they support the basic, even classic at this point, relational model. However, relational DBMSs may differ in certain details, such as the exact nature of their indexes, attribute data type options, and SQL query features, which must be known and taken into account during physical database design.

Hardware Characteristics Certain hardware characteristics, such as processor speeds and disk data transfer rates, though not directly parts of the physical database design process, are associated with it. Simply put, the faster the hardware, the more tolerant the system can be of a physical design that avoids relatively severe changes in the logical design.

PHYSICAL DATABASE DESIGN TECHNIQUES

Figure 8.3 lists several physical database design categories and techniques within each. The order of the categories is significant. Depending on how we modify the logical design to try to make performance improvements, we may wind up introducing new complications or even reintroducing data redundancy. Also, as noted in Figure 8.3, the first three categories do not change the logical design, whereas the last four categories do. So, the order of the categories is roughly from least to most disruptive of the original logical design. In this spirit, the only techniques that introduce data redundancy (storing **derived data, denormalization,** duplicating tables, and adding **subset tables**) appear at the latter part of the list.

> **Figure 8.3**
> Physical database design
> categories and techniques

Physical design categories and techniques that DO NOT change the logical design
- Adding External Features
  - Adding Indexes
  - Adding Views
- Reorganizing Stored Data
  - Clustering Files
- Splitting a Table into Multiple Tables
  - Horizontal Partitioning
  - Vertical Partitioning
  - Splitting-Off Large Text Attributes

Physical design categories and techniques that DO change the logical design
- Changing Attributes in a Table
  - Substituting Foreign Keys
- Adding Attributes to a Table
  - Creating New Primary Keys
  - Storing Derived Data
- Combining Tables
  - Combine Tables in One-to-One Relationships
  - Alternatives for Repeating Groups
  - Denormalization
- Adding New Tables
  - Duplicating Tables
  - Adding Subset Tables

Adding External Features

This first category of physical design changes, adding external features, doesn't change the logical design at all! Instead, it involves adding features to the logical design, specifically indexes and views. Although certain tradeoffs have to be kept in mind when adding these external features, there is no introduction of data redundancy.

Adding Indexes   If the name of the game is performance and since today's business environment is addicted to finding data on a direct access basis, then the use of indexes in relational database is a natural. There are two questions to consider.

The first question, is which attributes or combinations of attributes should you consider indexing in order to have the greatest positive impact on the application environment? Actually, there are two categories of possibilities. One category is attributes that are likely to be prominent in direct searches. These include:

- Primary keys.
- **Search attributes,** that is, attributes whose values you will use to retrieve particular records. This is true especially when the attribute can take on many different values. (In fact, some argue that it is not beneficial to build an index on an attribute that has only a small number of possible values.)

The other category is attributes that are likely to be major players in operations such as joins that will require direct searches internally. Such operations also include the SQL ORDER BY and GROUP BY commands that we will look at in the next chapter. It should be clear that a particular attribute might fall into both of these categories!

The second question is, what potential problems can be caused by building too many indexes? If it were not for the fact that building too many indexes can cause problems in certain kinds of databases, the temptation would be to build a large number of indexes for maximum direct access benefit. The issue here is the volatility of the data. Indexes are wonderful for direct searches. But when the data in a table is updated, the system must take the time to update the table's indexes, too. It will do this automatically, but it takes time. If several indexes must be updated, this multiplies the time it takes to update the table several times over. What's wrong with that? If there is a lot of update activity, the time that it takes to make the updates *and to update all of the indexes* could slow down the operations that are just trying to read the data for query applications, degrading query response time down to an unacceptable level!

One final point about building indexes: If the data volume, the number of records in a table, is very small, then there is no point in building any indexes on it at all (although some DBMSs will always require an index on the primary key). The point is that if the table is small enough, it is more efficient to just read the whole table into main memory and search by scanning it!

Figure 8.4 repeats the General Hardware Company relational database, to which we will add some indexes. We start by building indexes, marked indexes A–F, on the primary key attribute(s) of each table. Consider the SALESPERSON and CUSTOMER tables. If the application set requires joins of the SALESPERSON and CUSTOMER tables, the Salesperson Number attribute of the CUSTOMER table would be a good choice for an index, index G, because it is the foreign key that connects those two tables in the join. If we need to frequently find salesperson records on a direct basis by Salesperson *Name*, then that attribute should have an index, index H, built on it. Consider the SALES table. If we have an important, frequently run application that has to find the total sales for all or a range of the products, then the needed GROUP BY command would run more efficiently if the Product Number attribute was indexed as index I.

➤ **Figure 8.4**
The General Hardware
Company relational data-
base with some indexes

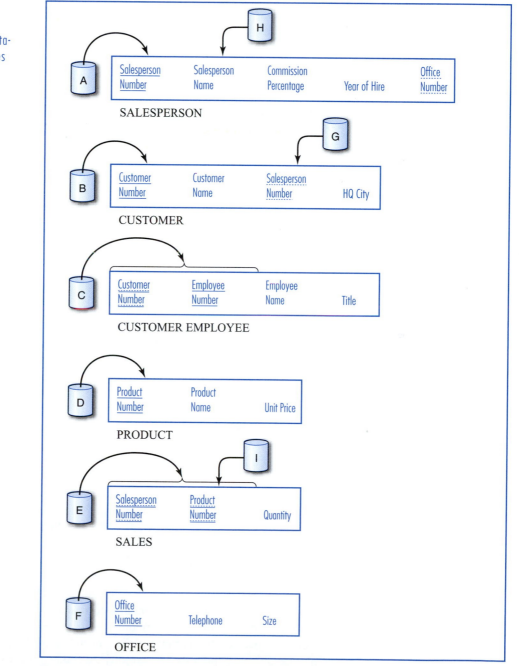

Adding Views Another external feature that doesn't change the logical design is the view. In a relational database, a **view** is what is more generally known in database management terms as a **logical view.** It is a mapping onto a physical table that allows an end-user to access only part of the table. The view can include a subset of the table's columns, a subset of the table's rows, or a combination of the two. It can even be based on the join of two tables. *No data is physically duplicated when a view is created.* It is literally a way of viewing just part of a table. For example, in the General Hardware Company SALESPERSON table, a view can be created that includes only the Salesperson Number, Salesperson Name, and Office Number attributes. A particular person can be given access to the view and then only sees these three columns. He is not even aware of the existence of the other two attributes of the physical table.

A view is an important device in protecting the security and privacy of data, an issue that we listed among the factors in physical database design. Using views to limit the access of individuals to only the parts of a table that they really need to do their work is an important means of protecting the company's data. As we will see later in this book, the combination of the view capability and the SQL GRANT command forms a powerful data protection tool.

Reorganizing Stored Data

The next level of change in physical design involves reorganizing the way data is stored on the disk without changing the logical design at all and thus without introducing data redundancy. We present one example of this type of modification.

Clustering Files Suppose that in the General Hardware Company business environment it is important to be able to frequently and quickly retrieve all of the data in a salesperson record together with all of the records of the customers for which that salesperson is responsible. Clearly, this would require a join of the SALESPERSON and CUSTOMER tables. Just for the sake of argument let's assume that this retrieval, including the join, does not work fast enough to satisfy the response time or throughput requirements. One solution, assuming that the DBMS in use supports it, might be the use of **clustered files.**

Figure 8.5 shows the General Hardware salesperson and customer data from Figure 5.14 arranged as clustered files. The logical design has not changed. Logically, the DBMS considers the SALESPERSON and CUSTOMER tables just as they appear in Figure 5.14. But physically, they have been arranged on the disk in the interleaved fashion shown in Figure 8.5. Each salesperson record is followed, physically on the disk, by the customer records with which it is associated. That is, each salesperson record is followed on the disk by the records of the customers for whom that salesperson is responsible. For example, the salesperson record for salesperson 137, Baker, is followed on the disk by the customer records for customers 0121, 0933, 1047, and 1826. Note that the foreign key value salesperson number 137 appears as a foreign key in each of those four customer records. So, if a query is posed to find a salesperson record, say Baker's record, and all of his associated customer records, performance will be improved because all five of the records are near each other on the disk, even though logically they come from two separate tables. Without the clustered files, Baker's record would be on one part of

the disk with all of the other salesperson records, and the four customer records would be on another part of the disk with the other customer records, resulting in slower retrieval for this kind of two-table, integrated query.

The downside of this clustering arrangement is that retrieving subsets of *only* salesperson records or *only* customer records is slower than without clustering. Without clustering, all of the salesperson records are near each other on the disk, which helps when retrieving subsets of them. With clustering, the salesperson records are scattered over a much larger area on the disk because they're interspersed with all of those customer records, making the retrieval of subsets of just salesperson records slower.

Splitting a Table into Multiple Tables

The three physical design techniques in this category arrange for particular parts of a table, either groups of particular rows or groups of particular columns, to be stored separately, on different areas of a disk or on different disks. Later in the book, when we discuss distributed database, we will see that this concept can even be extended to storing particular parts of a table in different cities.

Horizontal Partitioning In **horizontal partitioning,** the rows of a table are divided into groups, and the groups are stored separately on different areas of a disk or on different disks. This may be done for several reasons. One is to manage the different groups of records separately for security or backup and recovery purposes. Another is to improve data retrieval performance when, for example, one group of records is accessed much more frequently than the rest of the records in the table. Consider, for example, the need for accessing the records for sales managers in the CUSTOMER EMPLOYEE table of Figure 5.14c more frequently than the records of other customer employees. Separating out the frequently accessed group of records, as shown in Figure 8.6, means that they can be stored near each other in a concentrated space on the disk, which will speed up their retrieval. The records can also be stored on an otherwise infrequently used disk, so that the applications that use them don't have to compete excessively with other applications that need data on the same disk. The downside of horizontal partitioning is that a search of the entire table or the retrieval of records from more than one partition can be more complex and slower.

Vertical Partitioning   A table can also be subdivided by columns, producing the same advantages as horizontal partitioning. In this case, the separate groups, each made up of different columns of a table, are created because different users or applications require different columns. For example, as shown in Figure 8.7, it might be beneficial to split up the columns of the SALESPERSON table of Figure 5.14a, so that the Salesperson Name and Year of Hire columns are stored separately from the others. But note that in creating these vertical partitions, *each partition must have a copy of the primary key*, Salesperson Number in this example. Otherwise, in **vertical partitioning,** how would you be able to keep track of which rows in each partition go together to logically form the rows of the original table? In fact, this point leads to an understanding of the downside of vertical partitioning. A query that involves the retrieval of complete records, that is, data that is in more than one vertical partition, actually requires that the vertical partitions be *joined* to reunite the different parts of the original records.

Splitting Off Large Text Attributes   A variation on vertical partitioning involves splitting off large **text attributes** into separate partitions. Sometimes the records of a table have several numeric attributes and a long text attribute that provides a description of the data in each record. It might well be that frequent access of the numeric data is necessary and that the long text attribute is only accessed occasionally. The problem is that the presence of the long text attribute tends to spread the numeric data over a larger disk area and thus slows down retrieval of the

➤ **Figure 8.6**
Horizontal partitioning of the CUSTOMER EMPLOYEE table

Customer Number	Employee Number	Employee Name	Title
0933	30441	Levy	Sales Manager
1525	33779	Baker	Sales Manager

Customer Number	Employee Number	Employee Name	Title
0121	27498	Smith	Co-Owner
0121	30441	Garcia	Co-Owner
0933	25270	Chen	VP Sales
0933	48285	Morton	President
2198	27470	Smith	President
2198	30441	Jones	VP Sales
2198	33779	Garcia	VP Personnel
2198	35268	Kaplan	Senior Accountant

> **Figure 8.7**
> Vertical partitioning of the
> SALESPERSON table

Salesperson Number	Salesperson Name	Year of Hire
137	Baker	1995
186	Adams	2001
204	Dickens	1998
361	Carlyle	2001

Salesperson Number	Commission Percentage
137	10
186	15
204	10
361	20

numeric data. The solution is to split off the text attribute, *together with a copy of the primary key*, into a separate vertical partition and store it elsewhere on the disk.

Changing Attributes in a Table

Up to this point, none of the physical design techniques discussed has changed the logical design. They have all involved adding external features such as indexes and views, or physically moving records or columns on the disk as with clustering and partitioning.

The first physical design technique category that changes the logical design involves substituting a different attribute for a foreign key.

Substituting Foreign Keys   Consider the SALESPERSON and CUSTOMER tables of Figure 8.4. We know that Salesperson Number is a unique attribute and serves as the primary key of the SALESPERSON table. Say, for the sake of argument, that the Salesperson Name attribute is also unique, meaning that both Salesperson Number and Salesperson Name are candidate keys of the SALESPERSON table. Salesperson Number has been chosen to be the primary key, and Salesperson Name is an alternate key.

Now, assume that there is a frequent need to retrieve data about customers, including the *name* of the salesperson who is responsible for that customer. The CUSTOMER table contains the *number* of the Salesperson who is responsible for a customer but not the name. By now, we know that solving this problem requires a join of the two tables, based on the common Salesperson Number attribute. But if this is a frequent or critical query that requires high speed, we can improve the performance by *substituting* Salesperson Name for Salesperson Number as the foreign key in the CUSTOMER table, as shown in Figure 8.8. With Salesperson Name now contained in the CUSTOMER table, we can retrieve customer data, including the *name* of the responsible salesperson, *without having to do a performance-slowing join*. Finally, since Salesperson Name is a candidate key of the SALESPERSON table, using it as a foreign key in the CUSTOMER table still assures the ability to join the two tables when this is required for other queries.

➤ **Figure 8.8**
Substituting another candidate key for a foreign key

CUSTOMER			
Customer Number	Customer Name	Salesperson *Name*	HQ City

Adding Attributes to a Table

Another means of improving database performance entails modifying the logical design by adding attributes to tables. Here are two ways to do this.

Creating New Primary Keys   Sometimes a table simply does not have a single, unique attribute that can serve as its primary key. A two-attribute primary key, such as the combination of state and city names, might be okay. But there are circumstances in which the primary key of a table might consist of two, three, or more attributes and the performance implications of this may well be unacceptable. For one thing, indexing a multi-attribute key would likely be clumsy and slow. For another, having to use the multi-attribute key as a foreign key in the other tables in which such a foreign key would be necessary would probably also be unacceptably complex.

The solution is to invent a new, primary key for the table that consists of a single, new attribute. The new attribute will be a unique, serial number attribute, with an arbitrary unique value assigned to each record of the table. This new attribute will then also be used as the foreign key in the other tables in which such a foreign key is required. In the General Hardware database of Figure 8.4, recall that the two-attribute primary key of the CUSTOMER EMPLOYEE table, Customer Number and Employee Number, is necessary because customer numbers are only unique within each customer company. Suppose that General Hardware decides to invent a new attribute, Customer Employee Number, which will be its own set of employee numbers for these people that will be *unique across all of the customer companies*. Then, the current two-attribute primary key of the CUSTOMER EMPLOYEE table can be replaced by this one, new attribute, as shown in Figure 8.9. If the Customer Number, Employee Number combination had been placed in other tables in the database as a foreign key (it wasn't), then the two-attribute combination would be replaced by this new, single attribute, too. Notice that Customer Number is still necessary as a foreign key because that's how we know which customer company a person works for. Arguably, the old Employee Number attribute may still be required because that is still their employer's internal identifier for them.

Storing Derived Data   Some queries require that calculations be performed on the data in the database and that the calculated values be returned as the answers. If these same values have to be calculated over and over again, perhaps by one person

➤ **Figure 8.9**
Creating a new primary key attribute to replace a multi-attribute primary key

CUSTOMER EMPLOYEE				
Customer Employee Number	Customer Number	Employee Number	Employee Name	Title

or perhaps by many people, then it might make sense to calculate them once and store them in the database. Technically, this is a form of data redundancy, though a rather subtle form. If the "raw" data is ever updated without the stored, calculated values being updated as well, the accuracy or integrity of the database will be compromised.

To illustrate this point, let's add another attribute to General Hardware's CUSTOMER table. This attribute, called Annual Purchases in Figure 8.10a, is the expected amount of merchandise, in dollars, that a customer will purchase from General Hardware in a year. Remember that there is a one-to-many relationship from salespersons to customers, with each salesperson being responsible for several (or many) customers. Suppose that there is a frequent need to quickly find the total amount of merchandise each *salesperson* is expected to account for in a year, that is, the sum of the Annual Purchases attribute for all of the particular salesperson's customers. This sum could be recalculated each time it is requested for any particular salesperson, but that might take too much time. The other choice is to calculate the sum for each salesperson and store it in the database, recognizing that whenever a customer's Annual Purchases value changes, the sum for the customer's salesperson has to be updated, too.

The question then becomes, where do we store the summed annual purchases amount for each salesperson? Since the annual purchases figures are in the CUSTOMER table, your instinct might be to store the sums there. But where in the CUSTOMER table? You can't store them in individual customer records because each sum involves *several* customers. You could insert special "sum records" in the CUSTOMER table, but they wouldn't have the same attributes as the customer records themselves and that would be very troublesome. Actually, the answer is to store them in the SALESPERSON table. Why? Because there is one sum for each salesperson—again, it's the sum of the annual purchases of all of that salesperson's customers. So, the way to do it is to add an additional attribute, the Total Annual Customer Purchases attribute, to the SALESPERSON table, as shown in Figure 8.10b.

Figure 8.10
Adding derived data

CUSTOMER

<u>Customer Number</u>	Customer Name	<u>Salesperson Number</u>	HQ City	Annual Purchases

a. Annual Purchases attribute added to the CUSTOMER table.

SALESPERSON

<u>Salesperson Number</u>	Salesperson Name	Commission Percentage	Year of Hire	<u>Office Number</u>	Total Annual Customer Purchases

---

CUSTOMER

<u>Customer Number</u>	Customer Name	<u>Salesperson Number</u>	HQ City	Annual Purchases

b. Total Annual Customer Purchases attribute added to the SALESPERSON table as derived data.

Combining Tables

Three techniques are described below, all of which involve combining two tables into one. Each technique is used in a different set of circumstances. It should be clear that all three share the same advantage: if two tables are combined into one, then there must surely be situations in which the presence of the new single table allows us to avoid joins that would have been necessary when there were two tables. Avoiding joins is generally a plus for performance. But, at what price? Let's see.

Combination of Tables in One-to-One Relationships   Remember the one-to-one relationship between salespersons and offices in the General Hardware environment? Figure 8.11 shows the two tables combined into one. After all, if a salesperson can have only one office and an office can have only one salesperson assigned to it, there can be nothing wrong with combining the two tables. Since a salesperson can have only one office, a salesperson can be associated with only one office number, one (office) telephone, and one (office) size. A like argument can be made from the perspective of an office. Office data can still be accessed on a direct basis by simply creating an index on the Office Number attribute in the combined table.

Again, the advantage is that if we ever have to retrieve detailed data about a salesperson *and* his office in one query, it can now be done without a join. There are three negatives. One is that the tables are no longer logically as well as physically independent. If we want information just about offices, there is no longer an OFFICE table to go to. The data is still there, but we have to be aware that it is buried in the SALESPERSON/OFFICE table. Two, is that retrievals of salesperson data *alone* or of office data *alone* could be slower than before because the longer combined SALESPERSON/OFFICE records spread the combined data over a larger area of the disk. Three, as previously described, is that the storage of data about unoccupied offices is problematic and may require a reevaluation of which field should be the primary key.

Alternatives for Repeating Groups   Suppose that we change the business environment so that every salesperson has exactly two customers, identified respectively as their "large" customer and their "small" customer, based on annual purchases. The structure of Figure 8.4 would still work just fine. But because these **repeating groups** of customer attributes, one "group" of attributes (Customer Number, Customer Name, etc.) for each customer, are so well controlled, they can be folded into the SALESPERSON table. What makes them so well controlled is that there are exactly two for each salesperson and they can even be distinguished from each other as "large" and "small." This arrangement is shown in Figure 8.12. Note that the foreign key attribute of Salesperson Number from the CUSTOMER table is no longer needed.

➤ **Figure 8.11**
Combined SALESPERSON/
OFFICE table showing the
merger of two tables in a
one-to-one relationship

SALESPERSON/OFFICE						
Salesperson Number	Salesperson Name	Commission Percentage	Year of Hire	Office Number	Telephone	Size

SALESPERSON/CUSTOMERS										
Salesperson Number	Salesperson Name	Commission Percentage	Year of Hire	Office Number	Large Customer Number	Large Customer Name	Large Customer HQ City	Small Customer Number	Small Customer Name	Small Customer HQ City

➤ **Figure 8.12**   *Merging of repeating groups into another table*

Once again, this arrangement avoids joins when salesperson and customer data must be retrieved together. But as with the preceding one-to-one relationship case, retrievals of salesperson data *alone* or of customer data *alone* could be slower than before because the longer combined SALESPERSON/CUSTOMER records spread the combined data over a larger area of the disk. And retrieving customer data alone is now more difficult. In the one-to-one relationship case, we could simply create an index on the Office Number attribute of the combined table. In the combined table of Figure 8.12, however, there are *two* customer number attributes in each salesperson record. Retrieving records about customers alone would clearly take a greater amount of skill than before.

Denormalization   In the most serious of database performance dilemmas, when everything else that can be done in terms of physical design has been done, it may be necessary to take pairs of related, third normal form tables and to combine them, introducing possibly massive data redundancy. Why would anyone in his right mind want to do this? Because if after everything else has been done to improve performance, response times and throughput are still unsatisfactory for the business environment, eliminating run-time joins by recombining tables may mean the difference between a usable system and a lot of wasted money on a database (and application) development project that will never see the light of day. Clearly, if the physical designers decide to go this route, they must put procedures in place to manage the redundant data as updates are made to the data over time.

Figure 8.13 shows the denormalized SALESPERSON and CUSTOMER tables combined into one. The surviving table of the two in the one-to-many relationship will always be the table on the "many side" of the relationship. You can attach one set of salesperson data to a customer record; you cannot attach many sets of customer data to a single salesperson record without creating an even worse mess. The sample salesperson and customer data from Figure 5.14 is denormalized in Figure 8.14. (Figure 8.14 is identical to Figure 4.6. We used it earlier in the book to make a point about data redundancy when we were exploring that subject.) Since a salesperson can have several customers, a particular salesperson's data will be repeated for each customer he has. Thus the table shows that salesperson number 137's name is Baker *four times*, his commission percentage is 10 *four times*, and his year of hire

CUSTOMER							
Customer Number	Customer Name	Salesperson Number	HQ City	Salesperson Number	Salesperson Name	Commission Percentage	Year of Hire

➤ **Figure 8.13**   *The denormalized SALESPERSON and CUSTOMER tables as the new CUSTOMER table*

CUSTOMER							
Customer Number	Customer Name	Salesperson Number	HQ City	Salesperson Number	Salesperson Name	Commission Percentage	Year of Hire
0121	Main St. Hardware	137	New York	137	Baker	10	1995
0839	Jane's Stores	186	Chicago	186	Adams	15	2001
0933	ABC Home Stores	137	Los Angeles	137	Baker	10	1995
1047	Acme Hardware Store	137	Los Angeles	137	Baker	10	1995
1525	Fred's Tool Stores	361	Atlanta	361	Carlyle	20	2001
1700	XYZ Stores	361	Washington	361	Carlyle	20	2001
1826	City Hardware	137	New York	137	Baker	10	1995
2198	Western Hardware	204	New York	204	Dickens	10	1998
2267	Central Stores	186	New York	186	Adams	15	2001

➤ **Figure 8.14** The denormalized salesperson and customer data from Figure 5.12

was 1995 *four times*. The performance improvement better have been worth it because the integrity exposure is definitely there.

Adding New Tables

Finally, there is the concept of simply duplicating data. Occasionally, trying to maintain response time and throughput with the number of applications and users trying to share the same data may be beyond the capabilities of the hardware, software, and all of the other physical design techniques. At the risk of overt data redundancy (which hopefully will be managed), the only recourse is to duplicate the data.

Duplicating Tables   The direct approach is to duplicate tables and have different applications access the duplicates. This is exactly the opposite of the central database management concept of sharing data.

Adding Subset Tables   A somewhat less severe technique is to duplicate only those portions of a table that are most heavily accessed. These subset tables can then be assigned to different applications to ease the performance crunch. Data redundancy is still the major drawback, although obviously there is not as much of it as when the entire table is duplicated.

EXAMPLE: GOOD READING BOOKSTORES

Consider the Good Reading Bookstores database of Figure 5.16. Recall that there is a one-to-many relationship between the PUBLISHER and BOOK tables. A book is published by exactly one publisher, but a publisher publishes many books. That's why the Publisher Name attribute is in the BOOK table as a foreign key. A reasonable assumption is that there are several hundred publishers and many thousands of different books. If the various stores in the Good Reading chain carry different books to satisfy their individual clienteles, then there could be thousands of publishers and hundreds of thousands of different books.

Assume that Good Reading's headquarters frequently needs to quickly find the details of a book, based on either its book number or its title, together with details about its publisher. As stated, this would clearly require a join of the PUBLISHER and BOOK tables. If the join takes too long, resulting in unacceptable response times, throughput, or both, what are the possibilities in terms of physical design that can improve the situation? Here are several suggestions, although each has its potential drawbacks, as previously discussed.

- The Book Number attribute and the Book Title attributes in the PUBLISHER table can each have an index built on them to provide direct access, since the problem says that books are going to be searched for based on one of these two attributes.
- The two join attributes—the Publisher Name attribute of the PUBLISHER table and the Publisher Name attribute of the BOOK table—can each have an index built on them to help speed up the join operation.
- If the DBMS permits it, the two tables can be clustered, with the book records associated with a particular publisher stored near that publisher's record on the disk.
- The two tables can be denormalized, with the appropriate publisher data being appended to each book record (and the PUBLISHER table being eliminated), as:

Book Number	Book Title	Publication Year	Pages	Publisher Name	City	Country	Telephone	Year Founded

What if it was important to be able to quickly find the *number of different books* that Good Reading carries from a particular publisher? This information could be found by using the SQL COUNT function to count the number of that publisher's books when the query is asked. However, if this proves to be too slow, as it well might be, then the number of books from each publisher can be calculated and stored as an additional attribute of derived data in the PUBLISHER table, as:

Publisher Name	City	Country	Telephone	Year Founded	Number of Books

EXAMPLE: WORLD MUSIC ASSOCIATION

Consider the World Music Association (WMA) relational database of Figure 5.17. WMA has a problem in that there is a much larger number of retrieval requests for information about recordings by Beethoven and Mozart than for recordings by other composers. Since those records are scattered throughout the RECORDING table, performance tends to be slower than desired. A solution is to horizontally divide the RECORDING table into two partitions, one with the records for recordings by Beethoven and Mozart and the other with all of the other records of the table. These two partitions can be stored on different parts of the same disk or on different disks. Performance will be improved with the Beethoven and Mozart records separated out and concentrated together on a restricted disk area.

There is an application need to frequently and quickly retrieve salary data for the musicians on an individual and group basis. In the MUSICIAN table, the salary data is mixed in with other data (potentially much more data in each record than is shown in this example), which tends to slow down retrieval speeds. A solution is to create a vertical partition for the Annual Salary attribute, separating it from the rest of the attributes of the table. Remember that a copy of the primary key, in this case Musician Number, must accompany the nonkey attribute(s) being split off into a separate vertical partition. Thus one vertical partition will consist of the Musician Number and Annual Salary attributes, while the other will consist of Musician Number and all of the nonkey attributes except for the Annual Salary attribute. Storing these two vertical partitions on different parts of a disk or on different disks will enhance performance under the described application circumstances.

Assume that the COMPOSITION table has an additional attribute called "Description":

Composition Name	Composer Name	Year	Description

Description is a long, text attribute that allows written descriptions of compositions to be stored in the database. Although this is certainly useful, WMA has several applications that require frequent, fast access to the other attributes of the table. The bulky description data tends to spread the records over a wider area of the disk than would otherwise be the case. Again, this is really a special case of the vertical partitioning scenario. The solution is to break off the description data, together with a copy of the primary key, and store it elsewhere on the disk or on a different disk.

The next example involves the MUSICIAN table, and for this example we want to assume that the Musician Name attribute is unique. That means that now both Musician Number and Musician Name are candidate keys of the table and Musician Number has been chosen to be the primary key. It seems that there is an important application that requires the fast and frequent retrieval of musician names together with their college degree data but without their musician numbers. As currently structured, this would clearly require repeated joins of the MUSICIAN and DEGREE tables, which might cause unacceptable performance problems. Since the Musician *Name* attribute is unique and is a candidate key of the MUSICIAN table, a solution to this problem is to replace the Musician Number foreign key attribute in the DEGREE table with Musician Name:

Musician *Name*	Degree	University	Year

With Musician Name already in the DEGREE table, the retrieval situation described does not require a join. Moreover, the DEGREE table is still able to uniquely tie degrees to musicians, since Musician Name is unique.

Another possible solution to the more general problem of retrieving both detailed data about musicians *and* their degrees at the same time involves the concept of repeating groups. We know that there is a one-to-many relationship between musicians and degrees since a musician can have several degrees, but a degree is associated with only one musician. Suppose we assume that a musician can have at most three degrees. We can then eliminate the DEGREE table entirely by merging its data into the MUSICIAN table:

Musician Number	Musician Name	Instrument	Annual Salary	Orchestra Name	Degree #1	University #1	Year #1	Degree #2	University #2	Year #2	Degree #3	University #3	Year #3

This is possible because of the small, fixed maximum number of degrees and because of the ability to distinguish among them, in this case in a time sequence based on when they were awarded or by level, as bachelor's degree first, master's degree second. In this case, there will be null attribute values since not every musician has three degrees. Furthermore, there may be more programmer involvement since inserting new degree data or even retrieving degree data may require more informed and careful operations. But it certainly eliminates the join between the MUSICIAN table and the now defunct DEGREE table, which may be the modification necessary for acceptable performance.

EXAMPLE: LUCKY RENT-A-CAR

Consider the Lucky Rent-A-Car database of Figure 5.18. One issue with this company is the privacy of its customers' data. Some of its employees may need to access the entire CUSTOMER table, while others may need, for example, customer number and customer name data but not the more personal data, such as customer address and customer telephone. A restriction to accomplish this can be set up using views. One view can be created that includes the entire table; another can be created that includes only the Customer Number and Customer Name attributes. Using these two views in the SQL GRANT command, which we will discuss later in the book, different employees or groups of employees can be given full access to the CUSTOMER table or restricted access to only part of it.

The RENTAL table represents the many-to-many relationship between cars and customers, recording who rented which car on a particular date. The primary key is thus Car Serial Number, Customer Number, and Rental Date. Recall that Rental Date must be part of the primary key because a particular customer could have rented a particular car on more than one occasion. This three-attribute primary key is clumsy. An index built on it would be long and clumsy, and if it had to be used as a foreign key in another table, that would be clumsy, too. A solution is to add a new Rental Number attribute that will serve as a unique key of the table:

Rental Number	Car Serial Number	Customer Number	Rental Date	Return Date	Total Cost

Next, assume that the following table, which has data about the president of each manufacturer, has been added to the database.

Manufacturer Name	President Name	President Address	President Telephone	President E-mail

Since each company has exactly one president, there is a one-to-one relationship between manufacturers, represented by the existing MANUFACTURER table, and presidents, represented by the new PRESIDENT table. As is usually the case with such situations, it makes sense to have the two different entities represented in two different tables. However, if we ever need to retrieve both detailed manufacturer data and detailed president data, we will have to execute a join. If we have to do this frequently and with significant speed, it may make sense to combine the two tables together:

Manufacturer Name	Manufacturer Country	Sales Rep Name	Sales Rep Telephone	President Name	President Address	President Telephone	President E-mail

After all, since a company has only one president, it also has only one president name, one president address, and so forth. This arrangement results in a bulkier table that will be spread out over a larger disk area than either table alone, possibly slowing down certain retrievals. But it will avoid the join needed to retrieve manufacturer and president detailed data together.

Finally, here are examples of the physical design technique of adding new tables. Lucky Rent-A-Car's CAR table is accessed very frequently—so frequently, in fact, that it has become a performance bottleneck. The company has decided to duplicate the table and put each of the two copies on different disk devices so that some applications can access one disk and other applications the other disk. This will improve throughput. However, these two duplicate tables must be kept identical at all times and when any changes are made to them, the changes must be made to both copies simultaneously. Notice that while the CAR table may have to be read frequently for Lucky's rental operations, it only has to be updated when new cars are added to Lucky's inventory or existing cars are taken out of inventory. This makes the duplicate table technique practical because frequent changes that require the updating of both tables simultaneously would slow down the entire environment significantly.

In the CUSTOMER table, some large corporate customers' records are accessed much more frequently than the rest of the customer records. To help ease this performance bottleneck and to gather these customer records together in one disk area to further enhance performance, a subset table of *copies* of just these records can be created and stored elsewhere on the disk or on a different disk. Again, the issue of simultaneous updates of the duplicate data must be considered. Note the difference between creating a subset table and creating a horizontal partition. In the case of subset tables, a copy of the records is left behind in the original table; in the case of horizontal partitioning, no copy is left behind.

KEY TERMS

Clustered files	Horizontal partitioning	Search attribute
Data volatility	Logical view	Subset tables
Data volume	Performance	Text attribute
Database performance	Physical database design	Throughput
Denormalization	Repeating groups	Vertical partitioning
Derived data	Response time	View

QUESTIONS

1. What is physical database design?

2. Describe why physical database design is necessary.

3. Explain why the need to perform joins is an important factor affecting application and database performance.

4. Why does the degree to which data is dispersed over a disk affect application and database performance?

5. Explain why the volume of data access operations can adversely affect application and database performance.

6. Which "input" is the starting point for physical database design.

7. Describe how response time requirements and throughput requirements determine the overall performance level of the application and database environment.

8. Describe the characteristics of the data in the database that must be considered as inputs to the physical database design process. Why are they important?

9. Describe the characteristics of the applications that must be considered as inputs to the physical database design process. Why are they important?

10. Why do DBMS and hardware characteristics have to be taken into account in the physical design process?

11. Explain the statement, "Some physical database design techniques do and some do not change the logical design."

12. What attributes should be considered as candidates for having indexes built on them? What is the potential problem with building too many indexes?

13. What is a view? Which factors affecting application and database performance can be dealt with using views? Explain.

14. Describe the clustering files technique. What advantage is gained by using it? What is its disadvantage?

15. What is the difference between horizontal and vertical partitioning? What is their common advantage? Are their disadvantages different or the same? Explain.

16. Describe the physical design technique of substituting foreign keys. Under what circumstances would you use it?

17. Under what circumstances would you want to create a new, single-attribute primary key in a table? What would it accomplish?

18. Under what circumstances would you want to store derived data in a table? What would it accomplish?

19. Combining tables that are in a one-to-one relationship, combining tables involving well-controlled repeating groups, and denormalization all lead to the same performance advantage. What is it? Why is it important?

20. What is denormalization? Denormalization, while improving performance under certain circumstances, also leads to a serious problem. How does denormalization improve performance, and what is this major drawback?

21. Duplicating entire tables or parts of tables (subset tables) obviously introduces data redundancy. What is the advantage of doing this? Do you think it's worth the introduction of redundancy? Explain.

EXERCISES

1. Consider the following relational database that Best Airlines uses to keep track of its mechanics, their skills, and their airport locations. Mechanic number, airport name, and skill number are all unique fields. Size is an airport's size in acres. Skill Category is a skill's category, such as an engine skill, wing skill, or tire skill. Year Qualified is the year that a mechanic first qualified in a particular skill; Proficiency Rating is the mechanic's proficiency rating in a particular skill.

MECHANIC table				
Mechanic Number	Mechanic Name	Telephone	Salary	Airport Name

AIRPORT table				
Airport Name	City	State	Size	Year Opened

.SKILL table		
Skill Number	Skill Category	Skill

QUALIFICATION table			
Mechanic Number	Skill Number	Year Qualified	Proficiency Rating

Analyze each of the following situations and, using the physical database design techniques discussed in this chapter, state how you would modify the logical design shown to improve performance or otherwise accommodate it.

a. There is a high-priority need to quickly find any particular airport's data given only the airport's city and state.

b. There is a frequent need to find the total salary of all of the mechanics at any particular airport.

c. There is a high-priority need to quickly find any particular mechanic's data together with the data about the airport at which she works.

d. There is a frequent need to get a list of the names and telephone numbers of the mechanics who work at any particular airport, together with the airport's city and state.

e. Assume that there is an additional attribute called Skill Description in the SKILL table. This attribute is used to store lengthy descriptions of each skill. The problem is that its presence in the SKILL table is slowing down access to the rest of the data in the table, which is accessed much more frequently.

f. The need to access data about the ten largest airports in the country is much more frequent than the need to access data about the rest of the airports.

2. Consider the following relational database for the Quality Appliance Manufacturing Company. The

database is designed to track the major appliances (refrigerators, washing machines, dishwashers, etc.) that Quality manufactures. It also records information about Quality's suppliers, the parts they supply, the buyers of the finished appliances, and the finished goods inspectors. Note the following facts about this environment:

- Suppliers are the companies that supply Quality with its major components, such as electric motors, for the appliances. Supplier number is a unique identifier.

- Parts are the major components that the suppliers supply to Quality. Each part comes with a part number, but that part number is only unique within a supplier. Thus, from Quality's point of view, the unique identifier of a part is the combination of part number and supplier number.

- Each appliance that Quality manufactures is given an appliance number that is unique across all of the types of appliances that Quality makes.

- Buyers are major department stores, home improvement chains, and wholesalers. Buyer numbers are unique.

- An appliance may be inspected by several inspectors. There is a many-to-many relationship between appliances and inspectors.

- There are one-to-many relationships between suppliers and parts (Supplier Number is a foreign key in the PART table), parts and appliances (Appliance Number is a foreign key in the PART table), and appliances and buyers (Buyer Number is a foreign key in the APPLIANCE table).

SUPPLIER table

Supplier Number	Supplier Name	City	Country	Telephone

PART table

Part Number	Supplier Number	Part Type	Cost	Appliance Number

APPLIANCE table

Appliance Number	Appliance Type	Date of Manufacture	Buyer Number	Price

BUYER table

Buyer Number	Buyer Name	City	Country	Credit Rating

INSPECTOR table

Inspector Number	Inspector Name	Salary	Date of Hire

INSPECTION table

Appliance Number	Inspector Number	Date of Inspection	Score

Analyze each of the following situations and, using the physical database design techniques discussed in this chapter, state how you would modify the logical design shown to improve performance or otherwise accommodate it.

a. The Appliance Type attribute in the APPLIANCE table indicates whether an appliance is a refrigerator, washing machine, or the like. Refrigerator records are accessed much more frequently than the records of the other appliance types, and there are strict response time requirements for accessing them.

b. There is a frequent and very high-priority need to quickly retrieve detailed data about an appliance together with detailed data about the buyer who bought it.

c. Because of the large number of people trying to access the PART table and the fast response time needed, the PART table has become a bottleneck and the required response time is not being achieved.

d. Assume that the Buyer Name attribute in the BUYER table is unique. There is a high-priority need to quickly retrieve the following data about appliances: appliance number, appliance type, date of manufacture, and buyer *name*.

e. In the APPLIANCE table, there is a much more frequent need with strict response time requirements for accessing the price data (of course, together with the appliance number) than for accessing the rest of the data in the table.

MINICASES

1. Consider the following relational database for Happy Cruise Lines. It keeps track of ships, cruises, ports, and passengers. A "cruise" is a particular sailing of a ship on a particular date. For example, the seven-day journey of the ship *Pride of Tampa* that leaves on June 13, 2003, is a cruise. Note the following facts about this environment.

   - Both ship number and ship name are unique in the SHIP Table.
   - A ship goes on many cruises over time. A cruise is associated with a single ship.
   - A port is identified by the combination of port name and country.
   - As indicated by the VISIT table, a cruise includes visits to several ports, and a port is typically included in several cruises.
   - Both Passenger Number and Social Security Number are unique in the PASSENGER table. A particular person has a single Passenger Number that is used for all of the cruises that she takes.
   - The VOYAGE table indicates that a person can take many cruises, and a cruise, of course, has many passengers.

SHIP table				
Ship Number	Ship Name	Ship Builder	Launch Date	Gross Weight

CRUISE table				
Cruise Number	Start Date	End Date	Cruise Director	Ship Number

PORT table			
Port Name	Country	Number of Docks	Port Manager

VISIT table				
Cruise Number	Port Name	Country	Arrival Date	Departure Date

PASSENGER table				
Passenger Number	Passenger Name	Social Security Number	Home Address	Telephone Number

VOYAGE table			
Passenger Number	Cruise Number	Stateroom Number	Fare

Analyze each of the following situations and, using the physical database design techniques discussed in this chapter, state how you would modify the logical design shown to improve performance or otherwise accommodate it.

a. There is a need to list cruises by cruise number, but there is also a need to periodically list all of the cruises in order by start date.

b. There is a frequent need to quickly retrieve the data about a cruise together with the data about the ship that is used on the cruise.

c. There is a frequent need to quickly retrieve cruise data based on departure date.

d. Data about passengers from California must be accessed quickly and much more frequently than data about passengers from anywhere else.

e. There is a frequent need to quickly retrieve a list of the port managers of the ports at which the ship on any particular cruise will stop.

f. There is a frequent need to quickly find the total number of passengers who were on any particular cruise.

g. There is a frequent need to find the start and end dates of cruises as quickly as possible.

h. There is a frequent need to find cruise data based on ship *name. Hint:* The Ship Name attribute is unique.

2. Consider the following relational database for the Super Baseball League. It keeps track of teams in the league, coaches and players on the teams, work experience of the coaches, bats belonging to each team, and which players have played on which teams. Note the following facts about this environment:

   - The database keeps track of the history of all the teams that each player has played on and all the players who have played on each team.

- The database only keeps track of a coach's current team.
- Team number, team name, and player number are each unique attributes across the league.
- Coach name is only unique within a team (and we assume that a team cannot have two coaches of the same name).
- Serial number (for bats) is only unique within a team.
- In the Affiliation table, the years attribute indicates the number of years that a player played on a team; the batting average is for the years that a player played on a team.

TEAM table			
Team Number	Team Name	City	Manager

COACH table		
Team Number	Coach Name	Coach Telephone

WORK EXPERIENCE table			
Team Number	Coach Name	Experience Type	Years of Experience

BATS table		
Team Number	Serial Number	Manufacturer

PLAYER table		
Player Number	Player Name	Age

AFFILIATION table			
Player Number	Team Number	Years	Batting Average

Analyze each of the following situations and, using the physical database design techniques discussed in this chapter, state how you would modify the logical design shown to improve performance or otherwise accommodate it.

a. There is a frequent need to quickly find the total number of years that any particular player has played in the league (i.e., the total number of years played for all the teams a player played for).

b. There is a need to retrieve AFFILIATION table records directly based on batting averages.

c. The three-attribute primary key of the WORK EXPERIENCE table has been found to be cumbersome to use in queries and awkward to index.

d. There is a frequent and very high-priority need to quickly retrieve player name and age data together with the teams (identified by team number) they have played on, the number of years they played on the teams, and the batting averages they compiled.

e. Assume that we add the following Stadium table to the Super Baseball League relational database. Each team has one home stadium, which is what is represented in this table. Assume that a stadium can serve as the home stadium for only one team. Stadium name is unique across the league.

STADIUM table			
Stadium Name	Year Built	Size	Team Number

There is a frequent and high-priority need to quickly retrieve detailed team and stadium data together.

CHAPTER 9

RELATIONAL DATA RETRIEVAL: SQL

CHAPTER OBJECTIVES

After learning the material in this chapter, you will be able to:
- ✔ Describe SQL as a relational data manipulation language.
- ✔ Explain that you can create and update relational tables using SQL.
- ✔ Write SQL SELECT commands to retrieve relational data using a variety of operators, including GROUP BY, ORDER BY, and the built-in functions of AVG, SUM, MAX, MIN, and COUNT.
- ✔ Write SQL SELECT commands that join relational tables.
- ✔ Write SQL SELECT subqueries.
- ✔ Describe a strategy for writing SQL SELECT statements.
- ✔ Describe the principles of how a relational query optimizer works.

Photo Courtesy of Advance Auto Parts

ADVANCE AUTO PARTS

Advance Auto Parts is the second largest retailer of automotive parts and accessories in the United States. The company was founded in 1932 with three stores in Roanoke, Virginia, where it is still headquartered today. In the 1980s, with fewer than 175 stores, the company developed an expansion plan that brought it to over 350 stores by the end of 1993. It has rapidly accelerated its expansion since then and, with mergers and acquisitions, now has more than 2,400 stores and over 32,000 employees throughout the United States. Advance Auto Parts sells over 250,000 automotive components. Its innovative "Parts Delivered Quickly" (PDQ) system, which was introduced in 1982, allows its customers access to this inventory within 24 hours.

One of Advance Auto Parts' key database applications, its Electronic Parts Catalog, gives the company an important competitive advantage. Introduced in the early 1990s and continually upgraded since then, this system allows store personnel to look-up products they sell based on the customer's vehicle type. The system's records include part descriptions, images, and drawings. Once identified, store personnel pull an item from the store's shelves if it's in stock. If it's not in stock, then using the system they send out a real-time request for the part to the home office to check on the part's warehouse availability. Within minutes the part is picked at a regional warehouse and it's on its way. In addition to its use in the stores, the system is used by the company's purchasing and other departments.

The system runs on an IBM mid-range system at the company's headquarters and is built on the SQL Server DBMS. Parts catalog data, in the form of updates, is downloaded weekly from this system to a small server located in each store. Additional data retrieval at headquarters is accomplished with SQL. The 35-table database includes a Parts table with 2.5 million rows that accounts not only for all of the items in inventory but for different brands of the same item. There is also a Vehicle table with 31,000 records. These two lead to a 45 million record Parts Application table that describes which parts can be used in which vehicles.

Printed by permission of Advance Auto Parts

There are two aspects of data management: data definition and data manipulation. *Data definition,* which is operationalized with a **data definition language (DDL),** involves instructing the DBMS software on what tables will be in the database, what attributes will be in the tables, which attributes will be indexed, and so forth. *Data manipulation* refers to the four basic operations that can and must be performed on data stored in any DBMS or in any other data storage arrangement for that matter: data retrieval, data update, insertion of new records, and deletion of existing records. Data manipulation requires a special language with which users can communicate data manipulation commands to the DBMS. As a class, these are known as **data manipulation languages (DML).**

A standard language for data management in relational databases, known as **Structured Query Language (SQL),** was developed in the early 1980s. SQL incorporates both DDL and DML features. It was derived from an early IBM Corporation research project in relational database called System R. SQL has long since been declared a standard by the American National Standards Institute (ANSI) and by the International Standards Organization (ISO). Indeed, several versions of the standards have been issued over the years. Using the standards, many manufacturers have produced versions of SQL, which are all quite similar, at least at the level at which we will look at it in this book. These SQL versions are found in such mainstream DBMSs as DB2, Oracle, MS Access, Informix, and others.

SQL in its various implementations is used very heavily in practice today by companies and organizations of every description, Advance Auto Parts being one of countless examples.

SQL COMMANDS

SQL is a comprehensive database management language. The most interesting aspect of SQL and the aspect that is the most appropriate to study in an introduction to database management is its rich data retrieval capability. But before we go on to explore the SQL data retrieval command, which is called **SELECT,** we will take a brief look at some of the other SQL commands.

Building the Data Structure

First, in order to have a database to talk about, you have to be able to instruct the DBMS to create some **base tables.** These are the actual physical tables in which the data will be stored on the disk. The command that creates tables and tells the system what attributes will be in the tables is called the CREATE TABLE command. Using the CREATE TABLE command, you can also specify which attributes are primary and foreign keys and which attributes are unique. In addition, you can specify referential integrity constraints. If a table in the database is to be discarded, the command is the DROP TABLE command.

Another important feature of a relational database is its indexes. You build indexes with the CREATE INDEX command, which allows you to specify on which attribute(s) of which table an index is being built. You discard indexes with the DROP INDEX command.

A *logical view,* sometimes just called a view, is derived from one or more base tables. A view may consist of a subset of the columns of a single table, a subset of the rows of a single table, or both. It can also be the join of two or more base tables. The creation of a view in SQL does *not* entail the physical duplication of data in a base table into a new table. Instead, the view is a mapping onto the base table(s). It's literally a "view" of some part of the physical, stored data. Views are built using the CREATE VIEW command. Within this command, you specify the base table(s) on which the view is to be based and the attributes and rows of the table(s) that are to be included in the view. Interestingly, these specifications are made within the CREATE VIEW command using the SELECT statement, which we will discuss shortly in the context of data retrieval. Views can be discarded using the DROP VIEW command.

Data Manipulation Operations

Once the tables have been created, the focus changes to the standard data manipulation operations (besides data retrieval) of updating existing data, inserting new rows in tables, and deleting existing rows in tables. The commands are, respectively **UPDATE, INSERT,** and **DELETE.** In the UPDATE command, you have to identify which row(s) of a table are to be updated based on data values within those rows. Then you have to specify which columns are to be updated and what the new data values of those columns in those rows will be. In the INSERT command, you have to specify a row of data to enter into a table. In the DELETE command you have to specify which row(s) of a table are to be deleted based on data values within those rows.

DATA RETRIEVAL WITH THE SQL SELECT COMMAND

Introduction to the SQL SELECT Command

Data retrieval in SQL is accomplished with the SELECT command. You should understand a few fundamental ideas about the SELECT command before looking into the details of using it. The first point is that the SQL SELECT command is *not* the same thing as the relational algebra Select operator that we discussed earlier in the book. It's a bit unfortunate that the same word was used to mean two different things, but that's the way it is. The fact is that the SQL SELECT command is capable of performing relational Select, Project, and Join operations singly or in combination, and much more. We will demonstrate this in the following discussion.

SQL SELECT commands are considered, for the most part, to be declarative rather than procedural in nature. This means that you specify what data you are looking for rather than provide a logical sequence of steps that guide the system in *how* to find the data. As we will see later in this chapter, the relational DBMS analyzes the **declarative** SQL SELECT statement and creates an **access path,**—a plan for what steps to take to respond to the query. The exception to this and the reason for the qualifier "for the most part" at the beginning of this paragraph is that a feature of the SELECT command known as subqueries permits the user to specify a certain amount of logical control over the data retrieval process.

Another point is that SQL SELECT commands can be run in either a query or an embedded mode. In the query mode, the user types the command at a workstation and presses the Enter key. The command goes directly to the relational DBMS, which evaluates the query and processes it against the database. The result is then returned to the user at the workstation. Commands entered this way can normally also be stored and retrieved at a later time for repetitive use. In the embedded mode, the SELECT command is embedded within the lines of a higher-level language program and functions as an input or "read" statement for the program. When the program is run and the program logic reaches the SELECT command, the program executes the SELECT. The SELECT command is sent to the DBMS which, as in the query mode case, processes it against the database and returns the results, this time to the program that issued it. The program can then use and further process the returned data. The only tricky part to this is that traditional higher-level language programs are designed to retrieve one record at a time. As we know from the earlier discussion of relational algebra (and as we will shortly see with SQL), the result of a relational retrieval command is itself a relation. A relation that consists of a single row can resemble a record, but a relation of several rows, if anything, resembles several records. In the embedded mode, the program that issued the SQL SELECT command and receives the resulting relation back must treat the rows of the relation as a list of records and process them one at a time.

SQL SELECT commands can be issued against either the actual, physical database tables or against a logical view of one table or of several joined tables. Good business practice dictates that in the commercial environment, SQL

SELECT commands should be issued against such logical views rather than directly against the base tables. As we will see later in this book, this is a simple but effective security precaution.

Finally, the SQL SELECT command has a broad array of features and options, and we will only cover some of them at this introductory level. What is also very important, however, is that our discussion of the SELECT command and the features that we will cover will work in all of the major SQL implementations, such as Oracle, MS Access, SQL Server, DB2, Informix, and so on, possibly with minor syntax variations in some cases.

Basic Functions

The Basic SELECT Format   In the simplest SELECT command, we will indicate from which table of the database we want to retrieve data, which rows of that table we are interested in, and which attributes of those rows we want to retrieve. The basic format of such a SELECT statement is:

```
SELECT <columns>
FROM <table>
WHERE <predicates identifying rows to be included>;
```

We will illustrate the SQL SELECT command with the General Hardware Company database of Figure 5.14, which is reproduced here for convenience as Figure 9.1. As is traditional with SQL, the SQL statements will be shown in all capital letters, except for data values taken from the tables. Note that the attribute names in Figure 9.1 have been abbreviated for convenience and set in capital letters to make them easily recognizable in the SQL statements. Also, spaces in the names have been removed. The General Hardware database provides an example of a simple query that demonstrates the basic SELECT format:

"Find the commission percentage and year of hire of salesperson number 186."

The SQL statement to accomplish this would be:

```
SELECT COMMPERCT, YEARHIRE
FROM SALESPERSON
WHERE SPNUM=186;
```

How is this command constructed? The desired attributes are listed in the SELECT clause, the required table is listed in the FROM clause, and the restriction or predicate indicating which row(s) is involved is shown in the WHERE clause in the form of an equation. Notice that SELECT statements always end with a single semicolon (;) at the very end of the entire statement.

The result of this statement is:

COMMPERCT	YEARHIRE
15	2001

As is evident from this query, an attribute like SPNUM being used to search for the required rows, also known as a **search argument,** does not have to appear in the query result, as long as its absence does not make the result ambiguous, confusing, or meaningless.

➤ **Figure 9.1**
The General Hardware
Company relational
database

(a) SALESPERSON table

SPNUM	SPNAME	COMMPERCT	YEARHIRE	OFFNUM
137	Baker	10	1995	1284
186	Adams	15	2001	1253
204	Dickens	10	1998	1209
361	Carlyle	20	2001	1227

(b) CUSTOMER table

CUSTNUM	CUSTNAME	SPNUM	HQCITY
0121	Main St. Hardware	137	New York
0839	Jane's Stores	186	Chicago
0933	ABC Home Stores	137	Los Angeles
1047	Acme Hardware Store	137	Los Angeles
1525	Fred's Tool Stores	361	Atlanta
1700	XYZ Stores	361	Washington
1826	City Hardware	137	New York
2198	Western Hardware	204	New York
2267	Central Stores	186	New York

(c) CUSTOMER EMPLOYEE table

CUSTNUM	EMPNUM	EMPNAME	TITLE
0121	27498	Smith	Co-Owner
0121	30441	Garcia	Co-Owner
0933	25270	Chen	VP Sales
0933	30441	Levy	Sales Manager
0933	48285	Morton	President
1525	33779	Baker	Sales Manager
2198	27470	Smith	President
2198	30441	Jones	VP Sales
2198	33779	Garcia	VP Personnel
2198	35268	Kaplan	Senior Accountant

(Continues)

To retrieve the entire record for salesperson 186 the statement would change to:

```
SELECT *
FROM SALESPERSON
WHERE SPNUM=186;
```

resulting in:

SPNUM	SPNAME	COMMPERCT	YEARHIRE	OFFNUM
186	Adams	15	2001	1253

Figure 9.1 (Continued)
The General Hardware
Company relational
database

(d) PRODUCT table

PRODNUM	PRODNAME	UNITPRICE
16386	Wrench	12.95
19440	Hammer	17.50
21765	Drill	32.99
24013	Saw	26.25
26722	Pliers	11.50

(e) SALES table

SPNUM	PRODNUM	QUANTITY
137	19440	473
137	24013	170
137	26722	688
186	16386	1745
186	19440	2529
186	21765	1962
186	24013	3071
204	21765	809
204	26722	734
361	16386	3729
361	21765	3110
361	26722	2738

(f) OFFICE Table

OFFNUM	TELEPHONE	SIZE
1253	901-555-4276	120
1227	901-555-0364	100
1284	901-555-7335	120
1209	901-555-3108	95

The "*" in the SELECT clause indicates that all attributes of the selected row are to be retrieved. Notice that this retrieval of an entire row of the table is, in fact, a relational Select operation! Recall that a relational Select operation can retrieve one *or more* rows of a table, depending, in this simple case, on whether the search argument is a unique or nonunique attribute. The search argument is nonunique in the following query:

"List the salesperson numbers and salesperson names of those salespersons who have a commission percentage of 10."

```
SELECT SPNUM, SPNAME
FROM SALESPERSON
WHERE COMMPERCT=10;
```

which results in:

SPNUM	SPNAME
137	Baker
204	Dickens

The SQL SELECT statement can also be used to accomplish a relational Project operation. Recall that this is a vertical slice through a table involving all rows and some attributes. Since all of the rows are included in the Project operation, there is no need for a WHERE clause to limit which rows of the table are included. For example,

"List the salesperson number and salesperson name of all of the salespersons."

```
SELECT SPNUM, SPNAME
FROM SALESPERSON;
```

results in:

SPNUM	SPNAME
137	Baker
186	Adams
204	Dickens
361	Carlyle

To retrieve an entire table, that is, to have an SQL SELECT statement that places no restrictions on either the rows or the attributes, you would issue:

```
SELECT *
FROM SALESPERSON;
```

and have as the result:

SPNUM	SPNAME	COMMPERCT	YEARHIRE	OFFNUM
137	Baker	10	1995	1284
186	Adams	15	2001	1253
204	Dickens	10	1998	1209
361	Carlyle	20	2001	1227

Comparisons   In addition to equal (=), the standard comparison operators, greater than (>), less than (<), greater than or equal to (>=), less than or equal to (<=), and not equal to (<>) can be used in the WHERE clause.

"List the salesperson numbers, salesperson names, and commission percentages of the salespersons whose commission percentage is less than 12."

```
SELECT SPNUM, SPNAME, COMMPERCT
FROM SALESPERSON
WHERE COMMPERCT<12;
```

This results in:

SPNUM	SPNAME	COMMPERCT
137	Baker	10
204	Dickens	10

As another example:

"List the customer numbers and headquarters cities of the customers that have a customer number of at least 1700."

```
SELECT CUSTNUM, HQCITY
FROM CUSTOMER
WHERE CUSTNUM>=1700;
```

results in:

CUSTNUM	HQCITY
1700	Washington
1826	New York
2198	New York
2267	New York

ANDs and ORs   Frequently, there is a need to specify more than one limiting condition on a table's rows in a query. Sometimes, for a row to be included in the result it must satisfy more than one condition; this requires the Boolean **AND** operator. Sometimes a row can be included if it satisfies one of two or more conditions; this requires the Boolean **OR** operator.

AND   An example in which two conditions must be satisfied is:

"List the customer numbers, customer names, and headquarters cities of the customers that are headquartered in New York and that have a customer number higher than 1500."

```
SELECT CUSTNUM, CUSTNAME, HQCITY
FROM CUSTOMER
WHERE HQCITY='New York'
AND CUSTNUM>1500;
```

resulting in:

CUSTNUM	CUSTNAME	HQCIT
1826	City Hardware	New York
2198	Western Hardware	New York
2267	Central Stores	New York

Notice that customer number 0121, which is headquartered in New York, was not included in the results because it failed to satisfy the condition of having a customer number greater than 1500. With the AND operator, it had to satisfy both conditions to be included in the result.

OR   To look at the OR operator, let's change the last query to:

"List the customer numbers, customer names, and headquarters cities of the customers that are headquartered in New York or that have a customer number higher than 1500."

```
SELECT CUSTNUM, CUSTNAME, HQCITY
FROM CUSTOMER
WHERE HQCITY='New York'
OR CUSTNUM>1500;
```

results in:

CUSTNUM	CUSTNAME	HQCITY
0121	Main St. Hardware	New York
1525	Fred's Tool Stores	Atlanta
1700	XYZ Stores	Washington
1826	City Hardware	New York
2198	Western Hardware	New York
2267	Central Stores	New York

Notice that the OR operator really means one or the other *or both*. Customer 0121 is included because it is headquartered in New York. Customers 1525 and 1700 are included because they have customer numbers higher than 1500. Customers 1826, 2198, and 2267 are included because they satisfy both conditions.

Both AND and OR   What if both AND and OR are specified in the same WHERE clause? AND is said to be "higher in precedence" than OR, and so all

ANDs are considered before any ORs are considered. The following query, which has to be worded very carefully, illustrates this point:

"List the customer numbers, customer names, and headquarters cities of the customers that are headquartered in New York or that satisfy the two conditions of having a customer number higher than 1500 and being headquartered in Atlanta."

```
SELECT CUSTNUM, CUSTNAME, HQCITY
FROM CUSTOMER
WHERE HQCITY='New York'
OR CUSTNUM>1500
AND HQCITY='Atlanta';
```

The result of this query is:

CUSTNUM	CUSTNAME	HQCITY
0121	Main St. Hardware	New York
1525	Fred's Tool Stores	Atlanta
1826	City Hardware	New York
2198	Western Hardware	New York
2267	Central Stores	New York

Notice that since the AND is considered *first*, one way for a row to qualify being in the result is if its customer number is greater than 1500 and its headquarters city is Atlanta. With the AND taken first, it's that combination *or* the headquarters city has to be New York. If the OR operator was considered first, it would change the whole complexion of the statement. The best way to deal with this, especially if there are several ANDs and ORs in a WHERE clause, is with the use of parentheses. The rule is that *anything* in parentheses is done *first*. If the parentheses are nested, then whatever is in the innermost parentheses is done first and then the system works from there toward the outermost parentheses. Thus a "safer" way to write the last SQL statement would be:

```
SELECT CUSTNUM, CUSTNAME, HQCITY
FROM CUSTOMER
WHERE HQCITY='New York'
OR (CUSTNUM>1500
AND HQCITY='Atlanta');
```

If you really wanted the OR to be considered first, you could force it by writing the query as:

```
SELECT CUSTNUM, CUSTNAME, HQCITY
FROM CUSTOMER
WHERE (HQCITY='New York'
OR CUSTNUM>1500)
AND HQCITY='Atlanta';
```

This would mean that, with the AND outside of the parentheses, both of two conditions have to be met for a row to qualify for the results. One condition is that the headquarters city is New York or the customer number is greater than 1500. The other condition is that the headquarters city is Atlanta. Since for a given row the headquarters city can't be both Atlanta and New York, the situation looks grim. But, in fact, customer number 1525 qualifies. Its customer number is greater than 1500, which satisfies the OR of the first of the two conditions and its headquarters city is Atlanta, which satisfies the second condition. Thus both conditions are met for this and only this row.

BETWEEN, IN, and LIKE   **BETWEEN, IN,** and **LIKE** are three useful operators. BETWEEN allows you to specify a range of numeric values in a search; IN allows you to specify a list of character strings to be included in a search; and LIKE allows you to specify partial character strings in a "wildcard" sense.

BETWEEN   Suppose that you want to find the customer records for those customers whose customer numbers are between 1000 and 1700, inclusive (meaning that both 1000 and 1700, as well as all numbers in between them, are included). Using the AND operator, you could specify this as:

```
SELECT *
FROM CUSTOMER
WHERE (CUSTNUM>=1000
AND CUSTNUM<=1700);
```

Or you could use the BETWEEN operator and specify it as:

```
SELECT *
FROM CUSTOMER
WHERE CUSTNUM BETWEEN 1000 AND 1700;
```

With either way of specifying it the result would be:

CUSTNUM	CUSTNAME	SPNUM	HQCITY
1047	Acme Hardware Store	137	Los Angeles
1525	Fred's Tool Stores	361	Atlanta
1700	XYZ Stores	361	Washington

IN   Suppose that you want to find the customer records for those customers headquartered in Atlanta, Chicago, or Washington. Using the OR operator, you could specify this as:

```
SELECT *
FROM CUSTOMER
WHERE (HQCITY='Atlanta'
OR HQCITY='Chicago'
OR HQCITY='Washington');
```

Or you could use the IN operator and specify it as:

```
SELECT *
FROM CUSTOMER
WHERE HQCITY IN ('Atlanta', 'Chicago', 'Washington');
```

With either way of specifying it, the result would be:

CUSTNUM	CUSTNAME	SPNUM	HQCITY
0839	Jane's Stores	186	Chicago
1525	Fred's Tool Stores	361	Atlanta
1700	XYZ Stores	361	Washington

LIKE   Suppose that you want to find the customer records for those customers whose names begin with the letter "A." You can accomplish this with the LIKE operator and the "%" character used as a "wildcard" to represent any string of characters. Thus, "A%" means the letter "A" followed by any string of characters, which is the same thing as saying any word that begins with "A."

```
SELECT *
FROM CUSTOMER
WHERE CUSTNAME LIKE 'A%';
```

The result would be:

CUSTNUM	CUSTNAME	SPNUM	HQCITY
0933	ABC Home Stores	137	Los Angeles
1047	Acme Hardware Store	137	Los Angeles

Note that unlike BETWEEN and IN, in SQL there is no easy alternate way of accomplishing what LIKE is capable of.

In a different kind of example, suppose that you want to find the customer records for those customers whose names have the letter "a" as the second letter of their names. Could you specify "%a%"? No, because the "%a" portion of it would mean any number of letters followed by "a," which is not what you want. In order to make sure that there is just one character followed by "a", which is the same thing as saying that "a" is the second letter, you would specify "_a%." The "_" wildcard character means that there will be exactly one letter (any one letter) followed by the letter "a." The "%," as we already know, means that any string of characters can follow afterward.

```
SELECT *
FROM CUSTOMER
WHERE CUSTNAME LIKE '_a%';
```

The result would be:

CUSTNUM	CUSTNAME	SPNUM	HQCITY
0121	Main St. Hardware	137	New York
0839	Jane's Stores	186	Chicago

Notice that both the words "Main" and "Jane's" have "a" as their second letter. Also notice that, for example, customer number 2267 was not included in the result. Its name, "Central Stores," has an "a" in it, but it is not the second letter of the name. Again, the single "_" character in the operator LIKE "_a%" specifies that there will be one character followed by "a." If the operator had been LIKE "%a%," then Central Stores would have been included in the result.

Filtering the Results of an SQL Query   Two ways to modify the results of an SQL SELECT command are with the use of **DISTINCT** and of **ORDER BY.** It is important to remember that these two devices do not affect what data is retrieved from the database but rather how the data is presented to the user.

DISTINCT   In some circumstances the result of an SQL query may contain duplicate items; this duplication is undesirable. Consider the following query:

"Which cities serve as headquarters cities for General Hardware customers?"

This could be taken as a simple relational Project that takes the HQCITY column of the CUSTOMER table as its result. The SQL command would be:

```
SELECT HQCITY
FROM CUSTOMER;
```

which results in:

HQCITY

New York
Chicago
Los Angeles
Los Angeles
Atlanta
Washington
New York
New York
New York

Technically, this is the correct result, but why is it necessary to list New York four times or Los Angeles twice? Not only is it unnecessary to list them more than once, but doing so results in unacceptable clutter. Based on the way the query was stated, the result should have each city listed once. The DISTINCT operator is used to eliminate duplicate rows in a query result. Reformulating the SELECT statement as:

```
SELECT DISTINCT HQCITY
FROM CUSTOMER;
```

results in:

HQCITY

New York
Chicago
Los Angeles
Atlanta
Washington

ORDER BY   The ORDER BY clause simply takes the results of an SQL query and orders them by one or more specified attributes. Consider the following query:

"Find the customer numbers, customer names, and headquarters cities of those customers with customer numbers greater than 1000. List the results in alphabetic order by headquarters cities."

```
SELECT CUSTNUM, CUSTNAME, HQCITY
FROM CUSTOMER
WHERE CUSTNUM>1000
ORDER BY HQCITY;
```

This results in:

CUSTNUM	CUSTNAME	HQCITY
1525	Fred's Tool Stores	Atlanta
1047	Acme Hardware Store	Los Angeles
1826	City Hardware	New York
2198	Western Hardware	New York
2267	Central Stores	New York
1700	XYZ Stores	Washington

If you wanted to have the customer names *within the same city* alphabetized, you would write:

```
SELECT CUSTNUM, CUSTNAME, HQCITY
FROM CUSTOMER
WHERE CUSTNUM>1000
ORDER BY HQCITY, CUSTNAME;
```

This results in:

CUSTNUM	CUSTNAME	HQCITY
1525	Fred's Tool Stores	Atlanta
1047	Acme Hardware Store	Los Angeles
2267	Central Stores	New York
1826	City Hardware	New York
2198	Western Hardware	New York
1700	XYZ Stores	Washington

The default order for ORDER BY is ascending. The clause can include the term ASC at the end to make ascending explicit, or it can include DESC for descending order.

Built-In Functions

A number of so-called **built-in functions** give the SQL SELECT command additional capabilities. They involve the ability to perform calculations based on attribute values or to count the number of rows that satisfy stated criteria.

AVG and SUM   Recall that the SALES table shows the lifetime quantity of particular products sold by particular salespersons. For example, the first row indicates that Salesperson 137 has sold 473 units of Product Number 19440 dating back to when she joined the company or when the product was introduced. Consider the following query:

> *"Find the average number of units of the different products that Salesperson 137 has sold (i.e., the average of the quantity values in the first three records of the SALES table)."*

Using the AVG operator, you would write:

```
SELECT AVG(QUANTITY)
FROM SALES
WHERE SPNUM=137;
```

and the result would be:

AVG(QUANTITY)
_____
443.67

To find the total number of units of all products that she has sold, you would use the SUM operator and write:

```
SELECT SUM(QUANTITY)
FROM SALES
WHERE SPNUM=137;
```

and the result would be:

SUM(QUANTITY)
_____
1331

MIN and MAX   You can also find the minimum or maximum of a set of attribute values. Consider the following query:

> *"What is the largest number of units of Product Number 21765 that any individual salesperson has sold?"*

Using the MAX operator, you would write:

```
SELECT MAX(QUANTITY)
FROM SALES
WHERE PRODNUM=21765;
```

and the result would be:

MAX(QUANTITY)
_____
3110

To find the smallest number of units, you simply replace MAX with MIN:

```
SELECT MIN(QUANTITY)
FROM SALES
WHERE PRODNUM=21765;
```

and get:

MIN(QUANTITY)
_____
809

COUNT   COUNT is a very useful operator that counts the number of rows that satisfy a set of criteria. It is often used in the context of "how many of something" meet some stated conditions. Consider the following query:

"How many salespersons have sold Product Number 21765?"

Remember that each row of the SALES table describes the history of a particular salesperson selling a particular product. That is, each combination of SPNUM and PRODNUM is unique; there can only be one row that involves a particular SPNUM/PRODNUM combination. If you can count the number of rows of that table that involve Product Number 21765, then you know how many salespersons have a history of selling it. Using the notational device COUNT(*), we find that the SELECT statement is:

```
SELECT COUNT(*)
FROM SALES
WHERE PRODNUM=21765;
```

and the answer is:

COUNT(*)
―――――――
3

Don't get confused by the difference between SUM and COUNT. As we demonstrated above, SUM adds up a set of attribute values; COUNT counts the number of rows of a table that satisfy a set of stated criteria.

Grouping Rows

Using the built-in functions, we were able to calculate results based on attribute values in several rows of a table. In effect, we formed a *single* "group" of rows and performed some calculation on their attribute values. Many situations will require such calculations to be made on *several different groups* of rows. This is a job for the **GROUP BY** clause.

GROUP BY   A little earlier we found the total number of units of all products that a single, particular salesperson has sold. It seems reasonable that at some point we might want to find the total number of units of all products that *each* salesperson has sold. That is, we want to *group together* the rows of the SALES table that belong to *each* salesperson and calculate a value—the sum of the Quantity attribute values in this case—for each such group. Here is the way such a query might be stated:

"Find the total number of units of all products sold by each salesperson."

The SQL statement, using the GROUP BY clause, would look like this:

```
SELECT SPNUM, SUM(QUANTITY)
FROM SALES
GROUP BY SPNUM;
```

and the results would be:

SPNUM	SUM(QUANTITY)
137	1331
186	9307
204	1543
361	9577

Notice that GROUP BY SPNUM specifies that the rows of the table are to be grouped together based on having the same value in their SPNUM attribute. All of the rows for Salesperson Number 137 will form one group, all of the rows for Salesperson Number 186 will form another group, and so on. The Quantity attribute values in each group will then be summed – SUM(QUANTITY) – and the results returned to the user. But it is not enough to provide a list of sums:

1331

9307

1543

9577

These are indeed the sums of the quantities for each salesperson, but without identifying which salesperson goes with which sum, they are meaningless! That's why the SELECT clause includes both the SPNUM and the SUM(QUANTITY). Including the attribute(s) specified in the GROUP BY clause in the SELECT clause allows you to properly identify the sums calculated for each group.

An SQL statement with a GROUP BY clause may also include a WHERE clause. Thus the query:

> *"Find the total number of units of all products sold by each salesperson whose salesperson number is at least 150."*

would look like:

```
SELECT SPNUM, SUM(QUANTITY)
FROM SALES
WHERE SPNUM>=150
GROUP BY SPNUM;
```

and the results would be:

SPNUM	SUM(QUANTITY)
186	9307
204	1543
361	9577

HAVING   Sometimes there is a need to limit the results of a GROUP BY based on the values calculated for each group with the built-in functions. For example, take the last query above,

> *"Find the total number of units of all products sold by each salesperson whose salesperson number is at least 150."*

and modify it with an additional sentence so that it reads:

> *"Find the total number of units of all products sold by each salesperson whose salesperson number is at least 150. Only include salespersons whose total number of units sold is at least 5000."*

This would be accomplished by adding a **HAVING** clause to the end of the SELECT statement:

```
SELECT SPNUM, SUM(QUANTITY)
FROM SALES
```

```
WHERE SPNUM>=150
GROUP BY SPNUM
HAVING SUM(QUANTITY)>=5000;
```

and the results would be:

SPNUM	SUM(QUANTITY)
186	9307
361	9577

with Salesperson Number 204, with a total of only 1,543 units sold, dropping out of the results.

Notice that in this last SELECT statement, there are two limitations. One, that the Salesperson Number must be at least 150, appears in the WHERE clause, and the other, that the sum of the number of units sold must be at least 5,000, appears in the HAVING clause. It is important to understand why this is so. If the limitation is based on *individual attribute values* that appear in the database, then the condition goes in the WHERE clause. This is the case with the limitation based on the Salesperson Number value. If the limitation is based on *the group calculation performed with the built-in function*, then the condition goes in the HAVING clause. This is the case with the limitation based on the sum of the number of product units sold.

The Join

Up to this point, all of the SELECT features that we have looked at have been shown in the context of retrieving data from a single table. The time has come to look at how the SQL SELECT command accomplishes the join of two or more tables. To make a join work, two specifications must be made in the SELECT statement. One is that the tables to be joined must be listed in the FROM clause. The other is that the join attributes in the tables being joined must be declared and matched to each other in the WHERE clause. And there is one more point. Since two or more tables are involved in a SELECT statement that involves a join, the same attribute *name* may appear in more than one of the tables. When this happens, these attribute names must be "qualified" with a table name when used in the SELECT statement. All of this is best illustrated in an example.

Consider the following query, which we discussed earlier in this book:

"Find the name of the salesperson responsible for Customer Number 1525."

The SELECT statement to satisfy this query is:

```
SELECT SPNAME
FROM SALESPERSON, CUSTOMER
WHERE SALESPERSON.SPNUM=CUSTOMER.SPNUM
AND CUSTNUM=1525;
```

and the result is:

SPNAME

Carlyle

Let's take a careful look at this last SELECT statement. Notice that the two tables involved in the join, SALESPERSON and CUSTOMER, are listed in the FROM clause. Also notice that the first line of the WHERE clause

```
SALESPERSON.SPNUM=CUSTOMER.SPNUM
```

links the two join attributes: the SPNUM attribute of the SALESPERSON table (SALESPERSON.SPNUM) and the SPNUM attribute of the CUSTOMER table (CUSTOMER.SPNUM). The notational device of having the table name "." the attribute name is known as "qualifying" the attribute name. As we said earlier, this qualification is necessary when the same attribute name is used in two or more tables in a SELECT statement. By the way, notice in the SELECT statement that the attributes SPNAME and CUSTNUM don't have to be qualified because each appears in only one of the tables included in the SELECT statement.

Here is an example of a join involving three tables, assuming for the moment that salesperson names are unique:

> *"List the names of the products of which salesperson Adams has sold more than 2,000 units."*

The salesperson name data appears only in the SALESPERSON table, and the product name data appears only in the PRODUCT table. The SALES table shows the linkage between the two, including the quantities sold. And so the SELECT statement will be:

```
SELECT PRODNAME
FROM SALESPERSON, PRODUCT, SALES
WHERE SALESPERSON.SPNUM=SALES.SPNUM
AND  SALES.PRODNUM=PRODUCT.PRODNUM
AND  SPNAME='Adams'
AND  QUANTITY>2000;
```

which results in:

PRODNAME
_____

Hammer
Saw

Subqueries

A variation on the way that the SELECT statement, works is when one SELECT statement is "nested" within another in a format known as a *subquery*. This can go on through several levels of SELECT statements with each successive SELECT statement contained in a pair of parentheses. The execution rule is that the inner-most SELECT statement is executed first, and its results are then provided as input to the SELECT statement at the next level up. This procedure can be an alternative to the join. Furthermore, under certain circumstances this procedure *must* be used. These latter circumstances are common enough and important enough to include in this treatment of the SQL SELECT command.

Subqueries as Alternatives to Joins   Let's reconsider the first join example given above:

"Find the name of the salesperson responsible for Customer Number 1525."

If you methodically weave through the database tables to solve this query, as we discussed earlier in the book, you start at the CUSTOMER table, find the record for Customer Number 1525, and discover in that record that the salesperson responsible for this customer is Salesperson Number 361. You then take that information to the SALESPERSON table where you look up the record for Salesperson Number 361 and discover in it that the salesperson's name is Carlyle. Using a subquery, you can build this logic into an SQL statement as:

```
SELECT SPNAME
FROM SALESPERSON
WHERE SPNUM=
    (SELECT SPNUM
    FROM CUSTOMER
    WHERE CUSTNUM=1525);
```

and the result will again be:

SPNAME
_____

Carlyle

Follow the way that the description given above of how to methodically solve the problem is reconstructed as a SELECT statement with a subquery. Since the innermost SELECT (the indented one), which constitutes the subquery, is considered first, the CUSTOMER table is queried first, the record for Customer Number 1525 is found, and 361 is returned as the SPNUM result. How do we know that only one salesperson number will be found as the result of the query? Because CUSTNUM is a *unique attribute*, Customer Number 1525 can only appear in one record, and that one record only has room for one salesperson number! Moving along, Salesperson Number 361 is then fed to the outer SELECT statement, which, in effect, makes the main query, that is, the outer SELECT, look like:

```
SELECT SPNAME
FROM SALESPERSON
WHERE SPNUM=361;
```

and this results in:

SPNAME
_____

Carlyle

Notice, by the way, that in the SELECT statement, there is only one semicolon at the end of the entire statement, including the subquery.

When a Subquery Is Required   There is a very interesting circumstance in which a subquery *is required*. This situation is best explained with an example up front. Consider the following query:

"Which salespersons with salesperson numbers greater than 200 have the lowest commission percentage of any such salesperson?" (We'll identify salespersons by their salesperson number.)

This appears to be a perfectly reasonable request, and yet it turns out to be deceptively difficult. This is because the query really has two very different parts to it. First, the system has to determine what the lowest commission percentage is for salespersons with salesperson numbers greater than 200. Second, it has to see which of these salespersons has that lowest percentage. It's really tempting to try to satisfy this type of query with an SQL SELECT statement like:

```
SELECT SPNUM, MIN(COMMPERCT)
FROM SALESPERSON
WHERE SPNUM>200;
```

or perhaps:

```
SELECT SPNUM
FROM SALESPERSON
WHERE SPNUM>200
AND COMMPERCT=MIN(COMMPERCT);
```

But these *will not work*! It's like asking SQL to perform two separate operations and somehow apply one to the other in the correct sequence. This turns out to be asking too much. But there is a way to do it and it involves subqueries. In fact, we will ask the system to determine the minimum commission percentage *first*, in a subquery, and then use that information in the main query to determine which salespersons have it:

```
SELECT SPNUM
FROM SALESPERSON
WHERE SPNUM>200
AND COMMPERCT=
    (SELECT MIN(COMMPERCT)
    FROM SALESPERSON)
    WHERE SPNUM>200);
```

which results in:

SPNUM
___

204

The minimum commission percentage across all of the salespersons with salesperson numbers greater than 200 is determined *first* in the subquery and the result is 10. The main query, then, in effect looks like:

```
SELECT SPNUM
FROM SALESPERSON
WHERE SPNUM>200
AND COMMPERCT=10;
```

which yields the result of salesperson number 204, as shown.

Actually, this is a very interesting example of a required subquery. What makes it really interesting is why the predicate, SPNUM>200, appears in *both* the main query *and* the subquery. Clearly it has to be in the subquery because you must first find the lowest commission percentage among the salespersons with salesperson numbers greater than 200. But then why does it have to be in the main query, too? The answer is that the only thing that the subquery returns to the main query is a single number, specifically a commission percentage. *There is no memory passed on to the main query of how the subquery arrived at that value.* If you remove SPNUM>200 from the main query so that it now looks like:

```
SELECT SPNUM
FROM SALESPERSON
WHERE COMMPERCT=
    (SELECT MIN(COMMPERCT)
    FROM SALESPERSON)
    WHERE SPNUM>200);
```

you would find every salesperson *with any salesperson number* whose commission percentage is equal to the lowest commission percentage of the salespersons with salesperson numbers greater than 200. Of course, if for some reason you *do want* to find all of the salespersons, regardless of their salesperson number, who have the same commission percentage as the salesperson who has the lowest commission percentage of the salespersons with salesperson numbers greater than 200, then this last SELECT statement is exactly what you should write.

A Strategy for Writing SQL SELECT Commands

Before we go on to some more examples, it will be helpful to think about developing a strategy for writing SQL SELECT statements. The following is an ordered list of steps.

1. Determine what the result of the query is to be and write the needed attributes and functions in the SELECT clause. This may seem like an obvious statement, but it will pay to think this through carefully before going on. In fact, it is at this very first step that you must determine whether the query will require a GROUP BY clause or a subquery. If either of these is required, you should start outlining the overall SELECT statement by writing the GROUP BY clause or the nested SELECT for the subquery further down the page (or screen).

2. Determine which tables of the database will be needed for the query and write their names in the FROM clause. Include only those tables that are really necessary for the query. Sometimes this can be tricky. For example, you might need an attribute that is the primary key of a table, and you might be tempted to immediately include that table in the FROM clause. However, it could be that the attribute in question is a foreign key in another table that is *already* in the FROM clause for other reasons. It is then unnecessary to include the table in which it is the primary key unless, of course, other attributes from that table are needed, too.

3. If the query involves a join, begin constructing the WHERE clause by equating the join attributes from the tables that are in the FROM clause. Once this job is out of the way, you can begin considering the row limitations that must be stated in the WHERE clause.

4. Continue filling in the details of the WHERE clause, the GROUP BY clause, and any subqueries.

One final piece of advice: If you are new to writing SQL SELECT commands but you have a programming background, you may be tempted to avoid setting up joins and try writing subqueries instead. Resist this temptation for two reasons! One is that joins are an essential part of the relational database concept. Embrace them; don't be afraid of them. The other is that writing multiple levels of nested subqueries can be extremely error prone and difficult to debug.

EXAMPLE: GOOD READING BOOKSTORES

The best way to gain confidence in understanding SQL SELECT statements is to write some! And there are some further refinements of the SQL SELECT that we have yet to present. We will use the same three example databases that appeared in previous chapters, but, as with the General Hardware database, we will shorten the attribute names. We will state a variety of queries and then give the SELECT statements that will satisfy them, plus commentary as appropriate. You should try to write the SELECT statements yourself before looking at our solutions!

Figure 9.2 repeats the Good Reading Bookstores relational database from Figure 5.16. Here is a list of queries for Good Reading Bookstores.

Figure 9.2
Good reading Bookstores
Relational database

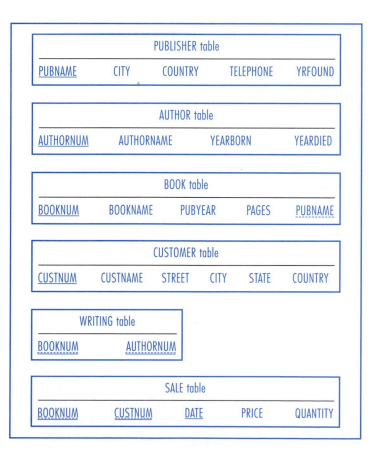

1. *"Find the book number, book name, and number of pages of all of the books published by London Publishing Ltd. List the results in order by book name."*

This query obviously requires the PUBNAME attribute, but it *does not* require the PUBLISHER table. All of the information needed is in the BOOK table, including the PUBNAME attribute, which is there as a foreign key. The SELECT statement is:

```
SELECT BOOKNUM, BOOKNAME, PAGES
FROM BOOK
WHERE PUBNAME='London Publishing Ltd.'
ORDER BY BOOKNAME;
```

2. *"How many books of at least 400 pages does Good Reading Bookstores carry that were published by publishers based in Paris, France?"*

This is a straightforward join between the PUBLISHER and BOOK tables that uses the built-in function COUNT. All of the attribute names are unique between the two tables, except for PUBNAME which must be qualified with a table name every time it is used. Notice that "Good Reading Bookstores" does not appear as a condition in the SELECT statement, although it was mentioned in the query. The entire database is about Good Reading Bookstores and no other! There is no BOOK-STORE CHAIN table in the database, and there is no STORENAME or CHAIN-NAME attribute in any of the tables.

```
SELECT COUNT(*)
FROM PUBLISHER, BOOK
WHERE PUBLISHER.PUBNAME=BOOK.PUBNAME
AND CITY='Paris'
AND COUNTRY='France'
AND PAGES>=400;
```

3. *"List the publishers in Belgium, Brazil, and Singapore that publish books written by authors who were born before 1920."*

Sometimes a relatively simple-sounding query can be fairly involved. This query actually requires four tables of the database! To begin with, we need the PUBLISHER table because that's the only place that a publisher's country is stored. But we also need the AUTHOR table because that's where author birth years are stored. The only way to tie the PUBLISHER table to the AUTHOR table is to connect PUBLISHER to BOOK, then to connect BOOK to WRITING, and finally to connect WRITING to AUTHOR. With simple, one-attribute keys such as there are in these tables, the number of joins will be one less than the number of tables. The FROM clause below shows four tables, and the first three lines of the WHERE clause show the three joins. Also, notice that since a publisher may have published more than one book with the stated specifications, DISTINCT is required to prevent the same publisher name from appearing several, perhaps many, times in the result. Finally, since we want to include publishers in three specific countries, we list the three countries as Belgium, Brazil, *and* Singapore. But in the SELECT statement, we have to indicate that for a record to be included in the result, the value of the COUNTRY attribute must be Belgium, Brazil, *or* Singapore.

```
SELECT DISTINCT PUBNAME
FROM PUBLISHER, BOOK, WRITING, AUTHOR
WHERE PUBLISHER.PUBNAME=BOOK.PUBNAME
AND BOOK.BOOKNUM=WRITING.BOOKNUM
AND WRITING.AUTHORNUM=AUTHOR.AUTHORNUM
AND COUNTRY IN ('Belgium', 'Brazil', 'Singapore')
AND YEARBORN<1920;
```

4. *"How many books did each publisher in Oslo, Norway; Nairobi, Kenya; and Auckland, New Zealand, publish in 2001?"*

The keyword here is "each." This query requires a separate total for each publisher that satisfies the conditions. This is a job for the GROUP BY clause. We want to group together the records for each publisher and count the number of records in each group. Each line of the result must include both a publisher name and count of the number of records that satisfy the conditions. This SELECT statement requires both a join and a GROUP BY. Notice the seeming complexity but the unambiguous beauty of the ANDs and ORs structure regarding the cities and countries.

```
SELECT PUBNAME, CITY, COUNTRY, COUNT(*)
FROM PUBLISHER, BOOK
WHERE PUBLISHER.PUBNAME=BOOK.PUBNAME
AND ((CITY='Oslo' AND COUNTRY='Norway')
   OR (CITY='Nairobi' AND COUNTRY='Kenya')
   OR (CITY='Auckland' AND COUNTRY='New Zealand'))
AND PUBYEAR=2001
GROUP BY PUBNAME;
```

5. *"Which publisher published the book that has the earliest publication year among all of the books that Good Reading Bookstores carries?"*

This query calls only for the name of the publisher, not the name of the book. This is a case that requires a subquery. First, the system has to determine the earliest publication year, and then it has to see which books have that earliest publication year. Once you know the books, their records in the BOOK table give you the publisher names. Since more than one publisher may have published a book in that earliest year, there could be more than one publisher name in the result. And since a particular publisher could have published more than one book in that earliest year, DISTINCT is required to avoid having that publisher's name listed more than once.

```
SELECT DISTINCT PUBNAME
FROM BOOK
WHERE PUBYEAR=
   (SELECT MIN(PUBYEAR)
   FROM BOOK);
```

➤ **Figure 9.3**
World Music Association
relational database

ORCHESTRA table

| ORCHNAME | CITY | COUNTRY | MUSICDIR |

MUSICIAN table

| MUSNUM | MUSNAME | INSTRUMENT | ANNSALARY | ORCHNAME |

DEGREE table

| MUSNUM | DEGREE | UNIVERSITY | YEAR |

COMPOSER table

| COMPOSERNAME | COUNTRY | DATEBIRTH |

COMPOSITION table

| COMPOSITIONNAME | COMPOSERNAME | YEAR |

RECORDING table

| ORCHNAME | COMPOSITIONNAME | YEAR | PRICE |

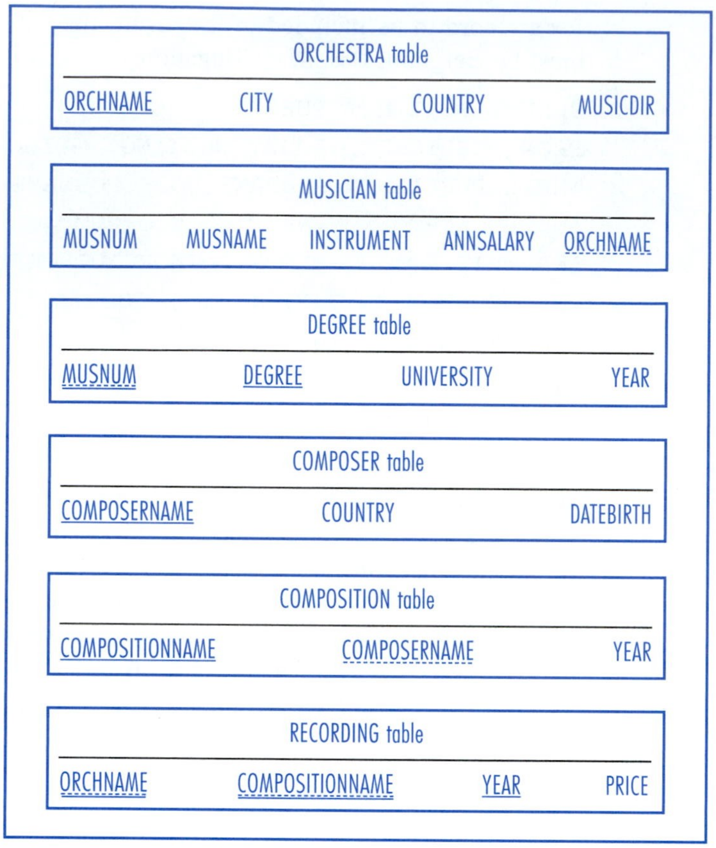

EXAMPLE: WORLD MUSIC ASSOCIATION

Figure 9.3 repeats the World Music Association relational database from Figure 5.17. Here is a list of queries for the World Music Association.

1. *"What is the total annual salary cost for all of the violinists of the Berlin Symphony Orchestra?"*

```
SELECT SUM(ANNSALARY)
FROM MUSICIAN
WHERE ORCHNAME='Berlin Symphony Orchestra'
AND INSTRUMENT='Violin';
```

2. *"Make a single list, in alphabetic order of all of the universities attended by the cellists of India."*

```
SELECT DISTINCT UNIVERSITY
FROM ORCHESTRA, MUSICIAN, DEGREE
WHERE ORCHESTRA.ORCHNAME=MUSICIAN.ORCHNAME
AND MUSICIAN.MUSNUM=DEGREE.MUSNUM
AND INSTRUMENT='Cello'
AND COUNTRY='India'
ORDER BY UNIVERSITY;
```

3. *"What is the total annual salary cost for all of the violinists of each orchestra located in Canada? Only include in the result those orchestras whose total annual salary for its violinists is in excess of $150,000."*

Since this query requires a separate total for *each* orchestra, the SELECT statement must rely on the GROUP BY clause. Since the condition that the total must be over 150,000 is based on figures calculated by the SUM built-in function, it must be placed in a HAVING clause rather than in the WHERE clause.

```
SELECT ORCHNAME, SUM(ANNSALARY)
FROM ORCHESTRA, MUSICIAN
WHERE ORCHESTRA.ORCHNAME=MUSICIAN.ORCHNAME
AND COUNTRY='Canada'
AND INSTRUMENT='Violin'
GROUP BY ORCHNAME
HAVING SUM(ANNSALARY)>150,000;
```

4. *"What is the name of the most highly paid pianist?"*

It should be clear that a subquery is required. First, the system has to determine what the top salary of pianists is, and then it has to find out which pianists have that salary.

```
SELECT MUSNAME
FROM MUSICIAN
WHERE INSTRUMENT='Piano'
AND ANNSALARY=
    (SELECT MAX(ANNSALARY)
    FROM MUSICIAN
    WHERE INSTRUMENT='Piano');
```

This is another example in which a predicate, INSTRUMENT='Piano' in this case, appears in *both* the main query *and* the subquery. Clearly it has to be in the subquery because you must first find out how much money the highest paid pianist makes. But then why does it have to be in the main query, too? The answer is that the only thing that the subquery returns to the main query is a single number, specifically a salary value. *There is no memory passed on to the main query of how the subquery arrived at that value.* If you remove INSTRUMENT='Piano' from the main query so that it now looks like:

```
SELECT MUSNAME
FROM MUSICIAN
WHERE ANNSALARY=
    (SELECT MAX(ANNSALARY)
    FROM MUSICIAN
    WHERE INSTRUMENT='Piano');
```

you would find every musician *who plays any instrument* whose salary is equal to *the highest paid pianist*. Of course, if for some reason you *do want* to find all of the musicians, regardless of the instrument they play, who have the same salary as the highest paid pianist, then this last SELECT statement is exactly what you should write.

5. *"What is the name of the most highly paid pianist of any orchestra in Australia?"*

This is the same idea as the last query, but it involves two tables, both of which must be joined in both the main query and the subquery. The reasoning for this is the same as in the last query. The salary of the most highly paid pianist in Australia must be determined first in the subquery. Then that result must be used in the main query where it must be compared *only* to the salaries of the Australian pianists.

```
SELECT MUSNAME
FROM MUSICIAN, ORCHESTRA
WHERE MUSICIAN.ORCHNAME=ORCHESTRA.ORCHNAME
AND INSTRUMENT='Piano'
AND COUNTRY='Australia'
AND ANNSALARY=
    (SELECT MAX(ANNSALARY)
    FROM MUSICIAN, ORCHESTRA
    WHERE MUSICIAN.ORCHNAME=ORCHESTRA.ORCHNAME
    AND INSTRUMENT='Piano'
    AND COUNTRY='Australia')
```

EXAMPLE: LUCKY RENT-A-CAR

Figure 9.4 repeats the Lucky Rent-A-Car relational database from Figure 5.18. Here is a list of queries for Lucky Rent-A-Car.

➤ **Figure 9.4**
Lucky Rent-A-Car relational database

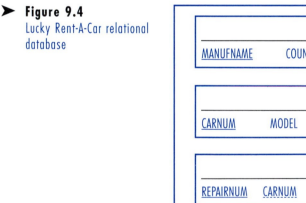

1. *"List the manufacturers whose names begin with the letter C or the letter D and that are located in Japan."*

```
SELECT MANUFNAME
FROM MANUFACTURER
WHERE (MANUFNAME LIKE 'C%'
OR MANUFNAME LIKE 'D%')
AND COUNTRY='Japan';
```

2. *"What was the average mileage of the cars that had tune-ups in August 2003?"*

```
SELECT AVG(MILEAGE)
FROM MAINTENANCE
WHERE PROCEDURE='Tune-Up'
AND DATE BETWEEN 'AUG-01-2003' AND 'AUG-31-2003';
```

The exact format for specifying dates may differ among SQL processors, and a given processor may have several options.

3. *"How many different car models do manufacturers in Italy make?"*

This query will use an interesting combination of COUNT and DISTINCT which may not work in all SQL processors. In this case, it literally counts the different models among the cars made in Italy. Since many different cars are of the same model, DISTINCT is needed to make sure that each model is counted just once.

```
SELECT COUNT(DISTINCT MODEL)
FROM MANUFACTURER, CAR
WHERE MANUFACTURER.MANUFNAME=CAR.MANUFNAME
AND COUNTRY='Italy';
```

4. *"How many repairs were performed on each car manufactured by Superior Motors during the month of March 2004? Only include cars in the result that had at least three repairs."*

```
SELECT CAR.CARNUM, COUNT(*)
FROM CAR, MAINTENANCE
WHERE CAR.CARNUM=MAINTENANCE.CARNUM
AND MANUFNAME='Superior Motors'
AND DATE BETWEEN 'MAR-01-2004' AND 'MAR-31-2004'
GROUP BY CAR.CARNUM
HAVING COUNT(*)>=3;
```

5. *"List the cars of any manufacturer that had an oil change in January 2004 and had at least as many miles as the highest mileage car manufactured by Superior Motors that had an oil change that same month."*

This is an example in which the specifications in the subquery are considerably different from the specifications in the main query.

```
SELECT MAINTENANCE.CARNUM
FROM MAINTENANCE
WHERE PROCEDURE='Oil Change'
```

```
AND DATE BETWEEN 'JAN-01-2004' AND 'JAN-31-2004'
AND MILEAGE>=
    (SELECT MAX(MILEAGE)
    FROM CAR, MAINTENANCE
    WHERE CAR.CARNUM, MAINTENANCE.CARNUM
    AND PROCEDURE='Oil Change'
    AND DATE BETWEEN 'JAN-01-2004' AND 'JAN-31-2004
    AND MANUFNAME='Superior Motors');
```

RELATIONAL QUERY OPTIMIZER

Relational DBMS Performance

An ever-present issue in data retrieval is performance: the speed with which the required data can be retrieved. In a typical relational database application environment (and as we've seen in the examples above), many queries require only one table. It is certainly reasonable to assume that such single-table queries using indexes, hashing, and the like should, more or less, not take any longer in a relational database system environment than they would in any other kind of file management system. But what about the queries that involve joins? Recall the detailed explanation of how a join works earlier in the book, which used the Salesperson and Customer tables as an example. These very small tables did not pose much of a performance issue, if the join was carried out in the worst case way, comparing every row of one table to every row of the other table, as was previously described. But what if we attempted to join a 1 million row table with a 3 million row table? How long do you think that would take—even on a large, fast computer? It might well take much longer than a person waiting for a response at a workstation would be willing to tolerate. This was one of the issues that caused a delay of almost ten years from the time that the first article on relational database was published in 1970 until relational DBMSs were first offered commercially almost ten years later.

The performance issue in relational database management has been approached in two different ways. One, the tuning of the database structure, **physical database design,** was covered in Chapter 8 of this book. The other way that the relational database performance issue has been approached is through highly specialized software in the relational DBMS itself. This software, known as a **relational query optimizer,** is in effect an expert system that evaluates each SQL SELECT statement sent to the DBMS and determines an efficient way to satisfy it.

Relational Query Optimizer Concepts

All major SQL processors (meaning all major relational DBMSs) include a query optimizer. Using a query optimizer, SQL attempts to figure out the most efficient way of answering a query, prior to actually responding to it. Certainly, a query that involves only one table should be evaluated to take advantage of aids such as indexes on pertinent attributes. But, again, the most compelling and interesting reason for having a query optimizer in a relational database system is to execute multiple-table, join types of operations without having to go through the very time-consuming, exhaustive row comparison process described earlier in the book. Exactly how a specific relational

DBMS's query optimizer works is typically a closely held trade secret. Retrieval performance is one way in which the vendors of these products compete with each other. Nevertheless, we can discuss some basic ideas here.

When an SQL query optimizer is presented with a new SELECT statement to evaluate, it seeks out information about the tables named in the FROM clause. This information includes:

- Which attributes of the tables have indexes built over them
- Which attributes have unique values
- How many rows each table has

The query optimizer finds this information in a special, internal database known as the **relational catalog,** which will be described further later in this book.

The query optimizer uses the information about the tables, together with the various components of the SELECT statement itself, to try to find an efficient way to retrieve the data required by the query. For example, in the General Hardware Company SELECT statement:

```
SELECT SPNUM, SPNAME
FROM SALESPERSON
WHERE COMMPERCT=10;
```

the query optimizer might check on whether the COMMPERCT attribute has an index built over it. If this attribute does have an index, the query optimizer might decide to use the index to find the rows with a commission percentage of 10. However, if the number of rows of the SALESPERSON table is small enough, the query optimizer might decide to read the entire table into main memory and scan it for the rows with a commission percentage of 10.

Another important decision that the query optimizer makes is how to satisfy a join. Consider the following General Hardware Company example that we looked at above:

```
SELECT SPNAME
FROM SALESPERSON, CUSTOMER
WHERE SALESPERSON.SPNUM=CUSTOMER.SPNUM
AND CUSTNUM=1525;
```

In this case, the query optimizer should be able to recognize that since CUSTNUM is a unique attribute in the CUSTOMER table and only one customer number is specified in the SELECT statement, only a single record from the CUSTOMER table, the one for customer number 1525, will be involved in the join. Once it finds this CUSTOMER record (hopefully with an index), it can match the SPNUM value found in it against the SPNUM values in the SALESPERSON records looking for a match. If it is clever enough to recognize that SPNUM is a unique attribute in the SALESPERSON table, then all it has to do is find the single SALESPERSON record (hopefully with an index) that has that salesperson number and pull the salesperson name (SPNAME) out of it to satisfy the query. Thus, in this type of case, an exhaustive join can be completely avoided.

When a more extensive join operation can't be avoided, the query optimizer can choose from one of several join algorithms. The most basic, and the one that we described earlier in the book as a Cartesian product, is known algorithmically as a **nested-loop join.** One of the two tables is selected for the outer loop and the other for the inner loop. Each of the records of the outer loop is chosen in succession, and, for each, the inner loop table is scanned for matches on the join attribute. If the query optimizer can determine that only a subset of the rows of the outer or inner tables is needed, then only those rows need be included in the **comparisons.**

A more efficient join algorithm than the nested-loop join is called the **merge-scan join,** but it can only be used if certain conditions are met. The principle is that for the merge-scan join to work, each of the two join attributes either has to be in sorted order or has to have an index built over it. An index, by definition, is in sorted order, and so, one way or the other, each join attribute has a sense of order to it. If this condition is met, then comparing every record of one table to every record of the other table as in a nested-loop join is unnecessary. The system can simply start at the top of each table or index, as the case may be, and move downwards, without ever having to move upwards.

KEY TERMS

Access path	DELETE	ORDER BY
AND/OR	DISTINCT	Nested-loop join
Base table	Embedded mode	Query
BETWEEN	GROUP BY	Relational query optimizer
Built-in functions	HAVING	Search argument
Comparisons	IN	SELECT
Data definition language (DDL)	INSERT	Structured Query Language (SQL)
Data manipulation language (DML)	LIKE	Subquery
Declarative	Merge-scan join	UPDATE

QUESTIONS

1. What are the four basic operations that can be performed on stored data?

2. What is Structured Query Language (SQL)?

3. Name several of the fundamental SQL commands and discuss the purpose of each.

4. What is the purpose of the SQL SELECT command?

5. How does the SQL SELECT command relate to the relational Select, Project, and Join concepts?

6. Explain the difference between running SQL in query mode and in embedded mode.

7. Describe the basic format of the SQL SELECT command.

8. In a general way, describe how to write an SQL SELECT command to accomplish a relational Select operation.

9. In a general way, describe how to write an SQL SELECT command to accomplish a relational Project operation.

10. In a general way, describe how to write an SQL SELECT command to accomplish a combination of a relational Select operation and a relational Project operation.

11. What is the purpose of the WHERE clause in SQL SELECT commands?

12. List and describe some of the common operators that can be used in the WHERE clause.

13. Describe the purpose of each of the following operators in the WHERE clause:
    a. AND
    b. OR
    c. BETWEEN
    d. IN
    e. LIKE

14. What is the purpose of the DISTINCT operator?

15. What is the purpose of the ORDER BY clause?

16. Name the five SQL built-in functions and describe the purpose of each.

17. Explain the difference between the SUM and COUNT built-in functions.

18. Describe the purpose of the GROUP BY clause. Why does the attribute in the GROUP BY clause also have to appear in the SELECT clause?

19. Describe the purpose of the HAVING clause. How do you make the decision of whether to place a row-limiting predicate in the WHERE clause or in the HAVING clause?

20. How do you construct a Join operation in an SQL SELECT statement?

21. What is a subquery in an SQL SELECT statement?

22. Describe the circumstances in which a subquery *must* be used.

23. What is a relational query optimizer? Why is it important?

24. How do relational query optimizers work?

25. What information does a relational query optimizer use in making its decisions?

26. What are some of the ways that relational query optimizers can handle joins?

EXERCISES

1. Consider the following relational database that Best Airlines uses to keep track of its mechanics, their skills, and their airport locations. Mechanic number (MECHNUM), airport name (AIRNAME), and skill number are all unique fields. SIZE is an airport's size in acres. SKILLCAT is a skill's category, such as an engine skill, wing skill, and tire skill. YEARQUAL is the year that a mechanic first qualified in a particular skill; PROFRATE is the mechanic's proficiency rating in a particular skill.

MECHANIC table				
MECHNUM	MECHNAME	TELEPHONE	SALARY	AIRNAME

AIRPORT table				
AIRNAME	CITY	STATE	SIZE	YEAROPENED

SKILL table		
SKILLNUM	SKILLNAME	SKILLCAT

QUALIFICATION table			
MECHNUM	SKILLNUM	YEARQUAL	PROFRATE

Write SQL SELECT commands to answer the following queries.

a. List the names and telephone numbers of all of the mechanics.

b. List the airports in California that are at least twenty acres in size and have been open since 1935. Order the results from smallest to largest airport.

c. List the airports in California that are at least twenty acres in size or have been open since 1935.

d. Find the average size of the airports in California that have been open since 1935.

e. How many airports have been open in California since 1935?

f. How many airports have been open in each state since 1935?

g. How many airports have been open in each state since 1935? Only include in your answer those states that have at least five such airports.

h. List the names of the mechanics who work in California.

i. Fan blade replacement is the name of a skill. List the names of the mechanics who have a proficiency rating of 4 in fan blade replacement.

j. Fan blade replacement is the name of a skill. List the names of the mechanics who work in California who have a proficiency rating of 4 in fan blade replacement.

k. List the total, combined salaries of all of the mechanics who work in each city in California.

l. Find the largest of all of the airports.

m. Find the largest airport in California.

2. Consider the following relational database for the Quality Appliance Manufacturing Company. The database is designed to track the major appliances (refrigerators, washing machines, dishwashers, etc.) that Quality manufactures. It also records information about Quality's suppliers, the parts they supply, the buyers of the finished appliances, and the finished goods inspectors. Note the following facts about this environment:

- Suppliers are the companies that supply Quality with its major components, such as electric motors, for the appliances. Supplier number is a unique identifier.

- Parts are the major components that the suppliers supply to Quality. Each part comes with a part number, but that part number is only unique within a supplier. Thus, from Quality's point of view, the unique identifier of a part is the combination of part number and supplier number.

- Each appliance that Quality manufactures is given an appliance number that is unique across all the types of appliances that Quality makes.

- Buyers are major department stores, home improvement chains, and wholesalers. Buyer numbers are unique.
- An appliance may be inspected by several inspectors. A many-to-many relationship exists between appliances and inspectors, as indicated by the INSPECTION table.
- There are one-to-many relationships between suppliers and parts (Supplier Number is a foreign key in the PART table), parts and appliances (Appliance Number is a foreign key in the PART table), and appliances and buyers (Buyer Number is a foreign key in the APPLIANCE table).

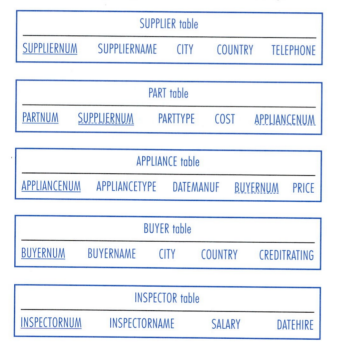

Write SQL SELECT commands to answer the following queries.

a. List the names, in alphabetic order, of the suppliers located in London, Liverpool, or Manchester, UK.

b. List the names of the suppliers that supply motors (see PARTTYPE) costing between $50 and $100.

c. Find the average cost of the motors (see PARTTYPE) supplied by supplier number 3728.

d. List the names of the inspectors who were inspecting refrigerators (see APPLIANCETYPE) on April 17, 2003.

e. What was the highest inspection score achieved by a refrigerator on November 3, 2003?

f. Find the total amount of money spent on Quality Appliance products by each buyer from Mexico, Venezuela, and Argentina.

g. Find the total cost of the parts used in each dishwasher manufactured on February 28, 2004. Only include in the results those dishwashers that used at least $200 in parts.

h. List the highest paid inspectors.

i. List the highest paid inspectors who were hired in 2002.

j. Among all of the inspectors, list those who earn more money than the highest paid inspector who was hired in 2002.

MINICASES

1. Consider the following relational database for Happy Cruise Lines. It keeps track of ships, cruises, ports, and passengers. A "cruise" is a particular sailing of a ship on a particular date. For example, the seven-day journey of the ship *Pride of Tampa* that leaves on June 13, 2003, is a cruise. Note the following facts about this environment.
   - Both ship number and ship name are unique in the SHIP able.
   - A ship goes on many cruises over time. A cruise is associated with a single ship.
   - A port is identified by the combination of port name and country.
   - As indicated by the VISIT table, a cruise includes visits to several ports and a port is typically included in several cruises.
   - Both Passenger Number and Social Security Number are unique in the PASSENGER table. A particular person has a single Passenger Number that is used for all of the cruises that she takes.

• The VOYAGE table indicates that a person can take many cruises, and a cruise, of course, has many passengers.

```
┌─────────────────────────────────────────────────────────┐
│                      SHIP table                          │
├─────────────────────────────────────────────────────────┤
│  SHIPNUM    SHIPNAME    BUILDER    LAUNCHDATE    WEIGHT   │
└─────────────────────────────────────────────────────────┘
```

```
┌─────────────────────────────────────────────────────────┐
│                      CRUISE table                        │
├─────────────────────────────────────────────────────────┤
│ CRUISENUM   STARTDATE   ENDDATE   DIRECTOR   SHIPNUM      │
└─────────────────────────────────────────────────────────┘
```

```
┌─────────────────────────────────────────────────────────┐
│                      PORT table                          │
├─────────────────────────────────────────────────────────┤
│ PORTNAME      COUNTRY       NUMDOCKS        MANAGER       │
└─────────────────────────────────────────────────────────┘
```

```
┌─────────────────────────────────────────────────────────┐
│                      VISIT table                         │
├─────────────────────────────────────────────────────────┤
│ CRUISENUM   PORTNAME   COUNTRY   ARRDATE   DEPDATE        │
└─────────────────────────────────────────────────────────┘
```

```
┌─────────────────────────────────────────────────────────┐
│                    PASSENGER table                       │
├─────────────────────────────────────────────────────────┤
│ PASSENGERNUM  PASSENGERNAME  SOCSECNUM  ADDRESS  PHONE    │
└─────────────────────────────────────────────────────────┘
```

```
┌─────────────────────────────────────────────────────────┐
│                      VOYAGE table                        │
├─────────────────────────────────────────────────────────┤
│ PASSENGERNUM      CRUISENUM      ROOMNUM        FARF      │
└─────────────────────────────────────────────────────────┘
```

Write SQL SELECT commands to answer the following queries.

a. Find the start and end dates of cruise number 35218.

b. List the names and ship numbers of the ships built by the Ace Shipbuilding Corporation that weigh more than 60,000 tons.

c. List the companies that have built ships for Happy Cruise Lines.

d. Find the total number of docks in all the ports in Canada.

e. Find the average weight of the ships built by the Ace Shipbuilding Corporation that have been launched since 2000.

f. How many ports in Venezuela have at least three docks?

g. Find the total number of docks in each country. List the results in order from most to least.

h. Find the total number of ports in each country.

i. Find the total number of docks in each country but only include those countries that have at least twelve docks in your answer.

j. Find the name of the ship that operated on (was used on) cruise number 35218.

k. List the names, addresses, and telephone numbers of the passengers who sailed on *The Spirit of Nashville* on cruises that began during July 2003.

l. Find the names of the company's heaviest ships.

m. Find the names of the company's heaviest ships that began a cruise between July 15, 2003, and July 31, 2003.

2. Consider the following relational database for the Super Baseball League. It keeps track of teams in the league, coaches and players on the teams, work experience of the coaches, bats belonging to each team, and which players have played on which teams. Note the following facts about this environment:

• The database keeps track of the history of all the teams that each player has played on and all f the players who have played on each team.

• The database only keeps track of the coach's current team.

• Team number, team name, and player number are each unique attributes across the league.

• Coach name is only unique within a team (and we assume that a team cannot have two coaches of the same name).

• Serial number (for bats) is unique only within a team.

• In the AFFILIATION table, the Years attribute indicates the number of years that a player played on a team; the batting average is for the years that a player played on a team.

```
┌─────────────────────────────────────────────────────────┐
│                      TEAM table                          │
├─────────────────────────────────────────────────────────┤
│ TEAMNUM      TEAMNAME      CITY          MANAGER          │
└─────────────────────────────────────────────────────────┘
```

```
┌─────────────────────────────────────────────────────────┐
│                      COACH table                         │
├─────────────────────────────────────────────────────────┤
│ TEAMNUM          COACHNAME           TELEPHONE            │
└─────────────────────────────────────────────────────────┘
```

```
┌─────────────────────────────────────────────────────────┐
│                  WORK EXPERIENCE table                   │
├─────────────────────────────────────────────────────────┤
│ TEAMNUM   COACHNAME   EXPERIENCETYPE   YEARSEXPERIENCE    │
└─────────────────────────────────────────────────────────┘
```

BATS table		
TEAMNUM	SERIALNUM	MANUFACTURER

PLAYER table		
PLAYERNUM	PLAYERNAME	AGE

AFFILIATION Table			
PLAYERNUM	TEAMNUM	YEARS	BATTINGAVG

Write SQL SELECT commands to answer the following queries.

a. Find the names and cities of all the teams with team numbers greater than fifteen. List the results alphabetically by team name.

b. List all of the coaches whose last names begin with "D" and who have between five and ten years of experience as college coaches (see YEARSEXPE-RIENCE and EXPERIENCETYPE).

c. Find the total number of years of experience of Coach Taylor on team number 23.

d. Find the number of different types of experience of Coach Taylor on team number 23.

e. Find the total number of years of experience of each coach on team number 23.

f. How many different manufacturers make bats for the league's teams?

g. Assume that team names are unique. Find the names of the players who have played for the Dodgers for at least five years (see YEARS in the AFFILIATION Table).

h. Assume that team names are unique. Find the total number of years of work experience of each coach on the Dodgers, but only include in the result those coaches who have more than eight years of experience.

i. Find the names of the league's youngest players.

j. Find the names of the league's youngest players whose last names begin with the letter "B."

CHAPTER 10

OBJECT-ORIENTED DATABASE MANAGEMENT

CHAPTER OBJECTIVES

After learning the material in this chapter, you will be able to:
✔ List several limitations in the relational database model.
✔ Describe the object-oriented database concept.
✔ Model data using such complex relationships as generalization and aggregation, and such concepts as inheritance and polymorphism.
✔ Describe the benefits of encapsulation.
✔ Describe the value of developing abstract data types.
✔ Explain what an object/relational database is.

HNEDAK BOBO GROUP

Hnedak Bobo Group (HBG) is a leading architecture and design firm headquartered in Memphis, TN, with a satellite office in Las Vegas, Nevada. The firm has twenty-eight registered architects and forty-three licensed professionals. HBG is organized into architecture, interior design, and construction management divisions, with three distinct specialty practice areas focused on the entertainment and hospitality industry, corporate buildings, and urban/historic/civic structures. Hnedak (pronounced like 'knee dak') Bobo is best known for its work in the gaming and hospitality industries and has been consistently ranked as one of the top firms in the United States for hospitality design (ranked second in late 2002 in a national survey of hotel and hospitality design firms conducted by *Hotel & Motel Management* Magazine). As for urban/historic/civic structures, Hnedak Bobo was responsible for the Peabody Place Mixed-Use project in Memphis, Tennessee, which, at the time of its construction, was the largest urban redevelopment project in the United States.

Hnedak Bobo Group uses a relational database application called the Contact Management and Lead Tracking System to keep track of its customers, potential customers, and potential projects or "leads." This is a critical system in this type of large project-oriented business and requires that an owner or principal of the firm be assigned as each potential project's "pursuit manager." The system tracks all phases of "lead development," starting with first hearing of a possible project. It then continues with estimating the project's potential for the firm, estimating the probability of getting the contract, and, eventually, to contract negotiation and signing. An important part of this ongoing effort is keeping in touch with the firm's customers and potential customers. To this end, the system maintains personal information about these people and is organized to maintain contact with them through greeting cards, gifts, a newsletter, and company announcements.

Hnedak Bobo's Contact Management and Lead Tracking System is stored as an MS Access relational database running on a Compaq server. The system was implemented in 1999. It employs canned, menu-based queries written in Visual Basic. The main database tables are a Contacts table with 5,500 records (meaning that they maintain contact with that number of people) and an Events table that tracks every meeting, telephone call, etc. with each contact. Another set of tables tracks the project leads and lead development phases.

Printed by permission of Hnedak Bobo Group

Traditional information systems (IS) and the applications within them have always maintained a clear separation between their programs and their data. Programs and data structures are designed separately, implemented separately, and stored on disk separately. Relational databases fit very well into this arrangement. For much of IS history the emphasis was on the programs, with the data structures and ultimately the data stored in them being a secondary consideration. Elsewhere in this book we discuss the fact that from a managerial point of view, the concept of data as a corporate resource has made significant inroads into changing the IS environment from this program-centric mentality into a more data-centric one.

On the technical side, an alternative approach to information systems and IS development, which comes under the broad heading of object orientation, began during the 1980s. This approach is, by its nature, more data-centric. It began with object-oriented programming, then object-oriented systems analysis and object-oriented systems design, and finally object-oriented database management, complete with object-oriented database management systems (OODBMS). A variety of OODBMSs have been developed and marketed commercially. We will take a brief look at the essential points of object-oriented database management in this chapter, but, as we do so, it is important to bear in mind that the commercial OODBMSs vary widely in the OODBMS features that they support either partially or fully.

WHAT'S MISSING IN THE RELATIONAL DATABASE CONCEPT?

Relational tables seem to do a good job of storing data for information systems, as we've seen in concept and in a variety of examples. So, what's missing? The answer to this question is a bit complicated. Many people would say that nothing is missing from the relational model (or, for that matter, in this context, from the hierarchical and network models that came before it). Others would point out that for certain kinds of complex applications, the relational model is lacking in support for the more complex data model features they need. Some even argue that all applications could benefit from certain additional features in terms of data integrity. Let's take a look at "what's missing" from the relational model. The answer to this question will also serve as an introduction to the main features of the object-oriented database model.

- Although the relational model is fine for dealing with unary, binary, and ternary relationships among entities, it does not directly provide support for more complex but important relationships among different subcategories or specialized categories of particular entities. This is known as generalization or **generalization/specialization** in the object-oriented database model. Nor does the relational model directly provide support for situations in which particular entities are constructed from other component entities. This is known as **aggregation** in the object-oriented database model.

- As in all traditional information systems, the separation of programs and databases exposes the data in the databases to being updated by a variety of programs. Of course, we assume that these programs are thoroughly tested and debugged. But since so many people are writing programs that can affect particular data, a hidden mistake can always pop up unexpectedly and cause errors in the data. This problem becomes even more serious as the sharing of data among different applications increases. It might be desirable to institute a system in which only a limited, controlled set of program segments is allowed to update particular data. Application programs would then make requests for the execution of these program segments to update the data. This approach could go a long way toward improving data integrity.

- The relational model supports only a limited number of relatively simplistic numeric and character-oriented data types, which are sufficient for most standard accounting, inventory, and other traditional business applications. But it does not directly support more complex data types that we increasingly encounter such as graphic images, photo images, video clips, audio clips, long text documents, and such mathematical constructs as matrices. The object-oriented database model allows for the creation of all these data types and any others that are needed with its abstract data-type feature.

The object-oriented database concept has several other features or advantages. One is that each unit of data or object has an object identifier that is permanent and unique among all objects of all types in the system. Another is that some OODBMSs are implemented as pointer-based systems, meaning that related objects are "connected" by their storage addresses, as opposed to the foreign key/join arrangement in relational databases. Some believe that this pointer-based approach is superior in performance to the multi-table join approach of relational databases when related data must be brought together. Ironically, relational database replaced the pointer-based approach of the earlier hierarchical and network DBMSs. Finally, it is argued that OODBMSs are the most natural data storage vehicles when object-oriented programming languages, such as C++, Smalltalk, and Java, are in use.

INTRODUCTION AND TERMINOLOGY

Earlier in this book, we defined an entity as an object or event in our environment that we want to keep track of. An entity set was defined as a collection of entities of the same type. Entities have properties that we called attributes. We then defined a data structure known as a record which contains all of the facts, the attributes, that we know about a given entity. The records about all of the entities in an entity set were collected together in a file. Finally, we spoke of a record type as a general description of all the records in a file—essentially a list of the kinds of attributes that describe each entity. And we spoke of a record occurrence as a specific set of attribute values that describe one of the entities.

Object-oriented data modeling has its own features and its own terminology, but it still must describe the entities, objects, and events in the real business environment. Having said that, we must first recognize that in object-oriented modeling, the term **object** is used to describe an advanced data structure that includes an entity's attributes *plus* **methods** or **operations** or **procedures** (program code!) that can operate on and modify the object's attribute values. This is obviously a major departure from the strict separation of data and program code that we're used to. In the same spirit in which we organized the records that described similar entities into a file, the objects that describe similar entities are known collectively as an **object class** or, simply, a **class.** Conversely, an instance or an occurrence of a class is an object.

This terminology is in keeping with the standard diagramming notation for object-oriented systems development, known as the **Unified Modeling Language (UML).** Introduced in 1997 by the Object Management Group (OMG), UML has nine standard diagrams that describe such features as the system's data, its business processes, its intended results, the components of its program code, and its hardware and software architectures. For our purposes, we will focus on the UML **class diagram,** which describes the system's data, including attributes of and relationships between the "objects." As before, we will demonstrate these OODBMS concepts in the context of the General Hardware Company example, as well as the other three running examples that we have used. Some of the details of the examples will have to be changed in order to demonstrate the object-oriented concepts, and we will carefully point out those changes as they occur.

COMPLEX RELATIONSHIPS

In our earlier discussion of data modeling using the entity-relationship model which led to relational database design, we saw the importance of being able to model unary, binary, and ternary one-to-one, one-to-many, and many-to-many relationships. The first question then is, can we model such complex *relationships* in UML class diagrams and can they be implemented in the OODBMS concept? The answer is definitely yes. It had better be yes because, as we know by now, those are fundamental relationships in any business environment. The point, however, is that UML class diagrams and ultimately OODBMS implementations go beyond those fundamental relationships to other, more specifically targeted kinds of relationships known as generalization and aggregation.

Generalization

Generalization, also known as generalization/specialization, is a relationship that recognizes that some kinds of entities can be subdivided into smaller, more specialized groups. All of the entities may have some common characteristics, but each of the smaller groups may have certain unique characteristics as well. For example, all movies have a producer and a director, but only animated movies have animation artists. All boats have hulls, owners, and registration numbers, but only sailboats have sails. All retail stores have names, addresses, and occupancy licenses, but only restaurants have health inspection scores and restaurant critic ratings; only gas stations have underground storage tanks; only supermarkets have produce departments and meat departments.

The General Hardware Company entity-relationship diagram of Figure 3.9 is reproduced here as Figure 10.1. Remember that General Hardware is a wholesaler that supplies retail stores such as hardware stores, and home improvement chains. Thus far, the only products that we've assumed General Hardware sells to its customers are

➤ **Figure 10.1**
The General Hardware
Company E-R diagram

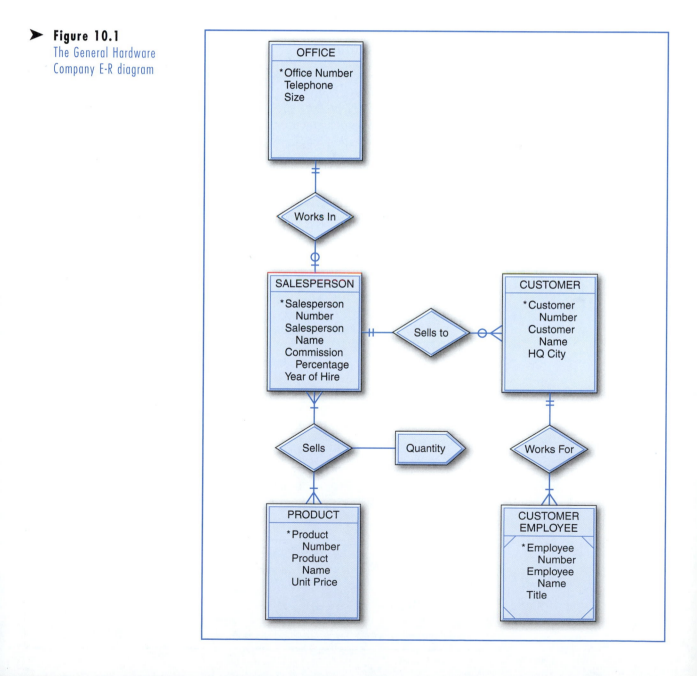

tools. But now General Hardware has decided to expand its product line beyond tools to include light fixtures and lumber. Figure 10.2 shows a generalization diagram that represents General Hardware's expanded product line and recognizes that while all of the products share some common attributes, different kinds of products have additional unique attributes. Each box in Figure 10.2 represents a class and has three sections separated by horizontal lines. At the top, in capital letters, is the class name; in the middle are the class attributes; and at the bottom are the class operations (although we're not showing any operations yet). The upward pointing arrows indicate generalizations. The diagram shows that there are three *kinds* of products: TOOLs, LIGHT FIXTUREs, and LUMBER. Furthermore, there are two kinds of tools: POWER TOOLs, and NONPOWER TOOLs.

Inheritance of Attributes

The PRODUCT class indicates that all products have three common attributes: Product Number, Product Name, and Unit Price. In fact, we say that all of the classes *below* PRODUCT *inherit* the attributes shown in PRODUCT; that is, they include these attributes among their own. In general, attributes are inherited downwards in these generalization diagrams. So,

- The attributes for POWER TOOLs are Product Number, Product Name, Unit Price (all from PRODUCT), Weight (from TOOL), and Amperes.
- The attributes for NONPOWER TOOLs are Product Number, Product Name, Unit Price, Weight, and Years of Warranty.

➤ **Figure 10.2**
General Hardware Company product generalization diagram

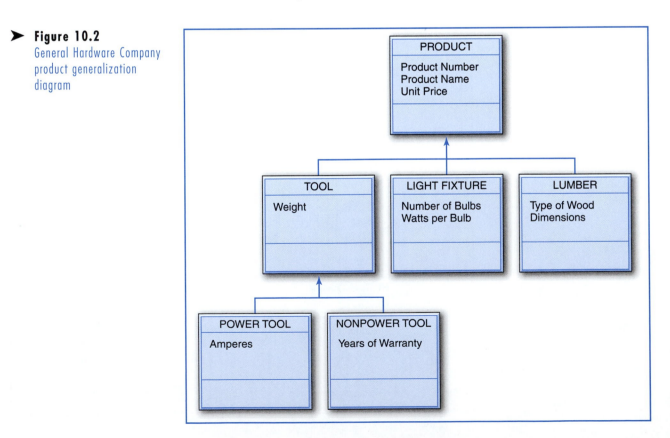

- The attributes for LIGHT FIXTUREs are Product Number, Product Name, Unit Price, Number of Bulbs, and Watts per Bulb.
- The attributes for LUMBER are Product Number, Product Name, Unit Price, Type of Wood, and Dimensions.

Operations, Inheritance of Operations, and Polymorphism

Figure 10.3 shows the addition of some operations to the diagram in Figure 10.2. Actually, there are three kinds of operations: constructor, query, and update. A constructor operation creates a new instance of a class, that is, a new object. An example in Figure 10.3 is Add Lumber, which is an operation that will add a new instance of LUMBER, that is, a new object, to the database when General Hardware starts carrying a new type or size of lumber in its wholesale inventory. A query operation returns data about the values of an object's attributes but does not update them. Calculate Discount in the PRODUCT class is an example of a query operation. The operation calculates a discount for a particular customer buying a particular product and returns the result to the user who issued the query, but does not store the result in the database. An update operation updates an object's attribute values. Change Unit Price in the PRODUCT class is an example of an update operation. From time to time, a product's unit price has to be changed, and the result is stored in the database as the new unit price.

Notice that Calculate Discount is an operation that applies to all products because operations are inherited downward in the same way that attributes are. Since there is nothing more said about the discount further down the hierarchy, we conclude

➤ **Figure 10.3**
General Hardware Company product generalization diagram with operations

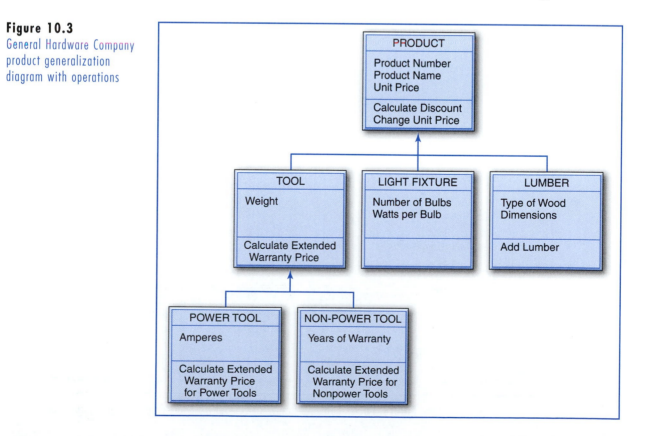

that the discount is calculated *in the same way* for all kinds of products. On the other hand, the diagram indicates that the Calculate Extended Warranty Price for TOOLs is performed differently for POWER TOOLs and for NONPOWER TOOLs. The operation is initially specified in the TOOLs box, but operation names in the POWER TOOL and NONPOWER TOOL boxes indicate that it changes in some way when it is inherited down to those boxes. Perhaps the presence of an electric motor in the power tools requires a different kind of calculation. This modification or refinement of operations as they are inherited downward is called **polymorphism.** (*Note:* Technically, the operations that are performed differently in the lower level objects can have the same name—simply Calculate Extended Warranty Price—in this example, even though they will perform differently for the different kinds of objects.)

Aggregation

Figure 10.4 shows the addition of the FRAME and BULBS classes, connected to the LIGHT FIXTURE class with a diamond-shaped symbol. This is not further generalization but is another type of relationship known as *aggregation*. In generalization, lower-level classes are kinds of upper-level classes (e.g., POWER TOOLs and NONPOWER TOOLs are both *kinds of* TOOLs). In aggregation, a class is shown to be composed of other classes. FRAMEs and BULBS are not kinds of LIGHT FIXTUREs; rather, each is *a part of* a LIGHT FIXTURE. As shown in Figure 10.4, each component class can have its own special attributes and conceivably, operations, too.

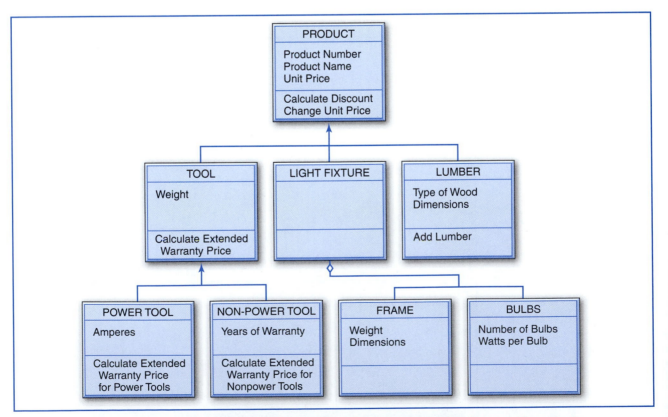

➤ **Figure 10.4** General Hardware Company product diagram with aggregation

The General Hardware Company Class Diagram

Figure 10.5 shows the complete General Hardware Company UML class diagram. The upper portion of the diagram is largely the same as the entity-relationship diagram

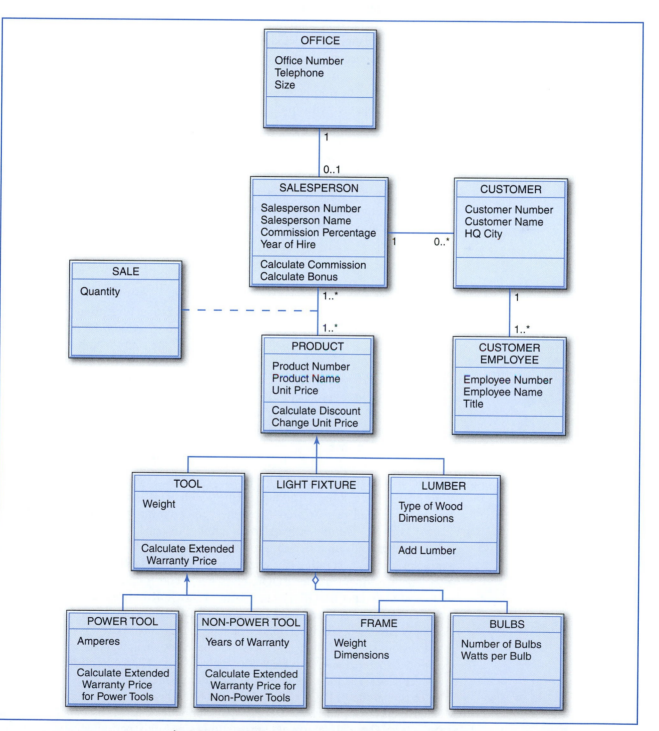

➤ **Figure 10.5**   General Hardware Company class diagram

of Figure 10.1. In converting the entity boxes to class boxes, we added some operations and changed some of the notation. In terms of one-to-one, one-to-many, and many-to-many relationships, in this notation "1" means exactly one, "0..1" means zero or one, "0..*" means zero-to-many, and "1..*" means one-to-many. Also note that the many-to-many relationship between SALESPERSON and PRODUCT requires an additional class (similar in concept to an associative entity) to show the nature of the many-to-many relationship, including any intersection data. This SALE class is attached to the connective line between the SALESPERSON and PRODUCT classes with a dashed line.

It is important to stop here for a moment and ask whether an ordinary relational database together with application programming could be used to implement all of the various kinds of relationships shown in Figure 10.5. The answer is yes, they could. But the point is that it would be up to the database designer and especially the application programmer *to manage* the various kinds of relationships in the database with the application code. This is as opposed to an OODBMS, which is designed to handle all of these relationships among its natural features. To stretch a term a bit, in the OODBMS concept, the database management system "understands" all of these kinds of relationships and is capable of directly managing data involved in them.

The Good Reading Bookstores Class Diagram

Good Reading Bookstores has decided to expand its product line to include periodicals (newspapers and magazines), music CDs, and movie videos/DVDs. The upper portion of Figure 10.6 is the class diagram version of the entity-relationship diagram of Figure 3.10, except that several changes have been made to reflect the change in product line. The BOOK entity type has become the PRODUCT class since there can now be several kinds of products, not just books. Similarly, PUBLISHER has become PRODUCING COMPANY to show that we are now dealing with publishers, music studios, and movie studios, and AUTHOR has become CREATOR to show that we are now dealing with authors, singers, and movie producers and directors.

A generalization hierarchy has been created under PRODUCT, which indicates that there are four kinds of products: BOOK, PERIODICAL, CD, and VIDEO/DVD. The three attributes in the PRODUCT class—Product Number, Product Name, and Year Created—are inherited downward to all four of the subordinate classes. *In addition*, a book has a number of pages; a periodical has a volume, a number, and a number of pages; a CD has a number of tracks, a total length in minutes, and a chart rating (the current popularity of the CD); and a video/DVD has a length in minutes. The BOOK class has a constructor-type operation, Add Book, that adds new BOOK instances, that is, BOOK objects, as new books are published and added to the store's inventory. PERIODICAL has a query-type operation associated with it that calculates the date that each periodical is to be removed from the store shelves if it has not been purchased by then. CD has an update-type operation associated with it that changes the value of a CD's Chart Rating attribute on a weekly basis as industrywide, new popularity charts come out.

Notice that the PERIODICAL class, and only this class, is associated with the ARTICLE class. Similarly, the CD class, and only this class, is associated with the SONG class. These are reasonable restrictions since only periodicals have articles and only CDs have songs. But this reveals an interesting point about generalization that we have not seen before. Thus far, the reason for setting up subordinate classes in a generalization hierarchy was to allow the subordinate classes to have distinct attributes and operations that the other subordinate classes don't have. Now, we see that there is a second reason for setting up subordinate classes: to be able to associate only selected subordinate classes with other classes!

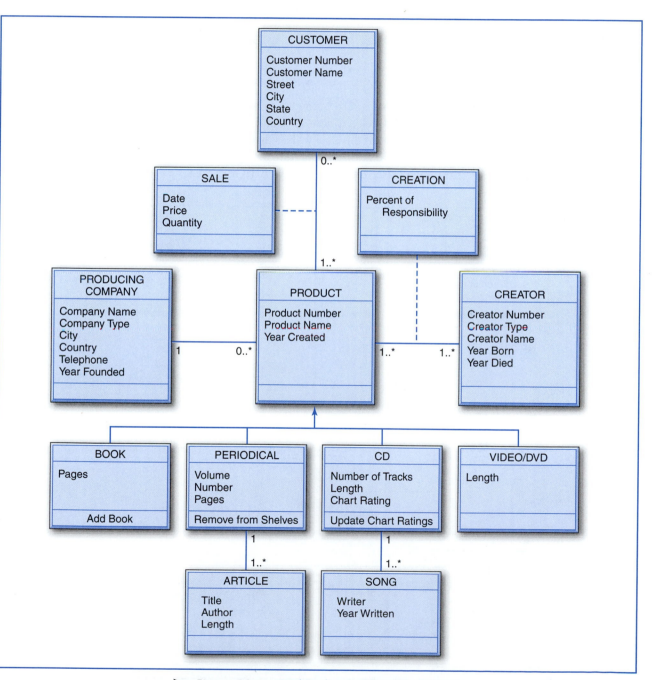

➤ **Figure 10.6**   Good Reading Bookstores class diagram

The World Music Association Class Diagram

The upper portion of Figure 10.7 is the class diagram version of the World Music Association entity-relationship diagram of Figure 3.11, with one major change. Instead of considering only symphonies, which were associated with orchestras, we are going to consider many kinds of compositions. Of course, different kinds of compositions are performed by different kinds of musical groups. So, the ORCHESTRA entity type in the E-R diagram of Figure 3.11 has become the GROUP class, and a generalization hierarchy has been constructed with subordinate classes ORCHESTRA, CHAMBER GROUP, and JAZZ GROUP.

The Lucky Rent-A-Vehicle Class Diagram

Lucky Rent-A-Car has expanded to become Lucky Rent-A-Vehicle! In addition to renting cars, Lucky is now renting limousines, trucks, airplanes, and helicopters. The upper part of the Lucky class diagram of Figure 10.8 looks very much like the Lucky entity-relationship diagram of Figure 3.12. The only difference is the change from the CAR entity-type to the VEHICLE class.

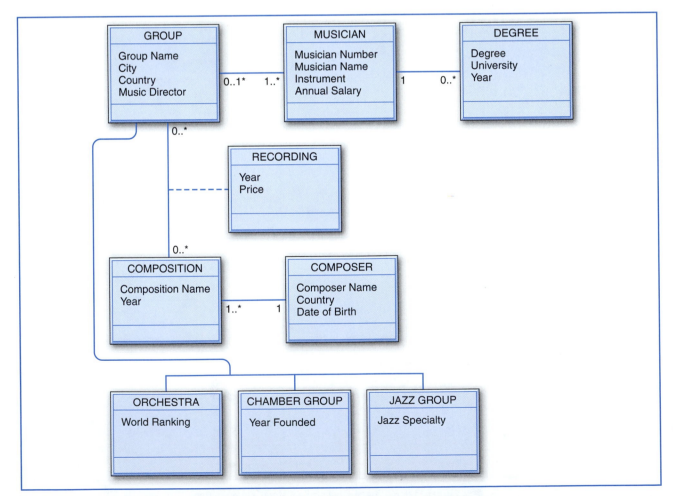

➤ **Figure 10.7** World Music Association class diagram

There is a two-level generalization hierarchy under VEHICLE. At the first level are the LAND (vehicle) and AIR (vehicle) classes. Then, at the next level down, a LAND vehicle can be a CAR, LIMOUSINE, or TRUCK, while an AIR vehicle can

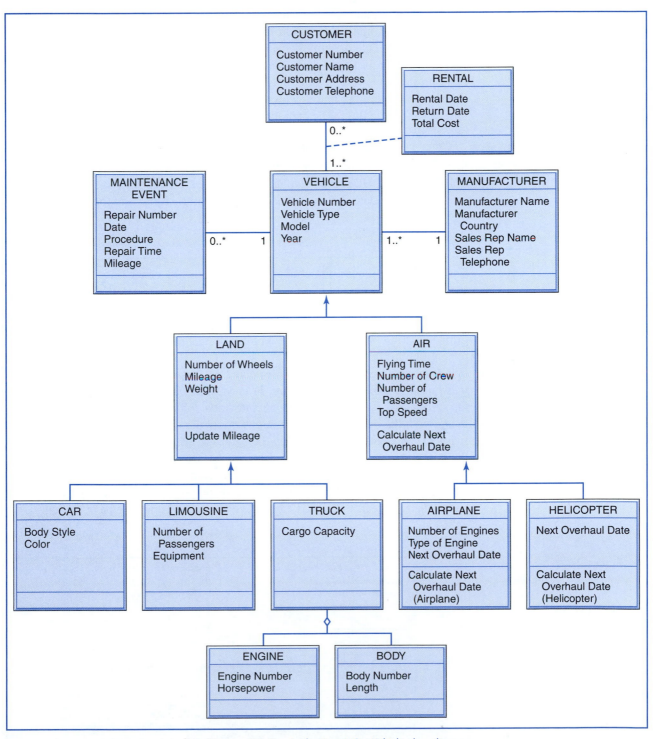

➤ **Figure 10.8** Lucky Rent-A-Car Vehicle class diagram

be an AIRPLANE or a HELICOPTER. Each CAR object will have nine attributes: Body Style and Color, plus four attributes inherited from VEHICLE and another three attributes inherited from LAND. Similarly, each LIMOUSINE will have nine attributes, each TRUCK will have eight attributes, each AIRPLANE will have eleven attributes, and each HELICOPTER will have nine attributes.

There is an update operation for all LAND vehicles to update their mileage attribute that is calculated in the same way for all three types of LAND vehicles; that is, no polymorphism is associated with this operation. On the other hand, the diagram indicates that there is polymorphism in the way that the Calculate Next Overhaul Date is inherited downward from the AIR class to the AIRPLANE and HELICOPTER classes. The operation will be somewhat different for each of those two classes.

The diamond-shaped symbol on the branch under the TRUCK class indicates that there is an aggregation diagram under it. Indeed, each TRUCK is composed of an ENGINE and a BODY, each with its own attributes. Notice that the company is interested in keeping data about engines and bodies for trucks but not for cars or limos.

ENCAPSULATION

Earlier, we introduced the concept that it might, in general, be a good idea to permit particular data to be updated only by a limited, controlled set of program segments. This would have the advantage of improving data integrity by eliminating the possibility of some less-than-fully-debugged or otherwise rogue program updating the data in some kind of inaccurate way. But how can such a concept be implemented?

A fascinating feature of object-oriented database management that implements these ideas is called **encapsulation.** In encapsulation, as illustrated in Figure 10.9, the attributes of a class or even an individual object are "encapsulated," stored together on the disk, with the operations that will act upon them. Yes, the program segments are actually stored within the database, which is a radical departure from the complete separation of data and programs that we always assumed in the relational database environment (as well as in the earlier navigational database environment). Furthermore, the OODBMS will only permit the attributes of the encapsulated objects to be updated by the encapsulated update-type operations. New

➤ **Figure 10.9**
An application program sends a message that triggers an encapsulated operation in an object

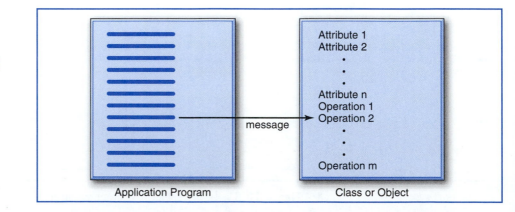

Application Program   Class or Object

class instances or objects will only be permitted to be created by the class's encapsulated constructor-type operations. Query-type operations would also be encapsulated, but since they do not update data, the data integrity issue is not a factor.

When an application program requires encapsulated data for any reason, it sends a **message** to one of the object's encapsulated operations to trigger it into action (Figure 10.9). The application program sends along any input data needed for the operation (for example, the number of years that an extended warranty is to be in effect for the Calculate Extended Warranty Price for Power Tools operation in General Hardware's POWER TOOL class in Figure 10.5). The encapsulated operation then executes its program code. Depending on the type of operation, it updates the object's attribute values, adds a new instance of a class or object, or simply returns data to satisfy a query.

ABSTRACT DATA TYPES

Data has traditionally fit into one of a small number of simple data types consisting of a few variations of character and numeric data. These are adequate to handle the kinds of attributes that we usually think of as being stored in a database. Names, addresses, descriptions, and so forth are stored as character data types. Attributes involving money and other numeric data that include fractional amounts are stored as decimal numbers. Serial numbers or quantity attributes that count a number of items are stored as integers. Furthermore, these simple data types have operations associated with them in the programming languages that use them. We take it for granted that we can add, subtract, multiply, and divide data stored in the numeric data types, but these operations are indeed associated with numeric data types and they are specifically not associated with character-type data.

Another interesting feature of object-oriented database management is the ability to create new, **abstract data types** and operations that are associated with them. But what kinds of data would require these new and perhaps exotic data types? Figure 10.10 illustrates some of them. In the increasingly rich data environments we

➤ **Figure 10.10**
Abstract data types

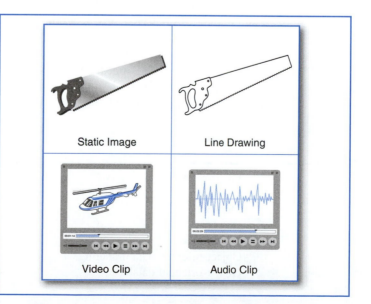

find ourselves in today, we may want to store static images, line drawings, video clips, and audio clips. For example, consider adding an attribute called Picture to the TOOL class of General Hardware's class diagram in Figure 10.5, so that one of the attributes of each tool is a photo of it. (This particular data type has been called a binary large object or BLOB.) Associated operations might include zoom and rotate. Consider adding an attribute called Flight to the HELICOPTER class of Lucky Rent-A-Vehicle's class diagram in Figure 10.8 to include a video clip of each helicopter flying. Associated operations might include pause or fast-forward. Or consider adding an attribute called Music to the CD class of Good Reading Bookstores' class diagram in Figure 10.6 to include an audio clip of one of a CD's songs. An associated operation might be adjust volume. It is worth emphasizing that part of the beauty of this concept is that the attributes that use these new data types are treated exactly like the less exotic attributes that merely use the simple character, decimal, and integer data types.

OBJECT/RELATIONAL DATABASE

When OODBMSs first became commercially available in the 1980s, they found some limited use in niche applications like storing an electric power company's power grid in a data format that could take advantage of the unique features of the object-oriented data approach. As we know by now, however, these OODBMSs didn't overwhelm the world of relational database and displace it. For, in spite of their new bells and whistles, the OODBMSs were lacking in several areas, including the superior query capabilities of SQL that everyone had become accustomed to with relational database. Yet their advanced features were too tempting to ignore.

Eventually, perhaps inevitably, relational database and **object-oriented database** came together in the form of hybrid relational database management systems with object-oriented features added to them. At first, these were called extended relational database systems but as they became more formalized, they became known as **object/relational database** systems. Imagine the General Hardware Company data stored as an object/relational database. A data structure for storing data about tools would essentially be a relational table that would include columns for Product Number, Product Name, Unit Price, Weight, *and Photo* (a photo of the tool), which would be stored as a static image-type of attribute (Figure 10.11). The attribute Photo could then appear in SQL statements just like the other attributes and could be processed as such, returning the photo to the user in a query or even matching a photo against the photos already in the table.

KEY TERMS

Abstract data type	Inheritance	Object/relational database
Aggregation	Message	Operation
Class	Method	Polymorphism
Class diagram	Object	Procedure
Complex relationships	Object class	Unified Modeling Language (UML)
Encapsulation	Object-oriented data modeling	
Generalization/specialization	Object-oriented database	

➤ **Figure 10.11**
The TOOL table in an
object/relational database

Product Number	Product Name	Unit Price	Photo
16386	Wrench	12.95	
19440	Hammer	17.50	
21765	Drill	32.99	
24013	Saw	26.25	
26722	Pliers	11.50	

QUESTIONS

1. Name and briefly describe three deficiencies in the relational database model.

2. In object-oriented terminology, what is an object? What is a class?

3. Describe the advanced relationship known as generalization. What are its benefits?

4. Describe how attributes are inherited in a generalization hierarchy.

5. What is an operation? Can operations be inherited? What is polymorphism?

6. Describe the advanced relationship known as aggregation. What are its benefits?

7. What is encapsulation in object-oriented database? What are its benefits?

8. What is an abstract data type (ADT)? What is the significance of having a database system that is capable of creating ADTs?

9. What is an object/relational database management system? What are its advantages?

EXERCISES

1. Draw an object-oriented class diagram, including traditional unary, binary, and ternary relationships, as well as generalization and aggregation relationships as needed, to represent the following business environment. Include all of the attributes and operations listed in the description.

The Houston, Texas, city government wants to develop an information system to keep track of the buildings in the city for both taxation and fire department dispatching purposes. The city will keep track of the address, year built, and owner of record of every building. It will also record the station number, address, and telephone number of each fire station. Each fire station has primary responsibility for a given set of buildings.

There are four types of buildings: single-family homes, apartment buildings, stores, and office buildings. The city wants to record the number of apartments in each apartment building, and the type of goods and annual sales volume of each store. It wants to record the number of floors in each office building. It must also keep track of the companies in each office building. An office building can have several or many companies in it; a company can have offices in several buildings. Each company has a name, telephone number, and a unique tax identification number. The city also wants to store the number of square feet that a particular company has in a particular office building. Single-family homes are made up of three parts: the house itself, a garage, and a shed. The city wants to keep track of the number of bedrooms, number of baths, and total floor space in the house, the capacity of the garage in number of cars, and the capacity of the shed in volume (cubic feet).

There is a tax calculation formula that is different for each of the four types of buildings.

2. Draw an object-oriented class diagram, including traditional unary, binary, and ternary relationships, as well as generalization and aggregation relationships as needed, to represent the following business environment. Include all of the attributes and operations listed in the description.

Reliable Home Warranty Company contracts with homeowners to repair their major appliances, electrical systems, and plumbing, all for a single annual fee. When a homeowner needs a repair, he calls Reliable and speaks to a dispatcher who sends a qualified technician from a participating repair company. The participating repair company then charges Reliable for the repair. Each dispatcher has an employee number, name, home address, and home telephone number. Each homeowner has a contract number, name, home address, home telephone number, and contract renewal date. Each job has a unique job number, date, and time. Each job is handled by one dispatcher and, obviously, involves one homeowner.

There are three kinds of jobs: appliance repair, electrical repair, and plumbing repair. For an appliance repair, the company wants to record the appliance type, its model number, its serial number, and the name of the appliance repair company assigned. In addition, Reliable wants to keep track of the manufacturer of the appliance. For each appliance manufacturer it lists the manufacturer name, headquarters address, and telephone number for parts ordering. There is a calculation for the charge that the appliance repair company makes to Reliable based on the type of appliance and the time spent. For a plumbing repair, Reliable keeps track of the name of the plumbing company and the length of time for the repair, but beyond that it makes a distinction between inside repairs and outside repairs such as to sewer lines or septic tanks. Charges from the plumbing company to Reliable are based on a specific plumbing charge formula but are calculated differently depending on whether the repair is an inside or outside repair. Also, for outside repairs, Reliable must record the distance from the house to the main sewer line or septic tank. For an electrical repair, Reliable tracks the length of time for the repair and the amount and type of wire used in the repair. There is a formula for calculating electrical repair charges based on time and the specialized materials used. Reliable must also keep certain information about the electrical contracting company assigned to the repair. This information includes the contractor's license number, name, address, and liability insurer. A particular electrical contracting company can be involved in many repairs.

MINICASES

1. In Minicase 1 of Chapter 3, you were asked to draw an entity-relationship diagram describing Happy Cruise Lines' business environment. We now report that Happy Cruise Lines has been acquired by MegaShip Lines, Inc., which has a fleet of oil tankers, container ships, and automobile transport ships. Thus, with the addition of Happy's cruise ships, MegaShip Lines will have four kinds of ships.

   a. Draw an object-oriented generalization diagram, including aggregation relationships as needed, to represent MegaShip's new business environment, with the following attributes and operations. All of MegaShip's ships have ship number, ship name, year built, weight, miles traveled, and next overhaul date attributes. In addition, cruise ships have passenger capacity and next health inspection date; oil tankers have oil capacity, container ships

   have number of containers, and automobile transport ships have number of automobile attributes. An operation determines the next overhaul date for all of the ships in the same manner. Another operation determines the next health inspection date for cruise ships. An operation calculates the next date for a ship to be refueled. This operation is the same for oil tankers, container ships, and automobile transport ships, but is different for cruise ships because of safety precautions regarding the passengers. Oil tankers are composed of a hull, one or more engines, and one or more oil storage tanks. An attribute of hull is length, an attribute of engine is horsepower, and an attribute of oil storage tank is capacity.

   b. Add the information given about cruise ships, cruises, and so on, in Chapter 3, Minicase 1, to the diagram in part (a), constructing a complete object-oriented class diagram.

2. In Minicase 2 of Chapter 3, you were asked to draw an entity-relationship diagram describing the Super Baseball League's business environment. We now report that the Super Baseball League has been absorbed into the Sensational Sports Federation (SSF). SSF divides its sports into two categories: team sports and individual sports. There are three team sports: baseball, basketball, and football; and two individual sports: golf and tennis. The central entity in each of these five sports is a "participant." In the team sports a participant is a team; in the individual sports a participant is an individual player. Every SSF participant (team or individual) has a participant number, participant name, sport (e.g., baseball, golf, etc.), and year affiliated with SSF. In addition, every team has a number of players, a home city and state, and a mascot. Every player in the individual sports has a name, home address, home telephone number, and annual income. Furthermore, golfers have a handicap; tennis players have a world ranking.

a. Draw an object-oriented generalization diagram to represent SSF's business environment.

b. Add the information given about baseball teams and associated entities in Minicase 2 of Chapter 3 to the diagram in part (a), constructing a complete object-oriented class diagram.

c. Add several operations to the class diagram in part (b), demonstrating polymorphism with some of them.

CHAPTER 11

DATA ADMINISTRATION, DATABASE ADMINISTRATION, AND DATA DICTIONARIES

CHAPTER OBJECTIVES

After learning the material in this chapter, you will be able to:

✔ Define and compare data administration and database administration.
✔ List and describe the advantages of data administration.
✔ List and describe the advantages of database administration.
✔ List and describe the responsibilities of data administration.
✔ List and describe the responsibilities of database administration.
✔ Explain the concept of metadata.
✔ List and describe such metadata realizations as passive and active data dictionaries, relational DBMS catalogs, and data repositories.

Photo Courtesy of ESPN

ESPN

ESPN, headquartered in Bristol, Connecticut, is a major sportscasting network whose ventures include cable television, radio, sports news, a magazine, and even wireless sports updates. ESPN acquires sports programming, broadcasts it, and stores it. The backbone of this complex operation is a database application called the Network Cable System (NCS). NCS is implemented in Oracle and runs on an IBM large-end Unix server.

Implemented in 1993, NCS is a cradle-to-grave system that tracks all of ESPN's broadcasting business from the time that programming is acquired until long after it is shown. It tracks and stores the contracts for the programming, schedules the programming, coordinates the commercial advertisements that will be shown during the broadcasts, and manages the tape library of current and historic sports footage. It even has pointers to digitally stored advertisements. Finally, it stores Nielsen ratings that indicate how many people watched its broadcasts, on a historic basis.

One of the main relational tables in the system is the Program Schedule table. With one record per sports event, this table coordinates the broadcast schedule for ESPN, ESPN2, ESPNNews, ESPNClassic, and other operations. There is also an Airings table and a Units table, with 12 million records dating back to 1993 that records commercials aired. These can be linked back to the events in the Program Schedule table. These database tables are used both in the operational and analytical modes. Operationally, on a day-to-day basis they, for example, manage the check-in and check-out of tapes from the tape library. But they are also used to analyze the historic broadcast, Nielsen, and advertising data to learn the effectiveness of the broadcasting and the value of the advertising.

Advanced technologies are only as effective as the people who guide them. This is true of jet airliners, X-ray imaging devices, nuclear power plants, and certainly computers! In the late 1960s, as early navigational database management systems were starting to come into use, a few forward-looking companies began to recognize the need for a department whose job it would be to manage the DBMS and its environment. As the years went by, some of these groups gained responsibility over data in non-DBMS files as well. In addition, some of them advanced from a position of managing data only on an operational basis to additionally performing strategic planning, policy setting, and other broader-based duties.

This chapter will describe the functions and groups that companies create to manage their data and their database environment. This "people side" of database management consists of two parts: data administration and database administration. **Data administration** is a planning and analysis function that is responsible for setting data policy and standards, for promoting the company's data as a competitive resource, for accounting for the use of data, and for providing liaison support to systems analysts during application development. The **database administration** function is more operationally oriented and is responsible for the day-to-day monitoring and management of the company's various active databases, as well as providing liaison support to program designers during application development. Database administration typically carries out many of the policies set by data administration. This chapter will also describe a class of software tools, known generically as **data dictionaries,** which the data administration and database administration functions can use to help manage their company's data.

THE ADVANTAGES OF DATA AND DATABASE ADMINISTRATION

The initial question that arises is, why do companies need these data and database administration departments? What value do they add? Are they just additional cost centers that don't produce revenue? Indeed, at one time or another, most companies have struggled with these questions but in today's heavily data-intensive, information-dependent business environment, these functions are recognized as being more important than ever. The reasons, as listed in Figure 11.1, are explained next.

Data as a Shared Corporate Resource

Data is a corporate resource, and it has taken its rightful place alongside money, plant and equipment, personnel, and other corporate resources. Virtually all aspects of business have become dependent on their information systems and the data flowing through them. Today's organizations could not function without their vast stores of personnel data, customer data, product data, supplier data, and so forth. Indeed, data may well be the most important corporate resource because, by its very nature, it describes all of the others. Furthermore, the effective use of its data can give a company a significant competitive advantage. Whether it is used for supply chain management, customer service, or advanced marketing applications, a company's data can have a real impact on its share of the marketplace and on its bottom-line profitability.

But all resources tend to be scarce (is there ever enough money to go around?), and there is typically internal competition for them. Data is no exception. As more and more corporate functions seek the same data for their work, bottlenecks can form and the speed of accessing the data can slow. Companies have responded in a variety of ways, including bringing in faster computers and making copies of the data for different applications. But the former has its limits, and the latter introduces the kind of multi-file redundancy that we argued against earlier in this book. Also, some companies have a policy of data "ownership" in which one of several corporate functions that share some particular data has the primary claim to it and often the ability to decide who else can use it.

What all of these considerations are leading to is simply this: Any shared corporate resource requires a dedicated department to manage it. How would a company handle its money without its finance and accounting departments? It makes little sense to have an important resource either not managed at all or managed part-time and half-heartedly by some group that has other responsibilities too. It also makes little sense to have any one of the groups competing for the shared resource also managing it—the resource manager must obviously be impartial when a dispute arises. The dedicated departments that manage the company's data are the data administration and database administration departments. Actually, the parallel between the two corporate resources, money and data, is reflected in the parallel of having two company functions to manage each. Finance and data administration, respectively take a more strategic or tactical-level view of each resource, whereas accounting and database administration, respectively, take a more operational-level view of them.

➤ **Figure 11.1**
The advantages of data and database administration

- Data as a shared corporate resource
- Efficiency in job specialization
- Operational management of data
- Managing externally acquired databases
- Managing data in the decentralized environment

Efficiency in Job Specialization

Many of the functions involved in the management of data are highly specialized and require specific expertise. They can range from long-range data planning to working with the idiosyncrasies of a particular database management system. This argues for a full-time staff of specialists who do nothing but manage a company's data and databases.

A good example, and one on which we have spent considerable time in this book, is database design. To do a really good job of both logical and physical database design requires considerable education and practice. The question then becomes one of who among the information systems personnel should be responsible for designing the company's main, shared databases. The systems analysts? The application programmers? Which systems analysts or application programmers? After all, there may be several or many application development projects, each with different systems analysts and application programmers assigned, that will share the same databases. It doesn't make a lot of sense to have any of these people design the databases, for at least two reasons. First, it is unreasonable to expect any of them to be as expert at designing databases as people who do it on a full-time basis. Second, if any one application development group designs the shared databases, they will tend to optimize them for their own applications and not take into account the needs of the other applications. The solution is to have application-independent, full-time database specialists (i.e., data and database administration personnel), who are experts at database design and who will optimize the database designs for the overall good of the company.

Operational Management of Data

At the operational level, for the day-to-day management of the company's production databases, an independent department must be responsible, for reasons that were set forth above. Since the data is likely to be shared among several or many corporate functions and users, the data should be managed by an independent group whose loyalty is to the overall company and not to any individual function. There is also the specific example that in the shared data environment there will always be some applications or users that depend on other applications or users to collect data and/or update the tables on a regular or irregular basis. So, it is prudent to have an independent data administration group keep track of who is responsible for updating which tables and to monitor whether they have kept to the expected schedule, for the benefit of all the others who use these tables.

Also, working with the databases at the operational level requires an in-depth knowledge of the DBMS in use, of the databases themselves, and of such specific skills and tasks as physical database design, database security, and backup and recovery. It is unreasonable to expect application programmers, systems analysts, or anyone else with their own focused duties to be experts in data management techniques. In short, it requires specialists.

Managing Externally Acquired Databases

In today's information systems environment, some databases are not designed by a company's own personnel but are acquired as part of purchased software packages.

A prominent example is Enterprise Resource Planning (ERP) software like the multi-function, integrated software sold by companies such as SAP and Peoplesoft. These packages consist of application modules that manage a variety of corporate functions (personnel, accounting, etc.). They typically include a central database shared by all of the application modules. When a company decides to go the ERP route, they are making an important commitment to having a shared data resource. Once again, the only arrangement that makes sense for the management of this shared resource is to have an independent group that is tasked with managing it for the overall good of the company.

Managing Data in the Decentralized Environment

With the advent of personal computers, local area networks, and new, user-friendly software in the 1980s, many companies decentralized at least some of their information systems work. These technologies permitted user departments all over the company to handle some or all of their information systems needs on their own, without having to rely on the central information systems organization. This arrangement has a variety of advantages and disadvantages (though a book on database management is not the place to go into them). Although such developments as ERP software with its centralized database concept have swung the pendulum back toward the centralized IS environment to some extent, decentralization is a fact of life to a greater or lesser degree in virtually all companies.

The question then, in terms of the advantages of data and database administration is, do we need these functions more or less in the **decentralized environment** than we do in the centralized environment? Some people might say that we don't need them. In fact, when the move toward decentralization began, one of the stated reasons was to reduce the "overhead" of the central IS department, and that included database administration. Furthermore, many people are quite content to develop their own databases on their PCs using MS Access and other such PC-based DBMSs. But there is a very strong argument that says that data and database administration are even *more important* in a decentralized environment than in a centralized one.

First of all, most large companies do not have totally decentralized IS; most have a hybrid centralized/decentralized environment. And if nothing else, the centralized portion includes a central, shared database, which certainly requires a database administration function to manage it. Moreover, with company data present in a variety of central databases, databases associated with local area networks, and even databases on PCs, the *coordinating role* of data administration is crucial. This coordinating role is a key responsibility of data administration, which is our next topic.

THE RESPONSIBILITIES OF DATA ADMINISTRATION

As information systems are used in all aspects of a company's business, data administrators find themselves playing key roles in the corporate environment. Those who understand what data a company possesses and how it flows both from department to department within the company and between the company and its customers, suppliers, and other external entities, are in the best position to understand how the company really functions. Data administrators often come from the ranks of systems analysts, and, indeed, some companies use the term **data analyst** to describe them. What are the responsibilities of the data administration function? They are listed in Figure 11.2 and discussed below.

Data Coordination

With data playing so prominent a role in the corporate environment, its accuracy is of the utmost importance. But in the centralized/decentralized environment, with data and copies of data scattered among mainframe computers, local area network servers, and even PCs, the possibility of inconsistency and error increases. There is nothing more annoying than two people making important presentations in a meeting and showing different figures that should be the same. It is up to the data administrators to keep track of the organization's data, including download schedules, update schedules and responsibilities, and data interchange with other companies. This is not to suggest that data administration should try to control all of the databases on all of the employees' PCs. That would be impossible. But total data anarchy is not desirable either, and so **data coordination** becomes the job of the data administrators, by which they maintain a reasonable amount of control over the company's data.

Data Planning

Data planning begins with determining what data will be needed for future company business efforts and the applications that will support them. This may be limited to data generated and used internally within the company. However, today it often means coordinating with other companies in a supply chain or acquiring external customer data for use in marketing. In either case, there is the need to plan for integrating the new data with the company's existing data. A number of methodologies have been developed to aid in data planning. These methodologies take into account the business processes that the company performs as part of its normal operations and add the data needed to support them. While they generally operate at a high "strategic" level and may not get into the details of individual attributes, they do provide a broad roadmap to work from.

Related to strategic data planning is the matter of what hardware and software will be needed to support the company's information systems operations in the future. The questions involved range from such relatively straightforward

➤ **Figure 11.2**

The responsibilities of data administration

- Data coordination
- Data planning
- Data standards
- Liaison to systems analysts and programmers
- Training
- Arbitration of disputes and usage authorization
- Documentation and publicity
- Data's competitive advantage

matters as how many disk drives will be needed to contain the data to broader issues of how much processing power will be needed to support the overall IS environment. Another data planning issue is how metadata and the data dictionary concept that we will discuss later in this chapter should be put to use. This involves what data should be stored in the data dictionary, to what uses the data dictionary should be put, who should interact with the data dictionary and how, and on what kind of schedule all of this should take place. Yet another data planning issue that occasionally faces companies is the migration of old, pre-database data and applications into the company's database environment. There is also the problem of migrating data from one DBMS to another, as the company's software infrastructure changes.

Data Standards

In order to reduce errors, improve performance, and enhance the ability of one IS worker to understand the work done by another, it is important for the data administration function to set standards regarding data and its use. One example of **data standards** is controlling the way that attribute names, table names, and other data-related names are formed. Attribute names must be meaningful and consistent. The company can't have the human resources department use Serial Number as the attribute name for employee numbers while at the same time the manufacturing department uses it for finished product serial numbers. Similarly, a problem arises if the human resources department tries to use Serial Number and Employee Number in different tables to represent the employee number. Another example of standards setting is insisting on consistency in the way the programs that access the database are written, especially in regard to the database call instructions. Care here can help to prevent database call-related performance problems, as well as to ease maintenance by having standard, readily understood instructions.

Data standards also come into play in the IS interactions between companies in supply chains. When data is exchanged using electronic data interchange (EDI) technology, adjustments have to be made to account for attribute structure and other differences in the information systems of the two companies involved.

Liaison to Systems Analysts and Programmers

In the role of liaison to application developers, data administrators (who are often called data analysts in this role) are responsible for providing support to the systems analysts and programmers in all matters concerning the data needed by an application. During the systems analysis phase of application development, the support may include help in determining what data is needed for the application and which of the data items needed for the application already exist in the active database.

Another aspect of such liaison activity, which is really a topic in itself, is the question of database design. Data analysts are generally involved in database design at some level, but the decision of what that precise level of involvement should be is dependent on a number of factors. In an IS environment in which the data administration organization is very strong and in which there is a significant amount of data sharing among different applications and different functional areas of the company, the data analysts may do all of the logical database design work themselves. Here again, they can stand as an impartial group creating the best design for the overall good of all the sharing users. The other choice is for the application developers to do the database design with either active consultation by the data analysts or approval responsibility after the fact by the data analysts. In the active consultation role, the data analysts lend their expertise to the effort, as well as determine how the new data should mesh with data in the existing database, if there is to be such a merging. In the approval role, the application developers (usually the lead programmers for this activity) design the database, which is then shown to the data analysts for discussion and approval.

Training

In some companies, data administration is responsible for training all those in the company who have a reason to understand the company's data and, in some cases, the DBMS environment. Management personnel should understand why the database approach is good for the company and for their individual functions specifically. Users must understand why the shared data is secure and private. Application developers must be given substantial training in how to work in the database environment, including training in database concepts, database standards, how to write DBMS calls in their programs, possibly how to do database design, how to use the data dictionary to their advantage, and in general, what services they can expect data and database administration to provide.

Arbitration of Disputes and Usage Authorization

To introduce the concept of **arbitration,** we should spend a moment on the question of **data ownership.** Who in a company "owns" a piece of data or a database? To be technical, since data is a resource of value to the company, the data "belongs" to the company's owners or stockholders. But in practical terms, in many companies data is controlled by its user or primary user. In this case, data and database administration act as custodians of the data in the sense of providing security, backup, performance monitoring, and other such services. In some companies with an advanced level of data sharing, ownership responsibility actually falls to data administration itself.

If ownership has been established and a new application requires the use of existing data, then it is the job of data administration to act as an intermediary and approach the owner of the data with the request for data sharing. This can also happen if someone in the company simply wants to query someone else's database. If there is a dispute over such data sharing, then the data administration group acts as an arbitrator between the disagreeing parties. Incidentally, the data administration group may also find itself acting as arbitrator between two database users who are sharing the same CPU and vying for better performance.

Documentation and Publicity

Using the data dictionary as its primary tool, the data management function is responsible for documenting the data environment. This **documentation** includes a description of the data and the databases, plus programs, reports, and which people have access to these items. A more complete list of such metadata items will be discussed later in this chapter with data dictionaries.

As a related issue, the data management group should perform a publicity function, informing potential users of what data already exists in the database. Knowing what data exists might encourage employees to think about how they can use the company's data to gain competitive advantages that did not previously exist. They may discover how to automate more of their work and to integrate their work more directly with related business processes that are already automated.

Data's Competitive Advantage

Earlier, we talked about the idea of data providing a competitive advantage for the company. Another point is that data administrators, by virtue of their knowledge of the company's data and the way it flows from one company function to another, are in a unique position to understand how the company "works." This is especially true since virtually all company functions today are dependent on information systems. Combining these two concepts, a very important and very high-profile responsibility of the data administration function is to respond to questions about how the company's business procedures can be adjusted or modified to improve the company's operating efficiency. This can also extend to data administration taking the initiative and making suggestions for improvement on its own. This capability, which can lead to decreased costs and improved profits for the company, makes data administration a particularly important company function.

THE RESPONSIBILITIES OF DATABASE ADMINISTRATION

Database administration is a technical function that is responsible for the day-to-day operations and maintenance of the DBMS environment, including such related tools as the data dictionary. This is quite analogous to the role of the systems programmers who are responsible for maintaining the mainframe operating systems. Like operating systems, DBMSs tend to include many highly product-specific features that require a thoroughly trained individual to handle. What are the responsibilities of the database administration function? They are listed in Figure 11.3 and are explained as follows.

➤ **Figure 11.3**
The responsibilities of database administration

- DBMS performance monitoring
- DBMS troubleshooting
- DBMS usage and security monitoring
- Data dictionary operations
- DBMS data and software maintenance
- Database design

DBMS Performance Monitoring

One of the key functions performed by database administration is **performance monitoring.** Using utility programs, the database administrators can gauge the performance of the running DBMS environment. This activity has a number of implications. It is important to know how fast the various applications are executing as part of ensuring that response time requirements are being met. Also, this type of performance information is pertinent to future hardware and software acquisition plans. Depending on the characteristics of the DBMS and the operating system under which it is running, the performance information may be used to redistribute the database application load among different CPUs or among different memory regions within a system. Finally, performance information can be used to ferret out inefficient applications or queries that may be candidates for redesign.

The database administrators must also interface with the IS organization's systems programming staff, which maintains the mainframe operating systems. The systems programmers will also have performance and troubleshooting responsibilities, which may overlap with those of the database administrators. The net of this is that it greatly facilitates matters if the two groups get along well with each other and can work together effectively.

DBMS Troubleshooting

Inevitably, a DBMS application will occasionally fail during execution, for reasons ranging from a bug in the application code to a hardware or system software failure. The question is, who do the users call when it happens? In a strongly controlled environment, the database administrators should be the **troubleshooting** interface. The key to the troubleshooting operation is to make an assessment of what went wrong and coordinate the appropriate personnel needed to fix it, including systems programmers, application programmers, and the data administrators themselves.

DBMS Usage and Security Monitoring

Database administrators keep track of which applications are running in the database environment and can track who is accessing the data in the database at any moment. Again, there are software utilities that enable them to perform these functions. Monitoring the users of the database environment is really done from several perspectives. One is the matter of **security:** making sure that only authorized personnel access the data. This includes the function of instructing the system to allow new users to access the database, as ordered by data administration personnel in conjunction with the data owners. Another perspective is that of **usage:** the need to maintain records on the amount of use the various users make of the database. This can have implications in future load balancing and performance optimizing work, and may also be used in allocating system costs among the various users and applications. A related concern is database auditing. Even assuming that only authorized users have accessed the database, reasons involving accounting and error correction require that a record be kept of who has accessed and who has modified which data items. Incidentally, if the data auditing function is to be performed, the tool that allows it to be accomplished is a journal or log, similar to the one used for backup and recovery. Depending on the nature of the auditing, this journal or log may have to record all simple data accesses as well as all data modifications.

Data Dictionary Operations

The database administration group is responsible for the operational aspects, as opposed to the planning aspects, of the data dictionary and any other metadata tools. It also provides dictionary access to other personnel such as systems analysts, generates periodic data dictionary reports as required by management, and provides management with answers to ad hoc questions about the data and the IS environment. For example, systems analysts developing a new application may want to find out if the data they need in the new application already exists in the company's databases. IS management will want periodic reports on the company's databases, including a list of the tables and their sizes. An ad hoc query may include which people had access to certain data that leaked out of the company! We will discuss this in more detail in the data dictionary section of this chapter.

DBMS Data and Software Maintenance

Database administration personnel will be involved with a wide range of data and software maintenance activities, to a greater or lesser degree depending on how the IS department is organized. These activities include installing new versions of the DBMS, installing "fixes" or "patches" (corrections) to the DBMS, performing backup and recovery operations (to be discussed in the next chapter), and any other tasks related to repairing or upgrading the DBMS or the database. One particular data maintenance activity is modifying the database structures as new tables and attributes are inevitably added. This is really also an issue of database design.

Database Design

In the mix of centralized and decentralized IS environments that exist today, there is a wide range in database administration responsibilities for database design. For the shared, central databases, database administration is responsible for physical database design and may also either be responsible for or be a participant in logical database design. Notice that their responsibility for physical database design is consistent with their expertise in the features (and idiosyncrasies!) of the DBMS in use and with their overall responsibility for the performance of the DBMS environment. For decentralized databases on LAN servers or even on PCs, the database administrator's role in database design is often more that of a consultant who is called in on request.

DATA DICTIONARIES

Introduction

The information systems function (and within it, the data and database administration functions) is responsible for managing data as a corporate resource. Not only does the data have to be stored, but like any other resource there have to be provisions for inputting more of it, outputting it (in the form of reports, query responses, data transmissions to supply chain partners, etc.), and, most certainly, processing it. To accomplish all of these functions requires people, equipment (i.e., computers, disks, networks, and so forth) and established procedures, standards, and policies. The question before us now is, how does IS management keep track of all of this? But then, how does *any* corporate function keep track of their resources and other responsibilities? With information systems, of course! Does that mean that IS management can keep track of *their own* resources and responsibilities with information systems? The apparent answer should be, yes, and perhaps even, obviously yes. But this has been a long and at times difficult road. Do you know the old story about the shoemaker's children being the last ones to get shoes (Figure 11.4)? The shoemaker was so busy making shoes for the other children of the town in order to make a living that his own children were the last ones to get shoes. Similarly, the IS function has been so busy developing and running systems to support all the other corporate functions that it took a long time before it could invest the resources to develop information systems to support itself.

What we are talking about here comes under the general term of **metadata,** literally data about data. What data does an IS function need to manage itself, and what kinds of tools can it employ to store and handle the data? For a long time, the term for such a metadata storage tool has been the **data dictionary,** literally a database *about* data. More recently, the term **data repository** has come into vogue. The term **data catalog** has also taken on certain specific meanings. We begin our discussion of these terms and their implications with a simple but concrete example of part of a data dictionary.

A Simple Example of Metadata

Figure 11.5 once again shows the General Hardware Company's relational database. Recall that among the entities that General Hardware has to keep track of are salespersons and customers. Each row of the SALESPERSON table describes one entity (i.e., one salesperson), and each column of the SALESPERSON table describes one kind of attribute or feature or fact about a salesperson. Similar statements can be

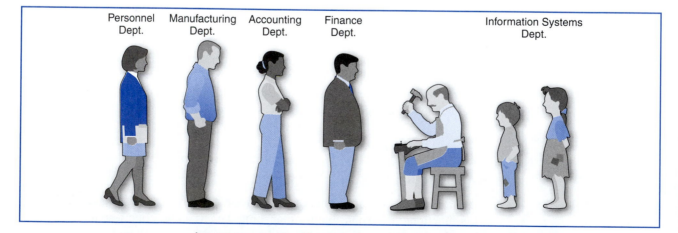

➤ **Figure 11.4**   The shoemaker's children are the last ones to get shoes

➤ **Figure 11.5**
The General Hardware
Company relational
database

SALESPERSON				
Salesperson Number	Salesperson Name	Commission Percentage	Year of Hire	Office Number

CUSTOMER			
Customer Number	Customer Name	Salesperson Number	HQ City

CUSTOMER EMPLOYEE			
Customer Number	Employee Number	Employee Name	Title

PRODUCT		
Product Number	Product Name	Unit Price

SALES		
Salesperson Number	Product Number	Quantity

OFFICE		
Office Number	Telephone	Size

made for the CUSTOMER table. Why are we repeating and belaboring these points this late in the book? To contrast them with the tables of a data dictionary. We know that the SALESPERSON and CUSTOMER tables exist to help the company's sales function conduct its business. Today, this kind of database support of company functions, provided by the company's information systems, is taken almost for granted. But do all company functions have database support? Sales, personnel, accounting, finance, product development, manufacturing, and customer support certainly do. But what about the information systems function, itself?

Figure 11.6 shows two of the tables of a simple data dictionary: a database designed to help the IS function manage its own responsibilities. Again, we know that the sales function wants to keep track of salespersons and customers. So what does the IS function want to keep track of? Two entities that IS must manage are the tables and attributes in the company's databases and, more broadly, in its IS environment. IS must have a complete list of all the tables in the company's databases (at least in its central, shared databases), as well as detailed data about the

➤ **Figure 11.6**
Two data dictionary tables

(a) TABLES table

Table Name	Table Length	Disk Number
Salesperson	500	A23
Customer	6,400	A23
Customer Employee	127,000	A23
Product	83,000	A47
Sales	273,000	A47
Office	600	A47

(b) ATTRIBUTES table.

Attribute Name	Attribute Type	Attribute Length
Salesperson Number	Numeric	3
Salesperson Name	Alphabetic	20
Commission Percentage	Numeric	2
Year of Hire	Numeric	4
Customer Number	Numeric	4
Customer Name	Alphabetic	20
HQ City	Alphabetic	15

tables. It also has to track the attributes that are in the tables. Thus Figure 11.6 shows a *TABLES table* and an *ATTRIBUTES table*—that's right, a data dictionary table listing the company's tables and a data dictionary table listing the attributes in the company's tables.

In the SALESPERSON table, each row represents one of the entities: a salesperson. In the CUSTOMER table, each row represents a customer. The equivalent in the data dictionary is that each row of the TABLES table represents one of the tables in the company's database and each row of the ATTRIBUTES table represents one of the attributes in the tables in the company's database. Thus, in this example, we see that each row of the TABLES table in Figure 11.6 represents one of the tables of General Hardware's database in Figure 11.5. Also, each row of the ATTRIBUTES table in Figure 11.6 represents one of the attributes in Figure 11.5.

If the sales function has decided that Salesperson Number, Salesperson Name, Commission Percentage, and Year of Hire are attributes that it must store for each salesperson, and Customer Number, Customer Name, Salesperson Number, and HQ City are attributes that it must store for each customer, what are the attributes for tables and attributes that IS feels it must store in the data dictionary? Figure 11.6a shows that the attributes for tables are Table Name, Table Length (number of records), and Disk Number (the disk on which the table is stored). The attributes for attributes (yes, that's correct, think about it!) shown in Figure 11.6b are Attribute Name, Attribute Type, and Attribute Length (in bytes).

As in any database, in addition to tracking the basic facts about the represented entities, a data dictionary must keep track of the relationships between the entities.

The data dictionary table in Figure 11.7 represents the many-to-many relationship between the tables and attributes shown in the data dictionary's TABLES table and ATTRIBUTES table. In terms of demonstrating the nature of the many-to-many relationship between tables and attributes, first Figure 11.7 obviously shows that each table has several attributes. But also notice that the Salesperson Number attribute is associated with two tables, both the SALESPERSON and CUSTOMER tables (because it is the primary key of the SALESPERSON table and is a foreign key in the CUSTOMER table).

Thus the tables of Figure 11.6 and Figure 11.7 contain metadata, data *about the company's data*. How is the data organized? What are the data structures called? Where is the data stored? How much data is there? This is the essence of metadata. Now let's see how it has evolved.

Passive and Active Data Dictionaries

Definitions and Distinctions   Commercially available data dictionaries, which date from the late 1970s, are passive in nature. Basically, a **passive data dictionary** is used just for documentation purposes. Data about the entities in the IS environment are entered into the dictionary and cross-referenced as one-to-many and many-to-many relationships. Requests for information in the form of reports and queries about the dictionary's contents are run as needed. The passive data dictionary is simply a self-contained database used for documenting the IS environment.

In contrast, an **active data dictionary** is one that interacts with the IS environment on a real-time basis. The nature of the interaction can be a matter of input into the data dictionary, output from it, or both. A data dictionary being active in terms of input means that an event taking place in the IS environment, such as the creation of a new database table, automatically results in new data (about this event) being input into the data dictionary. A data dictionary being active in terms of output means that responses from the dictionary are an integral part of running the IS environment. For example, the data dictionary may contain data about who in the company is authorized to access particular tables. If the data dictionary must be "consulted" for this data every time someone tries to access a table, then the data dictionary is considered to be active in the output sense.

Entities and Attributes   In the earlier example, we discussed tables and attributes as two possible data dictionary entities. Figure 11.8 shows a broader list of possibilities. This is not intended to be a complete list that fits the needs of all companies. In fact, one of the principles of the data dictionary concept is to make the data dictionary expandable and customizable to a company's particular needs.

The two classes of attributes for data dictionary entities are (1) those of a general nature that likely apply to any of the entities and (2) those specific to particular data dictionary entities. "Name" is an example of a general attribute. Most data dictionary entities must have a name or some

➤ **Figure 11.7**
A data dictionary table representing the many-to-many relationship between the TABLES table and the ATTRIBUTES table

Table Name	Attribute Name
Salesperson	Salesperson Number
Salesperson	Salesperson Name
Salesperson	Commission Percentage
Salesperson	Year of Hire
Customer	Customer Number
Customer	Customer Name
Customer	Salesperson Number
Customer	HQ City

➤ **Figure 11.8**
Data dictionary sample entities

- Data-Related Entities
  - Databases
  - Tables
  - Attributes
  - Web Pages
- Software-Related Entities
  - Application Programs
  - Database Management Systems
  - Jobs
- Hardware-Related Entities
  - Computers
  - Disks
  - Local Area Networks
- Outputs
  - Reports
  - Queries
- People

other identifier. By far, however, most data dictionary attributes are specific to particular entities. Some examples include the Value Range of a numeric attribute, the Length of a record or table row, the Home Address of a person, the Capacity of a disk, the Language that a program is written in, and so forth.

Relationships   The relationship between almost any pair of data dictionary entities can have value to IS management. Some examples of common data dictionary relationships and the entities involved are shown in Figure 11.9. With such relationships between the dictionary entities, data administration personnel can aid in new software development, data security and privacy, change management, and a host of other IS environment tasks.

Uses and Users   Data dictionaries can be of considerable use to a variety of people in the corporate environment in general as well as in the IS environment specifically. The heaviest users of the data dictionary will be IS management and the data administration and database administration functions under them. The data dictionary is fundamentally the database used to store the data about the data and computer resources that these various people are charged with managing. Whether producing periodic lists of databases or tables in the IS environment or responding to ad hoc queries about which personnel had access to data that leaked out of the company, the data dictionary is the information resource for IS.

Systems analysts and program designers can use the data dictionary in two major ways. One use is as a source of information about what entities, attributes, and so forth already exist in the IS environment, which might be needed in a new application development effort underway. If data needed for a new system already

➤ **Figure 11.9**
Data dictionary sample
relationships

- Table (or file) Construction: Which attributes (or fields) appear in which tables (or files).
- Security: Which people have access to which databases or tables or files.
- Impact of Change: Which programs might be affected by changes to which tables or files. (*Note:* This has become much less of an issue due to the data independence of relational databases.)
- Physical Residence: Which tables or files are on which disks.
- Program Data Requirements: Which programs use which tables or files.
- Responsibility: Which people are responsible for updating which databases or tables or files.

exists, then the new application may be able to use it. If there are existing database structures that the application can add on to in order to satisfy its requirements, then that might amount to a large cost saving. In those and related situations, the dictionary is the repository of data to be searched. The other dictionary use for systems analysts and designers is as a documentation device for the new information that is generated as a result of their application development efforts. In this way, the application developers have a natural vehicle for documentation, and the data dictionary has a natural way of being populated with data concerning new applications.

Corporate employees in all functions and at almost all levels can benefit from the data dictionary by using it to discover the available data in the company. Exploring new ways to use the data to improve their own responsibilities will help the company as a whole. Finally, there is the benefit to corporate management. As we said earlier, it becomes increasingly important for management to understand the nature of the data in its systems, which mirrors the workings of the organization, in order to have the best grasp on how the company functions.

Relational DBMS Catalogs

An integral part of every relational DBMS is its catalog. A **relational catalog** is a highly active but limited-scope data dictionary that is very closely tied in to the operations of the relational DBMS. Not surprisingly, the relational catalog is itself composed of relational tables and may be queried with standard SQL commands. Typical database entity data stored in relational catalogs include databases, tables, attributes, views, indexes, users, and disks. At the attribute level, the relational catalog will note such important facts as which attributes in the database are unique. Notice that all of these entities are very closely tied to the running of the relational DBMS. In contrast to general-purpose data dictionaries, relational catalogs do not include such entities as reports and nonrelational files.

The main purpose of the relational catalog is to accurately support the relational query optimizer. As we discussed earlier in the book, when a query is posed to the relational DBMS, the relational query optimizer tries to find an efficient way or *access path* to satisfy the query. In order to accomplish this, the optimizer must have a source of complete and absolutely accurate data about the database. It must know what attributes are in the tables, which attributes are indexed, which attributes are unique, and whatever other data will help it to come up with an efficient solution plan. It finds all of this data in the relational catalog. The point about the relational catalog being highly active, in data dictionary terms, is that in order for it to be absolutely accurate, it must be updated in a mechanical and automated way. The system can't take the chance that a human inputting data into the relational catalog might make a mistake. So, input to the relational catalog is accomplished programmatically as changes to the database environment occur. For example, if someone instructs the relational DBMS to create a new table, it does two things. It creates the new table, *and* it automatically inputs data about the new table into the relational catalog. This is the only way to ensure the accuracy of the relational catalog.

Another use of the relational catalog, which we spoke about generically when discussing data dictionaries, is to provide a roadmap through the database data for anyone who wants to query the data or explore new ways to use the data. The relational DBMS checks the user authorization data in the catalog before it allows a user to retrieve data he is requesting with a SELECT statement or to update, delete, or insert records in application tables.

Data Repositories

The latest realization of the metadata concept is known as the **data repository.** A data repository is, in effect, a large-scale data dictionary that includes entity types generated and needed by the latest IS technologies. One popular usage of the term *data repository* is associated with CASE (Computer Aided Software Engineering) software. In the CASE environment, the data repository holds the same types of data that traditional data dictionaries hold, as well as CASE-specific data such as reusable code modules. The term *data repository* has also been associated with object-oriented database environments in which OODBMS-specific entity types such as objects are included.

KEY TERMS

Active data dictionary	Data planning	Passive data dictionary
Arbitration	Data repository	Performance monitoring
Data administration	Data standards	Relational catalog
Data analyst	Database administration	Security monitoring
Data coordination	Decentralized environment	Troubleshooting
Data dictionary	Documentation	Usage monitoring
Data ownership	Metadata	

QUESTIONS

1. What is data administration?

2. What is database administration?

3. What are the advantages of having data administration and database administration departments?

4. Explain and defend the following statement: Data is a corporate resource and should be managed in the same manner in which other corporate resources are managed.

5. Why is it important to have data and database administration specialists from the point of view of efficiency in job specialization?

6. What is the importance of data and database administration from the point of view of externally acquired databases?

7. Defend the following statement: Data and database administration are even more important in the

decentralized IS environment than in the centralized one.

8. List and briefly explain five major responsibilities of data administration.

9. Why is it important that data administrators perform a data coordination role?

10. What kinds of planning do data administrators have to do regarding data?

11. Defend or refute the following statement: Current IS technologies and practices make having data standards more important than ever before.

12. In general, what are data administration's responsibilities to the professional and managerial employees of the company? Concentrate on training, publicity, and liaison tasks.

13. Why might data administration have to serve as the arbitrator of disputes?

14. List and briefly explain five major responsibilities of database administration.

15. Discuss database administration's role in performance monitoring and troubleshooting.

16. How do database administration's responsibilities to the data dictionary differ from those of data administration?

17. Describe the role of database administration in database design and explain why that role makes sense.

18. What is metadata?

19. What is a data dictionary?

20. Explain in your own words why a data dictionary in a relational DBMS environment would have a "*Tables* table."

21. What is the difference between an active and a passive data dictionary?

22. List some typical data dictionary entities.

23. List some typical uses of the data dictionary.

24. How does a relational catalog differ from a general-purpose data dictionary? What is its role in the relational DBMS environment?

25. How does a data repository differ from a general-purpose data dictionary?

EXERCISES

1. You have just been named Director of Data Administration of General Hardware Company. General Hardware maintains a large, central IS organization with several operational relational databases at its headquarters. It also has databases on several local area network servers, some of which are located at its headquarters and some of which are in regional offices. Of course, there are many relational databases on individual employees' PCs, too. Certain data is sent from the central databases to the LAN databases nightly.

   You have been given a free hand to create a data administration department and supporting database administration departments for General Hardware and its IS environment. Design your data and database administration functions. Include their responsibilities and explain how they will add value to the corporation.

2. Good Reading Bookstores Database.
   a. Create a data dictionary TABLES table and an ATTRIBUTES table and enter data in them for Good Reading Bookstores database, shown in Figure 7.21. Your answer should be based on the format shown in Figure 11.6. Use your judgment as to attribute type values, length values, and so forth.
   b. Create a RELATIONSHIPS table for this tables and attributes data, using the format in Figure 11.7.

3. Best Airlines Mechanics Database.
   a. Create a data dictionary TABLES table and an ATTRIBUTES table and enter data in them for Best Airlines' mechanics database, shown in Exercise 1 in Chapter 8. Your answer should be based on the format shown in Figure 11.6. Use your judgment as to attribute type values, length values, and so on.
   b. Create a RELATIONSHIPS table for this tables and attributes data, using the format in Figure 11.7.

MINICASES

1. Happy Cruise Lines.
   a. You have just been named Director of Data Administration of Happy Cruise Lines. Happy

Cruise Lines maintains a central IS organization with several operational relational databases on several large-server computers at its headquarters.

Each of its cruise ships has a medium-scale server on board with its own databases that help manage the running of the ship. Real-time transmissions are made between headquarters and the ships via satellite that keep both the headquarters and shipboard databases constantly up-to-date.

You have been given a free hand to create a data administration department and supporting database administration departments for Happy Cruise Lines and its IS environment. Design your data and database administration functions. Include their responsibilities and explain how they will add value to the corporation.

b. Create a data dictionary TABLES table and an ATTRIBUTES table and enter data in them for Happy Cruise Lines' database, shown in Minicase 1 in Chapter 5. Your answer should be based on the format shown in Figure 11.6. Use your judgment as to attribute type values, length values, and so on.

c. Create a RELATIONSHIPS table for this tables and attributes data, using the format in Figure 11.7.

2. Super Baseball League.

a. You have just been named Director of Data Administration of the Super Baseball League. The Super Baseball League maintains a substantially decentralized IS organization with the focus on the individual teams. Each team has a server at its stadium or offices near the stadium. The League has a server at its headquarters. Data collected at the team locations, such as player statistics updates and game attendance figures, is uploaded nightly to the server at league headquarters.

You have been given a free hand to create a data administration department and supporting database administration departments for the Super Baseball League and its IS environment. Design your data and database administration functions. Include their responsibilities and explain how they will add value to the corporation.

b. Create a data dictionary TABLES table and an ATTRIBUTES table and enter data in them for the Super Baseball League database (including the STADIUM table) shown in Minicase 2 in Chapter 5. Your answer should be based on the format shown in Figure 11.6. Use your judgment as to attribute type values, length values, and so forth.

c. Create a RELATIONSHIPS table for this tables and attributes data, using the format in Figure 11.7.

CHAPTER 12

DATABASE CONTROL ISSUES: SECURITY, BACKUP AND RECOVERY, CONCURRENCY

CHAPTER OBJECTIVES

After learning the material in this chapter, you will be able to:

✔ List the major data control issues handled by database management systems.
✔ List and describe the types of data security breaches.
✔ List and describe the types of data security measures.
✔ Describe the concept of backup and recovery.
✔ Describe the major backup and recovery techniques.
✔ Explain the problem of disaster recovery.
✔ Describe the concept of concurrency control.
✔ Describe such concurrency control issues and measures as the lost update problem, locks and deadlock, and versioning.

Photo Courtesy of Footstar

FOOTSTAR

Footstar is one of the largest footwear retailers in the United States, competing in two distinct sectors: discount and family footwear, and athletic footwear. Footstar sells one out of every eight pairs of shoes sold in America. Its stores include the

459-unit Footaction chain and the 95 Just For Feet superstores. In addition, it is the largest operator of licensed footwear departments, with over 5,000 such outlets in major department stores, discount stores, and pharmacy chains. In these, it sells shoes under brand names that include Thom McAn and Cobbie Cuddlers. Footstar is a $2.3 billion/year company and is headquartered in West Nyack, New York. The Footaction chain was founded in 1976 and the Just For Feet chain was founded in 1977.

In November 2001, Just For Feet rolled out its "Frequent Feet" customer loyalty program, which is enabled by a sophisticated database application. Customers are issued Frequent Feet cards. If the customer is a member of a family, each member of the family is issued one and their purchases count together towards the family's total. Every time a customer buys a pair of shoes at Just For Feet, the cashier asks for their card. (If they don't have their card with them, the records can be looked up online by their name or telephone number.) After a customer (or a family) buys three pairs of shoes, they get a discount. The discount increases after the sixth and ninth pairs. After they have bought twelve pairs, the thirteenth is free!

The Frequent Feet database is maintained in an Oracle DBMS running on a Unix IBM RS-6000 platform in Irving, Texas. Database integrity is enhanced by utilizing stored procedures that are called for data maintenance operations. If customers inquire about their Frequent Feet account in a store, a query is sent to the database in Irving which returns back their information within seconds. Footstar uses SQL Plus to run a variety of queries against the database, generating marketing data and mailing lists. It also runs regular reports to identify its top customers who are then sent further incentives including coupons and free offers. The Frequent Feet database has a Customer table with 12 million records and a Purchases table with 57 million records.

Printed by permission of Footstar

We've said that data is a corporate resource and that corporate resources must be carefully managed. Different corporate resources have different management requirements. Money must be protected from theft: equipment must be secured against misuse; buildings may require security guards. Data, too, is a corporate resource and has its own peculiar concerns, which we have termed **database control issues.** We will discuss the three main database control issues in this chapter. The first, **data security,** involves protecting the data from theft, from malicious destruction, from unauthorized updating, and more. The second, **backup and recovery,** refers to having procedures in place to recreate data that has been lost, for any reason. The third, **concurrency control,** refers to problems that can occur when two or more transactions or users attempt to update a piece of data simultaneously.

These very important issues require well-thought-out and standardized solutions. Indeed, entire books have been written about each one of them. Our goal in this chapter is to introduce each of these topics, discuss why they are important, explain what can go wrong, and highlight several of the main solutions for each.

DATA SECURITY

The Importance of Data Security

With data taking its place as a corporate resource and so much of today's business dependent on data and the information systems that process it, good data security is absolutely critical to every company and organization. A data security breach can dramatically affect a company's ability to continue normal functioning. Even beyond that, companies have a responsibility to protect data that often affects others beyond the company itself. Customer data, which, for example, can be financial, medical, or legal in nature, must be carefully guarded. When customers give a company personal data, they expect the company to be very careful in keeping it confidential. Banks must be sure that the money they hold, now in the form of data, cannot be tampered with or leaked outside of the bank. Individuals want personal information that insurance companies keep about them to remain confidential. Also, when a company has access to a trading partner's data in a supply chain arrangement, the partner company expects its data to remain secure. Governments, charged with protecting their citizens, must protect sensitive defense data from unauthorized intrusion. And the list goes on and on.

Types of Data Security Breaches

Data and the information systems that store and process it can be compromised in several different ways.

Unauthorized Data Access   Perhaps the most basic kind of data security breach is unauthorized data access; that is, someone obtains data that she is not authorized to see. This breech can range from seeing, say, a single record of a database table to obtaining a copy of an entire table or even an entire database. You can imagine an evil company wanting to steal a competitor's customer list or new product plans, the government of one country wanting to get hold of another country's defense plans, or even one person simply wanting to snoop on his neighbor's bank account. Sometimes the stolen data consists of computer passwords or security codes so that data or property can be stolen at a later time. And a variety of different people can be involved in the data theft, including a company's own employees, a trading partner's employees, or complete outsiders. In the case of a company's own employees, the situation can be considerably more complicated than that of an outsider breaking in and stealing data. An employee might have legitimate access to some company data but might take advantage of his access to the company's information systems to steal data he is not authorized to see. Or he might remove data from the company that he *is* authorized to see.

Unauthorized Data or Program Modification   Another exposure is unauthorized data modification. In this situation, someone changes the value of stored data that they are not entitled to change. Imagine a bank employee increasing her own bank account balance or that of a friend or relative. Or consider an administrative employee of a university changing a student's grade (or, for that matter, the student breaking into the university computer to change his own grade). In more sophisticated cases, a person might manage to modify one of a company's programs to modify data now or at a later time.

Malicious Mischief   The field of reference has to be expanded when it comes to discussing malicious mischief as a data security issue. To begin with, someone can corrupt or even erase some of a company's data. As with the theft of data, this can range from a single record in a table to an entire table or database. But there is even more to malicious mischief. Data can also be made unusable or unavailable by damaging the hardware on which it is stored or processed! Thus, in terms of malicious mischief, the hardware as well as the data has to be protected.

Methods of Breaching Data Security

Methods of breaching data security fall into several broad categories (Figure 12.1). Some of these methods require being on a company's premises, while others don't.

Unauthorized Computer Access   One method of stealing data is gaining unauthorized access to a company's computer and its data. This can be accomplished in a variety of ways. One is by "hacking" or gaining access from outside of the company. Some hackers are software experts who can exploit faults in a company's software. Others have stolen identification names and passwords and can enter a computer looking like legitimate users. As we suggested earlier, some data thieves actually are legitimate users: company employees who have authorized access to the company's computer system and who are intent on stealing data they are authorized to see or breaking into databases for which they do not have access. In all of these cases, data can be downloaded or copied and used illicitly from then on.

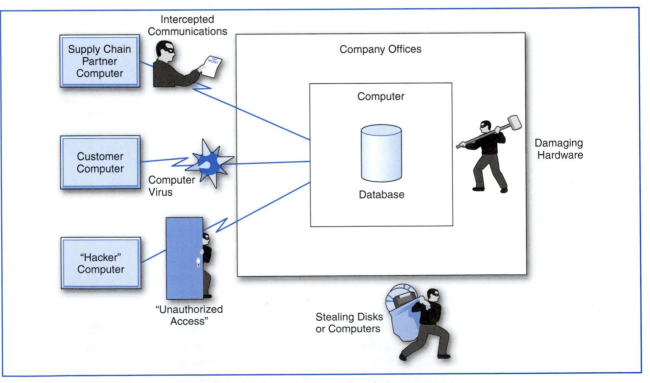

➤ **Figure 12.1**   Data security breaches

Intercepting Data Communications Intercepting data communications is the computer version of the old concept of **wiretapping.** Although data may be well protected in a company's computers, once it is transmitted outside of the company it becomes subject to being stolen while it is being transmitted. Some data transmission media are more subject to data interception than others. Tapping a simple twisted-pair telephone line or a coaxial cable takes skill but is feasible. When data is bounced off satellites, it is also subject to being intercepted. On the other hand, the light pulses going through fiber-optic transmission lines cannot be easily tapped.

Stealing Disks or Computers Can disks or even computers (with data on their hard drives) be stolen? That would have been difficult years ago when all computers were mainframes and all disks were very large. But today it is very possible. Zip Disks, 3.5" diskettes, and CDs all have the potential of being stolen from company offices or, for example, from hotel rooms in which company employees who are traveling are staying. Laptop computers can be stolen too and many have been stolen by organized teams of thieves as the laptops go through airport security stations. Even desktop computers have been stolen from company offices.

Computer Viruses A **computer virus** is a malicious piece of software that is capable of copying itself and "spreading" from computer to computer on diskettes and through telecommunications lines. Strictly speaking, a computer virus doesn't have to cause harm, but most are designed to do just that. Computer viruses have been designed to corrupt data, to scramble system and disk directories that locate files and database tables, and to wipe out entire disks. Some are designed to make so many copies of themselves that the sheer number of copies clogs computers and data communications lines. Computer viruses that travel along data communications lines are also called *worms.*

Damaging Computer Hardware All of the previous methods of breaching data security have something in common: they're all deliberate. However, this last category—damaging computer hardware—might be either deliberate or accidental. Even when accidental, the issue of damaging hardware has always been considered to fall into the realm of computer security. Computers and disks can and have been damaged in many ways, and it's not a matter of "high-tech" either. They have been damaged or ruined by fires, coffee spills, hurricanes, and disgruntled or newly fired employees with hammers or whatever other hard objects were handy. We will discuss security measures for these problems, but, in truth, no security measures for them are foolproof. That's one of the reasons that backup and recovery procedures, which we will discuss later in this chapter, are so very important.

Types of Data Security Measures

With the critical importance of data and all of the possible threats to data security, it is not surprising that the information systems industry has responded with an array of data security measures to protect the data and the hardware on which it is stored and processed (Figure 12.2).

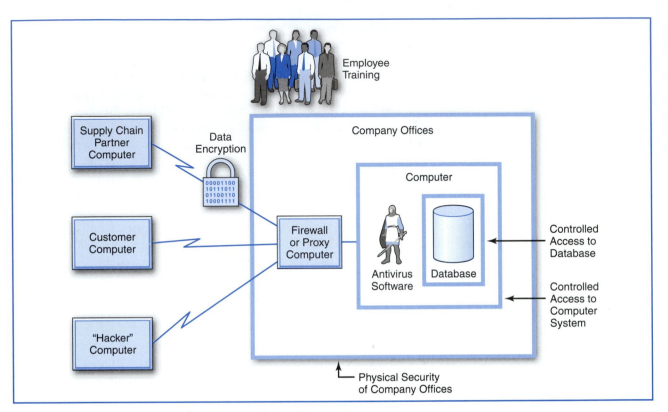

➤ **Figure 12.2**   Data security measures

Physical Security of Company Premises   In the 1950s, some progressive companies in New York and other large cities put their mainframe computers on the ground floor behind big picture windows so that everyone could see how, well, progressive they were. Those days are long gone. Today, suppose your company is located in a skyscraper that it might share with other companies. Where do you put your mainframe computer (or your several LAN servers which are often placed in the same room precisely for the security reasons we're talking about)? Here are some rules of thumb that have often been learned from hard experience.

- Don't put the computer in the basement because of the possibility of floods.
- Don't put the computer on the ground floor because of the possibility of a truck driving into the building, accidentally or on purpose. (I know of a company that had its computer center in a low-rise building adjoining an interstate highway. It eventually put up concrete barriers outside of the building because it was concerned about just this possibility.)
- Don't put the computer above the eighth floor because that's as high as fire truck ladders can reach.
- Don't put the computer on the top floor of the building because it is subject to helicopter landing and attack.
- If you occupy at least three floors of the building, don't put the computer on your topmost floor because its ceiling is another company's floor, and don't put the computer on your bottommost floor because its floor is another company's ceiling.

- Whatever floor you put the computer on, keep it in an interior space away from the windows.

Another physical security issue is personnel access to the computer room. Obviously, such access should be limited to those people who have a legitimate need to be in the room. Access to the room is controlled by one or a combination of:

- Something they know, such as a secret code to be punched in.
- Something they have, such as a magnetic stripe card, possibly combined with a secret code.
- Some part of them that can be measured or scanned. These **biometric systems** can be based on fingerprints, the dimensions and positions of facial features, retinal blood vessel patterns, or voice patterns.

There are also "electric-eye" devices that protect against a second person following right behind an authorized person into the secure room.

Believe it or not, a critical physical security issue involves the company's offices and cubicles. These contain PCs and possibly even LAN servers that contain their own data and provide access to the company's larger computers and to other PCs and servers. Such a simple procedure as locking your office door when you leave it, even for a short period of time, can be critical to data security. Logging off or going into a password-protected mode, especially when doorless cubicles are involved, is an alternative.

Controlled Access to the Computer System   What if someone has gained access to a company's offices and tries to access the computer system and its database from a PC or terminal of some sort from within? For that matter, what if someone tries to access a company's computer by dialing into it or otherwise accessing it through telecommunications lines from the outside? The first line of defense to prevent unauthorized entry to a computer system is the need for a combination of an identification tag and a **password** that goes with it to gain entry to the system. Identification tags are often publicly known (at least within the company), but to reduce the risk of someone else learning them, passwords must be kept secret, be changed periodically, and not be written down. Passwords should not appear on the terminal screen when they are typed in, and the user should create them himself so that there is less chance of his forgetting them. There are a variety of rules of thumb for creating passwords. They should not be too long or too short, say 6 to 12 characters. They should not be obvious, like a person's name. They should not be so difficult to remember that the person herself has to write them down, which is security exposure in itself because someone else could potentially see it.

Controlled Access to the Database   An additional layer of data security controls access to the data itself, once a legitimate user or an outsider has successfully gained entry to the computer system. This layer involves restricting access to specific data so that only specific people can retrieve or modify it. Some systems have such controls in the operating system or in other utility software. Basically, such controls consist of a grid that lists users on one axis and data resources, such as databases or tables on another axis, and indicates which users are authorized to retrieve or modify which data resources. Also, an additional layer of passwords, associated with the various data resources, can be introduced. Even after a legitimate user has given his system password to gain entry to the computer system, these additional passwords would be needed to gain access to specific data resources.

At the DBMS level a user cannot simply access any data he wants to; users have to be given explicit authorization to access data. Relational DBMSs have a very flexible and effective way of authorizing users to access data, which at the same time serves as an excellent data security feature. We are referring to the combination of the logical view, or simply the view concept, and the SQL **GRANT** command. With this combination, users, either individually or in groups (for example, everyone in the Accounting Department), can be restricted to accessing only certain database tables or only certain data within a database table. Furthermore, their access to this data can be restricted to read-only access or can include the ability to update data or even to insert new or delete existing rows in the table. The GRANT command is supported by several tables in the relational catalog.

How do these two features work in combination? First, using the CREATE VIEW statement, a view of a database table, consisting of a subset of the rows and/or columns, is created and given a name. This is done with an embedded SELECT statement! Isn't that clever? The desired rows and/or columns are identified just as if they were being retrieved, but instead of being retrieved they are labeled with a view name. Then, using the GRANT command, a user or a group of users is given access to *the view*, not to the entire table. In fact, they may not even be aware that there is more to the table than their subset. They simply use the view name in a SELECT statement for data retrieval as if it were a table name. But how is a user granted the authority to access data through the use of a view (or directly using a table name)? That's where the GRANT command comes in. The general form of the GRANT command is:

GRANT privileges ON (view or table) TO users [WITH GRANT OPTION].

Thus the database administrator grants the ability to read, update, insert, or delete (the "privileges") on a view or a table to a person or a group of people (the "users"). If the WITH GRANT OPTION is included, this person or group can in turn grant other people access to the same data.

Data Encryption   So far, all of the data security techniques that we've covered assume that someone tries to "break in" to the company's offices, its computer, or its DBMS. But data can be stolen in other ways, too. One is through wiretapping or otherwise intercepting some of the huge amounts of data that is transmitted today through telecommunications between a company and its trading partners or its customers. Another is by stealing a disk or a laptop computer outside of a company's offices, for example, in an airport. A solution to this problem is **data encryption.** When data is encrypted, it is changed, bit-by-bit or character-by-character, into a form that looks totally garbled. It can and must be reconverted, or decrypted, back to its original form to be of use. Data may be encrypted as it is sent from the company's computer, out onto telecommunications lines to protect against its being stolen while in transit. Or the data may actually be stored in an encrypted form on a disk, say on a diskette or on a laptop's hard drive, to protect against data theft if the diskette or laptop is stolen while an employee is traveling. Of course, highly sensitive data can also be encrypted on a company's disks within its mainframe computer systems or servers. This adds an additional level of security if someone successfully breaks into the computer system. Why not then simply encrypt all data wherever it may be? The downside is that it takes time to decrypt the data when you want to use it and to encrypt it when you want to store it, which can become a performance issue.

Data encryption techniques can range from simple to highly complex. The simpler the scheme, the easier it is for a determined person to figure it out and "break the code." The more complex it is, the more time it takes to encrypt and decrypt the data, although this potential performance problem has been at least partially neutralized by the introduction of high-performance hardware encryption "chips." Encryption generally involves a data conversion algorithm and a secret key. A very simple example of an alphabetic encryption scheme is as follows: Number the letters of the alphabet from A to Z as 1 to 26. For each letter in the data to be encrypted, add the secret key (some number in this case) to the letter's numeric value and change the letter to the letter represented by the new number. For example, if the key is 4, an A (value 1) becomes an E (since 1+4 = 5 and E is the fifth letter of the alphabet), a B becomes an F, and so on through the alphabet. W wraps around back to the beginning of the alphabet and becomes an A, X becomes a B, and so forth. The recipient must be aware of both the algorithm and the secret key so that it can work the algorithm in reverse and decrypt the data.

Modern encryption techniques typically encrypt data on a bit-by-bit basis using increasingly long keys and very complex algorithms. Consider the data communications case. The two major types of data encryption techniques are symmetric or **private key** and asymmetric or **public key encryption.** Private key techniques require the same long bit-by-bit key for encrypting and decrypting the data (hence the term *symmetric*). But this has an inherent problem. How do you inform the receiver of the data about the private key without *the key itself* being compromised en route? If the key itself is stolen, the intercepted data can be converted once the conversion algorithm is identified. Since there are only a few major conversion algorithms the security is in the key, not in having a great many different conversion algorithms.

The key transmission problem is avoided using algorithms that employ the very clever public key technique. In this technique there are two different keys: the public key that is used for encrypting the data and the private key that is used for decrypting it (hence the term *asymmetric*). *The public key is **not** capable of decrypting the data.* Thus the public key can be published for all the world to see. Anyone wanting to send data does so in complete safety by encrypting the data using the algorithm and the openly published public key. Only the legitimate receiver can decrypt the data because only the legitimate receiver has the private key that can decrypt the data with the published public key. The downside of the public key technique is that encrypting and decrypting tend to be slower than with the private key technique, resulting in slower application transactions when the public key technique is used.

A particularly interesting combination of private key and public key encryption is used in **Secure Socket Layer (SSL) technology** on the World Wide Web. Consider a person at home who wants to buy something from an online store on the Web. Her PC and its WWW browser are the client, and the online store's computer is the server. Both sides want to conduct the secure transaction using private key technology because it's faster, but they have the problem of one side picking a private key and getting it to the other side in a secure manner. Here are the basic steps in SSL:

1. The client contacts the server.

2. The server sends the client its *public key* for its public key algorithm (you'll see why in a moment). No one cares if this public key is stolen since it's, well, public!

3. The client, using a random number generator, creates a "session key," *the key for the private key algorithm* with which the secure transaction (the actual online shopping) will be conducted once everything is set up. But, as we've described, the problem now is how the client is going to securely transmit the session key it generated to the server, since both must have it to use the faster private key algorithm for the actual shopping.

4. Now, here is the really clever part of the SSL concept. The client is going to send the session key to the server securely, *using a public key algorithm and the server's **public key.*** The client encrypts the session key using the server's public key and transmits the encrypted session key to the server with the public key algorithm. It doesn't matter if someone intercepts this transmission because the server is the only entity that has the decrypting private key that goes with its public key!

5. Once the session key has been securely transmitted to the server, both the client and the server have it and the secure transaction can proceed using the faster private key algorithm.

Antivirus Software   Companies (and individuals!) employ *antivirus software* to combat computer viruses. Antivirus software uses two basic methods. One method is based on virus **signatures**—portions of the virus code that are considered to be unique to it. Vendors of antivirus software have identified known computer viruses and continually identify new ones and maintain an ever-growing, comprehensive list of their signatures. The antivirus software contains those signatures and on a real-time basis can check all messages and other traffic coming into the computer to see if any of the known viruses are trying to enter. The software can also, on request, scan disks of all types to check for viruses on them. The other antivirus method is for the software to constantly monitor the computer environment to watch for requests or commands for any unusual activity, such as, for example, a command to format a disk, therefore wiping out all of the data on it. The software will typically prevent the command from executing and will ask the person operating the computer whether she really wants this command to take place. It will take place, only if the operator responds that she does.

Firewalls   In today's business world with supply chain partners communicating with each other via computers over networks and with customers communicating with companies' Web sites over the Internet, a tremendous amount of data enters and leaves a company's computers every day over data communications lines. Unfortunately, this opens the possibility that a malicious person will try to break into a company's computers through these legitimate channels. Whether they are trying to steal, destroy, or otherwise harm the company's data, they must be stopped. Yet, these data communications channels must be kept open for legitimate business with the company's supply chain partners and customers.

One type of protection that companies use to protect against this problem is the **firewall**—software or a combination of hardware and software that protects a company's computer and its data against external attack via data communications lines. There are several types of firewalls. Some that are based purely on software involve checking the network address of the incoming message or components of the content of the message. An interesting firewall that is a combination of hardware and software is the **proxy server,** shown in Figure 12.3. With the proxy server, the message coming in from an outside computer does not go directly to the company's main computer, say a mainframe computer. Instead, it goes to a separate computer, the proxy server or firewall computer. The proxy server has software that takes apart the incoming message, extracts only those legitimate pieces of data that are supposed to go to the company's mainframe, reformats the data in a form the company's mainframe is expecting, and finally passes the reformatted data on to the company's main computer. In this way, no extraneous part of the incoming message, including any malicious code, ever reaches the company's main computer.

Training Employees   A surprisingly important data security measure is training the company's employees in good security practices, many of which are very simple and yet very important. What should the company tell its employees in terms of good data security practices? Here are a few samples:

- Log off your computer or at least lock your office door when you leave your office, even for just a few minutes.
- Don't write your computer password down anywhere.
- Don't respond to any unusual requests for information about the computer system (or anything else!) from anyone over the telephone. (People have phoned company personnel posing as employees of the company and told the person on the phone that they need their password to check out a problem in the computer system. And this trick has worked!)
- Don't leave diskettes or other storage media lying around your office.
- Don't take diskettes or other storage media out of the building.
- Don't assume that a stranger in the building is there legitimately without checking. (People have posed as telephone repairpersons to tap a company's data communications lines.)

➤ **Figure 12.3**
A firewall protecting a company's computer

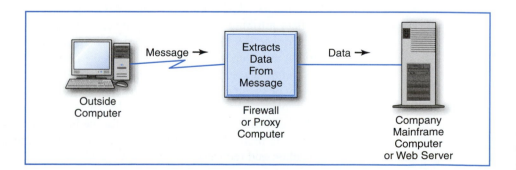

BACKUP AND RECOVERY

The Importance of Backup and Recovery

Regardless of how sophisticated information systems have become, we have to be prepared to handle a variety of events that can affect or even destroy data in a database. Trouble can come from something as simple as a legitimate user entering an incorrect data value or from something as overwhelming as a fire or some other disaster destroying an entire computer center and everything in it. Thus the consequences can range from a single data value being rendered inaccurate to all of the installation's databases being destroyed, with many other possibilities in between. In the information systems business, we have to assume that from time to time something will go wrong with our data, and so we have to have the tools available to correct or reconstruct it. These operations come under the heading of **backup and recovery.**

Backup Copies and Journals

The fundamental ideas in backup and recovery are fairly straightforward, and some have been around for a long time. They begin with two basic but very important tasks: backing up the database and maintaining a journal. First, there is back up. On a regularly scheduled basis, say once per week, a company's databases must be backed up or copied. The backup copy must be put in a safe place, away from the original in the computer system. (There have been cases of the copy being kept in the computer room only to have a fire destroy both the original and the copy.) There are several possibilities for storing the backup copy. For example, the backup copy may be kept in a fireproof safe in a nearby company building. Or it may be kept in a bank vault. Often, during the next backup cycle, the previous backup copy becomes the "grandfather copy" and is sent even farther away to a distant state or city for additional security.

The other basic backup and recovery task is maintaining a disk log or journal of all changes that take place in the data. This includes updates to existing records, the insertion of new records, and the deletion of existing records. Notice that it does *not* include the recording of simple read operations that *do not change* the stored data in any way. There are two types of database logs. One, which is variously called a **change log** or a **before and after image log,** literally records the value of a piece of data just before it is changed and the value just after it is changed. So, if an employee gets a raise in salary and the salary attribute value of his personnel record is to be changed from 15.00 (dollars per hour) to 17.50, the change log identifies the record by its unique identifier (e.g., its employee number) within its table name, the original salary attribute value of 15.00, and the new salary attribute value of 17.50. The other type of log, which is generally known as a **transaction log,** keeps a record of the program that changed the data and all of the inputs that the program used. A very important point about both kinds of logs is that a new log is started *immediately after* the data is backed up (i.e., a backup copy of the data is made). You'll see why in a moment.

Now, how are backups and logs used in backup and recovery operations? Actually, it depends on the *reason* for the backup and recovery operation, and, yes, there is more than one reason or set of circumstances that require some kind of backup and recovery.

Forward Recovery

First, let's consider the case of a calamity that destroys a disk or an only slightly lesser calamity that destroys a database or a particular database table. The disk or the database or the table has to be recreated, and the recovery procedure in this case is called **forward recovery** or **roll forward recovery** (the word "roll" in roll forward comes from the earlier use of tapes to record the logs). Let's look at this from the point of view of a lost table. To recreate the table that was lost, you begin by readying the last backup copy of the table that was made and readying the log with all of the changes that were made to the table *since* the last backup copy was made. The point is that the last backup copy is, well, a copy of the table that was lost, which is what you want, except that it doesn't include the changes to the data that were made *since* the backup copy was made. To fix this, a recovery program begins by reading the *first* log entry that was recorded *after* the last backup copy was made. In other words, it looks at the first change that was made to the table right after the backup copy was made. The recovery program updates the backup copy of the table with this log entry. Then, having gone back to the beginning of the log, it continues *rolling forward*, making every update to the backup copy of the table in the same order in which they were originally made to the database table itself. When this process is completed, the lost table has been rebuilt or recovered (Figure 12.4)! This process can be performed with either a change log or a transaction log. In the case of the change log, the "after images" are applied to the backup copy of the database. In the case of the transaction log, the actual programs that updated the database are rerun. This tends to be a simpler but slower process.

One variation of the process when a change log is used is based on the recognition that several changes may have been made to the same piece of data since the last backup copy of the table was made. If that's the case, then only the last one of the changes to the particular piece of data, which after all shows the value of this piece of data at the point that the table was destroyed, needs to be used in updating the database copy in the roll-forward operation. If the database environment is a

➤ **Figure 12.4**
Forward recovery

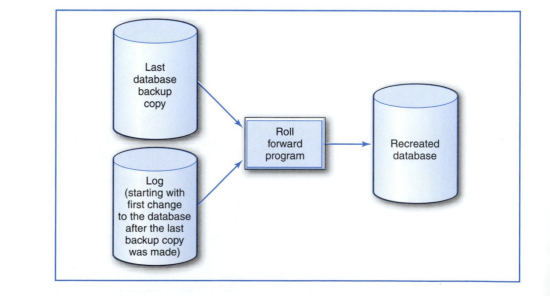

volatile one in which changes are made frequently and the same piece of data is commonly updated several times between backup operations, then the roll-forward operation, as we have described it, may be needlessly inefficient. Instead, it may be worthwhile to sort through the log prior to the roll-forward operation to find the *last* change made to each piece of data that was updated since the last backup copy was made. Then only those final changes need be applied to the backup copy in the roll-forward operation.

Backward Recovery

Now let's consider a different situation. Suppose that in the midst of normal operation an error is discovered that involves a piece of recently updated data. The cause might be as simple as human error in keying in a value or as complicated as a program ending abnormally and leaving in the database some, but not all, changes to the database that it was supposed to make. Why not just correct the incorrect data and not make a big deal out of this? Because in the interim, other programs may have read the incorrect data and made use of it, thus compounding the error in other places in the database.

So the discovered error—and in fact, all other changes that were made to the database *since* the error was discovered—must be backed out. The process is called **backward recovery,** or **rollback.** Essentially, the idea is to start with the database in its current state and the log positioned at the *last* entry that was made in it. (*Note:* backup copies of the database have nothing to do with this procedure.) Then a recovery program proceeds *backwards* through the log, resetting each updated data value in the database to its "before image", until it reaches the point where the error was made. Thus the program "undoes" each transaction in the reverse order (last-in, first-out) from which it was made (Figure 12.5). Once all of the data values in the tainted updates are restored to what they were before the data error occurred, the transactions that updated them must be rerun. This can be a manual process or, if a transaction log was maintained as well as a change log,

➤ **Figure 12.5**
Backward recovery

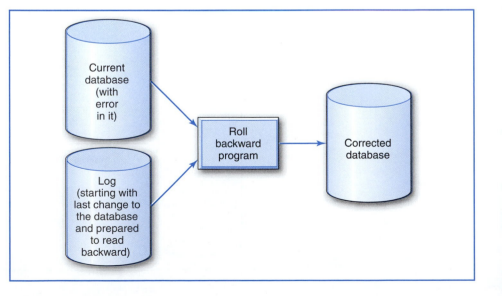

a program can *roll forward* through the transaction log, automatically rerunning all of the transactions from the point that the data error occurred.

Here is another note about backward recovery: Some systems can automatically initiate a roll-backward operation to undo the changes made to the database by a partially completed and then halted or failed transaction. This is called **dynamic backout.** There are situations in which it is helpful to restore the database to a point at which there is confidence that all changes made to the database up to that point are accurate. Some systems are capable of writing a special record to the log, known as a **checkpoint,** which specifies this kind of stable state.

Duplicate or Mirrored Databases

A backup and recovery technique of a very different nature is known as **duplicate** or **mirrored databases.** Two copies of the entire database are maintained, and both are updated simultaneously (Figure 12.6). If one is destroyed, the applications that use the database can just keep on running with the duplicate database. This is a relatively expensive proposition but allows continuous operation in the event of a disk failure, which may justify the cost for some applications. By the way, this arrangement is of no help in the case of erroneous data being entered (see backward recovery, above) because the erroneous data will be entered in both copies of the database!

The greater the "distance" between the two mirrored copies of the database, the greater the security. If both are on the same disk (not a good idea!) and the disk fails or is destroyed, both copies of the database are lost. If the two copies are on different disks but are in the same room and a fire hits the room, both might be destroyed. If they are on disks in two different buildings in the same city, that's much better, but a natural disaster such as a hurricane could affect both. Thus companies sometimes keep duplicate databases literally hundreds of miles apart to avoid such natural disasters.

Disaster Recovery

Speaking of natural disasters, the author lived through Hurricane Andrew in Miami, Florida, in August 1992 and learned about disaster recovery first-hand! The information systems of two major companies and a host of smaller ones

Figure 12.6

Mirrored databases

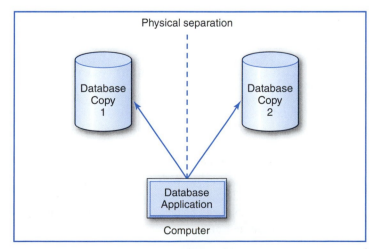

were knocked out of service by the hurricane. Companies in Miami whose buildings sustained major roof and window damage actually found fish that the hurricane had lifted out of the ocean deposited in their computers. They also discovered that when the salt water from the ocean saturated the ceiling tiles in their offices, wet flakes from the tiles fell down onto their computer equipment, ruining some of it. A company that thought that it was keeping its database backup copies in a safe place in another part of the city didn't take into account that the roof of the backup site would not stand up to a major hurricane, and so it lost its backup copies.

As the term implies, **disaster recovery** refers to rebuilding an entire information system or significant parts of one, after a catastrophic natural disaster such as a hurricane, tornado, earthquake, building collapse, or even a major fire. Several approaches can be taken to prepare for such disasters to information systems. They tend to be expensive or complex or both, but with today's critical dependence on information systems, companies that want to be careful and prepared have little choice. The possibilities include the following:

- Maintain totally mirrored systems (not just databases) in different cities.
- Contract with a company that maintains hardware similar to yours so that you can be up and running again quickly after a disaster. The companies that provide these so-called **hot sites** make money by contracting their services with many companies, assuming that they will not all suffer a disaster and need the hot site at the same time.
- Maintain space with electrical connections, air conditioning, and so on, into which new hardware can be moved if need be. These so-called **cold sites** are not nearly as practical as they once were because of the online nature and mission-critical character of today's information systems. They would simply take too long to get up and running.
- Make a **reciprocal arrangement** with another company with hardware similar to yours to aid each other in case one suffers a disaster. Obviously, the two companies should be in different industries and must not be competitors!
- Build a computer center that is relatively disaster proof. After Hurricane Andrew, one of the large affected companies in Miami rebuilt their computer center in a building they started referring to as "the bunker."

CONCURRENCY CONTROL

The Importance of Concurrency Control

Today's application systems, especially those that run within the database environment, assume that many people using these systems will require access to the same data at the same time. Modern hardware and systems software are certainly capable of supporting such shared data access. One very common example of this capability is in airline reservations, where several different reservations clerks, as well as customers on the Web, may have simultaneous requests for seats on the same flight. Another example is in an industrial or retail inventory application in which several employees on an assembly line or in an order fulfillment role seek to update the same item in inventory simultaneously.

When concurrent access involves only simple retrieval of data, there is no problem. But when concurrent access requires data modification, the two or more users attempting to update the data simultaneously have a rather nasty way of interfering with each other, which doesn't happen if they are merely performing data retrievals. This is the case in the airline reservations and inventory examples, since selling seats on flights and using items in inventory require that the number of seats or inventory items left be revised downwards, (i.e., many of the database accesses involve updates). The result can be inaccurate data stored in the database!

The Lost Update Problem

Using the airline reservations application as an example, let's see what can happen with simultaneous updates (Figure 12.7). Before we begin the example, bear in mind that we are not talking about simultaneous updates only at the "microsecond" level. As you are about to see, the problem can occur when the time spans involved are in seconds or minutes. Suppose that there are twenty-five seats left on Acme Airlines flight 345 on March 12. One day, at 1:45 P.M., a reservations clerk, Ms. Brown receives a telephone call from a customer who is thinking about booking four seats on that particular flight. Brown retrieves the record for the flight from the database, notes that there are twenty-five seats available, and begins to discuss the price and other details with her customer. At 1:48 P.M., another reservations clerk, Mr. Green, receives a call from another customer with a larger family who is considering booking six seats on the very same flight. Green retrieves the record for the flight from the database and notes that twenty-five seats are available. At 1:52 P.M., Brown's customer decides to go ahead and book four seats on the flight. Brown completes the transaction, and four seats are deducted from the number of seats available on the flight, updating the database record to show that there are now twenty-one seats available. Then, at 1:56 P.M., Green's customer decides to book six seats on the flight. Green completes this transaction, and six seats are deducted from the number of seats (25) that Green thought were available on the flight, leaving the database showing that nineteen seats are now available.

> **Figure 12.7**
> The lost update problem

Time	Ms. Brown	Mr. Green
1:45 PM	Reads the record Finds 25 seats left	
1:48 PM		Reads the record Finds 25 seats left
1:52 PM	Deducts 4 seats and writes updated record indicating 21 seats left	
1:56 PM		Deducts 6 seats and writes updated record indicating 19 seats left

But at this point the record should show 15 seats left!

So, the record for flight 345 on March 12 now shows that there are nineteen seats available. But shouldn't it be only fifteen, since a total of ten seats were sold? Yes, but the point is that neither of the clerks knew that the other was in the process of selling seats on the flight at the same time that the other was. Both Brown and Green started off with the knowledge that there were twenty-five seats left. When Brown deducted four seats, for a couple of minutes the record showed that there were twenty-one seats left. But then when Green deducted his six, he was deducting them from the original twenty-five seats that he saw when he originally retrieved the record from the database and not from the twenty-one seats that were left after Brown's sale. This is known as the **Lost Update Problem.**

By the way, you might question the *likelihood* of two clerks going after the same record simultaneously in a large airline reservations system. Have you ever tried to book a reservation on a flight from New York to Miami for Christmas week the week before Christmas week? The likelihood of this kind of conflict is very real in the airline reservations application and in countless other applications of every type imaginable.

Locks and Deadlock

The usual solution to this problem is to introduce what are known as software **locks.** When a user begins an update operation on a piece of data, the DBMS locks that data. Any attempt to begin another update operation on that same piece of data will be blocked, or "locked out," until the first update operation is completed and its lock on the data is released. This effectively prevents the Lost Update Problem. The level or "granularity" of lockout can vary. Lockout at a high level, for instance, at the level of an entire table, unfortunately prevents much more than that one particular piece of data from being modified while the update operation is going on, but is a low-overhead solution since only one lock is needed for the entire table. Lockout at a lower level, the record level for instance, doesn't hold up the rest of the table from being accessed or even updated when one of its records is being updated, but is a comparatively high-overhead solution because there must be a lock that can be set on every record.

Unfortunately, as so often happens, the introduction of this beneficial device itself causes other problems that did not previously exist. Follow the next scenario (Figure 12.8): Consider an inventory situation in which clerks must find out if a sufficient quantity of *each of two* parts, say nuts and bolts, are available to satisfy an order. If there are enough parts, then the clerks want to take the parts from inventory and update the quantities of the remaining parts in the database. Each clerk can only fill the order if enough of both parts are available. Each clerk must access and lock the record for one of the two parts while accessing the record for the other part. Proceeding with the scenario, suppose two clerks, Mr. White and Ms. Black, each request a quantity of nuts and bolts. White happens to list the nuts before the bolts in his query. At 10:15 A.M., he accesses and locks the record for nuts. Ms. Black happens to list the bolts before the nuts in her query. At 10:16 A.M., she accesses and locks the record for bolts. Then, at 10:17 A.M., White tries to access the record for bolts but finds it locked by Black. And 10:18 A.M., Black tries to access the record for nuts but finds it locked by White. Both queries then wait endlessly for each other to release what they each need to proceed. This is called **deadlock** or *the deadly embrace.* It actually bears a close relationship to the grid-lock traffic problem that major cities worry about during rush hour.

➤ **Figure 12.8**
Deadlock

Time	Mr. White	Ms. Black
10:15 A.M.	Gets and locks the record for nuts	
10:16 A.M.		Gets and locks the record for bolts
10:17 A.M.	Tries to get (and lock) the record for bolts but finds it locked by Ms. Black	
10:18 A.M.		Tries to get (and lock) the record for nuts but finds it locked by Mr. White

DEADLOCK!

Does the prospect of deadlock mean that locks should not be used? No, because there are techniques for handling deadlock, which fall into two classes: deadlock prevention and deadlock detection. Outright deadlock prevention sounds desirable but turns out to be difficult. Basically, a transaction would have to lock all of the data it will need, assuming it can even figure this out at the beginning of the transaction. (Often the value of one piece of data that a program retrieves determines what other data it needs.) If the transaction finds that some of the data it will need is unavailable because another transaction has it locked, all it can do is release whatever data it has already locked and start all over again.

So the usual way to handle deadlock is to allow it to occur, detect it when it does, and then abort one of the deadlocked transactions, allowing the other to finish. The one that was backed out can then be run again. One way to detect deadlock is through a timeout, meaning that a query has been hung up waiting for so long that the assumption is that it must be deadlocked. Another way to detect deadlock is by maintaining a **resource usage matrix** that dynamically keeps track of which transactions or users are waiting for which pieces of data. Software can continuously monitor this matrix and determine when a deadlock situation has occurred.

Versioning

Another way to deal with concurrent updates, known as **versioning,** does not involve locks at all. Basically, each transaction is given a copy or "version" of the data that it needs for an update operation, regardless of whether any other transaction is using the same data for an update operation at the same time. Each transaction records its result in its own copy of the data. Then each transaction tries to update the actual database with its result. At that point, monitoring software checks to see if there is a conflict between two or more transactions trying to update the same data at the same time. If there is, the software allows one of the transactions to update the database and makes the other(s) start over again. The hope is that conflicts will not occur often, allowing the applications to proceed along more efficiently without the need for locks.

KEY TERMS

Antivirus software	Deadlock	Private key encryption
Backup and recovery	Disaster recovery	Proxy server
Backward recovery	Duplicate database	Public key encryption
Before and after image log	Dynamic backout	Reciprocal arrangement
Biometric systems	Firewall	Resource usage matrix
Change log	Forward recovery	Rollback
Checkpoint	GRANT	Roll forward recovery
Cold site	Hot site	Secure Socket Layer (SSL) technology
Computer virus	Lock	Signature
Concurrency control	Lost update problem	Transaction log
Data encryption	Mirrored database	Versioning
Data security	Password	Wiretapping
Database control issues	Physical security	

QUESTIONS

1. Explain why data security is important.

2. Compare unauthorized data access with unauthorized data modification. Which do you think is the more serious issue? Explain.

3. Name and briefly describe three methods of breaching data security. Which one do you think is potentially the most serious? Explain.

4. How does the physical security of company premises affect data security?

5. How do magnetic stripe cards and fingerprints compare in terms of physical security protection?

6. Describe the rules for creating a good password.

7. Explain how the combination of views and the SQL GRANT command limit access to a relational database.

8. What is data encryption and why is it important to data security?

9. In your own words, describe how Secure Socket Layer (SSL) technology works.

10. In your own words, describe how a proxy server firewall works.

11. Explain why backup and recovery is important.

12. What is a journal or log? How is one created?

13. Describe the two different problems that forward recovery and backward recovery are designed to handle. Do mirrored databases address one of these two problems or yet a third one? Explain.

14. In your own words, describe how forward recovery works.

15. In your own words, describe how backward recovery works.

16. What is disaster recovery? Can the techniques for backup and recovery be used for disaster recovery?

17. Explain why concurrency control is important.

18. What is the lost update problem?

19. What are locks and how are they used to prevent the lost update problem?

20. What is deadlock and how can it occur?

EXERCISES

1. A large bank has a headquarters location plus several branches in each of the cities in a particular region of the country. As transactions are conducted at each branch, they are processed online against a relational database at headquarters. You have been hired as the bank's Director of Data Security. Design a comprehensive set of data security measures to protect the bank's data.

2. The bank in Exercise 1, which is totally dependent on its relational database, must be able to keep running in the event of the failure of any one table on one disk drive, in the event of a major disaster hitting its headquarters computer, or in the event of any catastrophe in between these two extremes. Describe the range of techniques and technologies that you would implement to enable the bank to recover from this wide range of failures.

3. The Tasty Seafood Restaurant is a large restaurant that specializes in fresh fish and seafood. Because of how important its reputation for freshness is to Tasty, it brings in a certain amount of each type of fish daily and, while trying to satisfy all of its customers, would rather run out of a type of fish than carry it over to the next day. After taking a table's order, a waiter enters the order into a touch-screen terminal that is connected to a computer in the kitchen. The order is sent from the touch-screen terminal to the computer only after all of it has been entered.

   At 8:00 P.M. there are ten servings of salmon, fifteen servings of flounder, and eight orders of trout left in the kitchen. At 8:03 P.M., waiter Frank starts entering an order that includes five servings of salmon, six of flounder, and four of trout. At the same time, on another touch-screen terminal, waitress Mary starts entering an order that includes one serving of salmon, three of flounder, and two of trout. At 8:05 P.M., before the other two have finished entering their orders, waitress Tina starts entering an order that includes six servings of salmon, one of flounder, and five of trout. Frank finishes entering his order at 8:06 P.M. Mary at 8:07 P.M., and Tina at 8:09 P.M.

   a. What would the result of all of this be in the absence of locks?

   b. What would the result be with a locking mechanism in place?

   c. What would happen if versioning was in use?

4. Construct examples of the lost update problem, the use of locks, deadlock, and versioning for the case of a joint bank account (i.e., two people who have access to the same bank account).

MINICASES

1. Happy Cruise Lines is headquartered in New York and in addition has regional offices in the cruise port cities of Miami, Houston, and Los Angeles. New York has a large server and several LANs. Each of the other three sites has a single LAN with a smaller server. The company's four offices communicate with each other via land-based telecommunications lines. The company's ships, each of which has a server on board, communicate with the New York headquarters via satellite. Also located in New York is the company's Web site, through which passengers and travel agents can book cruises.

   a. Devise a data security strategy for Happy Cruise Lines, incorporating appropriate data security measures.

   b. Happy Cruise Line's main relational database (see Minicase 1 in Chapter 5), located in New York, is considered critical to the company's functioning. It must be kept up and running as consistently as possible, and it must be quickly recoverable if something goes wrong. Devise backup and recovery and disaster recovery strategies for the company.

   c. A particularly popular Christmas-week cruise is booking up fast. There are only a few cabins left, and the company wants to be careful to not "overbook" the cruise. With customers, travel agents, and the company's own reservations agents all accessing the database at the same time, devise a strategy that will avoid overbooking.

2. The Super Baseball League maintains a substantially decentralized IS organization, with the focus on the individual teams. Each team has a server with a LAN at its stadium or offices near the stadium. The League has a server with a LAN at its Chicago headquarters. The league as well as each of the teams maintain a Web site at their locations. People can get general information about the league at the league's Web site; they can get information about the individual teams as well as buy game tickets through each team's Web site. Data collected at the team locations, such as player statistics updates and game attendance figures, is uploaded nightly to the server at league headquarters via telephone lines.

   a. Devise a data security strategy for the Super Baseball League, incorporating appropriate data security measures.

   b. The Super Baseball League's main relational database (see Minicase 2 in Chapter 5), located at its headquarters in Chicago, is, for the most part, a repository of data collected from the teams. The league wants to keep the headquarters database up and running, but it is more important to keep the individual team databases in their stadiums or offices up and running with as little downtime as possible. Devise backup and recovery and disaster recovery strategies for the Super Baseball League.

   c. Fans can order or buy tickets from the individual teams over the telephone, through the teams' Web sites, or in person at the teams' box offices. All of this activity takes place simultaneously. Devise a strategy that will avoid a particular seat for a particular game being sold more than once.

CHAPTER 13

CLIENT/SERVER DATABASE AND DISTRIBUTED DATABASE

CHAPTER OBJECTIVES

After learning the material in this chapter, you will be able to:

✔ Describe the concepts and advantages of the client/server database approach.
✔ Describe the concepts and advantages of the distributed database approach.
✔ Explain how data can be distributed and replicated in a distributed database.
✔ Describe the problem of concurrency control in distributed database.
✔ Describe the distributed join process.
✔ Describe data partitioning in a distributed database.
✔ Describe distributed directory management.

Photo Courtesy of Hasbro

HASBRO

Hasbro is a worldwide leader in children's and family leisure time entertainment products and services, including the design, manufacture, and marketing of games and toys ranging from traditional to high tech. Headquartered in Pawtucket, Rhode Island,

Hasbro was founded in 1923 by the Hassenfeld Brothers, hence the eventual company name. Over the years, the Hasbro family has expanded through internal growth plus acquisitions that include Milton Bradley (founded in 1860), Parker Brothers (founded in 1883), Tonka, Kenner, and Playskool. Included among its famous toys are MR. POTATO HEAD®, G.I. Joe®, Tonka Trucks®, Play Doh®, Easy Bake Oven®, Transformers®, Furby®, Tinkertoy®, and the games Monopoly® (the world's all-time, best-selling game), Scrabble®, Chutes and Ladders®, Candy Land®, The Game of Life®, Risk®, Clue®, Sorry®, and Yahtzee®.

Hasbro keeps track of this wide variety of toys and games with a database application called PRIDE (Product Rights Information Database), which was implemented in 2001. PRIDE's function is to track the complete life cycle of Hasbro's contract to produce or market each of its products. This includes the payment of royalties to the product's inventor or owner, Hasbro's territorial rights to sell the product by country or area of the world, distribution rights by marketing channel, various payment guarantees and advances, and contract expiration and renewal criteria. A variety of Hasbro departments use PRIDE, including accounting for royalty payments, marketing for worldwide marketing plans, merchandising, product development, and legal departments throughout the world.

PRIDE utilizes the Sybase DBMS and runs on an IBM RS-6000 Unix platform. Actual scanned images of the contracts are stored in the database. The system is designed to store amendments to the contracts, including keeping track of which amendments were in effect at any point in time. It is also designed to incorporate data corrections and to search the scanned contracts for particular text. The main database table is the Contract Master table, which has 7,000 records and a variety of sub-tables containing detailed data about royalties, territories, marketing channels, agents, and licensors. These tables produce a variety of customizable reports and queries. The data can also be exported to MS Excel for further processing in spreadsheets.

Printed by permission of Hasbro

Simply put, the question in this chapter is: "Where is the database located?" In many situations, the obvious answer is, "It's in the computer itself!" That is, it is located on one of the computer's disk drives. If the computer in question is a stand-alone personal computer, of course the database is stored on the PC's hard drive or on one of the PC's removable disks. (Where else could it be?!) The same can be and often is true of much larger computer systems. A company can certainly choose to have its databases stored in its mainframe computer, while providing access to the computer and its databases on a broad, even worldwide scale.

Over the years, two arrangements for locating data other than "in the computer itself" have been developed. Both arrangements involve computers connected to each other on networks. One, known as **client/server database,** is for personal computers connected together on a local area network. The other, known as **distributed database,** is for larger, geographically dispersed computers located on a wide area network. The development of these networked data schemes has been driven by a variety of technical and managerial advantages, although, as is so often the case, there are some disadvantages to be considered, as well.

CLIENT/SERVER DATABASE

A **local area network (LAN)** is an arrangement of personal computers connected together by communications lines (Figure 13.1). It is local in the sense that the PCs must be located fairly close to each other, say within a building or within several nearby buildings. Additional components of the LAN that can be utilized or shared by the PCs can be other, often more powerful **server** computers and peripheral devices such as printers. The PCs on a LAN can certainly operate independently, but they can also communicate with each other. If, as is often the case, a LAN is set up to support a department in a company, the members of the department can communicate with each other, send data to each other, and share such devices as a high-speed printer. Finally, a **gateway computer** on the LAN can link the LAN and its PCs to other LANs, to one or more mainframe computers, or to the Internet.

If one of the LAN's main advantages is the ability to share resources, then certainly one type of resource to share is data contained in databases. For example, the personnel specialists in a company's personnel department might all have to have access to the company's personnel database. But then, what are the options for locating and processing shared databases on a LAN? In terms of location, the basic concept is to store a shared database on a LAN server so that all of the PCs (also known as **clients**) on the LAN can access it. In terms of processing, there are a few possibilities in this **two-tiered client/server arrangement.**

The simplest tactic is known as the **file server approach.** When a client computer on the LAN needs to query, update, or otherwise use a file on the server, the entire file (yes, that's right, the entire file) must be sent from the server to that client. All of the querying, updating, or other processing is then performed in the client

> **Figure 13.1**
> Local area network (LAN)

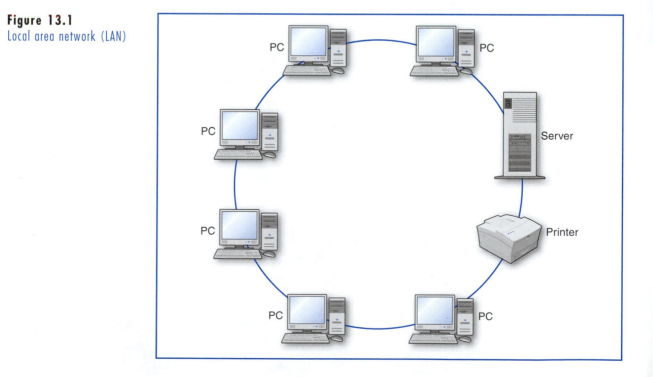

computer. If changes were made to the file, the entire file is then shipped back to the server. Clearly, for files of even moderate size, shipping entire files back and forth across the LAN with any frequency will be very costly. In terms of concurrency control, obviously the entire file must be locked while one of the clients is updating even one record in it. Other than providing a rudimentary file-sharing capability, this arrangement's drawbacks render it not very practical or useful.

A much better arrangement is variously known as the **database server** or **DBMS server approach.** Again, the database is located at the server, but this time, the processing is split between the client and the server, and there is much less data traffic on the network. Say that someone at a client computer wants to query the database at the server. The query is entered at the client, and the client computer performs the initial keyboard and screen interaction processing, as well as initial syntax checking of the query. The system then ships the query over the LAN to the server where the query is actually run against the database. Only the results are shipped back to the client. Certainly, this is a much better arrangement than the file server approach! The network data traffic is reduced to a tolerable level, even for frequently queried databases. Also, security and concurrency control can be handled at the server in a much more contained way. The only real drawback to this approach is that the company must invest in a sufficiently powerful server to keep up with all of the activity concentrated there.

Another issue involving the data on a LAN is the fact that some databases can be stored on a client PC's own hard drive while other databases that the client might access are stored on the LAN's server. This is also known as a two-tier approach, (Figure 13.2). Software has been developed that makes the *location* of the data *transparent* to the user at the client. In this mode of operation, the user issues a query at the client, and the software first checks to see if the required data

➤ **Figure 13.2**
Two-tier client/server
database

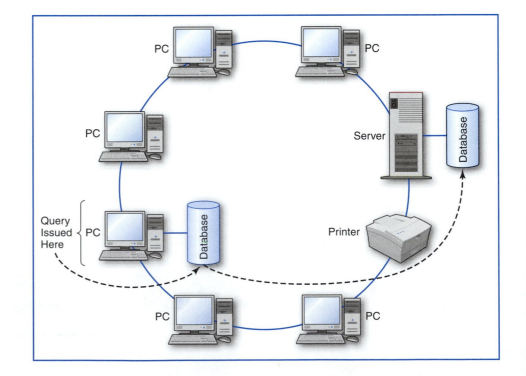

is on the PC's own hard drive. If it is, the data is retrieved from it, and that is the end of the story. If it is not there, then the software automatically looks for it on the server. In an even more sophisticated three-tier approach (Figure 13.3), if the software doesn't find the data on the client PC's hard drive or on the LAN server, it can leave the LAN through a gateway computer and look for the data on, for example, a large, mainframe computer that may be reachable from many LANs.

In another use of the term **three-tier approach,** the three tiers are the client PCs, servers known as **application servers,** and other servers known as database servers, (Figure 13.4). In this arrangement, local screen and keyboard interaction is still handled by the clients, but they can now request a variety of applications to be performed at and by the application servers. The application servers, in turn, rely on the database servers and their databases to supply the data needed by the applications. Though certainly well beyond the scope of LANs, an example of this kind of arrangement is the World Wide Web on the Internet. The local processing on the clients is limited to the data input and data display capabilities of browsers such as Netscape's Communicator and Microsoft's Internet Explorer. The application servers are the computers at company Web sites that conduct the companies' business with the "visitors" working through their browsers. The company application servers in turn rely on the companies' database servers to provide the necessary data to complete the transactions. For example, when a bank's customer visits his bank's Web site, he can initiate lots of different transactions, ranging from checking his account balances to transferring money between accounts to paying his credit card bills. The bank's Web application server handles all of these transactions. It, in turn, sends requests to the bank's database server and databases to retrieve the current account balances, add money to one account while deducting money from another in a funds transfer, and so forth.

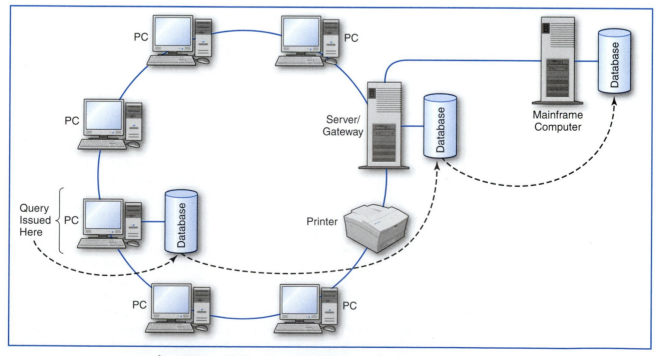

➤ **Figure 13.3**   Three-tier client/server database

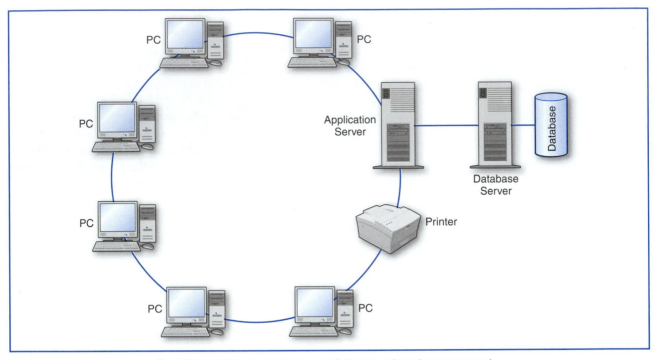

➤ **Figure 13.4**   Another type of three-tier client/server approach

DISTRIBUTED DATABASE

The Distributed Database Concept

In today's world of universal dependence on information systems, all sorts of people need access to companies' databases. In addition to a company's own employees, these include the company's customers, potential customers, suppliers, and vendors of all types. It is possible for a company to have all of its databases concentrated at one mainframe computer site with worldwide access to this site provided by telecommunications networks, including the Internet. Although the management of such a centralized system and its databases can be controlled in a well-contained manner and this can be advantageous, it poses some problems as well. For example, if the single site goes down, then everyone is blocked from accessing the databases until the site comes back up again. Also the communications costs from the many far-flung PCs and terminals to the central site can be expensive. One solution to such problems, and an alternative design to the centralized database concept, is known as **distributed database.**

The idea is that instead of having one, centralized database, we are going to spread the data out among the cities on the distributed network, each of which has its own computer and data storage facilities. All of this **distributed data** is still considered to be a single logical database. When a person or process anywhere on the distributed network queries the database, it is not necessary to know where on the network the data being sought is located. The user just issues the query, and the result is returned. This feature is known as **location transparency.** This can become rather complex very quickly, and it must be managed by sophisticated software known as a **distributed database management system** or distributed DBMS.

Distributing the Data Consider a large multinational company with major sites in Los Angeles, Memphis, New York (which is corporate headquarters), Paris, and Tokyo. Let's say that the company has a very important transactional relational database that is actively used at all five sites. The database consists of six large tables, named A, B, C, D, E, and F, and response time regarding queries made to the database is an important factor. If the database was centralized, the arrangement would look like Figure 13.5, with all six tables located in New York.

The first and simplest idea in distributing the data would be to disperse the six tables among the five sites. If particular tables are used at some sites more frequently than at other sites, it would make sense to locate the tables at the sites at which they are most frequently used. Figure 13.6 shows that we have kept Tables A and B at New York, while moving Table C to Memphis, Tables D and E to Tokyo, and Table F to Paris. Say that we moved Table F to Paris because it is used most frequently there. With Table F in Paris, the people there can use it as much as they want to without running up any telecommunications costs, as opposed to when the table used to be in New York. Furthermore, the Paris employees can exercise **local autonomy** over the data, taking responsibility for its security, backup and recovery, and concurrency control.

Unfortunately, distributing the database in this way has not relieved some of the problems that we had with the centralized database, and it has introduced a couple of new ones. The main problem that is carried over from the centralized approach is availability. In the centralized approach of Figure 13.5, if the New York

> **Figure 13.5**
> Centralized database

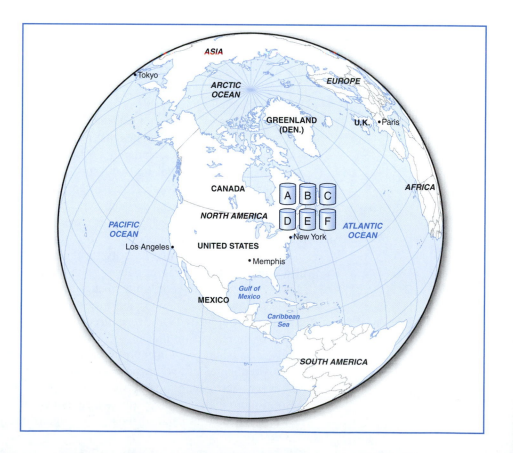

➤ **Figure 13.6**
Distributed database with
no data replication

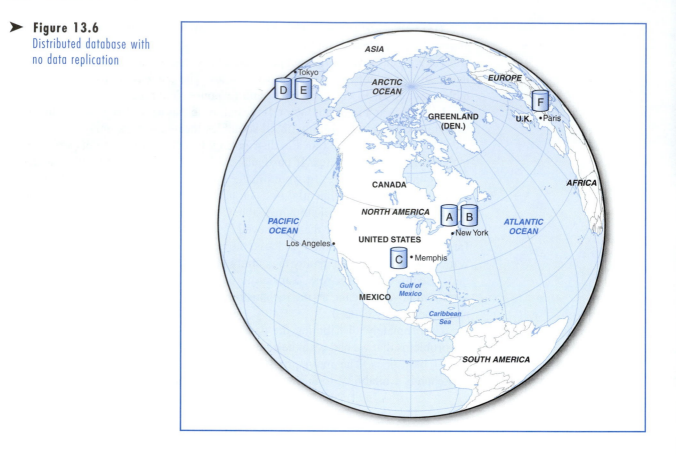

site went down, no other site on the network could access Table F (or any of the other tables). In the dispersed approach of Figure 13.6, if the Paris site goes down, Table F is equally unavailable to the other sites. A new problem that crops up in Figure 13.6 has to do with joins. When the database was centralized at New York, a query issued at any of the sites that required a join of two or more of the tables could be handled in the standard way by the computer at New York. The result would then be sent to the site that issued the query. In the dispersed approach, a join might require tables located at different sites! Though not an insurmountable problem, this would obviously add some major complexity (and we will discuss this further later in this chapter). Furthermore, although we could (and did) make the argument that local autonomy is good for issues like security control, an argument can also be made that security for the overall database can better be handled at a single, central location. Clearly, the simple dispersal of database tables as shown in Figure 13.6 is of limited benefit.

Let's introduce a new option into the mix. Suppose that we allow database tables to be duplicated—the term used with distributed database is **replicated**—at two or more sites on the network. This idea has both advantages and, unfortunately, disadvantages. On the plus side, the first advantage is availability. If a table is replicated at two or more sites and one of those sites goes down, everyone everywhere else on the network can still access the table at the other site(s). Also, if more than one site requires frequent access to a particular table, the table can be replicated at each of those sites, again minimizing telecommunications costs during data access. And copies of a table can be located at sites that have tables with which it may have to be joined, allowing the joins to take place at those sites without having the complexity of having to join tables across multiple sites. On the down side, if a table is replicated at several sites, it becomes more of a security risk. But the biggest problem that data replication introduces is that of concurrency control. As we have already seen, concurrency control is an issue even without replicated tables; with replicated tables, it becomes even more complex. How do you keep data consistent when it is replicated in tables on three continents? More about this issue later.

Assuming, then, that data replication has some advantages and that we are willing to deal with the disadvantages, what are the options for where to place the replicated tables? Figure 13.7 shows the maximum approach of replicating every table at every site. It's great for availability and for joins, but it's the absolute worst arrangement regarding concurrency control. Every change to every table has to be reflected at every site. It's also a security nightmare, and, by the way, it takes up a lot of disk space.

The concept in Figure 13.8 is to have a copy of the entire database at headquarters in New York and to have each table replicated exactly once at one of the other sites. Again, this improves availability, at least to the extent that each table is now at two sites. Because each table is at only two sites, the security and concurrency exposures are limited. Any join that has to be executed can be handled at

➤ **Figure 13.7**
Distributed database with maximum data replication

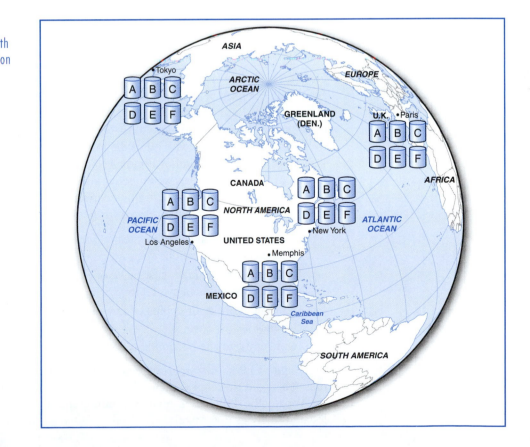

➤ **Figure 13.8**
Distributed database
with one complete copy
in one city

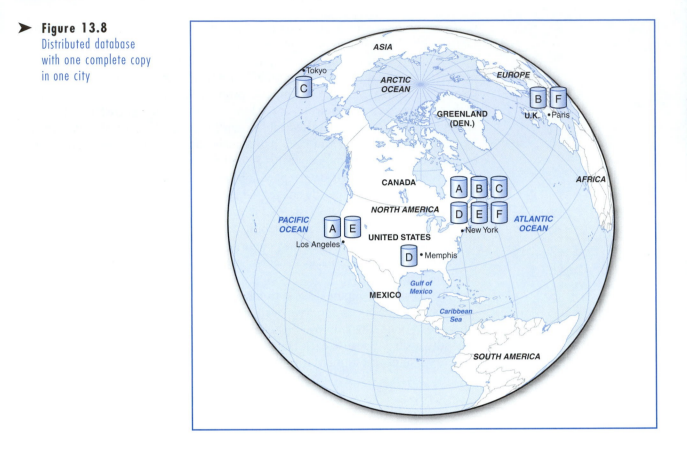

New York. So, this arrangement sounds pretty good, but it is limiting. What if a particular table is used heavily at both Tokyo and Los Angeles? We would like to place copies of it at both of those sites, but we can't because the premise is to have one copy in New York and only one other copy elsewhere. Also, New York would tend to become a bottleneck, with all of the joins and many of the other accesses being sent there. Still, the design of Figure 13.8 appears to be an improvement over the design of Figure 13.7. Can we do better still?

The principle behind making this concept work is flexibility in placing replicated tables where they will do the most good. We want to:

• Place copies of tables at the sites that use them most heavily in order to minimize telecommunications costs.
• Ensure that there are at least two copies of important or frequently used tables to realize the gains in availability.
• Limit the number of copies of any one table to control the security and concurrency issues.
• Avoid any one site becoming a bottleneck.

Figure 13.9 shows an arrangement of replicated tables based on these principles. There are two copies each of Tables A, B, E, and F, and three copies of Table D. Apparently, Table C is relatively unimportant or infrequently used, and it is located solely at Los Angeles.

➤ **Figure 13.9**
Distributed database
with targeted data
replication

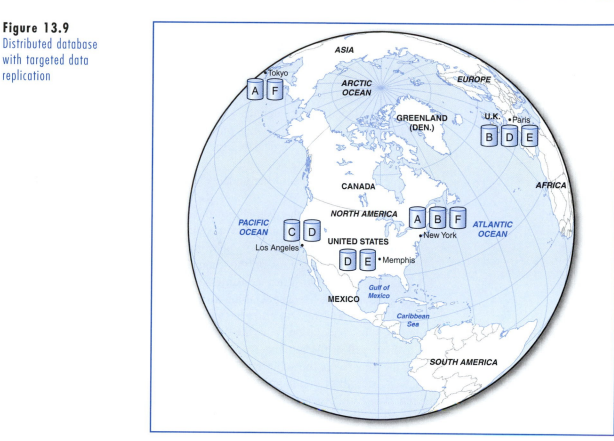

Concurrency Control in Distributed Database

Earlier in the book we discussed concurrency control in terms of the problems involved in multiple people or processes trying to update a record at the same time. When we allow replicated tables to be dispersed all over the country or the world in a distributed database, the problems of concurrent update expand, too. The original possibility of the "lost update" is still there. If two people attempt to update a particular record of Table B in New York at the same time, everything that we said about the problem of concurrent update earlier in the book remains true. But now, in addition, look at what happens when geographically dispersed, replicated files are involved. In Figure 13.9, if one person updates a particular value in a record of Table B in New York at the same time that someone else updates the very same value in the very same record of Table B in Paris, the results are going to be wrong. Or if one person updates a particular record of Table B in New York and then right after that a second person reads the same record of Table B in Paris, that second person is not going to get the latest, most up-to-date data. The protections that we discussed earlier that can be put into place to handle the problem of concurrent update in a single table are not adequate to handle the new, expanded problem.

If the nature of the data and of the applications that use it can tolerate retrieved data not necessarily being up-to-the-minute accurate, then several "asynchronous" approaches to updating replicated data can be used. For example, the site at which the data was updated, New York in the above example involving Table B, can simply send a message to the other sites that contain a copy of the same table, in this case Paris which also has a copy of Table B, in the hopes that the update will reach Paris reasonably quickly and that the computer in Paris will update that record in Table B right away. In another asynchronous scheme, one of the sites can be chosen to accumulate all of the updates to all of the tables. That site can then transmit the changes to all of the other sites on a regularly scheduled basis. Or each table can have one of the sites be declared the "dominant" site for that table. All of the updates for a particular table can be sent to the copy of the table at its dominant site, which can then transmit the updates to the other copies of the table on some timed or other basis.

But if the nature of the data and of the applications that use it require that all of the data in the replicated tables worldwide always be consistent, accurate, and up-to-date, then a more complex synchronous procedure must be put into place. Although there are variations on this theme, the basic process for accomplishing this is known as the **two-phase commit.** This process works as follows. Each computer on the network has a special log file in addition to its database tables. So, in Figure 13.9, each of the five cities has one of these special log files. Now, when an update is to be made at one site, the distributed DBMS has to do several things. It has to freeze all of the replicated copies of the table involved, send the update out to all the sites with the table copies, and then be sure that all the copies were updated. After all of that happens, all of the replicated copies of the table will have been updated and processing can resume. Remember that for this to work properly, either all of the replicated files have to be updated or none of them must be updated. What we don't want is for the update to take place at some of the sites and not at the others, which would obviously leave inconsistent results. Let's look at an example using Table D in Figure 13.9. Copies of Table D are located in Los Angeles, Memphis, and Paris.

Say that someone issues an update request to a record in Table D in Memphis. In the first or "prepare" phase of the two-phase commit, the computer in Memphis sends the updated data to Los Angeles and Paris. The computers in all three cities write the update to their logs (but *not* to their actual copies of Table D, at this point). The computers in Los Angeles and Paris attempt to lock their copies of Table D to get ready for the update. If another process is using their copy of Table D, then they will not be able to do this. Los Angeles and Paris then report back to Memphis whether or not they are in good operating shape and whether or not they were able to lock Table D. The computer in Memphis takes in all of this information and then makes a decision of whether to go ahead with the update or to abort it. If Los Angeles and Paris report back that they are up and running and were able to lock Table D, then the computer in Memphis will decide to go ahead with the update. If the news from Los Angeles and Paris was bad, Memphis will decide not to go ahead with the update. So, in the second or "commit" phase of the two-phase commit, Memphis sends its decision to Los Angeles and Paris. If it decides to complete the update, then all three cities transfer the updated data from their logs to their copy of Table D. If Memphis decides to abort the update then none of the sites transfers the updated data from their logs to their copy of Table D. All three copies of Table D remain as they were, and Memphis can start the process all over again.

The two-phase commit is certainly a complex, costly, and time-consuming process. It should be clear that the more volatile the data in the database is, the less attractive is this type of synchronous procedure for updating replicated tables in the distributed database.

Distributed Joins

Let's take a look at the issue of **distributed joins,** which came up earlier. In a distributed database in which no single computer (no single city) in the network contains the entire database, there is the possibility that a query will be run from one of the computers that requires a join of two or more tables that are not all at the same computer. Consider the distributed database design in Figure 13.9. Let's say that a query issued at Los Angeles requires the join of Tables E and F. First of all, neither of the two tables is located at Los Angeles, the site that issued the query. Then, notice that none of the other four cities contains a copy of both Tables E and F. That means that there is no one city to which the query can be sent for complete processing, including the join.

In order to handle this type of distributed join situation, the distributed DBMS must have a sophisticated capability to move data from one city to another to accomplish the join. Earlier in the book, we described the idea of the relational DBMS's relational query optimizer as an expert system that figures out an efficient way to respond to and satisfy a relational query. Similarly, the distributed DBMS must have its own built-in expert system that is capable of figuring out an efficient way to handle a request for a distributed join. This distributed DBMS expert system will work hand-in-hand with the relational query optimizer, which will still be needed to determine which records of a particular table are needed to satisfy the join, among other things. In the example of the query issued from Los Angeles that requires a join of Tables E and F, there are several options:

- Figure out which records of Table E are involved in the join and send copies of them from either Memphis or Paris (each of which has a copy of Table E) to either New York or Tokyo (each of which has a copy of the other table involved in the join, Table F). Then, execute the join in whichever of New York or Tokyo was chosen to receive the records from Table E and send the result back to Los Angeles.

- Figure out which records of Table F are involved in the join and send copies of them from either New York or Tokyo (each of which has a copy of Table F) to either Memphis or Paris (each of which has a copy of the other table involved in the join, Table E). Then, execute the join in whichever of Memphis or Paris was chosen to receive the records from Table F and send the result back to Los Angeles.

- Figure out which records of Table E are involved in the join and send copies of them from either Memphis or Paris (each of which has a copy of Table E) to Los Angeles, the city that initiated the join request. Figure out which records of Table F are involved in the join and send copies of them from either New York or Tokyo (each of which has a copy of Table F) to Los Angeles. Then, execute the join in Los Angeles, the site that issued the query.

How does the distributed DBMS decide among these options? It must consider:

- The number and size of the records from each table involved in the join.
- The distances and costs of transmitting the records from one city to another to execute the join.
- The distance and cost of shipping the result of the join back to the city that issued the query in the first place.

For example, if only twenty records of Table E are involved in the join while all of Table F is needed, then it would make sense to send copies of the twenty Table E records to a city that has a copy of Table F. The join can then be executed at the Table F city and the result sent back to Los Angeles. The arrangement of tables in Figure 13.9 suggests that, one solution would be to send the twenty records from Table E in Memphis to New York, one of the cities with Table F. The query could then be executed in New York and the result sent to Los Angeles, which issued the query. Why Memphis and New York rather than Paris and Tokyo, the other cities that have copies of Tables E and F, respectively? Because the distance (and probably the cost) between Memphis and New York is much less than the distances involving Paris and Tokyo. Finally, what about the option of shipping the data needed from both tables to Los Angeles, the city that issued the query, for execution? Remember, the entirety of Table F is needed for the join in this example. Shipping all of Table F to Los Angeles to execute the join there would probably be much more expensive than the New York option.

Partitioning or Fragmentation

Another option in the distributed database bag of tricks is known as **partitioning** or **fragmentation.** This is actually a variation on the theme of file partitioning that we discussed in the context of physical database design, earlier in the book.

In horizontal partitioning, a relational table can be split up so that some records are located at one site, other records are located at another site, and so on. Figure 13.10 shows the same five-city network that we have been using as an example, with another table, Table G, added. The figure shows that subset G1 of the records of Table G is located in Memphis, subset G2 is located in Los Angeles, and so on. A simple example of this would be the company's employee table: the records of the employees who work in a given city are stored in that city's computer. Thus G1 is the subset of records of Table G consisting of the records of the employees who work in Memphis, G2 is the subset consisting of the employees who work in Los Angeles, and so forth. This makes sense when one considers that most of the query and access activity on a particular employee's record will take place at his work location. The drawback is that when one of the sites, say the New York headquarters location, occasionally needs to run an application that requires accessing the employee records of everyone in the company, it must collect them from every one of the five sites.

In vertical partitioning, the columns of a table are divided up among several cities on the network. Each such partition must include the primary key attribute(s) of the table. This arrangement can make sense when different sites are responsible for processing different functions involving an entity. For example, the salary attributes of a personnel table might be stored in one city while the skills attributes of the table might be stored in another city. Both partitions would include the employee number, the primary key of the full table. Note that to bring the different

➤ **Figure 13.10**
Distributed database
with data partitioning/
fragmentation

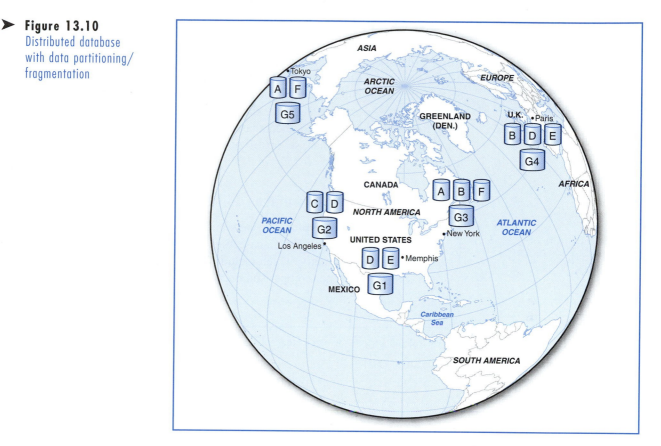

pieces of data about a particular employee back together again in a query would require a multi-site join of the two fragments of that employee's record.

Can a table be partitioned both horizontally and vertically? Yes, in principle! Can horizontal and vertical partitions be replicated? Yes, again, in principle! But bear in mind that the more exotic such arrangements become, the more complexity there is for the software and the IT personnel to deal with.

Distributed Directory Management

In the discussion on distributed database up to this point we've been taking the notion of location transparency for granted. That is, we've been assuming that when a query is issued at any city on the network, the system simply "knows" where to find the data it needs to satisfy the query. But that knowledge has to come from somewhere, and that place is in the form of a directory. A distributed DBMS must include a directory that keeps track of where the database tables, the replicated copies of database tables (if any), and the table partitions (if any) are located. Then, when a query is presented at any city on the network, the distributed DBMS can automatically use the directory to find out where the required data is located and maintain location transparency. That is, the person or process that initiated the query does not have to know where the data is, whether or not it is replicated, or whether or not it is partitioned.

Which brings up an interesting question. Where should the directory itself be stored? As with the matter of how to distribute the database tables themselves, there are a number of possibilities, some relatively simple and others more complex, with many of the same kinds of advantages and disadvantages that we've already discussed. The entire directory could be stored at only one site, copies of the directory could be stored at several of the sites, or a copy of the directory could be stored at every site. Actually, since the directory must be referenced for every query issued at every site and since the directory data will only change when new database tables are added to the database, database tables are moved, or new replicated copies or partitions are set up (all of which would be fairly rare occurrences), the best solution generally is to have a copy of the directory at every site.

Distributed DBMS Advantages and Disadvantages

At this point, it will be helpful to review and summarize the advantages and disadvantages of the distributed database concept and its various options. Figure 13.11 provides this summary, which includes the advantages and disadvantages of a centralized database, for comparison purposes.

➤ **Figure 13.11**
Advantages and disadvantages of centralized and distributed database approaches

---

Centralized Database—Like Figure 13.5

Advantages:
- Single site provides high degree of security, concurrency, and backup and recovery control.
- No need for a distributed directory since all of the data is in one place.
- No need for distributed joins since all of the data is in one place.

Disadvantages:
- All data accesses from other than the site with the database incur communications costs.
- The site with the database can become a bottleneck.
- Possible availability problem: if the site with the database goes down, there can be no data access.

Dispersing Tables on the Network (without replication or partitioning)—Like Figure 13.6

Advantages:
- Local autonomy.
- Reduced communications costs because each table can be located at the site that most heavily uses it.
- Improved availability because portions of the database are available even if one or some of the sites are down.

Disadvantages:
- Several sites have to be concerned with security, concurrency, and backup and recovery.
- Requires a distributed directory and the software to support location transparency.
- Requires distributed joins.

(Continues)

➤ **Figure 13.11 (Continued)**
Advantages and disadvantages of centralized and distributed database approaches

Targeted Data Replication—Like Figure 13.9

Advantages in addition to the advantages of dispersed tables:

• Greatly reduced communications costs for read-only data access because copies of tables can be located at multiple sites that most heavily use them.

• Greatly improved availability because if a site with a database table goes down, there may be another site with a copy of that table.

Disadvantages in addition to the disadvantages of dispersed tables:

• Multi-site concurrency control when data in replicated tables is updated.

Partitioned Tables—Like Figure 13.10

Advantages:

• Greatest local autonomy because data at the record or column level can be stored at the site(s) that most heavily use it.

• Greatly reduced communications costs because data at the record or column level can be stored at the site(s) that most heavily use it.

Disadvantages:

• Retrieving all or a large portion of a table may require multi-site accesses.

STATE OF TENNESSEE—DEPARTMENT OF SAFETY

Tennessee, with 5.7 million people and an area of over 42,000 square miles, is the 16th largest U.S. state in population and the 36th largest in size. Tennessee became the 16th state of the U.S. in 1796. Its principal cities are Memphis, Nashville (the capital), Knoxville, and Chattanooga. Tennessee's leading industries include printing, publishing, chemicals, fabricated metals, and automobile manufacturing. Almost one-half of the state's land is dedicated to 80,000 farms with the major products being cattle, hardwood lumber, dairy products, and cotton. Centrally located in the U.S., the state is also known as a major distribution center. As with all states, the Tennessee state government is responsible for a wide variety of public services, including the collection and management of state taxes, the management and maintenance of state parks, and the management of various social services for its citizens. The state's Department of Safety is responsible for services such as the licensing of motor vehicles and drivers, and the enforcement of laws covering the operation of motor vehicles.

The Department of Safety maintains a Driver's License System database application that tracks the state's driver's licenses. Implemented in 1978, the database stores basic name and address data as well as data that specifies the type of license and any restrictions such as required corrective lenses. In 1996, an extension to the application was implemented that captures and stores both a photograph of the driver and the driver's signature in a digital format or "image." All of this data, including the photo and signature, is incorporated into the actual physical driver's license. The images are captured at each driver's licensing location and transmitted online to the database for storage. All of the data, including the images, can be queried and retrieved online using canned queries.

Running on an IBM OS/390 mainframe computer located in the capital, Nashville, the database application is an interesting hybrid of two different types of databases and DBMSs. The original application that stores the name and address and license type data, and which dates from 1978, is implemented in IBM's IMS DBMS. The 1996 extension that stores the photos and signatures is implemented in IBM's DB2 relational DBMS. The relational database currently holds approximately 7 million photo and signature images, including driver photos taken for previous license renewals.

Printed by permission of State of Tennessee—Department of Safety

KEY TERMS

Application server	Distributed join	Partitioning
Client	Distributed directory management	Replicated data
Client/server database	File server approach	Server
Database server	Fragmentation	Three-tiered client/server approach
Database server approach	Gateway computer	Two-phase commit
Distributed data	Local area network (LAN)	Two-tiered client/server approach
Distributed database	Local autonomy	
Distributed database management	Location transparency	

QUESTIONS

1. What is a client/server database system?

2. Explain the database server approach to client/server database.

3. What are the advantages of the database server approach to client/server database compared to the file server approach?

4. What is data transparency in client/server database? Why is it important?

5. Compare the two-tier arrangement of client/server database to the three-tier arrangement.

6. What is a distributed database? What is a distributed database management system?

7. Why would a company be interested in moving from the centralized to the distributed database approach?

8. What are the advantages of locating a portion of a database in the city in which it is most frequently used?

9. What are the advantages and disadvantages of data replication in a distributed database?

10. Describe the concept of asynchronous updating of replicated data. For what kinds of applications would it work or not work?

11. Describe the two-phase commit approach to updating replicated data.

12. Describe the factors used in deciding how to accomplish a particular distributed join.

13. Describe horizontal and vertical partitioning in a distributed database.

14. What are the advantages and disadvantages of horizontal partitioning in a distributed database?

15. What are the advantages and disadvantages of vertical partitioning in a distributed database?

16. What is the purpose of a directory in a distributed database? Where should the directory be located?

17. Discuss the problem of directory management for distributed database. Do you think that as an issue, it is more critical, less critical, or about the same as the distribution of the data itself? Explain.

EXERCISES

1. Australian Boomerang, Ltd., wants to design a distributed relational database. The company is headquartered in Perth and has major operations in Sydney, Melbourne, and Darwin. The database involved consists of five tables, labeled A, B, C, D, and E, with the following characteristics:

   Table A consists of 500,000 records and is heavily used in Perth and Sydney.

   Table B consists of 100,000 records and is frequently required in all four cities.

   Table C consists of 800 records and is frequently required in all four cities.

   Table D consists of 75,000 records. Records 1–30,000 are most frequently used in Sydney. Records 30,001–75,000 are most frequently used in Melbourne.

   Table E consists of 20,000 records and is used almost exclusively in Perth.

   Design a distributed relational database for Australian Boomerang. Justify your placement, replication, and partitioning of the tables.

2. Canadian Maple Trees, Inc., has a distributed relational database with tables in computers in Halifax, Montreal, Ottawa, Toronto, and Vancouver. The database consists of twelve tables, some of which are replicated in multiple cities. Among them are tables A, B, and C, with the following characteristics.

   Table A consists of 800,000 records and is located in Halifax, Montreal, and Vancouver.

   Table B consists of 100,000 records and is located in both Halifax and Toronto.

   Table C consists of 20,000 records and is located in Ottawa and Vancouver.

   Telecommunications costs among Montreal, Ottawa, and Toronto are relatively low, while telecommunications costs between those three cities and Halifax and Vancouver are relatively high.

   A query is issued from Montreal that requires a join of tables A, B, and C. The query involves a single record from table A, 20 records from table B, and an undetermined number of records from table C. Develop and justify a plan for solving this query.

MINICASES

1. Consider the Happy Cruise Lines relational database of Minicase 1 in Chapter 5. The company has decided to reconfigure this database as a distributed database among its major locations: New York, which is its headquarters, and its other major U.S. ports: Miami, Los Angeles, and Houston. Distributed and replicated among these four locations, the tables have the following characteristics:

   SHIP consists of twenty records and is used in all four cities.

   CRUISE consists of 4,000 records. CRUISE records are used most heavily in the cities from which the cruise described in the record began.

   PORT consists of forty-two records. The records that describe Atlantic Ocean ports are used most heavily in New York and Miami. The records that describe Caribbean Sea ports are used most heavily in Houston and Miami. The records that describe Pacific Ocean ports are used most heavily in Los Angeles.

VISIT consists of 15,000 records and is used primarily in New York and Los Angeles.

PASSENGER consists of 230,000 records and is used primarily in New York and Los Angeles.

VOYAGE consists of 720,000 records and is used in all four cities.

Design a distributed relational database for Happy Cruise Lines. Justify your placement, replication, and partitioning of the tables.

2. Consider the Super Baseball League relational database of Minicase 2 in Chapter 5. The league has decided to organize its database as a distributed database with replicated tables. The nodes on the distributed database will be Chicago (the league's headquarters), Atlanta, San Francisco (where the league personnel office is located), and Dallas. The tables have the following characteristics:

TEAM consists of twenty records and is located in Chicago and Atlanta.

COACH consists of eighty-five records and is located in San Francisco and Dallas.

WORKEXP consists of 20,000 records and is located in San Francisco and Dallas.

BATS consists of 800,000 records and is located in Chicago and Atlanta.

PLAYER consists of 100,000 records and is located in San Francisco and Atlanta.

AFFILIATION consists of 20,000 records and is located in Chicago and San Francisco.

STADIUM consists of twenty records and is located only in Chicago.

Assume that telecommunications costs among the cities are all about the same.

Develop and justify a plan for solving the following queries:

a. A query is issued from Chicago to get a list of all the work experience of all the coaches on the Dodgers.

b. A query is issued from Atlanta to get a list of the names of the coaches who work for the team based at Smith Memorial Stadium.

c. A query is issued from Dallas to find the names of all the players who have compiled a batting average of at least .300 while playing on the Dodgers.

CHAPTER 14

THE DATA WAREHOUSE

CHAPTER OBJECTIVES

After learning the material in this chapter, you will be able to:
- ✔ Compare the data needs of transaction processing systems with those of decision support systems.
- ✔ Describe the data warehouse concept and list its main features.
- ✔ Compare the enterprise data warehouse with the data mart.
- ✔ Design a data warehouse.
- ✔ Build a data warehouse, including the steps of data extraction, data cleaning, data transformation, and data loading.
- ✔ Describe how to use a data warehouse with online analytic processing and data mining.
- ✔ List the types of expertise needed to administer a data warehouse.
- ✔ List the challenges in data warehousing.

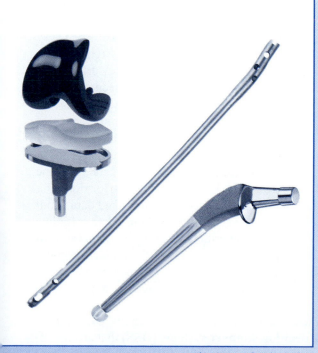

Photo Courtesy of Smith & Nephew

SMITH & NEPHEW

Smith & Nephew is a leader in the manufacture and marketing of medical devices. Headquartered in London, UK, the company has over 7,000 employees and has operations in thirty-four countries. Smith & Nephew focuses on three areas of medical device technology, each run by a separate business unit. In orthopedics, Smith & Nephew is a leading manufacturer of knee, hip, and shoulder replacement joints, as well as products that aid in the repair of broken bones (see photo). In endoscopy, the company is the world leader in arthroscopic surgery devices for minimally invasive surgery of the knee and other joints. Lastly, the company is the world leader in providing products and techniques for advanced wound management. All of this from a beginning in 1856 when Thomas J. Smith opened a pharmaceutical chemist shop in Hull, England. And, yes, he later brought his nephew into the company.

Smith & Nephew supports its orthopedics products business with a state-of-the-art data warehouse. This data warehouse incorporates daily sales and inventory data from its operational SAP system plus global data and data from external sources regarding finance and market data. It provides a decision support environment for sales administrators who must manage and realign sales territories, marketing specialists who have to analyze market potentials, product managers, and logistics managers. The data warehouse is also used to support an executive information system for reporting the company's results to the Orthopedic Executive Staff.

Implemented in 1999, the data warehouse is built on the Oracle RDBMS and runs on Hewlett-Packard Unix hardware. Queries are generated through Oracle query products as well as native SQL. Smith & Nephew's data warehouse architecture employs the classic star schema design, with several major subject areas. These and their fact tables include U.S. sales, global sales, budget, and inventory. The dimension tables, for example for global sales, include customer, time, and product. This arrangement allows historical sales data to be compiled by customer, sales territory, time period, product, and so forth.

Printed by permission of Smith & Nephew

Generally, when we think about information systems, we think about what are known as operational or **transaction processing systems (TPS).** These are the everyday application systems that support banking and insurance operations, manage the parts inventory on manufacturing assembly lines, keep track of airline and hotel reservations, support Web-based sales, and so on. These are the kinds of application systems that most people quickly associate with the information systems field, and, indeed, these are the kinds of application systems that we have used as examples in this book. The databases that support these application systems must have several things in common, which we ordinarily take for granted. They must have up-to-the-moment current data, they must be capable of providing direct access and very rapid response, and they have to be designed for sharing by large numbers of users.

But the business world has other needs of a very different nature. These needs generally involve management decision making and typically require analyzing data that has been accumulated over some period of time. They often don't even require the latest, up-to-the-second data! We've already seen Smith & Nephew's needs for managing its marketing activities. Another example occurs in the retail store business, when management has to decide how much stock of particular items they should carry in their stores during the October-December period this year; they are going to want to check on the sales volume for those items during the same three-month period in each of the last five years. If airline management is considering adding more flights between two cities (or dropping existing flights), they are going to want to analyze lots of accumulated data about the volume of passenger traffic between those two cities in their existing flights. If a company is considering expanding its operations into a new geographical region, management will want to study the demographics of the region's population and the amount of competition it will have from other companies, very possibly using data that it doesn't currently have but will have to acquire from outside sources.

In response to such management decision-making needs, there is another class of application systems, known as **decision support systems (DSS)** that are specifically designed to aid managers in these tasks. The issue for us in this book about database management concerns what kind of database is needed to support a DSS. In the past, files were developed to support individual applications that we would now classify as DSS applications. For example, the five-year sales trend analysis for retail stores described above has been a fairly standard application for a long time and was always supported by files developed for it alone. But as DSS activity has mushroomed, along with the rest of information systems growth, having separate files for each DSS application is wasteful, expensive, and inefficient, for several reasons:

- Different DSS applications often need the same data, causing duplicate files to be created for each application. As with any set of redundant files, they are wasteful of storage space and update time, and they create the potential for data integrity problems (although as we will see a little later, data redundancy in dealing with largely historical data is not as much of a concern as it is with transactional data).
- While particular files support particular DSS applications, they tend to be inflexible and do not support closely related applications that require slightly different data.
- Individual files tied to specific DSS applications do nothing to encourage other people and groups in the company to use the company's accumulated data to gain a competitive advantage over the competition.
- Even if someone in the company is aware of existing DSS application data that they could use to their own advantage (really, to the company's advantage), they generally can't get access to it because it is "owned" by the application for which it was created.

When we talked about the advantages of data sharing earlier in this book, the emphasis was on data in transactional systems. But the factors listed above regarding data for decision support systems, which in their own way largely parallel the reasoning for having shared transactional databases, inevitably led to the concept of broad-based, shared databases for decision support. These DSS databases have come to be known as **data warehouses.** In this chapter, we will discuss the nature, design, and implementation of data warehouses. Later in the chapter we will briefly touch upon some of their key uses.

THE DATA WAREHOUSE CONCEPT

Informally, a data warehouse is a broad-based, shared database for management decision making that contains data that has been accumulated over time. Imagine that at the end of every week or month, you gather up all of the company's sales data for that period and you append it to all of the accumulated sales data that is already in the data warehouse. Keep on doing this and eventually you will have several years of company sales data that you can search and query and on which you can perform all sorts of calculations.

More formally and in more detail, the classic definition of a data warehouse is that it is, "a **subject oriented, integrated, non–volatile,** and **time variant** collection of data in support of management's decisions."[1] In addition, the data in the warehouse must be high quality, may be aggregated, is often denormalized, and is not necessarily absolutely current (Figure 14.1). Let's take a look at each of these data warehouse characteristics.

---

[1] W.H., Inmon, *Building the Data Warehouse,* 2nd ed., (Hoboken, NJ: John Wiley & Sons, 1996).

➤ **Figure 14.1**
Characteristics of data
warehouse data

- The data is subject oriented
- The data is integrated
- The data is non-volatile
- The data is time variant
- The data must be high quality
- The data may be aggregated
- The data is often denormalized
- The data is not necessarily absolutely current

The Data Is Subject Oriented

The data in transactional databases tends to be organized according to the company's TPS applications. In a bank, this might mean the applications that handle the processing of accounts; in a manufacturing company, it might include the applications that communicate with the suppliers to maintain the necessary raw materials and parts on the assembly line; in an airline, it might involve the applications that support the reservations process. Data warehouses are organized around subjects, really the major entities of concern in the business environment. Thus subjects may include sales, customers, orders, claims, accounts, employees, and other entities that are central to the particular company's business.

The Data Is Integrated

Data about each of the subjects in the data warehouse is typically collected from several of the company's transactional databases, each of which supports one or more applications that have something to do with the particular subject. Some of the data, such as additional demographic data about the company's customers, may be acquired from outside sources. All of the data about a subject must be organized or integrated in such a way that it provides a unified, overall picture of all the important details about the subject over time. Furthermore, while being integrated, the data may have to be "transformed." For example, one application's database tables may measure the company's finished products in centimeters, while another may measure them in inches. One may identify countries of the world by name, while another may identify them by a numeric code. One may store customer numbers as an integer field, while another may store them as a character field. In all of these and in a wide variety of other such cases, the data from these disparate application databases must be transformed into common measurements, codes, data types, and so forth, as they are integrated into the data warehouse.

The Data Is Non-Volatile

Transactional data is normally updated on a regular, even frequent basis. Bank balances, raw materials inventories, airline reservations data, are all updated as the balances, inventories, and number of seats remaining, respectively, change in the normal course of daily business. We describe this data as volatile—subject to constant change. The data in the data warehouse is non-volatile. Once data is added to the data warehouse, it doesn't change. The sales data for October 2000 is whatever it was. It was totaled up, added to the data warehouse at the end of October 2000, and that's that. It will never change. Changing it would be like going back and rewriting history. The only sense in which the data in the data warehouse is updated is when data for the latest time period, the time period just ended, is appended to the existing data.

The Data Is Time Variant

Most transactional data is, simply, "current." A bank balance, an amount of raw materials inventory, the number of seats left on a flight, are all the current, up-to-the-moment figures. If someone wants to make a withdrawal from his bank account, the bank doesn't care what the balance was ten days ago or ten hours ago. The bank wants to know what the *current* balance is. There is no need to associate a date or time with the bank balance; in effect, the data's date and time would always be *now*. (To be sure, *some* transactional data must include timestamps. A health insurance company may keep six months of claim data online, and such data clearly requires timestamps.) On the other hand, data warehouse data, with its historic nature, always includes some kind of a timestamp. If we are storing sales data on a weekly or monthly basis and we have accumulated ten years of such historic data, each weekly or monthly sales figure obviously must be accompanied by a timestamp indicating the week or month (and year!) that it represents.

The Data Must Be High Quality

Transactional data can actually be somewhat forgiving of at least certain kinds of errors. In the bank record example, the account balance must be accurate, but if there is, say, a one-letter misspelling of the street name in the account holder's street address, that probably will not make a difference. This will not affect the account balance, and the post office will probably still deliver the account statements to the right house. But what if the customer's street address is actually spelled correctly in other transactional files? Consider a section of a data warehouse in which the subject is customer. It will be crucial to establish an accurate set of customers for the data warehouse data to be of any use. But with the address misspelling in one transactional file, when the data from that file is integrated with the data from the other transactional files, there will be some difficulty in reconciling whether the two different addresses both represent one customer, or whether they actually represent two different customers. This must be investigated and a decision made as to whether the records from the different files represent one customer or two different customers. It is in this sense that the data in the data warehouse must be of higher quality than the data in the transactional files.

The Data May Be Aggregated

When the data is copied and integrated from the transactional files into the data warehouse, it will often be aggregated or summarized for at least three reasons. One is that the type of data that management requires for decision making is generally summarized data. When trying to decide how much stock to order for a store for next December based on the sales data from the last five Decembers, the monthly sales figures are obviously useful, but the individual daily sales figures during those last five Decembers probably don't matter much. The second reason for having **aggregated data** in the data warehouse is that the sheer volume of all the historic detail data would make the data warehouse unacceptably huge in many cases. (They tend to be large as it is!) And the third reason is that if the detail data was stored in the data warehouse, the amount of time that it would take to summarize the data for management every time a query was posed would often be unacceptable. Having said all of that, the decision support environment is so broad that there are some situations within it that *do* call for detail data and, indeed, some data warehouses do contain at least some detail data.

The Data Is Often Denormalized

One of the fundamental truths about database that we encountered earlier in the book was that data redundancy improves the performance of read-only queries but takes up more disk space, requires more time to update, and introduces the exposure of data integrity problems when the data has to be updated. But in the case of the data warehouse, we have already established that the data is non-volatile. The *existing* data in the data warehouse never has to be updated. That makes the data warehouse a horse (or a database) of a different color! If the company is willing to tolerate the substantial additional space taken up by the redundant data, it can gain the advantage of the improved query performance that redundancy provides without paying the penalties of increased update time and potential data integrity problems because the existing data is historic and never has to be updated!

The Data Is Not Necessarily Absolutely Current

This is really a consequence of the kind of typical time schedule for loading new data into the data warehouse and was implied in "The Data Is Time Variant" sub-section, above. Say that you load the week-just-ended sales data into the data warehouse every Friday. The following Wednesday, a manager queries the data warehouse for help in making a decision. The data in the data warehouse is not "current" in the sense that sales data from last Saturday through today, Wednesday, is not included in the data warehouse. The question is, does it matter? The answer is, probably not! For example, the manager may have been performing a five-year sales trend analysis. When you're looking at the last five years of data, including or not including the last five days of data will probably not make a difference.

HILTON HOTELS

Hilton Hotels is one of the world's premiere lodging companies. Since opening its first hotel in 1919, Hilton has grown to a worldwide presence of over 2,000 hotel properties today. Headquartered in Beverly Hills, California, the company operates hotels under the names Hilton, Conrad, Doubletree, Embassy Suites, Hampton Inn, Hampton Inns and Suites, Hilton Garden Inn, and Homewood Suites by Hilton. Among the most famous Hilton Hotels are the Beverly Hilton in Beverly Hills, California, the Waldorf Astoria in New York City, and the Hilton Hawaiian Village.

A leader in information technology in its industry, one of Hilton's leading-edge database applications is its Guest Profile Manager (GPM). This is a customer relationship management (CRM) system that strives to achieve guest recognition and guest acknowledgement at all customer "touch points." These include email, contact at the hotel front desk, special channels on the in-room television, the Audix voice mail system, and on post-stay surveys. For example, in the CRM spirit of developing a personalized relationship with the customer, when a guest checks-in to any Hilton property, the front desk clerk receives information on their terminal that allows them to say, "Welcome back to Hilton, Mr. Smith," or "Welcome, Ms. Jones. I understand this is your first visit to this hotel (or to Hilton Hotels)." Both the front desk clerk and the housekeeping staff also get information on customer preferences and past complaints such as wanting a room with good water pressure and not wanting a noisy room. Targeted customers such as frequent guests might find fruit baskets, bottled water, or bathrobes in their rooms. The system even prepares personalized voice mail message greetings on the guest's in-room telephone answering system.

The system, which was inaugurated in March 2002, uses an Informix DBMS on a Sun Microsystems platform. The database contains both current reservations information and guest history, making it an interesting hybrid of a transaction processing system and a data warehouse. The pending reservations relation contains about two million records, while the one-year "stay summary" contains 60 million records. The database is shared for reservations, CRM, and other purposes. In addition, some of the data is copied into an offline data mart for marketing query purposes, using SQL Server as the DBMS and SAS software. Some of the data is organized in a classic data mart "star schema" arrangement using Epiphany software. In addition to Hilton's access by its hotels and marketing staff, Hilton provides their guests with access to their own records, including their history data, through the Hilton Web site.

Photo Courtesy of Hilton Hotels

Printed by permission of Hilton Hotels

TYPES OF DATA WAREHOUSES

Thus far, we have been using the term *data warehouse* in a generic sense. Although there are some further variations and refinements, there are basically only two kinds of data warehouses. One is called an **enterprise data warehouse (EDW),** and the other is called a **data mart (DM)** (Figure 14.2). The factors that distinguish the two are twofold: their size and the portion of the company that they service (which tend to go hand-in-hand), and the manner in which they are created and have new data appended to them (which are also related).

The Enterprise Data Warehouse (EDW)

The enterprise data warehouse is a large-scale data warehouse that incorporates the data of an entire company or of a major division, site, or activity of a company.

➤ **Figure 14.2**
The enterprise data warehouse and data marts

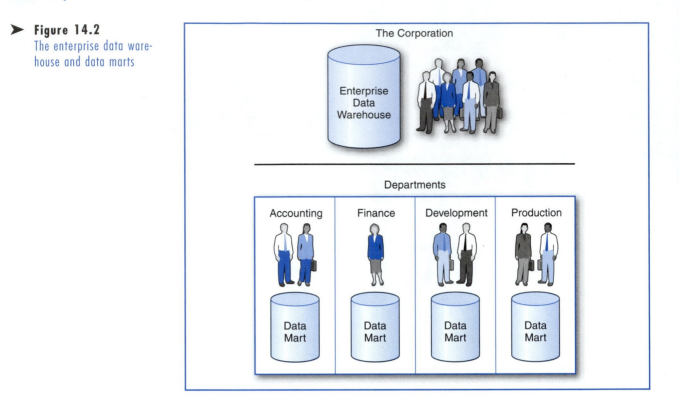

Both Smith & Nephew and Hilton Hotels employ such large-scale data warehouses. Depending on its nature, the data in the EDW is drawn from a variety of the company's transactional databases as well as from externally acquired data, requiring a major data integration effort. In data warehouse terminology, a full-scale EDW is built around several different subjects. The large mass of integrated data in the EDW is designed to support a wide variety of DSS applications and to serve as a data resource with which company managers can explore new ways of using the company's data to its advantage. Many EDWs restrict the degree of denormalization because of the sheer volume of data that large-scale denormalization would produce.

The Data Mart (DM)

A data mart is a small-scale data warehouse that is designed to support a small part of an organization, say a department or a related group of departments. As we saw, Hilton Hotels copies data from its data warehouse into a data mart for marketing query purposes. A company will often have several DMs. Data marts are based on a limited number of subjects (possibly one) and are constructed from a limited number of transactional databases. They focus on the business of a department or group of departments and thus tend to support a limited number and scope of DSS applications. Because of the DM's smaller initial size, there is more freedom to denormalize the data. Managerially, the department manager may feel that she has more control with a local DM and a greater ability to customize it to the department's needs.

Which to Choose: The EDW, the DM, or Both?

Should a company have an EDW, multiple DMs, or both? This kind of decision might be the result of careful planning, or it might simply evolve as a matter of management style or even just happenstance. Certainly, some companies have very deliberately and with careful planning decided to invest in the development of an EDW. There are also companies that have made the conscious decision to develop a series of DMs instead of an EDW. In other situations, no careful planning took place at all. There have been situations in managerially decentralized companies in which individual managers decided to develop DMs in their own departments. At times DMs have evolved from the interests of technical people in user departments.

In companies that have both an EDW and DMs, there are the questions of, which came first? and were they developed independently or were they derived from each other? This can go either way. In regards to data warehousing, the term *top-down development* implies that the EDW was created first and then later data was extracted from an EDW to create one or more DMs initially and on an ongoing basis. Assuming that the company has made the decision to invest in an EDW, this can make a great deal of sense. For example, once the data has been scrutinized and its quality improved (see Data Cleaning below) as it was entered into the EDW, downloading portions of it to DMs retains the high quality without putting the burden for this effort on the department developing the DM. Development in the other direction is possible, too. A company that has deliberately or as a matter of circumstance developed a series of independent DMs may decide, in a *bottom-up development* fashion to build an EDW out of the existing DMs. Clearly, this would have to involve a round of integration and transformation beyond those that took place to create the individual DMs.

DESIGNING A DATA WAREHOUSE

Introduction

Data warehousing has become a broad topic with many variations in its use, and so it comes as no surprise that there are a variety of ways to design data warehouses. Two of the characteristics of data warehouses are central to any such design: the subject orientation and the historic nature of the data. That is, the data warehouse (or each major part of the data warehouse) will be built around a subject and have a temporal (time) component to it. Data warehouses are often referred to as **multidimensional databases** because each occurrence of the subject is referenced by an occurrence of each of several **dimensions** or characteristics of the subject, one of which is time. For example, in a hospital patient tracking and billing system, the subject might be charges, and dimensions might include patient, date, procedure, and doctor. When there are just two dimensions, for example, the charges for particular patients on particular dates, they can easily be visualized on a flat piece of paper (Figure 14.3). When there are three dimensions, for example, the charges for particular procedures performed on particular patients on particular dates, they can be represented as a cube and still be drawn on paper (Figure 14.4). When there are four (or more) dimensions—the charges for particular procedures ordered by particular doctors performed on particular patients on particular dates—it takes some

➤ **Figure 14.3**
Hospital patient tracking
and billing system data with
two dimensions

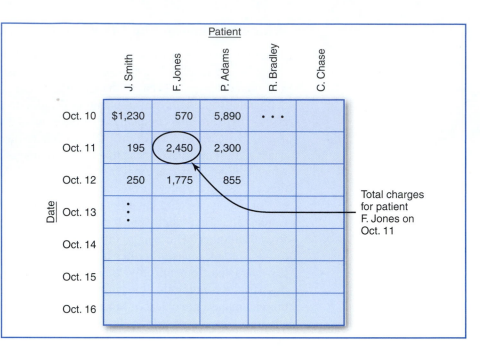

Total charges
for patient
F. Jones on
Oct. 11

➤ **Figure 14.4**
Hospital patient tracking
and billing system data with
three dimensions

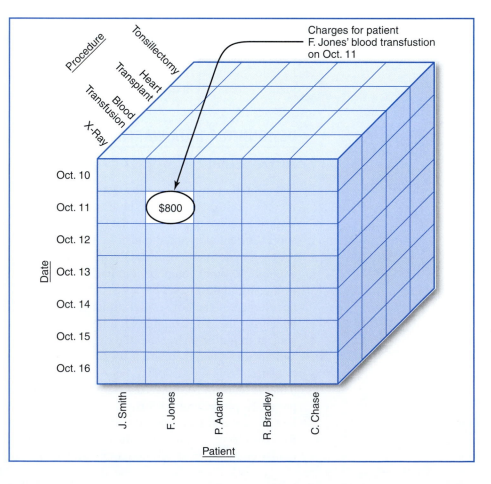

Charges for patient
F. Jones' blood transfustion
on Oct. 11

imagination (although there are techniques for combining dimensions that bring the visual representation back down to two or three dimensions). Certain data warehouse products on the market have special-purpose data structures to store such multidimensional data. But there is also much interest in storing such data in relational databases. A way to store multidimensional data in a relational database structure is with a model known as the **star schema.** The name comes from the visual design in which the subject is in the middle and the dimensions radiate outwards, as the rays of a star. As noted earlier, Smith & Nephew employs the star schema design for its data warehouse, as does Hilton Hotels for at least part of its data warehouse environment.

General Hardware Company Data Warehouse

Figure 14.5 repeats the General Hardware relational database, and Figure 14.6 shows a star schema for the General Hardware Company, with SALE as the subject. Star schemas have a "fact table," which represents the data warehouse

➤ **Figure 14.5**

The General Hardware Company relational database

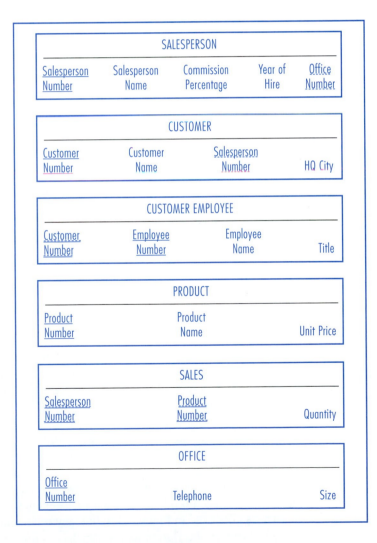

➤ **Figure 14.6**
General Hardware Company
data warehouse star schema
design

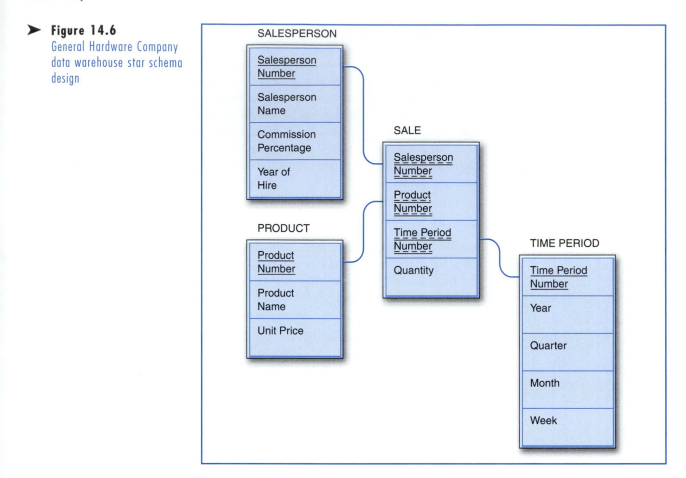

"subject" and several "dimension tables." In Figure 14.6, SALE is the fact table, and SALESPERSON, PRODUCT, and TIME PERIOD are the dimension tables. The dimension tables will allow the data in the fact table to be studied from many different points of view. Notice that there is a one-to-many relationship between each dimension table entity and the fact table entity. Furthermore, the "one side" of the relationship is always the dimension table, and the "many side" of the relationship is always the fact table. For a particular salesperson there are many sales records, but each sales record is associated with only one salesperson. The same is true of products and time periods.

To begin to understand and see this concept come to life, refer back to the SALES table in Figure 14.5, in which General Hardware keeps track of how many units of each product each salesperson has sold in *the most recent* time period, say in the last week. But what if we want to record and keep track of the sales for the most recent week, and the week before that, and the week before that, and so on going back perhaps five or ten years? That is a description of a data warehouse. The SALE table in the star schema of Figure 14.6 also reflects General Hardware's sales by salesperson and product but with a new element added: time. This table records the quantity of each product that each salesperson sold in each time period stored.

The SALE table in Figure 14.6, like any relational table, has to have a primary key. As shown in the figure, its primary key is the combination of the Salesperson

Number, Product Number, and Time Period Number attributes. But each of those attributes also serves as a foreign key. Each one leads to one of the dimension tables, as shown in Figure 14.6. Some historic data can be obtained with the fact table alone. Using the fact table, the SALE table, alone, we could, for example, find the total number of units of a particular product that a particular salesperson has sold for the entire time that the historic sales records have been kept, assuming we know both the product's product number and the salesperson's salesperson number. We would simply add the Quantity values in all of the SALE records for that salesperson and product. But the dimension tables provide a whole new dimension! For example, focusing in on the TIME PERIOD's Year attribute and taking advantage of this table's foreign key connection to the SALE table, we could refine the search to find the total number of units of a particular product that a particular salesperson sold in a particular single year or in a particular range of years. Or focusing in on the PRODUCT table's Unit Price attribute and the TIME PERIOD table's Year attribute, we could find the total number of units of expensive (unit price greater than some amount) products that each salesperson sold in a particular year. To make this even more concrete, suppose that we want to decide which of our salespersons who currently are compensated at the 10 percent commission level should receive an award based on their sales of expensive products over the last three years. We could sum the quantity values of the SALE table records by grouping them based on an attribute value of 10 in the Commission Percentage attribute of the SALESPERSON table, an attribute value greater than 50 (dollars) in the Unit Price attribute of the PRODUCT table, and a Year attribute representing each of the last three years in the TIME PERIOD table. The different combinations and possibilities are almost endless.

Figure 14.7 shows some sample data for General Hardware's star schema data warehouse. The rows shown in the SALE table are numbered on the left, just for convenience in this discussion. Look at the TIME PERIOD table in Figure 14.7. First, it is clear from the TIME PERIOD table that a decision was made to store data by the week and not by any smaller unit, such as the day. In this case, even if the data in the transactional database is being accumulated daily, it will be aggregated into weekly data in the data warehouse. Notice that the data warehouse began in the first week of the first month of the first quarter of 1997 and that this week was given the Time Period Number value of 001. The week after that was given the Time Period Number value of 002 and so on to the latest week stored. Now, look at the SALE table. Row 10 indicates that salesperson 137 sold 59 units of product 24013 during time period 103, which according to the TIME PERIOD table was the second week of the third month of the fourth quarter of 1998 (i.e., the second week of December 1998). Row 17 of the SALE table shows that salesperson 204 sold 44 units of product 16386 during time period 331, which was the third week of May 2003. Overall, as you look at the SALE table from row 1 down to row 20, you can see the historic nature of the data and the steady, forward time progression as the Time Period Number attribute starts with time period 001 in the first couple of records and steadily increases to time period 331 in the last batch of records.

Good Reading Bookstores Data Warehouse

Does Good Reading Bookstores need a data warehouse? Actually, this is a very good question, the answer to which is going to demonstrate a couple of important points

➤ **Figure 14.7**
General Hardware Company
data warehouse sample data

SALESPERSON

Salesperson Number	Salesperson Name	Commission Percentage	Year of Hire
137	Baker	10	1995
186	Adams	15	2001
204	Dickens	10	1998
361	Carlyle	20	2001

PRODUCT

Product Number	Product Name	Unit Price
16386	Wrench	12.95
19440	Hammer	17.50
21765	Drill	32.99
24013	Saw	26.25
26722	Pliers	11.50

TIME PERIOD

Time Period Number	Year	Quarter	Month	Week
001	1997	1	1	1
002	1997	1	1	2
003	1997	1	1	3
⋮				
101	1998	4	3	1
102	1998	4	3	2
103	1998	4	3	3
104	1998	4	3	4
⋮				
329	2003	2	2	1
330	2003	2	2	2
331	2003	2	2	3

(Continues)

about data warehouses. At first glance, the answer to the question seems to be, maybe not! After all, the sales data in Good Reading's transactional database *already carries a date attribute*, as shown in the SALE table of Figure 5.16. Thus it looks like Good Reading's transactional database is already historic! But Good Reading does need a data warehouse for two reasons. One is that while Good Reading's transactional database performs acceptably with perhaps the last couple of months of data in it, its performance would degrade to an unacceptable level if we tried to keep ten years of data

➤ **Figure 14.7 (Continued)**
General Hardware Company
data warehouse sample data

	Salesperson Number	Product Number	Time Period Number	Quantity
		SALE		
1	137	16386	001	57
2	137	24013	001	129
3	137	16386	002	24
4	137	24013	002	30
		⋮		
5	137	16386	102	85
6	137	24013	102	36
7	204	16386	102	111
8	204	24013	102	44
		⋮		
9	137	16386	103	47
10	137	24013	103	59
11	204	16386	103	13
12	204	24013	103	106
		⋮		
13	137	16386	331	63
14	137	24013	331	30
15	186	16386	331	25
16	186	24013	331	16
17	204	16386	331	44
18	204	24013	331	107
19	361	16386	331	18
20	361	24013	331	59

in it. The other reason is that the kinds of management decision making that require long-term historic sales data do not require daily data. Data aggregated to the week level is just fine for Good Reading's decision-making purposes, and having the data stored on a weekly basis saves a lot of time compared with having to retrieve and add up much more data to answer every query if the data is stored at the day level.

Figure 14.8 shows the Good Reading Bookstores data warehouse star schema design. The fact table is SALE, and each of its records indicates how many of a particular book a particular customer bought in a particular week (again, here, week is the lowest level time period) and the price that the customer paid per book. For this to make sense, there must be a company rule that the price of a book cannot change in the middle of a week, since each SALE table row has space to store only one price to go with the total quantity of that book purchased by that customer during that week. The design in Figure 14.8 also has a feature that makes it a **snowflake design.** One of the dimension tables, BOOK, leads to yet another dimension table, PUBLISHER. Consistent with the rest of the star schema, the snowflake relationship is one-to-many, "inward" toward the center of the star. A publisher publishes many books, but a book is associated with only one publisher.

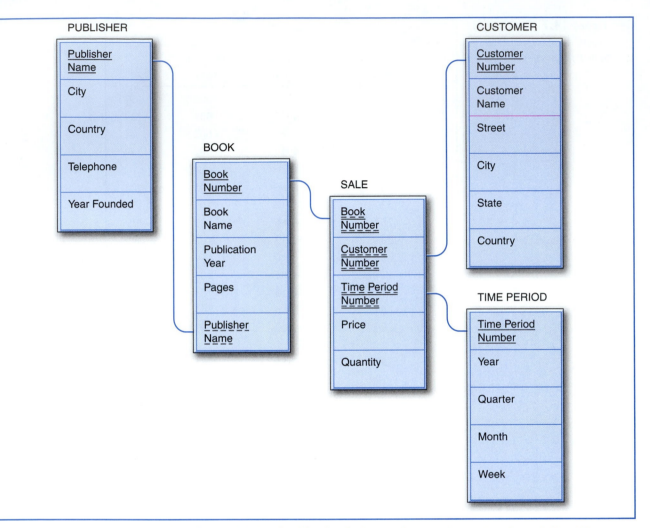

➤ **Figure 14.8** Good Reading Bookstores data warehouse star schema design with snowflake feature

To help in deciding how many copies of *Moby Dick* to order for their stores in Florida during the upcoming Christmas season, Good Reading could check on how many copies of *Moby Dick* were purchased in Florida during each of the last five Decembers. This query would require the Book Name attribute of the BOOK table, the State and Country attributes of the CUSTOMER table, and the Year and Month attributes of the TIME PERIOD table. To help in deciding whether to open more stores in Dallas, TX, Good Reading could sum the total number of all books purchased in all of their existing Dallas stores during each of the last five years. The snowflake feature expands the range of query possibilities even further. Using the Country attribute of the PUBLISHER table, the State and Country attributes of the CUSTOMER table, and the Quarter and Year attributes of the TIME PERIOD table, they could find the total number of books published in Brazil that were purchased by customers in California during the second quarter of 1999.

Lucky Rent-A-Car Data Warehouse

Like Good Reading Bookstores' transactional database, Lucky Rent-A-Car's transactional database, shown in Figure 5.18, already carries a Date attribute (two, in fact) in its RENTAL table. The reasoning for creating a data warehouse for Lucky is based on the same argument that we examined for Good Reading, that its transactional database would bog down under the weight of all of the data if we tried to store ten years or more rental history data in it. Interestingly, in the Lucky case, the data warehouse is still going to store the data down to the day level (resulting in a *huge* data warehouse). Why? In the rental car business, it is important to be able to check historically whether, for example, more cars were rented on Saturdays over a given time period than on Tuesdays. Assuming we consider Sunday to be day 1 of the week, Saturday is day 7 of the week and Tuesday is day 3.

Figure 14.9 shows the Lucky Rent-A-Car data warehouse star schema design. The fact table is RENTAL. In this case, as implied above, the fact table does *not* contain aggregated data. Every car rental transaction is recorded for posterity in the data warehouse. Notice that this data warehouse has a snowflake feature as the

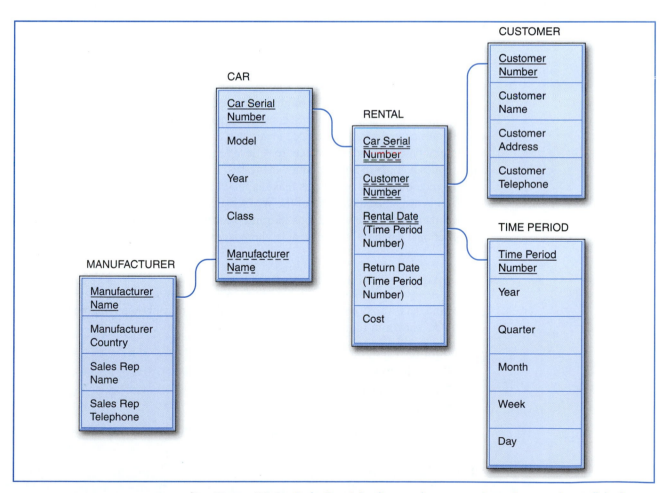

➤ **Figure 14.9**   Lucky Rent-A-Car data warehouse star schema design with snowflake feature

CAR dimension table is connected outwards to the MANUFACTURER table. The query possibilities are very rich in this data warehouse. Lucky could ask how many mid-size (the CAR table's Class attribute) General Motors cars were rented on the weekends in July of each of the last five years. To identify some of their most valuable customers for marketing purposes, Lucky could identify the customers (and create a name and address list for them) who rented full-size cars at least three times for at least a week each time, during the winter months of each of the last three years. Or using the Manufacturer Country attribute of the MANUFACTURER table in the snowflake, they could find the amount of revenue (based on the RENTAL table's Cost attribute) that they generated by renting Japanese cars during the summer vacation period in each of the last eight years.

What about a World Music Association Data Warehouse?

Did you notice that we didn't talk about a data warehouse for the World Music Association (WMA), whose transactional database is shown in Figure 5.17? If there were to be such a data warehouse, its most likely subject would be RECORDING, for the essence of their business is to keep track of different recordings made of different compositions by various orchestras. There is already a Year attribute in the RECORDING table of Figure 5.17. In this sense, the main data of the World Music Association's transactional database is already "timestamped," as was Good Reading Bookstores' and Lucky Rent-A-Car's data. We gave reasons for creating data warehouses for Good Reading and for Lucky, so what about WMA? First, the *essence* of the WMA data is **historic.** We might be just as interested in a recording made fifty years ago as one made last year. Second, by its nature, the amount of data in a WMA-type transactional database is much lower than the amount of data in a Good Reading or Lucky-type transactional database. The latter two transactional databases contain daily sales records in high-volume businesses. Even on a worldwide basis, the number of recordings that orchestras make is much smaller in comparison. So, the conclusion is that since the nature of the WMA transactional database blurs with what a WMA data warehouse would look like and the amount of (historic) data in the WMA transactional database is manageable, there is no need for a WMA data warehouse.

BUILDING A DATA WAREHOUSE

Once the data warehouse has been designed, there are four steps in actually building it. As shown in Figure 14.10, these are:

- **Data Extraction**
- **Data Cleaning**
- **Data Transformation**
- **Data Loading**

Let's take a look at each of these steps.

Data Extraction

Data extraction is the process of copying the data from the transactional databases in preparation for loading it into the data warehouse. There are several important

➤ **Figure 14.10**
The four steps in building a
data warehouse

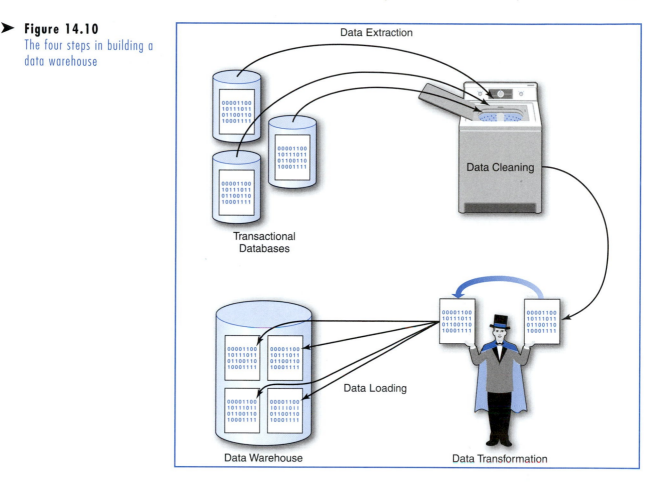

points to remember here. One is that this is not a one-time event. Obviously, there must be an initial extraction of data from the transactional databases when the data warehouse is first built, but after that it will be an ongoing process, performed at regular intervals, perhaps daily, weekly, or monthly, when the latest day's, week's, or month's transactional data is added to the data warehouse. Another point is that the data is likely to come from several transactional databases. Specific data (that means not necessarily all of the data) in each transactional database is copied and merged to form the data warehouse. There are pitfalls along the way that must be dealt with as, for example, the employee serial number attribute may be called "Employee Number" in one transactional database and "Serial Number" in another. Or, looking at it another way, the attribute name "Serial Number" may mean employee serial number in one database and finished goods serial number in another.

Some of the data entering into this process may come from outside of the company. For example, some companies are in the business of selling demographic data about people to companies that want to use it for marketing purposes. This process is known as **data enrichment.** Figure 14.11 shows enrichment data added to Lucky Rent-A-Car's data warehouse CUSTOMER dimension table from Figure 14.9. Notice that in the data enrichment process, age, income, and education data are added, presumably from some outside data source. Lucky might use

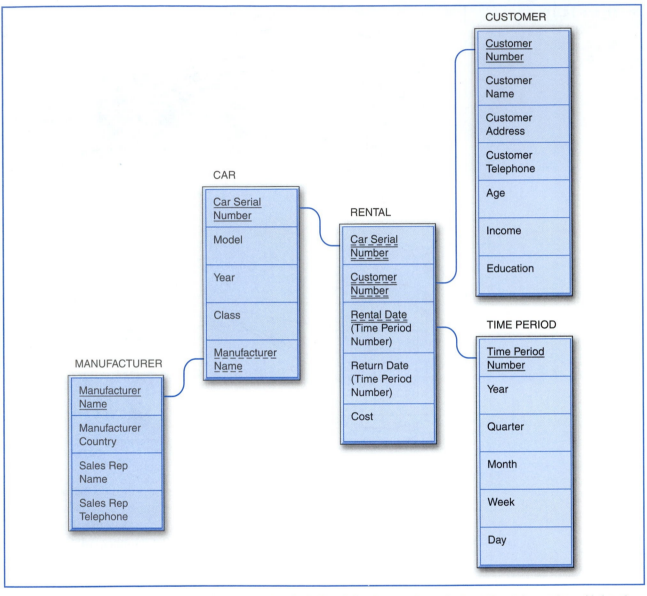

➤ **Figure 14.11**   Lucky Rent-A-Car data warehouse design with enrichment data added to the CUSTOMER table

this data to try to market the renting of particular kinds of cars to customers who fall into certain demographic categories. We will talk more about this later in the section on Data Mining.

Data Cleaning

Transactional data can have all kinds of errors in it, which may or may not affect the applications that use it. For example, if a customer's name is misspelled but the Post Office can correctly figure out to whom to deliver it, no one may ever bother to fix the error in the company's customer table. On the other hand, if a billing amount is much too high, the assumption is that the customer will notice it and demand that it be corrected. Data warehouses are very sensitive to data errors, and as many such errors as possible must be "cleaned" (the process is also referred to as "cleansed" or "scrubbed") as the data is loaded into the data warehouse. The point is that, depending on their nature, if data errors make it into the data warehouse, they can throw off the totals and statistics generated by the queries that are designed to support management decision making, compromising the value of the data warehouse.

There are two steps to cleaning transactional data in preparation for loading it into a data warehouse. The first step is to identify the problem data, and the second step is to fix it. Identifying the problem data is generally a job for a program since having people scrutinize the large volumes of data typically found today would simply take too long. Fixing the identified problems can be handled by using sophisticated artificial intelligence programs or by creating exception reports for employees to scrutinize. Figure 14.12 shows sample data from two of Good Reading Bookstores' transactional database tables (see Figure 5.16). The row numbers on the left are solely for reference purposes in this discussion. Each table has several errors that would have to be corrected as the data is copied, integrated, and aggregated into a data warehouse. Some of the errors shown may be less likely than others to actually turn up in today's more sophisticated application environment, but as a group they make the point that there are lots of potential data hazards out there.

Four errors or possible errors in the CUSTOMER table in Figure 14.12a are as follows:

- *Missing Data:* In row 1, the City attribute is blank. It's possible that a program could check an online "white pages" listing of Tennessee (State = "TN" in row 1), look for a Mervis at 123 Oak St. and in that way discover the city and automatically insert it as the City value in row 1. But it should also be clear that this type of error could occur in data for which there is no online source of data with which to cross check. In that case, the error may have to be printed in an error report for an employee to look at.

- *Questionable Data:* Rows 2 and 6, each of which has a different customer number, both involve customers named Gomez who live at 345 Main Ave., Columbus, USA. But one city is Columbus, Ohio ("OH") and the other is Columbus, Georgia ("GA"), each of which is a valid city/state combination. So, the question is whether these are really two different people who happen to have the same name and street address in two different cities named Columbus, or if they are the same person, one of the state designations is wrong, and there should only be one customer number.

- *Possible Misspelling:* Rows 3 and 8 have different customer numbers but are otherwise identical except for a one-letter difference in the customer name, "Taylor" versus "Tailor." Do both rows refer to the same person? For the sake of argument, say that an online white pages is not available but a real estate listing indicating which addresses are single-family houses and which are apartment buildings is. A program could be designed to assume that if the address is a single-family house, there is a misspelling and the two records do refer to the same person. On the other hand, if the address is an apartment building, they may, indeed, be two different people.

(a) CUSTOMER table

	Customer Number	Customer Name	Street	City	State	Country
1	02847	Mervis	123 Oak St.		TN	USA
2	03185	Gomez	345 Main Ave.	Columbus	OH	USA
3	03480	Taylor	50 Elm Rd.	San Diego	CA	USA
4	06837	Stevens	876 Leslie Ln.	Raleigh	NC	USA
5	08362	Adams	1200 Wallaby St.	Brisbane		Australia
6	12739	Gomez	345 Main Ave.	Columbus	GA	USA
7	13848	Lucas	742 Ave. Louise	Brussels		Belgium
8	15367	Tailor	50 Elm Rd.	San Diego	CA	USA
9	15933	Chang	48 Maple Ave.	Toronto	ON	Canada
10	18575	Smith	390 Martin Dr.	Columbus	RP	USA
11	21359	Sanchez	666 Ave. Bolivar	Santiago		Chile

(b) SALE table

	Book Number	Customer Number	Date	Price	Quantity
1	426478	03480	May 19, 2003	32.99	1
2	077656	18575	May 19, 2003	19.95	21
3	365905	06837	May 19, 2003	24.99	3
4	645688	21359	May 20, 2003	49.50	1
5	474640	15367	May 34, 2003	3200.99	1
6	426478	08362	June 03, 2003	32.99	2
7	276432	03480	June 04, 2003	30.00	1
8	365905	12738	June 04, 2003	24.99	1
9	276432	06837	June 05, 2003	30.00	5
10	327467	18575	June 12, 2003	-32.99	2
11	426478	06837	June 15, 2003	32.99	1

➤ **Figure 14.12**   Good Reading Bookstores sample data prior to data cleaning

- *Impossible Data:* Row 10 has a state value of "RP." There is no such state abbreviation in the United States. This must be flagged and corrected either automatically or manually.

There are also four errors or possible errors in the SALE table in Figure 14.12b. The data in this table is more numeric in nature than the CUSTOMER table data:

- *Questionable Data:* In row 2, the quantity of a particular book purchased in a single transaction is 21. This is possible but generally unlikely. A program may be designed to decide whether to leave it alone or to report it as an exception, depending on whether the type of book that it is makes it more or less likely that the quantity is legitimate.

- *Impossible/Out-of-Range Data:* Row 5 indicates that a single book cost $3,200.99. This is out of the possible range for book prices and must either be corrected based on the system knowing what the correct price is for that book (based on the book number) or reported as an exception.
- Apparently Incorrect Data: The Customer Number in row 8 is invalid. We don't have a customer with customer number 12738, but we do have a customer with customer number 12739 (see row 6 of the CUSTOMER table in part a of the figure). Someone would have to look into this one.
- *Impossible Data:* Row 10 shows a negative price for a book, which is impossible.

Data Transformation

As the data is extracted from the transactional databases, it must go through several kinds of **data transformations** on its way to the data warehouse:

- We have already talked about the concept of data from different transactional databases being merged to form the data warehouse tables. This is indeed one of the major data transformation steps.
- In many cases, the data will be aggregated as it is being extracted from the transactional databases and prepared for the data warehouse. Daily transactional data may be summed to form weekly or monthly data as the lowest level of data storage in the data warehouse, in terms of time period.
- Units of measure used for attributes in different transactional databases must be reconciled as they are being merged into common data warehouse tables. This is especially common if one transactional database uses the metric system and another uses the English system. Miles and kilometers, pounds and kilograms, gallons and liters, all have to go through a conversion process in order to wind up in a unified way in the data warehouse.
- Coding schemes used for attributes in different transactional databases must be reconciled as they are being merged into common data warehouse tables. For example, states of the United States could be represented in different databases by their full names, two-letter postal abbreviations, or with a numeric code from 1 to 50. Countries of the world could be represented by their full names, standard abbreviations used on vehicles, or with a numeric code. Another major issue along these lines is the different ways that dates can be stored.
- Sometimes values from different attributes in transactional databases are combined into a single attribute in the data warehouse, or the opposite occurs and a multi-part attribute is split apart. Consider the first name and last name of employees or customers as an example of this.

Data Loading

Finally, after all of the extracting, cleaning, and transforming, the data is ready to be loaded into the data warehouse. We would only repeat here that after the initial load, a schedule for regularly updating the data warehouse must be put in place, whether it is done on a daily, weekly, monthly, or some other designated time period basis. Remember, too, that data marts that use the data warehouse as their source of data must also be scheduled for regular updates.

USING A DATA WAREHOUSE

We have said that the purpose of a data warehouse is to support management decision making. Indeed, such decision support and the tools of its trade are major topics by themselves and not something that we want to go into in great detail here. Still, it would be unsatisfying to leave the topic of data warehouses without considering how they are used. We will briefly discuss two major data warehouse usage areas: **online analytic processing (OLAP)** and **data mining.**

Online Analytic Processing

Online Analytic Processing is a decision support methodology based on viewing data in multiple dimensions. Actually, we began approaching this topic earlier in the chapter when we described the two-, three-, and four-dimension scenarios for recording hospital patient tracking and billing data. There are many OLAP systems on the market today. As we said before, some employ special-purpose database structures designed specifically for multidimensional OLAP-type data. Others, known as relational OLAP or ROLAP systems store multidimensional data in relational databases using the star schema design that we have already covered.

How can OLAP data be used? The OLAP environment's multidimensional data is very well suited for querying and for multi-time period trend analyses, as we saw in the star schema discussion. In addition, several other data search concepts are commonly associated with OLAP:

- **Drill-Down:** This concept refers to going back to the database and retrieving finer levels of data detail than you have already retrieved. If you begin with monthly aggregated data, you may want to go back and look at the weekly or daily data, if the data warehouse supports it.

- **Slice:** A slice of multidimensional data is a subset of the data that focuses on a single value of one of the dimensions. Figure 14.13 is a slice of the patient data "cube" of Figure 14.4, in which a single value of the patient attribute, F. Jones, is nailed down and the data in the other dimensions is displayed.

- **Pivot or Rotation:** While helpful in terms of visualization, this is merely a matter of interchanging the data dimensions, for example, interchanging the data on the horizontal and vertical axes in a two-dimensional view, for visualization purposes.

Data Mining

As huge data warehouses are built and data is increasingly thought of as a true corporate resource, a natural movement toward squeezing more and more of a competitive advantage out of the company's data has taken place. This is especially true when it comes to the data warehouse which, after all, is not intended to support daily operations but is there to help management improve the company's competitive position in any way that it can. Certainly, one major kind of use of the data warehouse is the highly flexible data search and retrieval capability represented by OLAP-type tools and techniques. Another major kind of use falls under the heading of data mining.

➤ **Figure 14.13**
A 'slice' of the hospital
patient tracking and billing
system data

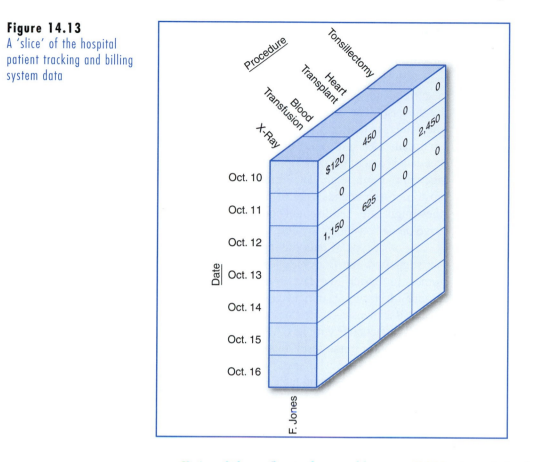

Data mining refers to the searching out of hidden knowledge in the company's data that can give the company a competitive advantage in its marketplace. This would be impossible for people to do by studying the data manually because they would immediately be overwhelmed by the sheer amount of data present in the company's data warehouse. It must be done by software. In fact, very sophisticated data mining software has been developed that uses several advanced statistical and artificial intelligence techniques that go by such names as:

- Case-based learning
- Decision trees
- Neural networks
- Genetic algorithms

Describing these techniques is beyond the scope of this book, which, after all, is about database management, not about decision support. But it's worth taking a quick look at a couple of the possibilities from an application or user's point of view.

One type of data mining application is known as **market basket analysis.** For example, consider the data collected by a supermarket as it checks out its customers by scanning the bar codes on the products they're purchasing. The company might have software study the collected market baskets, each of which is literally the goods that a particular customer bought in one trip to the store. The software might try to discover whether certain items "fall into" the same market basket more frequently than would otherwise be expected. That last phrase is important because some combinations of items in the same market basket are too obvious or common to be of any value. For example, finding eggs and milk being bought together frequently is not news. On the other hand, a piece of data mining folklore has it that one such study was done and discovered that people who bought disposable diapers also frequently bought beer (you can draw your own conclusion as to why this might be the case). The company could use this to advantage by stacking some beer near the diapers in its stores so that when people come in to buy diapers, they might make an impulse decision to buy the beer sitting next to it, too. Another use of market basket data is part of the developing marketing discipline of customer relationship management. If, through data mining, a supermarket determines that a particular customer who spends a lot of money in the store often buys a particular product, they might offer her discount coupons for that product as a way of rewarding her and developing "customer loyalty" so that she will keep on coming back to the store.

Another type of data mining application looks for patterns in the data. Earlier, we suggested that Lucky Rent-A-Car might buy demographic data about its customers to "enrich" the data about them in its data warehouse. Once again, consider Figure 14.11 with its enriched (Age, Income, and Education attributes added) CUSTOMER dimension table. Suppose, and this is quite realistic, that Lucky joined its RENTAL fact table with its CAR and CUSTOMER dimension tables, including only such attributes in the result that would help it identify its most valuable customers, for example, those who spend a lot of money renting "luxury" class cars. Figure 14.14 shows the resulting table, with the rows numbered on the left for convenience here. The Class and Manufacturer Name attributes came from the CAR table, the Cost attribute (the revenue for a particular rental transaction) came from the RENTAL table, and the Customer Number, Age, Income, and Education attributes came from the CUSTOMER table. Although it would take much more data than this to find statistically significant data patterns, the sample data in this figure gives you a rough idea of what a pattern might look like. Rows 2, 5, 8, and 11 all involve rentals of luxury class cars with high-cost (revenue to the company) figures. As you look across these rows to the customer demographics, you find "clusters" in age, income, and education. These expensive, luxury car rental transactions all involved people in their mid-40s in age, with high income and education levels. On the other hand, rows 10 and 14 involved people who also had high income and education levels. But these people were not in their mid-40s in age and they did not rent luxury cars and run up as big of a bill. With enough such data, Lucky might conclude that it could make more money by heavily promoting its luxury cars to customers in their mid-40s with high income and education levels. If its competitors have not realized this, then Lucky has gained a competitive advantage by "mining" its data warehouse.

ADMINISTERING A DATA WAREHOUSE

Earlier in this book we discussed the issues of managing corporate data and databases with people called data administrators and database administrators. As a huge database, the data warehouse requires a serious level of management. Further, with its unique character, it requires a strong degree of personnel specialization in its management (some have even given the role its own name of **data warehouse administrator**). Managing the data warehouse requires three kinds of heavily overlapping employee expertise:

	Class	Manufacturer Name	Cost	Customer Number	Age	Income	Education
			CAR/RENTAL/CUSTOMER				
1	Compact	Ford	320	884730	54	58,000	B.A.
2	Luxury	Lincoln	850	528262	45	158,000	M.B.A.
3	Full-Size	General Motors	489	109565	48	62,000	B.S.
4	Sub-Compact	Toyota	159	532277	25	34,000	High School
5	Luxury	Lincoln	675	155434	42	125,000	Ph.D.
6	Compact	Chrysler	360	965578	64	47,500	High School
7	Mid-Size	Nissan	429	688632	31	43,000	M.B.A.
8	Luxury	Lincoln	925	342786	47	95,000	M.A.
9	Full-Size	General Motors	480	385633	51	72,000	B.S.
10	Compact	Toyota	230	464367	64	200,000	M.A.
11	Luxury	Jaguar	1170	528262	45	158,000	M.B.A.
12	Sub-Compact	Nissan	89	759930	29	28,000	B.A.
13	Full-Size	Ford	335	478432	57	53,500	B.S.
14	Full-Size	Chrysler	328	207867	29	162,000	Ph.D.

➤ **Figure 14.14** Lucky Rent-A-Car enriched data, integrated for data mining

- Business Expertise
  - An understanding of the company's business processes that underlies an understanding of the company's transactional data and databases.
  - An understanding of the company's business goals to help in determining what data should be stored in the data warehouse for eventual OLAP and data mining purposes.
- Data Expertise
  - An understanding of the company's transactional data and databases for selection and integration into the data warehouse.
  - An understanding of the company's transactional data and databases to design and manage data cleaning and data transformation, as necessary.
  - Familiarity with outside data sources for the acquisition of enrichment data.
- Technical Expertise
  - An understanding of data warehouse design principles for the initial design.
  - An understanding of OLAP and data mining techniques so that the data warehouse design will properly support these processes.
  - An understanding of the company's transactional databases in order to manage or coordinate the regularly scheduled appending of new data to the data warehouse.
  - An understanding of how to handle very large databases in general (as the data warehouse will inevitably be) with their unique requirements for security, backup and recovery, being split across multiple disk devices, and so forth.

The other issue in administering a data warehouse is metadata, that is, the data warehouse must have a data dictionary to go along with it. The data warehouse is a huge data resource for the company and has great potential for giving the company a competitive advantage. But for this to happen, the company's employees have to understand what data is in it! And for two reasons. (1) to think about how to use the data to the company's advantage, through OLAP and data mining, and (2) to actually access the data for processing with those techniques.

CHALLENGES IN DATA WAREHOUSING

Data warehousing presents a distinct set of challenges. Many companies have jumped into data warehousing with both feet, only to find that they bit off more than they could chew and had to back off. Often, they try again with a more gradual approach and eventually succeed. Many of the pitfalls of data warehousing have already been mentioned at one point or another in this chapter. These include the technical challenges of data cleaning and finding more "dirty" data than expected, problems associated with coordinating the regular appending of new data from the transactional databases to the data warehouse, and difficulties in managing very large databases, which, as we have said, the data warehouse will inevitably be. There is also the separate challenge of building and maintaining the data dictionary and making sure that everyone who needs it understands what's in it and has access to it.

Another major challenge of a different kind is trying to satisfy the user community. In concept, the idea is to build such a broad, general data warehouse that it will satisfy all user demands. In practice, decisions have to be made about what and how much data it is practical to incorporate in the data warehouse at a given point in time and at a given point in the development of the data warehouse. Unfortunately, it is almost inevitable that some users will not be satisfied in general with the data at their disposal and others will want the data warehouse data to be modified in some way to produce better or different results. And that's not a bad thing! It means that people in the company understand or are gaining an appreciation for the great potential value of the data warehouse and they are impatient to have it set up the way that will help them help the company the most— Even if that means that the data included in the data warehouse and its design are a perpetually moving target.

KEY TERMS

Aggregated data	Decision support system (DSS)	Online analytic processing (OLAP)
Data cleaning	Dimension	Pivot or rotation
Data enrichment	Drill-down	Slice
Data extraction	Enterprise data warehouse (EDW)	Snowflake design
Data loading		Star schema
Data mart (DM)	Historic data	Subject oriented
Data mining	Integrated	Time variant
Data transformation	Market basket analysis	Transaction processing system (TPS)
Data warehouse	Multidimensional database	
Data warehouse administrator	Non-volatile	

QUESTIONS

1. What is the difference between transactional processing systems and decision support systems?

2. Decision support applications have been around for many years, typically using captive files that belong to each individual application. What factors led to the movement from this environment toward the data warehouse?

3. What is a data warehouse? What is a data warehouse used for?

4. Explain each of the following concepts. The data in a data warehouse:

   a. Is subject oriented.

   b. Is integrated.

   c. Is non-volatile.

   d. Is time variant.

   e. Must be high quality.

   f. May be aggregated.

   g. Is often denormalized.

   h. Is not necessarily absolutely current.

5. What is the difference between an enterprise data warehouse and a data mart?

6. Under what circumstances would a company build data marts from an enterprise data warehouse? build an enterprise data warehouse from data marts?

7. What is a multidimensional database?

8. What is a star schema? What are fact tables? What are dimension tables?

9. What is a snowflake feature in a star schema?

10. After a data warehouse is designed, what are the four steps in building it?

11. Name and describe three possible problems in transactional data that would require data cleaning before the data can be used in a data warehouse.

12. Name and describe three kinds of data transformations that might be necessary as transactional data is integrated and copied into a data warehouse.

13. What is online analytic processing (OLAP)? What does OLAP have to do with data warehouses?

14. What do the following OLAP terms mean?

    a. Drill-down

    b. Slice

    c. Pivot or rotation

15. What is data mining? What does data mining have to do with data warehouses?

16. Describe the ideal background for an employee who is going to manage the data warehouse.

17. Describe the challenges involved in having the data warehouse satisfy the user community.

EXERCISES

1. Video Centers of Europe, Ltd., data warehouse:

   a. Design a multidimensional database using a star schema for a data warehouse for the Video Centers of Europe, Ltd., business environment described in the diagram associated with Exercise 2 in Chapter 3. The subject will be "rental" which represents a particular tape or DVD having been rented by a particular customer. As stated in Exercise 2 in Chapter 3, be sure to keep track of the rental date and the price paid. Include a snowflake feature based on the actor, movie, and tape/DVD entities.

   b. Describe three OLAP uses of this data warehouse.

   c. Describe one data mining use of this data warehouse.

2. Best Airlines, Inc., data warehouse: In exercises earlier in the book, we saw the following relational database, which Best Airlines uses to keep track of its mechanics, their skills, and their airport locations. Mechanic number, airport name, and skill number are all unique fields. Size is an airport's size in acres. Skill Category

is a skill's category, such as an engine skill, wing skill, or tire skill. Year Qualified is the year that a mechanic first qualified in a particular skill; Proficiency Rating is the mechanic's proficiency rating in a particular skill.

MECHANIC table				
Mechanic Number	Mechanic Name	Telephone	Salary	Airport Name

AIRPORT table				
Airport Name	City	State	Size	Year Opened

SKILL table		
Skill Number	Skill Name	Skill Category

QUALIFICATION table			
Mechanic Number	Skill Number	Year Qualified	Proficiency Rating

MAINTENANCE EVENT table			
Airplane Number	Activity Number	Date	Mechanic Number

We now add the following tables to the database that record data about airplanes and maintenance performed on them. A maintenance event is a specific maintenance activity performed on an airplane.

AIRPLANE table			
Airplane Number	Airplane Model	Year Manufactured	Passenger Capacity

MAINTENANCE ACTIVITY table			
Activity Number	Activity Name	Expected Duration	Required Frequency

a. Design a multidimensional database using a star schema for a data warehouse for the Best Airlines, Inc., airplane maintenance environment described by the complete seven-table relational database shown above. The subject will be maintenance event. Include snowflake features as appropriate.

b. Describe three OLAP uses of this data warehouse.

c. Describe one data mining use of this data warehouse.

MINICASES

1. Happy Cruise Lines data warehouse:

a. Design a multidimensional database using a star schema for a data warehouse for the Happy Cruise Lines business environment described in Minicase 1 in Chapter 3. The subject will be "passage," which represents a particular passenger booking on a particular cruise. As stated in Exercise 1 in Chapter 3, be sure to keep track of the fare that the passenger paid for the cruise and the passenger's satisfaction rating of the cruise.

b. Describe three OLAP uses of this data warehouse.

c. Describe one data mining use of this data warehouse.

2. Super Baseball League data warehouse:

a. Design a multidimensional database using a star schema for a data warehouse for the Super Baseball League business environment described in Minicase 2 in Chapter 3. The subject will be "affiliation," which represents a particular player having played on a particular team. As stated in Exercise 2 in Chapter 3, be sure to keep track of the number of years that the player played on the team and the batting average he compiled on it.

b. Describe three OLAP uses of this data warehouse.

c. Describe one data mining use of this data warehouse.

CHAPTER 15

DATABASE AND THE INTERNET

CHAPTER OBJECTIVES

After learning the material in this chapter, you will be able to:

✔ List the four differences between the Internet database environment and the standard database environment.
✔ Describe the database connectivity issues in the Internet environment.
✔ Describe the expanded set of data types found in the Internet environment.
✔ Describe such database control issues as performance, availability, scalability, and security and privacy in the Internet environment.
✔ Describe the significance of data extraction into XML in the Internet environment.

Photo Courtesy of Amazon.com

AMAZON.COM

When one thinks of online shopping, one of the first companies that comes to mind is certainly Amazon.com. This highly innovative company, based in Seattle, Washington, was one of the first online stores and has consistently been one of the most successful. Amazon.com seeks to be the world's most customer-centric company, where customers can find and discover anything they might want to buy online. Amazon.com and sellers list millions of unique new and used items in categories such as electronics, computers, kitchen products and housewares, books, music, DVDs, videos, camera and photo items, toys, baby and baby registry, software, computer and video games, cell phones and service, tools and hardware, travel services, magazine subscriptions and outdoor living products. Through Amazon Marketplace, zShops and Auctions, any business or individual can sell virtually anything to Amazon.com's millions of customers. Demonstrating the reach of the Internet, Amazon.com has sold to people in over 220 countries.

Initially implemented in 1995 and continually improved ever since, Amazon.com's "order pipeline" is a very sophisticated, information-intensive system that accepts, processes, and fulfills customer orders. When someone visits Amazon.com's Web site, its system tries to enhance the shopping experience by offering the customer products on a personalized basis, based on past buying patterns. Once an order is placed, the system validates the customer's credit card information and sends the customer an email order confirmation. It then goes through a process of determining how best to fulfill the order, including deciding which of several fulfillment sites from which to ship the goods. When the order is shipped, the system sends the customer an email shipping confirmation. Throughout the entire process, the system keeps track of the current status of each order at any point in time.

Amazon.com's order pipeline system is totally built on relational database technology. Most of it uses Oracle running on Hewlett Packard Unix systems. In order to achieve high degrees of scalability and availability, the system is organized around the concept of distributed database including replicated data that is updated simultaneously at several domestic and international locations. The system is integrated with the Oracle Financials enterprise resource planning (ERP) system and the transactional data is shared with the company's accounting and finance functions. In addition, Amazon.com has built a multi-terabyte data warehouse that imports its transactional data and creates a decision support system with a menu-based facility system of its own design. Programs utilizing the data warehouse send personally targeted promotional mailers to the company's customers.

Amazon.com's database includes hundreds of individual tables. Among these are catalog tables listing its millions of individual books and other products, a customer table with millions of records, personalization tables, promotional tables, shopping cart tables that handle the actual purchase transactions, and order history tables. An order processing sub-system that determines which fulfillment center to ship goods from uses tables that keep track of product inventory levels in these centers.

Printed by permission of Amazon.com

One of the fascinating things about successful, new technologies is that after they've been around for awhile it's hard to imagine how we ever did without them. Automobiles and airplanes have always been a part of the lives of anyone reading this book. Computers are almost too obvious in this regard. What about photocopiers, as an example? How did we ever get along without photocopiers, what we used to routinely call "Xerox machines?" But even they have been in substantial use for well over forty years at this point. Then, there is the **Internet.** How did we ever get along without the Internet? The Internet has become such a huge part of our lives so quickly that it's easy to forget that widespread commercial use of the

Internet began only in the mid-1990s. Do you remember when there was no Amazon.com? It seems like it was always there!

Aside from e-mail and file transfers, we associate the Internet with that most exciting of applications, **electronic commerce.** It's amazing how we as individuals can shop online, bank online, get our news online, get all sorts of entertainment online, and search for every kind of information imaginable, all within the broad scope of e-commerce. Companies have found new ways of selling to each other, forming alliances with each other, disposing of excess inventory, and, generally speaking, turning the world into a global marketplace. And the essence of all of this e-commerce activity is data stored in databases. When you look through a company's product selections, the data comes from a database. When you place an order with a company, the order goes into a database. When you check your bank account balance, you're querying a database. Even reading newspapers online involves retrieving data from specialized text databases.

The question for us in this chapter is, what is *different* about the Internet database environment from a database environment that does not specifically involve the Internet? Well, first of all, what's *not* different? The fact is that most (but not all) e-commerce databases are relational databases and many are transactional in nature. The concepts of relational database and the rules for designing relational databases are the same for transactional e-commerce applications as they are for any other transactional applications. SQL and other standard query tools can be and are used in the e-commerce environment, too. Yet, there are some differences between the Internet database environment and the non-Internet environment. So, what's different? We will organize the answer to this question into four categories

- Database Connectivity Issues
- Expanded Set of Data Types
- Database Control Issues
- Data Extraction into XML

DATABASE CONNECTIVITY ISSUES

In a simple database environment, the application program, the database management system, and even the data (during execution), are all contained within and run within the hardware of a single computer. Figure 15.1 illustrates this arrangement when the computer is a stand-alone PC, but a similar situation could be described for a much larger computer with multiple simultaneous users as well.

Earlier in this book we talked about client/server systems. In the simplest client/server systems, there are two classes of computers, as shown in Figure 15.2. The client computers are end-user PCs that are all connected to a server computer on a local area network. The server contains the application programs, the database management system, and the database, which all of the clients share. When an end-user wants to run an application or retrieve data from the shared database, the client computers handle the initial processing of the request. This is the presentation or graphical user interface aspect. Then the data is sent on to the server for processing by the application code, including data retrieval from the shared database, as necessary. The server then returns the results to the client PC where the client is again responsible for formatting the screen display.

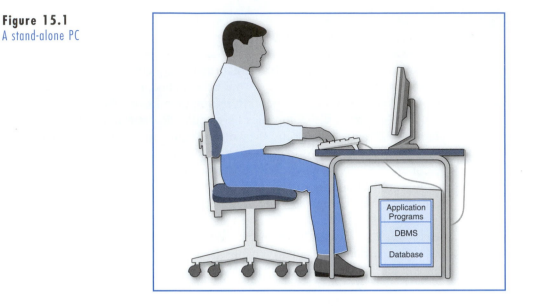

Although we usually associate the term **client/server system** with a system built on a local area network, in a broad sense the **World Wide Web (WWW)** can be considered to be a massive client/server system built on the Internet (Figure 15.3). The clients are the PCs that individuals and companies use to connect to the Internet. The **browsers** in the PCs, such as Netscape Navigator and Microsoft's Internet Explorer, constitute the software that handle the **client side** screen presentation duties. The servers are the company Web servers with which people at their

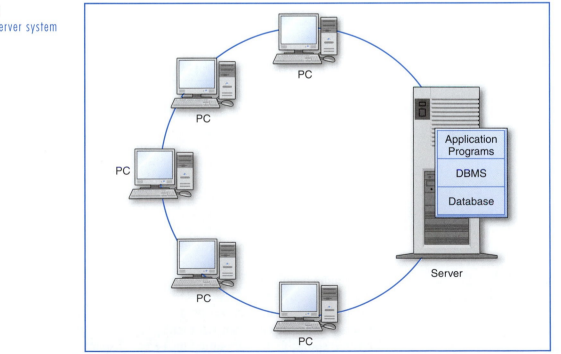

➤ **Figure 15.3**
The World Wide Web as a
client/server system

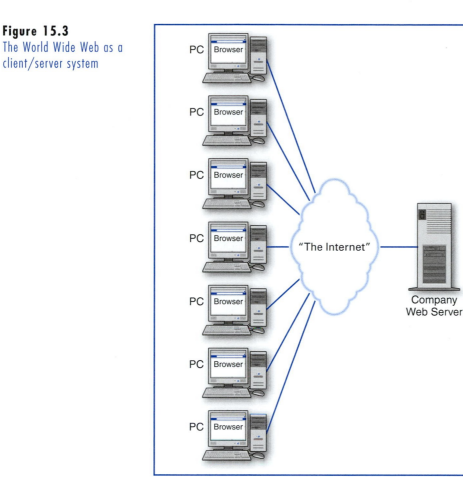

PCs communicate as they participate in the world of e-commerce. With this expansion of the idea of a client/server system, the World Wide Web, built on the Internet, qualifies as the world's largest client/server system!

But there is more to it than that, which shouldn't be surprising considering the much larger scale of a company's Web site and Web server compared with the server on a typical LAN. Let's talk about the hardware first, then the software. In the discussion earlier in the book on client/server database systems, we suggested the possibility of having a database server as a separate computer from the application server (Figure 13.4). This is a common arrangement in larger Web sites. Figure 15.4 shows the hardware components of the Web, including the disks containing the databases. There are three levels of computers in this arrangement: the client PCs, the Web server, and the database server. How does this **database connectivity** take place? Using an example, let's talk about this at two levels of detail—first, at a high level and then at a somewhat more detailed level that will introduce some of the specialized software that has been developed for the Web environment. Remember, this book is about database management systems, and so our goal in this discussion is to connect the ultimate user into the database.

Suppose that Good Reading Bookstores has developed a Web site to sell books to consumers online and that you are about to become one of its customers. Follow along in Figure 15.4. You sit down at your PC, establish contact

➤ **Figure 15.4**
Basic hardware components
of the Web to database
connection

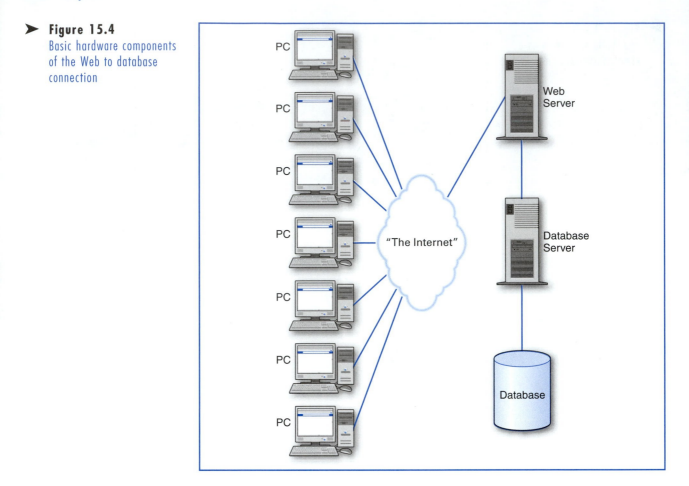

with your Internet Service Provider (ISP) (such as America Online or Microsoft's MSN), and enter the URL or Web address, www.GoodReadingBookstores.com. The browser software in your PC sends a message to Good Reading's Web server and establishes a "session" or connection with it. The Web server sends your browser Good Reading's **home page** which your browser displays on your monitor. Suppose that you are shopping for a particular book. On the home page is a space for you to fill-in the book's name. So, from the information systems point of view, what you are really trying to do, at this point, is to search the BOOK table in Good Reading's database, repeated here as Figure 15.5, to see if Good Reading carries this particular book. You type the book's name in the space on the home page display and press the Enter key. The book name is transmitted on the Internet to the application running in Good Reading's Web server. This application sends a command to the relational DBMS in Good Reading's database server, ordering it to perform the look-up operation in the database. This could very well be done with an SQL command embedded in the application running in the Web server. Then, everything flows in reverse. The relational DBMS retrieves the data from the database, sends it to the application in the Web server, which then sends it back over the Internet to the browser in your PC. The browser displays it for you, either showing information about the book or stating that Good Reading doesn't carry it. If the book is in stock and you

➤ **Figure 15.5**
The Good Reading
Bookstores relational
database

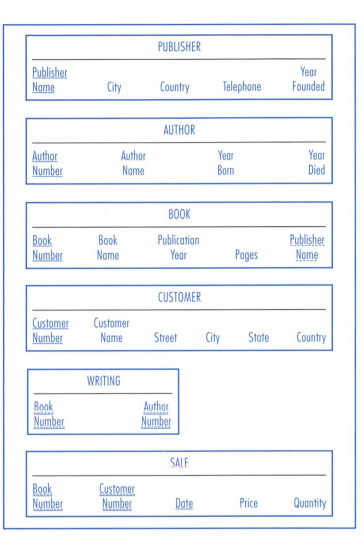

want to buy it, the transaction continues with message traffic passing back and forth between you and your browser on the **client side** and the Web server on the **server side.** Every time that the database must be accessed, the application in the Web server passes a command to the database server, which queries the database and returns the result.

Now, using Figure 15.6, let's take a bit more of a detailed look at the same Good Reading Bookstores scenario, introducing some of the specialized Web software that has been introduced. When your browser sends a message to the Web server (and vice versa), the message follows the rules of the Transmission Control Protocol/Internet Protocol (TCP/IP), which all Internet traffic (including, e.g., e-mail) must follow, and the Hypertext Transfer Protocol (HTTP), which is an additional protocol layer for World Wide Web traffic on the Internet. TCP specifies how the message is broken up into smaller "packets" for transmission. IP deals with the address of the computer to which the message is being sent. At the Web level, HTTP indicates the type of browser in the client and other information needed to format Web pages. But what happens once the message reaches the Web server, and, in particular, how is access to the database accomplished?

➤ **Figure 15.6**
Basic software components
of the Web to database
connection

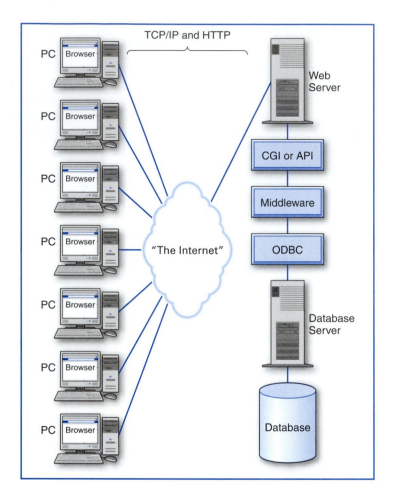

With the kind of self-contained computer and database environment that was illustrated in Figure 15.1, all of the hardware and software are designed to work together from beginning to end. The problem that must be addressed in the Web database environment is that there can be different kinds of hardware even just between the Web server and the database server, different kinds of application software languages, different browsers on the client side, and a variety of different kinds of data, not just data in relational databases. In order to tie all of these variable and assorted pieces together and make them work together, there have to be specialized interfaces and specialized software known as **middleware.**

Again, consider the application program that manages Good Reading's online sales process running in the Web server and follow the diagram in Figure 15.6. First, in order for the application software running in the Web server to connect with software outside of the Web server, there must be agreed upon interfaces and, indeed, there are. The original such interface is called the Common Gateway Interface (CGI). Later, another such interface with certain performance advantages was developed, and it is known as the Application Program Interface (API). These interfaces have software "scripts" associated with them that allow them to exchange data between the application in the server and the databases controlled by the database server. The connection to the databases could be made directly at this point, but again, with the prospect of different database management systems and different kinds of data involved, it made sense for another level of standards to be created to smooth out the differences and have one standard way of accessing the data. The most common set of such standards is called **Open Database Connectivity (ODBC),** which is designed as an interface to relational databases. Another, with its own set of features, is called **Java Database Connectivity (JDBC).** Other standards exist for various kinds of nonrelational data.

Because of the importance of connecting the applications in the Web server with the databases in the database server, various companies have developed specialized middleware with a variety of broad features, capabilities, and connectivity options. Among the products of this type on the market are Cold Fusion, Oracle Application Server, Microsoft Active Server Pages (ASP), and others.

EXPANDED SET OF DATA TYPES

Most of the data in traditional transactional databases are of two basic "types": numeric and character. These **data types** are all we generally need for accounting data, inventory data, marketing data, production data, and so forth. Indeed, all of the database examples in this book have used only numeric and character data. But there are other kinds of data, and this subject came up once before in this book in the discussion of object-oriented database (see Figure 10.10). There can be large text blocks (e.g., newspaper stories or descriptions of entities of any kind), **graphic images** (e.g., industrial design images or maps), photographs, **video clips** (or entire movies), and **audio clips** (or recordings). Specialized applications have focused on these special data types. For example, newspaper composition deals with large text blocks and photos; geographic information systems (GIS) are based on maps as graphic images.

But the Internet and its World Wide Web has created a new emphasis on this assortment of data types in a way that no previous information systems environment ever did. Think of the Web sites that you have visited. The displays coming to you in the form of Web pages don't exactly look like reams of accounting data! Certainly, they contain numbers and short character strings, but they also contain photographs, graphic images, animated graphic images, large text blocks (in online newspapers, magazines, etc.), video clips, and audio clips. The point for us is that databases that support Web sites must be capable of storing, searching, and retrieving this wide variety of data.

Relational DBMS vendors have added features to their products that support these various text and multimedia data types. Oracle has a category of data types known as the large object (LOB) category that includes data types:

- **Binary LOB (BLOB)**—Up to four gigabytes of unstructured binary data, suitable for graphic images, photographs, video clips, and audio clips.
- **Binary File (BFILE)**—A pointer to up to four gigabytes of "read-only" unstructured binary data stored in a file external to the database.
- **Character LOB (CLOB)**—Up to four gigabytes of character data suitable for large text files or documents.
- **National Character LOB (NCLOB)**—Up to four gigabytes of data suitable for large text files or documents in languages based on pictographs or non-Latin characters.

An older category of data types used for multimedia data known as RAW, including the data types RAW and LONG RAW, is no longer recommended.

The object/relational DBMS Informix Universal Server provides another style of handling multimedia and large text data using "Data Blades." Among these are:

- The data type IMAGE, which can be used as a general-purpose image data type. Or a data type may be defined for each of the common image formats, including JPEG, GIF, TIFF, and others.
- The data type DOC, which is used for storing large text blocks.
- A set of data types, including point, line, polygon, path, and circle, which can be used for storing a variety of graphic images.

DATABASE CONTROL ISSUES

Managing an Internet database environment presents several unique challenges in comparison to managing a database environment in a system that is specifically not connected to the Internet. Having said that, we must recognize that today, most systems are either directly connected to the Internet or are connected to other systems that are. Thus, in the Internet database environment, the general public potentially has access (planned or unplanned access as with hackers) to the company's databases. Furthermore, the public response to the applications that involve the Internet are often unpredictable, meaning that the load on the system and on access to the databases can change rapidly. These and other challenges require a special emphasis on:

- Performance
- **Availability**
- **Scalability**
- Security and Privacy

Performance

We have all experienced widely different performance levels when interacting with Web sites on the Internet. Response time, the elapsed time from pressing the Enter key or clicking on a "Go" icon, to having the Web server's response as a new Web page fully displayed on your monitor, can vary greatly. In business-to-consumer electronic commerce, for example, a consumer's lack of tolerance for poor performance at one Web site can easily cause him to click over to a competitor's site. The complexity of the Internet and Web environment provides many potential reasons for poor performance, including whether your connection to the Internet is through a 56K modem or a broadband connection, the level of hardware at your Internet service provider, the speed of the Web server you are interacting with and associated facilities at the Web site, and so forth. From the point of view of the company and its Web site, another major factor is the amount of traffic coming in from the Internet.

Internet traffic to a Web site, the number of people or companies trying to access it simultaneously, can vary greatly and because of a variety of factors such as:

- The time of day (which must be considered on a worldwide basis)
- The season of the year (e.g., the Christmas shopping season)

- The rapidly growing popularity of a Web site
- A major new product introduction
- A major event (e.g., the Victoria's Secret annual fashion show which has overwhelmed its Web site)

These spikes, some of them huge, in Internet traffic require serious predictive capacity planning. The trick is that the companies want to be able to maintain reasonable response time during the spikes without spending large amounts of money to buy a lot of extra computer equipment that will sit idle much or most of the time. Accomplishing this takes some serious planning and significant expertise.

Of course, system performance is also affected by software design and, in particular for our interest here by database design. Thus the chapter earlier in the book on physical database design is of particular interest in the Internet database environment. The various performance-boosting physical design techniques that we discussed are applicable, including denormalization, at least for relatively static database tables such as product lists in some industries.

In addition, we will mention two performance-boosting techniques that are of particular interest in the Web database environment. For the first one, take another look at Figure 15.4. When a query comes in from a PC and is passed from the Web server to the database server to the database, often the same or a different end-user is going to use the retrieved data again fairly soon. If a copy of that data can be held somewhere outside of the database on a temporary basis for the next time it is requested, then two benefits can be gained. Not only can the response time for future retrievals of that data be improved, but the amount of traffic between the Web server and the database server can be decreased, which helps to improve the performance of other accesses to the database. This concept of **database persistence** can be accomplished with a **query cache,** a special dedicated memory associated with the Web server or with a proxy server attached to it, to hold a copy of the retrieved data on a temporary basis. A second performance-boosting technique is used in situations where company employees can write SQL queries to access data over the Internet (or over an internal Intranet). Those queries that are run on a repetitive basis can be stored or "canned" and then called when needed. In this way, the system can avoid having to spend time going through query optimization and coming up with an efficient access path every time the query is run, a concept that was discussed in general earlier in the book.

Availability

A company's Web site and the databases that it accesses should be available to the public at all times. This is especially true if the company is expecting to receive traffic to the site on a worldwide basis, which, after all, is one of the hallmarks of e-commerce. Three o'clock in the morning in one part of the world is the middle of the day in another, and so the system really has to be up all of the time. An information system may be unavailable for several reasons:

- Because of a system or telecommunications failure
- Because of the failure of a support system, such as an electrical outage
- Because of a planned down period for system maintenance.
- Because of excessive traffic that clogs the system

Here again, the challenge is to make the information systems and their databases available "24/7" without going overboard in terms of cost. Regarding system failure, electrical outages, and planned maintenance time, redundant computer hardware and such accessories as electrical generators and batteries will do the job. The trick is to accomplish this at a reasonable cost. Excessive traffic is another story. Legitimate traffic spikes, as discussed above, can certainly reduce availability. But computer viruses that reproduce many copies of themselves and automated "robots" searching Web sites for information can clog systems, too. These must be prevented or the system must be constantly monitored by software that watches for such conditions.

One technique used to improve availability is known as **clustering.** A cluster of several servers is built, each with its own replicated copy of the database. As queries come in over the Web, sophisticated software checks the activity on each of the servers and their databases and performs **load balancing,** sending each particular query to a server that is relatively idle at that moment.

Scalability

Some electronic commerce efforts, in both "pure" e-commerce start-up companies and established companies, have experienced rapid growth. In one case, the growth rate of traffic to the Web site was estimated at 1,000 to 4,000 percent per year in the early years. This is certainly good news for any company that experiences it! But the information system that supports this Web site and its traffic growth must be scalable; that is, it must be capable of growing in size without adversely affecting the operations of the site. It is thus imperative that hardware and software be chosen that is capable of rapid and major expansion.

Security and Privacy

Earlier in the book we discussed data security at some length. Now, think of the Internet database environment in which all of the traditional data security concerns are still present but in addition, the information system is exposed to the whole world through its Web site! And that is not an exaggeration. In the business-to-consumer e-commerce environment the company *wants* as many people as possible to "visit" its Web site and buy its products. That also means that hackers, data thieves, virus writers, and anyone else with mischief on their minds has an openly published entry point into the company's information system. Obviously, this requires heavy-duty security, such as:

- Separating the different parts of the information system so that they run on different computers. Thus the Web server and the database server should be different computers, as shown in Figure 15.4. Furthermore, these should be separated from the rest of the company's information system by being on a separate LAN.
- Making major use of firewalls. As we discussed earlier, firewalls can be separate "proxy" computers that extract data from incoming messages and pass the data on in a different format to the Web server. Figure 15.7 is a re-drawing of the hardware arrangement in Figure 15.4 with the inclusion of a firewall computer. Firewalls can also be software-based, checking incoming messages for viruses and other suspicious code. And additional firewalls, including additional middleware (see Figure 15.6), can be placed between the Web server and the database server to catch any malicious code that gets through the initial firewall. Firewalls can also be placed between the Web server and the rest of the company's information systems.

> **Figure 15.7**
> A firewall between the
> Internet and the Web server

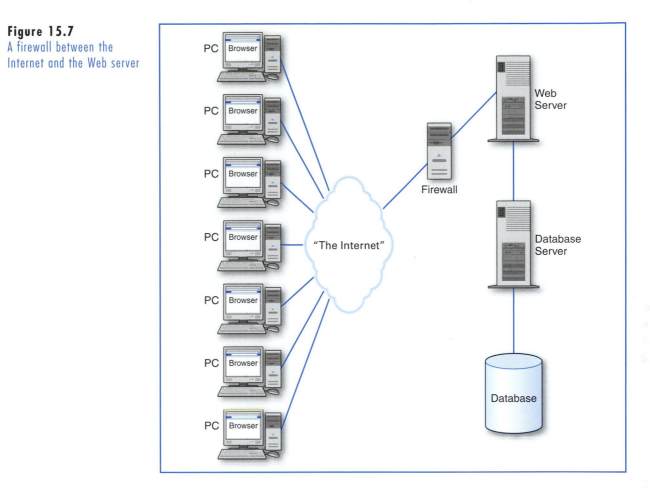

Closely related to the issue of security is the issue of privacy. Companies have long held personal data about their customers in their databases. What is different in the Internet database environment is, first, that the companies are communicating digitally with their customers through their Web sites, including passing their personal data, over the Internet. This requires the use of encryption so that the data cannot be intercepted and read while in transit over the Internet. Second, the collected personal data in the company's database makes a tempting target for someone out to steal such data. And, again, the database is potentially accessible through the company's public Web site, which brings us back to the discussion about firewalls and such, above.

BAPTIST MEMORIAL HEALTH CARE

Baptist Memorial Health Care Corp., headquartered in Memphis, Tennessee, operates a total of seventeen hospitals in Arkansas, Mississippi, and Tennessee. Its flagship hospital, Baptist Memorial Hospita—Memphis, is a 706-bed tertiary care teaching hospital, closely affiliated with University of Tennessee Medical School. Baptist Memphis annually has more than 28,000 admissions, 53,000 emergency department visits, 25,000 surgeries, and 125,000 outpatient visits. Located on the same campus are the Baptist Heart Institute and the Baptist Memorial Hospital for Women.

Photo Courtesy of Baptist Memorial Health Care

Baptist Memphis has a state-of-the-art relational database application called "Baptist MD," which was implemented in 2000. Supporting approximately 1,400 physicians and physician staff employees, the central feature of Baptist MD is a Web site on which a wide variety of patient data can be stored. This includes patient history, pathology reports, blood tests, and radiology results. The site can also store and display X-ray and MRI images. A special feature of the site is real-time fetal monitoring with which a physician can remotely check on the changing condition of the fetus via the Web site while the mother is in labor. The system provides each physician with a "My Patient" list, from which the physician can select one of their current patients to check their condition. The physician's office staff also has access to the Web site for record keeping purposes. Being Web based, physicians can check on their patients from anywhere that they can log onto the Internet. In one critical case, a physician was contacted by the hospital and was able to access the Web site and make a decision about a patient while out of the state on vacation.

Baptist MD is based on the Microsoft SQL Server DBMS, running on a Compaq server. It relies on the use of XML to deal with all of the different kinds of data in its Web site presentations. The system by its very nature is oriented around queries. These are menu driven, with menu selections triggering SQL queries. The relational database's main tables are a physician table with physician qualifications and patient admitting authority, a patient table that contains about 45,000 records (including a 90-day history), a results table which typically has ten to twenty test results and so forth per patient, and a users table with additional information about the physicians and the physician office staff employees who have access to the database.

Printed by permission of Baptist Memorial Health Care Corporation

DATA EXTRACTION INTO XML

As the final topic on Internet database, we will briefly touch on the subject of the Extensible Markup Language, **XML**, and how it relates to database management. First, some background. You are probably aware that when a Web server sends a Web page to your PC, the text and data in the page comes formatted in **HyperText Markup Language (HTML).** Embedded HTML "tags" literally mark up the text and data, instructing your PC's browser on how to display the page on your monitor. In the Good Reading Bookstores example, if the place on the Web page at which you are to enter the title of the book that you're searching for is labeled, "Book Title" and this label is to appear in boldface type on your monitor, it will come from the server looking like:

<h1><b>Book Title</b><h1>

which instructs your browser to display it in boldface type (the "b" in <b>). Okay, but what does this have to do with database management? We're getting there.

HTML is derived from a broader markup language called the **Standard Generalized Markup Language (SGML).** As you can see from HTML, SGML is capable of handling the formatting of displayed text and data. But SGML is also capable of indicating the *meaning* of data. It is on this capability that XML, which is also derived from SGML, focuses. Figure 15.8 shows how the attributes in the BOOK table in Good Reading's database (Figure 15.5) would be represented in an XML document type definition (DTD). Figure 15.9 shows some actual BOOK table data described by XML based on the DTD of Figure 15.8. Notice that each actual attribute in Figure 15.9, each piece of data, is accompanied by tags that indicate its *meaning*. XMLs ability to handle different kinds of data is put to good use by Baptist MD, as noted earlier. This XML capability is indeed important in the Web database environment. But beyond this ability of XML to represent data in a generalized way that incorporates the meaning of the data with the data itself, what does XML have to do with database management?

➤ **Figure 15.8**
XML Document Type Definition (DTD) for Good Reading Bookstores' BOOK data

```
<!ELEMENT book>
<!ELEMENT booknumber (#PCDATA)>
<!ELEMENT bookname (#PCDATA)>
<!ELEMENT publicationyear (#PCDATA)>
<!ELEMENT pages (#PCDATA)>
<!ELEMENT publishername (#PCDATA)>
```

➤ **Figure 15.9**
XML for a Good Reading Bookstores' book

```
<book>
<booknumber>374566</booknumber>
<bookname>Catch-22</bookname>
<publicationyear>1955</publicationyear>
<pages>443</pages>
<publishername>Simon and Schuster</publishername>
```

Finally, the answer to this question goes straight to the heart of e-commerce and the countless databases that support it. Modern companies are interconnected in automated **supply chains** in which their information systems applications send data to each other over telecommunications networks. This is not a new concept. For many years this activity has been accomplished with **electronic data interchange (EDI).** For example, an automobile manufacturer's parts inventory management system might recognize that it is starting to run short of tires on the assembly line. When the number of tires falls below a preset "reorder point," it automatically sends a message to an application in the tire manufacturer's computer ordering more tires. This type of process could also apply to Good Reading Bookstores and the publishers or book wholesalers that supply its stores. But a classic problem in EDI has been the different data formats in the databases of the supply chain partners. In order to automatically exchange data in an EDI arrangement, two companies have to go to a lot of trouble to match up attribute names, types, lengths, and so forth, with each other. Furthermore, a particular company has to go through this with *each* of its supply chain partners. It can be done and it is done, but it is a grueling, time-consuming process.

The beauty of XML in this regard is that it provides an independent layer of data definition that is separate from the particular formatting of each company's data in their databases. Again, consider Good Reading Bookstores but broaden the view and realize that there are many bookstores and bookstore chains, and many publishers and book wholesalers. Assume that every one of these companies agrees to use a single, standard XML description of books. Furthermore, each company will arrange to have software convert their stored book data to the standard XML format. Then, they can all freely exchange book data with each other (Figure 15.10). For example, if Good Reading has to order books from Publisher A, its software will convert the book data in its database needed for the order to the XML standard. When Publisher A receives Good Reading's order in the XML standard, its software will convert the data from the XML standard to its own format and go on to process the order. And, of course, this works in both directions. So, as long as Good Reading can convert its data to the XML standard, it can assume that *every* publisher it deals with can go on to convert the XML standard data to that publisher's data format, and vice versa from the publishers to the bookstores.

KEY TERMS

Audio clip
Availability
Binary file (BFILE)
Binary large object (BLOB)
Browser
Character large object (CLOB)
Client side
Clustering
Data type
Database connectivity
Database persistence
Electronic commerce

Electronic data interchange (EDI)
Graphic image
Home page
HyperText Markup Language (HTML)
Internet
Java Database Connectivity (JDBC)
Load balancing
Middleware
National character large object (NCLOB)

Open Database Connectivity (ODBC)
Query cache
Scalability
Server side
Standard Generalized Markup Language (SGML)
Supply-chain
Video clip
World Wide Web (WWW)
XML

➤ **Figure 15.10**
XML as an independent
layer of data definition

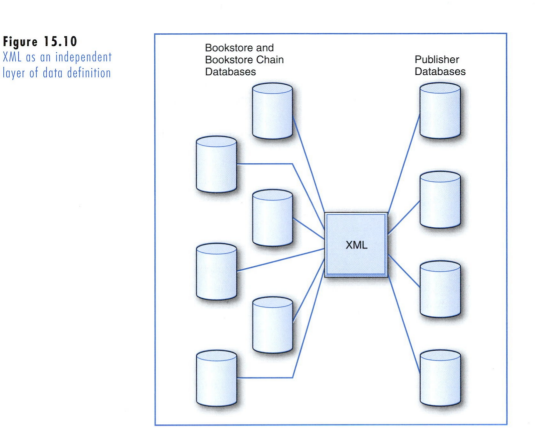

QUESTIONS

1. Explain why the World Wide Web is like a giant client/server system.

2. One of the principles of client/server systems is that the processing functions are divided among different computers in the system. Explain this division of labor in the World Wide Web.

3. Describe the arrangement of computers and disks at a Web site.

4. Describe the various software components needed to reach a database within a Web site.

5. Why is it important to have standardized software interfaces between the various Web site components?

6. List three multimedia data types that might be required for a Web site.

7. What is a BLOB? What is a CLOB? What are they used for?

8. List some factors that can affect response time in e-commerce.

9. List some factors that can cause large variations in the number of people trying to access a Web site simultaneously.

10. What can a company do to handle spikes in traffic to its Web site?

11. What does availability mean? Why is it important in the e-commerce environment?

12. What factors or events can affect a Web site's availability?

13. What does scalability mean? Why is it important in the e-commerce environment?

14. What is different about data security concerns in the Internet environment vs. the non-Internet environment?

15. What techniques or equipment can be employed for data security in the Internet environment?

16. Why is data privacy a concern in the e-commerce environment?

17. What is XML, and why is it useful regarding database in the e-commerce environment?

EXERCISES

1. Consider Lucky Rent-A-Car's Web site, which contains its database, as described in Figure 5.18. Describe, in detail, the steps that would be taken with both hardware and software to reach the database when a customer is making a reservation for a rental car over the Web.

2. Consider the World Music Association's Web site, which contains its database, as described in Figure 5.17. Describe, in detail, the steps that would be taken with both hardware and software to reach the database when a customer is searching for information about recordings of Beethoven's Fifth Symphony.

3. Describe three different uses for nontraditional data types in the Web sites of:

   a. Good Reading Bookstores
   b. World Music Association
   c. Lucky Rent-A-Car

MINICASES

1. Happy Cruise Lines.

   a. Consider Happy Cruise Lines' Web site, which contains its database, as described in Minicase 1 of Chapter 5. Describe, in detail, the steps that would be taken with both hardware and software to reach the database when an employee is gathering statistics about a particular cruise, such as the total revenue (the sum of the fares paid) for the cruise.

   b. Describe three different uses for nontraditional data types in the Happy Cruise Lines Web site.

2. Super Baseball League.

   a. Consider the Super Baseball League's Web site, which contains its database, as described in Minicase 2 of Chapter 5. Describe, in detail, the steps that would be taken with both hardware and software to reach the database to produce a list of the work experiences of a particular coach on a particular team.

   b. Describe three different uses for nontraditional data types in the Super Baseball League Web site.

INDEX